Rock Island Public Library
401 - 19th Street
Rock Island, IL 61201-8143

JUN   2006

D1195686

A MARYLAND BRIDE
IN THE DEEP SOUTH

Priscilla "Mittie" Bond

Priscilla Munnikhuysen Bond Papers, Mss. 2155, Louisiana and Lower Mississippi Valley Collection, LSU Libraries, Baton Rouge, La.

A Maryland Bride
in the
Deep South

THE CIVIL WAR DIARY OF
PRISCILLA BOND

EDITED, WITH AN INTRODUCTION, BY
KIMBERLY HARRISON

LOUISIANA STATE UNIVERSITY PRESS ✦ BATON ROUGE

PUBLISHED WITH THE ASSISTANCE OF THE
V. Ray Cardozier Fund

Published by Louisiana State University Press
Copyright © 2006 by Louisiana State University Press
All rights reserved
Manufactured in the United States of America
FIRST PRINTING

DESIGNER: Melanie O'Quinn Samaha
TYPEFACE: Adobe Caslon
TYPESETTER: The Composing Room of Michigan, Inc.
PRINTER AND BINDER: Edwards Brothers, Inc.

LIBRARY OF CONGRESS CATALOGING-IN-PUBLICATION DATA

Bond, Priscilla, 1838–1866.
A Maryland bride in the Deep South : the Civil War diary of Priscilla Bond / edited, with an introduction, by Kimberly Harrison.
    p. cm.
Includes bibliographical references and index.
ISBN 0-8071-3143-1 (cloth : alk. paper)
    1. Bond, Priscilla, 1838–1866—Diaries. 2. Women—Louisiana—Diaries. 3. Wives—Louisiana—Diaries. 4. Louisiana—History—Civil War, 1861–1865—Personal narratives. 5. United States—History—Civil War, 1861–1865—Personal narratives. 6. Plantation life—Louisiana—Houma Region—History—19th century. 7. Houma Region (La.)—Social life and customs—19th century. 8. Abbeville (La.)—Social life and customs—19th century. 9. Baltimore (Md.)—Biography. 10. United States—History—Civil War, 1861–1865—Social aspects. I. Harrison, Kimberly, 1969– II. Title.
E605.B69 2006
976.3′5105′092—dc22

2005023217

Maps by Mary Lee Eggart
The paper in this book meets the guidelines for permanence and durability of the Committee on Production Guidelines for Book Longevity of the Council on Library Resources. ⊗

For Jeremy

Contents

Preface

PRISCILLA "MITTIE" MUNNIKHUYSEN BOND began writing in the diary presented here in 1858, when she was nineteen years old. It is likely that she had kept a diary before, but the two books that span from 1858 to 1865 are the only ones that have survived. Bond writes of her life as a member of a prominent family living at Maiden Lane, the Munnikhuysen family home outside Baltimore, Maryland. In 1861 she married Howard Bond, the son of one of south Louisiana's wealthy sugarcane planters, and soon after moved with her husband to his family's plantation, Crescent Place, in Terrebonne Parish, near Houma, Louisiana. In Louisiana, Bond experienced the Civil War, first on her in-laws' plantation and then, in 1862, as a refugee in Abbeville, where she was immersed in, what seemed to her, a strange new culture of south Louisiana.

Bond's diary tells a compelling story. It presents multiple conflicts that the reader hopes to see resolved. Conflicts surround Bond's marriage as she questions her abilities to perform the duties of a wife and as she vacillates in her feelings for Howard. When Howard joins the war effort, questions arise both about his survival and about whether he will return to Louisiana after Confederate defeat or leave his family and flee to Mexico. Another conflict involves Bond's separation from her home, one marked by close relationships and frequent interaction with many relatives—aunts, uncles, cousins, siblings, and parents. Leaving behind one's close family—both nuclear and extended—was a momentous event for a woman like Bond. By marrying Howard and moving to Louisiana, she lost the security of these relationships and therefore, understandably, feared leaving Maryland, especially amid threats of war, to go to what she called the "strange land" of south Louisiana. Once in Louisiana, she expressed her longing for home and her increasing determination to return to her family. Also, throughout the Civil War, Bond struggled against deteriorating health, specifically with consumption. Other perhaps more minor battles, yet influential ones in shaping her daily life and outlook, occurred between Bond and her in-laws and among the inhabitants of

Abbeville, all of whom were experiencing the hardships of war and many the discomforts of refugee life.

While to date many women's wartime diaries have been published, Bond's differs from those now available in important ways. Beginning in 1858, it provides valuable insight into the years leading up to the Civil War, showing the war's impact on a young woman as she came into maturity during such turbulent times and as she experienced war separated from her family and family home. In addition, Bond's diary carries us through the entire Civil War and provides insight into the wartime culture of a unique area—south Louisiana—as seen by a young, devoutly Protestant woman from Maryland. It contributes to historical discussions such as those initiated by scholars including Joan Cashin, who articulates the differences between the old and the frontier south, and Jean Friedman, who shows the importance of family for southern women.[1] Bond's diary provides scholars with evidence to extend such work as it offers a Maryland woman's view of life, slavery, and family relationships in Civil War south Louisiana. Also, with the scope of the diary, we see how Bond worked to redefine herself, often using her diary to do so, in response to the hardships of war. We see how the war challenged dominant southern ideals as Bond began to lose confidence in traditional relationships, even that between husband and wife.

The diary provides a personal look into the Civil War and Louisiana history. Priscilla Bond did not have aspirations to public life. Unlike Mary Chesnut, the most famous of Civil War diarists, Bond did not aim to publish her diary. Also, unlike Chesnut, she did not extend her critiques of her surroundings to broader societal criticisms. When her diary begins, in 1858, she describes a world centered around her faith and her family. She is concerned with her own spiritual growth and the well-being of those close to her. This is still the world that Bond wishes for in 1865, as the war ends. The perspective that Bond allows us is very different from that of Chesnut, yet it is valuable all the same. The war pushed Bond to independence, and her voice strengthened even as her health declined, yet her experiences during the war did not change her commitment to her family in Maryland or to her God.

I first read Bond's diary in 1996, when I was completing an editing project for a graduate seminar. I was engaged by Bond's story, by her voice, which developed gradually as she continued to write and to mature, and by the narrative structure of the diary. I spent more time with the diary than I needed to in order to finish my project, hoping eventually to revisit it. I remain intrigued by Bond's story, a very personal one that evolves during a critical time and that touches upon crucial is-

---

1. See Cashin, *Family Venture;* and Friedman, *Enclosed Garden.*

sues in U.S. history. A number of historians, including Drew Gilpin Faust and Eugene Genovese, have made use of Bond's diary in their scholarship, recognizing her importance in providing insight into southern women's views of slavery and of the war's impact on women's self-perception and identity.[2] Bond's diary was deposited at Hill Special Collections in 1966 by Mrs. Hazel L. McNeal, Bond's great-niece. It has not previously been edited and has been published only on microfilm through Anne Firor Scott's series *Southern Women and Their Families in the Nineteenth Century: Papers and Diaries.*

2. Faust, *Mothers of Invention,* 18; Faust, "Altars of Sacrifice," 1211; Genovese, *Roll, Jordon, Roll,* 72.

Acknowledgments

MANY PEOPLE HAVE HELPED ME with this project. At Louisiana State University's Hill Memorial Library, Faye Phillips, Associate Dean for Special Collections, first introduced me to Bond's diary, and, once I began to pursue the publication, Tara Zachary Laver worked with me on permissions and encouraged the project. Judy Bolton helped me finalize the Louisiana illustrations. During my research I met with valuable assistance in both Maryland and Louisiana historical societies and public libraries. Particularly helpful were Henry C. Peden Jr. and John Hartman of the Historical Society of Harford County and Carlos Crockett at the Terrebonne Parish Library in Houma.

The Florida International University Office of the Provost/Foundation award provided needed course release time, and my department chairs, Don Watson and Carmela McIntire, also generously allowed me research time. The Biscayne Bay library staff was invaluable, specifically Steve Switzer and others who assisted me with many interlibrary loans.

I have been particularly fortunate in having excellent scholars provide feedback throughout this project. John Sacher generously read multiple drafts of the introduction. I have benefited from his insights and expert knowledge of nineteenth-century Louisiana. Carol Mattingly talked to me about this project for many years, and she also read and commented on my drafts, offering invaluable suggestions. I feel incredibly fortunate to have her as a mentor and friend. Also, as readers for a related project, Andrea Lunsford and Maureen Goggin provided helpful and supportive advice for rhetorically interpreting Bond's diary. The anonymous LSU Press readers' detailed and careful responses helped me hone the edition's focus and sharpen my interpretations. Shaun Mcguire also read the manuscript, more times than he bargained for, both in graduate seminars and outside of class. His suggestions led me to revisions that have helped make Bond's writing more accessible.

I am appreciative of the help I have received at LSU Press. Sylvia Frank Rodrigue expressed initial interest in Bond's diary and encouraged me to pursue the project. Rand Dotson has been the epitome of professionalism and guided the project through its last stages. Elizabeth Gratch gave careful and kind attention to the manuscript during copyediting.

Friends, especially Jeffrey and Dina Knapp, Cindy Chinelly, John Dufresne, Bruce Harvey, Liz Cortlander, Denise Duhamel, and Nick Carbo, have sustained me throughout this project with humor and excellent dinner parties. My family has always encouraged me, offering unconditional support. Much love and gratitude are due my father, mother, and Aunt Erma. Finally, Jeremy Rowan has been supportive, understanding, and encouraging through the many stages of this project's development. He read the manuscript at its various stages and offered his expertise as a historian. He also shared with me both the frustrations and the excitements that this project has brought, and I am very grateful to him.

A MARYLAND BRIDE
IN THE DEEP SOUTH

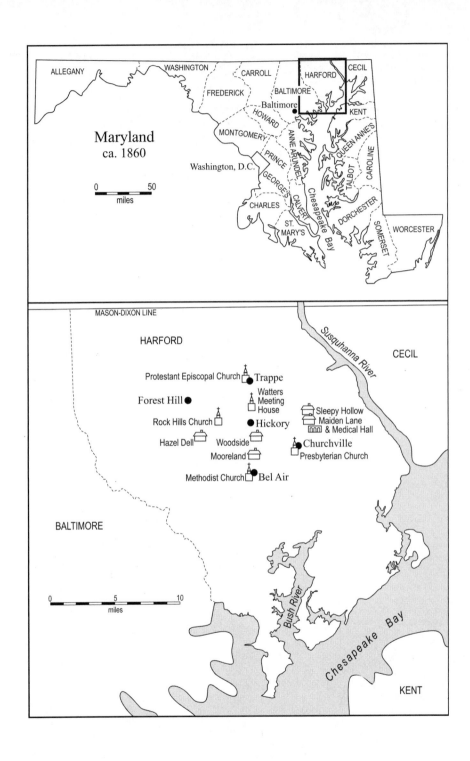

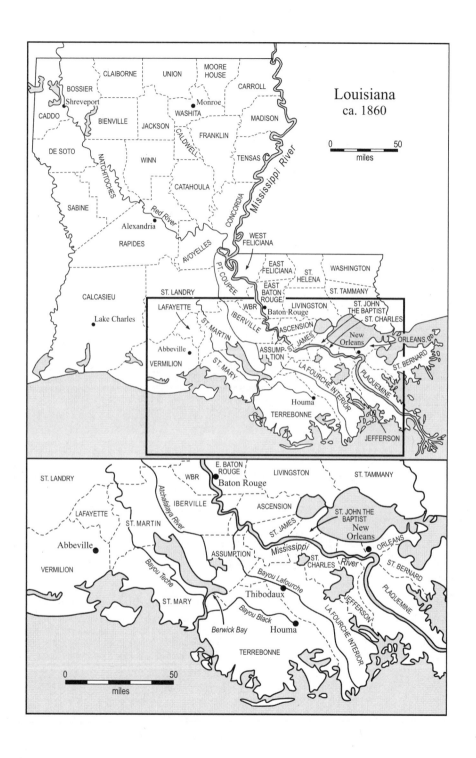

Louisiana
ca. 1860

Introduction

PRISCILLA ELIZABETH "MITTIE" MUNNIKHUYSEN BOND was born into a prominent, well-respected, and comfortable middle-class family in Harford County, Maryland, in 1838. The county, established in 1773, is located in northern Maryland, next to Baltimore. Many of Bond's relatives descended from original settlers. The Munnikhuysen social circle included the area's respected doctors, lawyers, judges, politicians, ministers, and farmers. Bond's family home, Maiden Lane, still stands in the Thomas Run Valley, in the town of Bel Air. The two-story wood frame and stone home figures prominently in the diary as a representation of family, warmth, and security. From one of her bedroom windows, in front of which Bond enjoyed writing, she had views of the Thomas Run Valley, woods, and hills.[1]

Through Bond's writing of both her diary and letters, we see various sides of her personality. She was a disciplined journal writer and often offered explanations when she was prevented from writing. Her longest absence from her diary was from the summer of 1862 to 1863, after the Bond plantation was burned. Even during this period it seems that she kept a record of her activities, as she provided a narrative of her experiences—complete with specific dates—when she again wrote in her diary. At times Bond comes across as whimsical and humorous, although more often she seems somber and concerned about speaking and acting appropriately. She had high expectations for herself and for others, and many of her entries concern her desire for self-improvement. Often to that end, she valued reading, writing, and self-reflection. Bond was physically attractive, as we can see in the photographs that survive and by the compliments that she records. She enjoyed horseback riding and attending church meetings. She also appreciated fine dresses and liked to dance—two luxuries that she often denied herself as she attempted to uphold the tenets of nineteenth-century Methodism.

Bond's life in Maryland was largely defined by family responsibilities and religious duties. Her entries, especially those of 1858, describe a life busy with visiting and receiving guests, many of whom were her relatives. At times she recoiled from

1. The house has been extended since the time Bond lived there and is now called the "Old Munnikhuysen Place."

her social duties, preferring to spend time with her diary and books. Still, her life was defined by an extended network of family members. As scholars have recognized, nineteenth-century women, particularly in the South, frequently constructed their identities in relation to their families and relied upon extended family networks for emotional fulfillment. Understanding the importance of family for southern women of this time is necessary for understanding Bond's perspective.[2]

Bond's father, John Anthony Munnikhuysen, was first-generation Dutch American. His father, John, arrived in Baltimore from Holland in 1783, established himself as a merchant, and later married Mary Howard. After John Munnikhuysen died, at the age of forty-one, Mary Howard married Parker Hall Lee, a member of an established Colonial family.[3] In 1818 John Anthony purchased from his stepfather the house that would become Maiden Lane and two hundred and forty acres of land on which to plant corn. Likely, the Munnikhuysens' connection with the Lee family enabled John Anthony to marry Bond's mother, Priscilla Ann Bond, a member of another large and prominent local family. The couple had three children in addition to Priscilla: Frances Howard, who was called Fannie (b. 1834), William Temminck (b. 1836), and Ann Lee (b. 1845). According to the 1860 census, the Munnikhuysen family owned real estate valued at eight thousand dollars and a personal estate worth a thousand dollars.[4] At this time, the family did not own slaves, but living in their home were three black servants; Bond often mentions Charlotte, who was thirty-five years old in 1860, and Betsy, who was nine.

The culture into which Bond was born differed drastically from that which she entered when she married Howard Bond and moved to Louisiana. In the nineteenth century, northern Maryland was largely a white and free labor society.[5] Only 16 percent of the population was black, and less than 5 percent were slaves. In 1850, 14,413 whites resided in Harford County, in contrast to 2,777 free blacks and 2,166

2. In particular, Friedman, in *The Enclosed Garden,* has shown the importance of kinship networks for women in the context of the nineteenth-century antebellum South. See also Fox-Genovese, "Family and Female Identity in the Antebellum South," 15–31. Fox-Genovese maintains that southern women defined themselves in relation to family membership.

3. In 1790 Parker Lee owned seventeen slaves, as stated in the 1790 U.S. census, population schedule, Harford County, Md., Parker Lee household, National Archives microfilm publication M637, roll 3.

4. 1860 U.S. census, population schedule, Harford County, Md., John Munnikhuysen household, National Archives microfilm publication M653, roll 476.

5. Fields, *Slavery and Freedom on the Middle Ground,* 6. As Fields explains, the northern part of the state consists of the following counties: Allegany, Baltimore, Carroll, Frederick, Harford, and Washington. In this area during the nineteenth century, industry was growing and becoming a significant part of the economy. In contrast, the southern counties (Anne Arundel, Calvert, Charles, Prince George, Montgomery, and St. Mary) depended on agriculture.

slaves.[6] Throughout the northern counties in 1860 white citizens totaled 366,649, in comparison to 13,327 slaves.[7] Most Maryland slaveholders had only one slave, while half of them owned fewer than three; only 10 percent held fifteen or more slaves.[8] Although Bond's parents did not own slaves, other of her family members and friends did. One of the largest slaveholders in Bond's Maryland social circle was her uncle William T. Munnikhuysen, who owned eight slaves.[9] Most of the Maryland families that Bond mentions had at least one member who was a slave-holder. Those who did not own slaves hired free blacks or slaves from local slave owners to work as cooks and household servants.

The relatively small number of slaves in the state can be partially explained by the agricultural production and the geography. In northern Maryland, the main crop during the nineteenth century was grain, and its cultivation did not require year-round slave labor. Instead of maintaining an unneeded slave population throughout the year, farmers depended on the large free black population as la-borers. Also, Maryland's location as a border state meant that it was watched closely by neighboring free states; as Robert Brugger concludes, "Maryland slave-holders had to be especially concerned with their image in the public eye."[10] Ow-ing to Maryland's location, antislavery ideas could flow easily across state bor-ders.[11] As a result, the issue of slavery was frequently under debate. In the 1820s, discussions about slavery raged in the northern counties of Maryland, and Har-ford citizens, along with those in Baltimore and Frederick counties, petitioned for a law that would gradually extinguish slavery. While slavery was not abolished as a result of the petitions, it did decline in the state. Some of the decrease was due to slaveholders moving their slaves to the South or West, but others freed their slaves, many of whom moved to Baltimore.[12] For some white Marylanders, how-ever, the large number of free blacks began to cause unease. Nat Turner's 1831 slave uprising in Virginia increased white citizens' discomfort, and they began to call for

6. U.S. Bureau of the Census, *Seventh Census of the U.S., 1850,* 220.

7. Fields, *Slavery and Freedom,* 6, 70.

8. Fields, *Slavery and Freedom,* 24.

9. 1860 U.S. census, slave schedule, Md., National Archives microfilm publication; in 1860 William reported owning real estate valued at eighteen thousand dollars and a personal estate worth five thou-sand dollars. 1860 U.S. census, Harford County, Md., William T. Munnikhuysen household, National Archives microfilm publication M653, roll 476. He was the father of Howard Munnikhuysen, Bond's friend. Also see the "List of Principal Friends" for more information regarding slaveholders in Bond's Maryland social circle.

10. Brugger, *Maryland,* 246.

11. See Fields, *Slavery and Freedom,* 4; and Brugger, *Maryland,* 245.

12. Brugger, *Maryland,* 210–11.

actions ranging from abolishing slavery to enslaving free blacks. Legislators chose a middle ground by restricting the rights of free blacks. They also established the Maryland State Colonization Society and set policies that encouraged free blacks to remove to Africa.[13]

Priscilla Bond was part of this society in which the institution of slavery had been historically under scrutiny. Yet at the same time she would have been aware of local slaveholders' concerns regarding the influence of abolitionists and the maintenance of slavery as an institution. John Brown's raid at Harpers Ferry in October 1859 is the first political subject that Bond broaches in her diary, an event that caused apprehension among slaveholding and non-slaveholding whites in Maryland.[14] At least partially as a result of white fear, southern rights Democrats gained control of both houses in the General Assembly in the 1859 election. In 1860 the General Assembly heard petitions from planters and slaveholders who wanted to end manumission. A member of a House of Delegates committee stated his intention to force the state to declare itself southern or to "go into the arms of the abolitionists."[15]

Before Bond left Maryland for Louisiana, in January 1861, the public world was beginning to infiltrate the domestic sphere of a Maryland southern belle as hints of national turmoil found expression, albeit briefly, in Bond's diary. As she was contemplating her marriage, both her public and private worlds were in upheaval. With southern states seceding from the Union beginning in December 1860, she prepared to leave not only her life as a belle but also the comfort and security of her family home.

When Bond married, she married into her extended family.[16] Howard's parents, Joshua and Rebecca Bond, were both originally from Maryland but had established their home in Terrebonne Parish, Louisiana, by the late 1830s, taking part in the westward migration from the southern seaboard to the frontier South, likely motivated by a slowing seaboard economy in the 1820s and 1830s.[17] While Bond's

13. Brugger, *Maryland,* 212–13.

14. As Fields concludes, "Hysteria concerning the raid subsided in Maryland with surprising rapidity, but alarm at its frightening implications did not" (76).

15. Quoted in Brugger, *Maryland,* 268.

16. Her grandmother on her father's side, Mary Howard, and Bond's mother were descendants of Peter Bond, who moved to Harford County from Anne Arundel in 1660; see Preston, *History of Harford County Maryland,* 206–9. The families were also connected through the Howard family, as Rebecca Bond's family name was Howard. Thus, Priscilla Bond calls her mother-in-law "Cousin" Rebecca.

17. Howard Bond was born in 1839 in Louisiana, according to 1850 census records. Joshua Bond, however, was not listed in the 1840 Louisiana census. 1850 U.S. census, population schedule, Terrebonne Parish, La., J. B. Bond household; National Archive microfilm publication M432, roll 241; and 1840 U.S.

own family was comparatively financially comfortable and respected in their community, Howard's family was extremely wealthy. Josh was one of the parish's most successful sugarcane growers, owning thirteen hundred acres of land and 115 slaves.[18] In Louisiana he formed a partnership with Robert Ruffin Barrow, one of the area's most powerful men, who made his fortune as a planter and canal operator. In the 1850 census, in partnership with Barrow, Josh Bond listed assets worth $90,000. By the 1860 census, his wealth had increased significantly, as he independently claimed real estate worth $52,000 and personal property of $137,400. His plantation, Crescent Place, was located on Bayou Black, near the Terrebonne Parish seat of Houma.

By marrying Howard, Priscilla Bond made a very advantageous marriage, moving into the elite planter class. Howard, before his marriage, had lived in Houma while he studied with a local doctor and ran a store, likely a pharmacy. While interested in science, he was also showing himself to be a businessman, with his store and with stock in one of Barrow's canal companies. Although he had been born in Louisiana, he often spent time in Maryland and oversaw some of his father's property there. He and his new wife, however, began their married life with his family, living at Crescent Place. Other occupants of the main house included his younger brothers, Wilmore (Wellie) and Barrow (named after Josh's business partner, Robert Ruffin Barrow), and his young sister, Louisa. Laura Bond, a cousin from Maryland, was also a guest at Crescent Place when Bond arrived. In Terrebonne Parish Bond's social circle consisted not primarily of middle-class professionals, as it did in Maryland, but of leading planter families such as the Barrows.

Bond, when arriving in Louisiana, would have found the southeast portion of the state dotted with sugar plantations. Many of the large landowners of Terrebonne had purchased Acadian-owned small farms to create large sugar plantations, and in 1861 there were 1,291 operating cane plantations.[19] The sugar region was one of the wealthiest and most opulent plantation districts in the country.[20] An 1850 *Debow's Review* article described the area as having "many extensive plantations, highly cultivated, neatly arranged" along the several bayous and noted that the area displayed richness despite having only recently been established, in 1822 (147).[21]

Behind the image of opulence and wealth were the many slaves who made the sugarcane planters' success possible. While the Acadian farmers had owned few

census, population schedule, Terrebonne Parish, La., National Archives microfilm publication M704, roll 129.

18. Menn, *Large Slaveholders of Louisiana*, 414–15.
19. Roland, *Louisiana Sugar Plantations during the Civil War*, 3.
20. Pace, "'It Was Bedlam Let Loose,'" 389.
21. Price, "Terrebonne Parish, Louisiana," 147.

slaves, the new plantation owners needed slave labor to run the large plantations. On Crescent Place, Josh Bond's 115 slaves lived on the grounds in slave quarters and would have likely formed relatively "mature and stable" slave communities.[22] The slave culture that Bond encountered in south Louisiana contrasted sharply with what she had been accustomed to in Harford, where the average slave lived in the owner's household and, because of the small slaveholdings, did not often form family networks.[23] Perhaps most surprising to Bond would have been that the white population was the minority. Throughout sugarcane country, slaves outnumbered whites 88,439 to 60,356.[24] In Terrebonne Parish, the free population was 5,306, and slaves numbered 6,785. Harford County, in sharp contrast, was home to 21,615 free citizens and 1,800 slaves.[25]

Bond soon realized that the culture of southern Louisiana was not that of the established seaboard. Instead, as a relatively new plantation society, Terrebonne Parish retained characteristics of the frontier South, a world in which the planters who had migrated there struggled to build wealth and to assert independence from the constraints of the traditional southern family. Houma, the parish seat, was founded in 1834. In 1841 a settler found that Houma had only "three or four little houses" and described the area as "a complete wilderness" with "nearly all kinds of wild animals abound[ing], deer, bear, etc."[26] Even in 1861, the physical terrain and climate would have seemed harsh, with extreme storms and humidity, stark swamplands, and the accompanying mosquitoes that gave Bond so much trouble. Bond portrays her new home as one of physical beauty but also of violence, one in which the whip was used frequently and in which citizens carried guns. As Joan Cashin has shown, the men who succeeded as planters on the southern frontier often adopted the values of "masculine independence" and braved the harsh landscape and initial rough living conditions to increase their wealth more rapidly than they could if they remained in the old South. Cashin explains that male planter migrants "adopted more aggressive, self-absorbed forms of behavior" than had their fathers.[27] Viewing Josh Bond as a product of the southern frontier culture

22. Malone, *Sweet Chariot*, 39.

23. Fields, *Slavery and Freedom*, 24.

24. Rodrigue, *Reconstruction in the Cane Fields*, 11.

25. U.S. Bureau of the Census, *Statistics of the United States (including mortality, property, &c.,) in 1860*, 194, 214.

26. Randolph A. Bazet, "Houma—An Historical Sketch," *Centennial Celebration, Houma, Louisiana, May 10–13, 1934* (Morgan City, La., 1934), 9, quoted in Becnel, *Barrow Family and the Barataria and Lafourche Canal*, 13.

27. Cashin, *Family Venture*, 99. Cashin explains that this masculine independence impacted both gender and racial relationships as men rejected the paternalist, reciprocal relationships that were fos-

helps explain Priscilla Bond's dislike of her father-in-law, her disgust at his behavior, and her fear of his influence over Howard.

Bond also found that her acquaintances in Louisiana were not, on the whole, as educated as her community in Maryland. The literacy rate in Terrebonne was indeed lower than that in Harford, with 19 percent of the free Terrebonne population illiterate compared to less than 1 percent of the Harford free population.[28] Additionally, the parish was home to many French-speaking Creoles; in 1840 two-thirds of the families in Terrebonne Parish were of French descent, and by 1850 over 90 percent of the residents were born in the state. Bond was indeed an outsider in southern Louisiana, especially in a parish such as Terrebonne that had maintained its French heritage.

Before Bond had time to grow accustomed to her life in an elite planter family, the Civil War began to play out in southern Louisiana, causing her to flee her new home and to separate from her new husband. In 1862 Howard was accused of leading an ambush on Union soldiers in which two were killed. In retaliation, his store was plundered, and buildings at Crescent Place, including the main house, were burned. Josh, along with his sons Wellie and Barrow, fled for Texas, taking along many of the slaves. Priscilla, Rebecca, Louisa ("Sis"), and a small number of household slaves traveled to Abbeville, where they were joined for a time by Howard, who, devoted to the Confederate cause, actively participated in the war, first by fighting with local militia and later enlisting as a private in the Twenty-sixth Regiment of the Louisiana Infantry.[29] In the spring of 1863, he began serving in the Ordnance Department and then in August 1864 was appointed state chemist. Both positions required him to live near Shreveport, Louisiana, in the northern part of the state and far from his wife.

In her diary, in place of listing visitors, Bond began to list battles, most frequently writing about local battles, a focus that offers insight into how the Civil War was viewed in south Louisiana. Tracking Priscilla's movements immediately after Crescent Place burned is at times tricky. She spent approximately two weeks with the Winders, wealthy planters in the parish, and then traveled to Thibodaux, Louisiana, to meet Howard. The diary entries written in July do not state where she was but hint that she might have been back at Crescent Place staying in properties that Federal forces had spared. In August 1862, Bond was in New Iberia, where she spent two months, and then she visited a friend in St. Mary Parish. On

---

tered on the Seaboard. As a result, women often grew more dependent on men and slaves endured mistreatment as slave owners "tended to equate masculinity with mistreating slaves."

28. See U.S. Census Bureau, *Seventh Census,* 480, 225. Also see Crete, *Daily Life in Louisiana,* 117. Crete notes the inferior state of Louisiana schools.

29. Booth, *Records of Louisiana Confederate Soldiers and Louisiana Confederate Commands,* 2:30.

28 October she, her mother-in-law, Rebecca, Sis, and at least two slaves, Mintty and Amanda, began their journey to Abbeville, where they arrived on 4 November.

Often separated from Howard, Bond was forced to make a place for herself in south Louisiana. Accustomed to support and understanding of family and friends in Maryland, she found that forging relationships in a new culture and during hardships of war was difficult. At times her strong identification with Maryland caused problems with her new community, and she had to defend herself against the title of "Yankee." Maryland, a border state, was of divided loyalties with the majority opposing secession. Confederate loyalists, however, were vocal, particularly in Baltimore, where a mob attacked the Sixth Massachusetts Regiment on 19 April 1861 as it passed through the city. While Maryland governor Thomas Hicks was a Unionist, the legislature in 1861 was prepared to accept southern independence or, at least, to remain neutral; the federal government intervened, suspending habeas corpus in the state and arresting state and local officials. Perhaps to protect herself from the accusations of being a Yankee, Bond often reported rumors that her home state had joined the Confederacy.

In the last years of the Civil War, Bond struggled to accept her situation, which was becoming increasingly dire. While she was in delicate health before leaving Maryland, her consumption continued to progress, and she writes of days spent in bed and fears of and sometimes wishes for death. In the latter sections of the diary, Bond writes of coughing blood and of various medical treatments. She also notes increasing prices, her decreasing finances, and the scarcity of supplies in Abbeville. In many of these entries, she writes in a detached tone, as if she were observing herself, as if she can hardly see her desperate situation as reality. Bond seems to have difficulty reconciling the image of herself as touched by war with that of her prewar self—a young woman concerned largely with marriage, dress, God, and family—not with survival. During the last months of the Civil War, she writes less frequently as she waits to hear from her husband, who failed to write or return home with other soldiers. Although sparse, her entries during this period are characterized by uncertainty yet also by determination and strength.

In the early years of the war, Bond had expressed her patriotism and support of the Confederacy occasionally in her diary. Without doubt she identified herself as a southerner, but her support of the war, even at its beginning, pales in comparison to that of her fellow diarists, such as Ellen Renshaw House, Grace Brown Elmore, and Sarah Morgan. In September 1860, she writes of making wreaths for a "grand mass meeting," and while she enjoyed the dignitaries' speeches, she does not discuss the views expressed. Similarly, in November 1860, she mentions attending a Democratic political rally, and a few days later she notes that the election takes place. Still, however, she does not reflect upon her own political views, and the election results figure little in her diary, eclipsed by her engagement. Once fighting commenced, she only rarely contemplates the political reasons for the war. An exception is her entry of 25 August 1863, in which she voices the view that the soldiers were fighting to protect southern property: she writes, "Poor soldiers— some are barefooted & ragged—but they are fighting for rights our foes (*the detestable Yankees*) would deprive of us. 'Fighting for the property we gained by honest toil.'" Yet in this entry she does not develop her own position, offering, instead, an uncredited quotation to explain the causes of war. She expresses her political opinion most strongly and emotionally in an 1861 letter to her mother in which she wishes for Maryland's secession.

From the outbreak of fighting, Bond's primary desire was to keep her family together, and she resisted Howard's participation in the war. She was not persuaded by the southern wartime rhetoric, as expressed in newspapers, from pulpits, in literature, and songs, that urged women to give up their men stoically to the battlefield. Bond differed from the many young women diarists of the time who, in exasperation, decried their sex and wished to be men so that they could actively engage in the war.[30] Unlike many women of her class who enthusiastically participated in the war effort by raising funds or gathering supplies for the troops, Bond did not actively participate in sewing circles or in local benefits for the Confederate cause.[31] Although she was sensitive to being labeled a Yankee, being from a border state, by October 1864 she writes: "They say I'm a Yankee—but if wanting peace is Yankee—then *I am one.* I am tired of *Disunion* of husband & wife." By the end of the war, her prevailing desire was to return to Maryland, whether or not it meant Confederate defeat.[32]

Bond's compelling story contributes to our understanding of the Civil War— what it meant for women and its impact on families and individual identities. The

30. For more discussion on southern women's frustrations with the limitations of their gender during war, see Faust, "Altars of Sacrifice," 1206–7. Diarists Sarah Morgan, writing in Baton Rouge, and Kate Stone, in northeastern Louisiana, also frequently stated their desire to be a man so that they could participate in the war.

31. When she first arrived in Terrebonne, Bond attended a sewing circle and pledged to make six shirts. She completed only one, however, and, in order to preserve her social standing, Howard was required to pay to cover the work. In a letter to her mother of 19 May 1861, she explains that her lack of participation was due to sickness.

32. Bond's view echoes that of many other southern women during the last years of the war. Many had initially believed that, by fighting the war, their men were protecting their families and property, but, as southern property was destroyed and as men were killed and maimed, women's support of the war waned. They longed for the restoration of their families, even if it meant the collapse of the Confederacy. Rable, *Civil Wars;* and Faust, *Mothers of Invention,* provide further discussion on this view.

diary also provides insight into the importance of literacy and the functions of rhetoric for southern women of privileged classes. Bond's diary served an important function in forming her identity; it was a rhetorical tool that allowed her, through writing about her speech acts, past and future, to come to terms with societal expectations of women's roles, which changed with men away at war. Many of her diary entries are self-persuasive as she used her writing and the space of the diary to motivate herself to act, to speak, and even to think appropriately. Like most nineteenth-century women of her class and culture, she was aware of her responsibilities to behave according to gender norms. She wrote in order to persuade herself to accept societal restrictions but also to negotiate expectations, trying to decide how far she could deviate and still remain comfortably within her culture's definition of proper womanhood.

Woven throughout Bond's story are the prominent themes of slavery, evangelical religion, and kinship. Her perspective in these areas is particularly valuable as she sees the institutions of slavery, the family, and the church from two very different viewpoints—as a belle in a prominent Maryland community and then as wife of a wealthy south Louisiana planter during the war. Gradually, we begin to see her confidence shaken in the southern paternalism that shaped both her views of gender and race relations. Her religious faith and devotion to her family home, however, remain strong and sustain her throughout the war and up to her death. Adding another dimension to her story, Bond's failing health impacts the way that she writes and how she views her world. She came of age and experienced the Civil War while suffering with pulmonary tuberculosis, or consumption, as it was called in the nineteenth century. She also provides insight into an area that has often been overlooked in discussions of the Civil War—the bayous of south Louisiana.

In order to provide a full context for reading Bond's writing, here I will discuss major themes of the diary, highlighting its rhetorical purposes. In many instances these themes blend together—as, for example, questions of slavery necessarily involve issues of religion and gendered identity. I also provide detail about the Civil War in south Louisiana to offer further insight into Bond's perspective.

A WOMAN'S "LOT": COURTSHIP AND MARRIAGE

Much of Bond's early diary deals with her courtship and details her life in Maryland amid her large extended family, providing insight into antebellum courtship on the eve of the Civil War and showing how one woman made her decision to marry by negotiating societal dictates, personal fears and desires, and her family's reservations and expectations. By marrying Howard, the son of an elite planter, Bond made an advantageous match and one that was likely opportune for her family, as Bond hints at financial difficulties.[33] The marriage, however, came at the cost of disrupting Bond's close community of immediate and extended family.[34]

In spite of marrying on the eve of war and with the promise of economic and social advantage, in many ways Bond's courtship was like that of other women of her class: she and Howard engaged in courtship rituals, writing love letters when he was in Louisiana, fending off cousins' questions about the romance, visiting relatives, and carving initials in "their" tree.[35] Playing a common courtship game, Bond tested Howard's feelings for her. This is most obvious when she breaks off the engagement in June 1860, when Howard fears that he cannot return to Maryland for the summer as he had promised.[36] Additionally, their courtship was "flooded with a vocabulary of personal wish, romantic choice, profound contrast between the sexes, emotional crisis, and transcendent pleasure."[37] Bond's entries about Howard before their marriage are frequently marked by doubt, reluctance, and anguish.

Like other belles at mid-century, Bond had high expectations for her future husband, wanting him to be her "ideal" and frequently admitting that he fell short.[38] Because husbands had complete legal, physical, and financial control over their wives, nineteenth-century women had to feel confident that their future husbands would fulfill their end of the bargain, serving as protectors, leaders, and providers. Moreover, by mid-century, marriage was intended not only to provide se-

33. Bond mentions money several times before her marriage. On 2 September 1859, for example, she wishes she had spending money, and a few days later, on the tenth, writes that she almost "forgot" to pay her shopping bill. Tellingly, after receiving a letter from Howard, she hopes that she will not act for "worldly gain" (13 December 1859). In her entry of 2 January 1861, she writes of trimming a hat for her sister to save money. She is pleased when Howard sends barrels of sugar from Louisiana and is troubled when Josh cannot send more because of the war. Additionally, Bond's cousins (also their neighbors and at least occasional business associates of John Anthony's) the Govers become bankrupt. More insight into the family's finances is provided in the letters, especially that of John Anthony to William and from Bond to Ann Lee when she discusses finding money to travel from Louisiana to Maryland.

34. In analyzing the writings of Sarah Gayle, Fox-Genovese, in "Family and Female Identity," finds that throughout her adulthood Gayle remained psychologically close to her birth family and turned to memories of her life with them when she was depressed (30). Gayle's example coincides with what we see in Bond's diary as she drew strength from the images of her Maryland home.

35. For more detail on courtship rituals, see Stowe, *Intimacy and Power in the Old South.*

36. Lystra, in *Searching the Heart,* shows that such testing rituals were frequent and important in nineteenth-century courtships as they proved to the lovers, especially to women, the more vulnerable member of the couple, that the relationship was strong and committed.

37. Stowe, *Intimacy and Power,* 51.

38. For more on nineteenth-century American women's anxiety regarding marriage, see Scott, *Southern Lady;* Stowe, *Intimacy and Power;* and Laas, *Love and Power in the Nineteenth Century.*

curity but also "true love."[39] Bond's quest to find her ideal can be compared to that of other southern diarists such as Sarah Morgan, who despaired of ever finding her "lord and master," her "Beau Ideal,"[40] and Emma Holmes, who longed for a "master spirit" whom she would "love to obey."[41] Diarist Ella Gertrude Clanton Thomas described her future husband, Jefferson Thomas, as the "polar star of my existence," expressing no doubt that he was worthy of her adoration and that she was making a correct choice.[42]

Bond, however, does not describe (or idealize) Howard as her master. In fact, she often shows herself as being in control: when Howard was home, he was frequently in bed sick and required her help. When she was sick and he attempted to lance her boil, he cut her artery and almost fainted. She often directed her own medical treatment, even though Howard was a trained chemist.[43] Her expectations differed, perhaps partly because she and Howard were close in age, unlike many young southern women, who married older men. Howard was nine months younger than she and at twenty-one was well below the average marriage age of men of his class.[44] Bond clearly saw her role in their relationship as a helpmate and frequently offered him advice. Also, unlike many of her contemporaries, who looked primarily to other women for emotional support, she required such sustenance from Howard, expecting him, for example, to understand her reluctance to leave home.

Bond, while at times expressing her love for Howard during their courtship and while certainly having affection for him, most often indicates that her love is not strong enough for her to sacrifice her Maryland home. Although she frequently voices reservations about her feelings for Howard, she also writes of the engagement as her choice, and she prays for guidance in choosing correctly. Her father, in a letter to her brother, states that she is free to make her own choice regarding Howard's offer. Nevertheless, Bond felt pressure to accept the proposal, as evident when she explains her resistance as a sin and writes of marriage to Howard as her duty and responsibility.[45] As Steven Stowe has shown, personal choice, romance,

39. Rothman, *Hands and Hearts;* and Tracey, *Plots and Proposals,* provide further discussion about the importance of romance during this period.

40. Morgan, *Sarah Morgan,* 60.

41. Holmes, *Diary of Miss Emma Holmes,* 201.

42. See entries of 9 July and 24 August 1852. Thomas chose to marry Jefferson Thomas despite her father's reservations. Virginia Burr, editor and scholar of Thomas's diaries, interprets Thomas's decision to marry as having been based on romantic love. See Burr, "Woman Made to Suffer and Be Strong," 215–32.

43. See her letter of 19 May 1861.

44. The average age for planter men to marry was twenty-six. See Bleser and Heath, "Clays of Alabama," 138.

45. Her view of resistance to marriage as sinful is clearly seen in her entry of 31 May 1860.

wealth, and family connections all played parts in southern courtship. Stowe explains that in the South "no one suggested that choosing a mate was a matter of simple personal preference, as it increasingly was among the propertied classes of the North."[46] Thus, when Bond writes of her choice in regard to her marriage, she refers not only to her personal desires but also to the desires and expectations of her community.

At times fighting her own desires, she turned to her diary. A majority of her entries before her marriage were self-persuasive—at times even self-coercive—as she worked to shape herself into the ideal image of a Christian woman and self-sacrificing future wife. Bond compared herself to her own mother, who appeared to her the epitome of wifely virtue—"meek and gentle kind affectionate and forbearing"—and she usually found herself deficient.[47] She frequently wished for the characteristics that would make her a "good wife," using her diary to lament her shortcomings while at the same time reinforcing in herself desired behaviors. She wrote about her romantic feelings for Howard, often chastising herself for her lack of feelings and trying to persuade herself that she was capable of loving him.

While Bond expressed reluctance to marry and to take on the role of wife, her primary concern was that marrying Howard also meant moving to Louisiana. Becoming a wife would be hard enough, but doing so away from her mother and support network often seemed more than she could bear. For antebellum women, moving away from family into their husband's home, even when it was within walking distance of their parents' home, was often traumatic and fraught with emotions. When the move was farther, the emotional impact could be devastating. As Joan Cashin found, southern women who followed their husbands in migrating to the Southwest commonly compared the move to death.[48]

Bond's father and brother, William, had reservations about the marriage. They disliked Howard's father, Josh, and doubted that Bond could be happy in his household.[49] Even before moving to Louisiana, Bond herself writes reservedly of Josh, fearing his influence on Howard.[50] William had firsthand experience living with the Bonds because he had moved to Terrebonne in the fall of 1859 to work

46. Stowe, *Intimacy and Power*, 101.

47. Entry of 15 December 1858.

48. Cashin, *Family Venture*, 45. Bond associates moving west with death. See especially her entry of 16 July 1858, in which she writes about her friend Jimmy Watters's departure for the West; she assumes that with his departure he is lost to her and wishes him a happy life and peaceful death. Also, in her entry of 16 October 1858, her thoughts of her own death are closely related to those about moving to Louisiana.

49. See John Anthony's letter of 14 January 1860 in app. 2.

50. See, for example, her entry of 22 May 1860.

with Josh on his plantation. While his letters home to Harford have not survived, Bond hints in her diary that he wrote negatively about his experiences.[51] Tellingly, after receiving letters from William, she frequently contemplates her own future, questioning whether she can leave Maryland and often becoming sick or depressed as a result. On 9 February 1860, for example, after recording her father's receipt of a letter from William, Bond writes of feeling sad, and two days later she took to her bed sick. William himself could not stomach living in Louisiana with the Bonds, and he cut his stay short, returning to Maryland unexpectedly in May 1860. After his return home, Bond again became depressed, likely after hearing stories of life on Josh's plantation. Yet, even with her father and brother's reservations about Josh, Bond does not indicate that they attempted to prevent the marriage, unlike those families studied by Stowe in which southern fathers were willing to use "paternalist persuasion" to influence their daughters' choice of husbands.[52] Perhaps the Munnikhuysen men were motivated by the social and economic implications of the match; this is unlikely, however, as John Anthony did not unduly pressure William to stay in Louisiana despite financial benefit. Bond's father, it seems, was indeed sincere when he said that his daughter's choice was her own.

Bond does not explain her mother's views on her engagement except to say that her mother gave her advice and reminded her to be a "true woman," a term that implies self-sacrifice and women's domestic responsibilities. It is after one of her talks with her mother that Bond turns to her diary to lament her failure as a woman: "Oh! what a sinner I am," she writes; "will a man ever be benefited by me."[53] Taking such evidence into account, it seems likely that Bond's mother did not disapprove of the marriage. Perhaps she did not object because of the blood ties that bound the families (her own maiden name was Bond). Likely, she saw the marriage as one that united her family and promised her daughter security. As Nancy Theriot points out, while belles in the mid-nineteenth century valued companionship and love in choosing their mates, their mothers and grandmothers would have held more stringently to the view of marriage as a family affair.[54]

---

51. Bond associates William's trip to Louisiana with danger and temptation; when she thinks of him in the Deep South, she fears the influence of "evil." See her entries of 12 October, 8 November, 7 December, and 14 December 1859. Likely, she refers to both the dangers and temptations of the slave culture. Some southern women lamented slavery for its negative influence on white men. Bond's contemporary and fellow Methodist Keziah Brevard, for example, in her diary entry of 20 February 1861, writes of her relief that she had no sons, as she was sure they would be corrupted by slavery. See Brevard, *Plantation Mistress on the Eve of the Civil War*, 92.

52. Stowe, *Intimacy and Power*, 100.

53. Entry of 31 May 1860.

54. Theriot, *Mothers and Daughters in Nineteenth-Century America*, 36.

When Bond explains her decision to marry in her journal, the tone and content of her announcement emphasizes the pragmatic—not the romantic—reasons for her marriage. She writes, "My Dr. thinks it better for me to marry now as my health is very bad and this climate is killing me."[55] Unlike the heroines of domestic novels so popular at mid-century, she links her decision to marry firmly with practicality. While it is obvious that she had affection for Howard, she was part of a culture that evaluated women's worth based on the marriages that they made, and Bond certainly realized that she was making a good match, one that reflected well not only on her but on her family.[56]

The impending war had little impact on Bond's own decision to marry except that the national uncertainty exacerbated her discomfort at leaving home. Bond married on 15 January 1861 and was traveling to Louisiana when the state seceded from the Union. If Josh Bond's wealth had influenced her decision to marry so that she could benefit her own family, she soon realized that war disrupted her plans, as Josh was prevented from even sending sugar to Maryland because of the federal navy's blockade of area ports in the spring of 1861.[57] The doubts that Bond had expressed about Howard became silent after their marriage, and she wrote only positively of Howard until the last years of the war.[58]

THE WAR'S IMPACT ON FEMALE ROLES: A "TRUE WOMAN"

On 29 September 1861, Bond admonishes herself to meet crises of war as her mother would: "I must be a 'true woman.' Oh how often those words Have rung in my ears! 'Be a true woman, Mit.' Those are my mother's words."[59] The cult of domesticity and true womanhood are now staple terms in most discussions of nineteenth-century women's roles. Exploring the ideology of true womanhood during the Civil War, historians recognize that many women were forced to cast aside traditionally feminine behaviors that simply did not work for them in the context of war, prudently revising notions of true womanhood in order to survive. Questions

55. Entry of 25 December 1860.

56. The young southern lady "played a vital role in upholding and enhancing her family's reputation." Roberts, *Confederate Belle*, 16.

57. In *Reconstruction in the Cane Fields*, Rodrigue explains that economic difficulty began for many south Louisiana sugar planters before the blockade (32). As early as November 1860, sugar prices were unstable.

58. In *Intimacy and Power* Stowe also notes that women who expressed much doubt before marriage often wrote positively about their husbands after marriage (154). He finds such expression to be part of the planter life of ritual, which cemented elite power and wealth (154).

59. Bond's mother's advice to be a "true woman" obviously had significant influence on Bond. In addition to writing her mother's words in her diary, she records them in two letters, those written on 19 May 1861 and 4 December 1863.

remain about what extent women internalized these role changes and how new responsibilities shaped their sense of identity.[60] Bond's story contributes to such historical discussions. Shaped by war, her understanding of true womanhood changed. She could not simply follow her mother's model but had to create new and acceptable roles for herself that allowed her safety as a refugee in an unfamiliar environment (without her husband to protect her) and that enabled her to take on responsibilities that she never anticipated, such as sugar speculating and family financial management.[61]

As the war intervened early in her marriage, Bond had to struggle to define herself as a wife to a frequently absent husband. Looking at the war's impact on marriage, scholars conclude that southern marriages often underwent changes. Henry Walker, Carol Bleser, and Frederick Heath, for example, have examined elite Alabama families and concluded that the war created changes in gender and power dynamics within the marriage.[62] Bond's example allows us to look at the war's impact on marriage through another lens, analyzing how the war shaped a newlywed's ability to define herself as a wife. For Bond, identifying herself as a wife was difficult during the war, when gender roles were in upheaval. Bond's situation was made worse because her relationship with Howard's mother was tumultuous, and Bond did not look to her mother-in-law, Rebecca, as a role model. In fact, Rebecca's criticisms of Bond, of Howard, and of their relationship complicated Bond's ability to define herself as a wife and daughter-in-law. The criticisms perhaps became more hurtful as Howard's visits and letters decreased.

Bond turned to her diary to counter the negative images of herself that Rebecca presented, and she wrote of events that reinforced her identity as a desirable and

60. Welter explored the term *true woman* in her influential 1966 article "Cult of True Womanhood." Historians who have explored the impact of the Civil War on women's roles and identities include Drew Gilpin Faust, much of whose work explores the impact of the war on women. See also Rable, *Civil Wars;* and Whites, *Civil War as a Crisis in Gender.* Rable's and Cashin's essays in Clinton and Silber, *Divided Houses,* suggest that women gained a greater sense of independence during the war. In the same collection, however, Bynum presents evidence that such independence was weakened in postwar years. Rable, "'Missing in Action'"; Cashin, "'Since the War Broke Out'"; Bynum, "Reshaping the Bonds of Womanhood."

61. See Bond's letters home to Maryland, in which she discusses these roles. She does not discuss them in detail in her diary; instead, she uses her diary to prepare and strengthen herself to perform new roles.

62. Walker, "Power, Sex, and Gender Roles"; and Bleser and Heath, "Clays of Alabama." Walker studies one family, the Claytons, to show that in one couple's marriage the wife gained autonomy during the war that lasted beyond the fighting. Similarly, Bleser and Heath find that Virginia Clay emerged from the war the stronger spouse. Both articles maintain that the war produced profound changes in the internal dynamics of individual marriages.

capable woman, often providing details of compliments she received.[63] As she notes compliments from men other than Howard, she falls back on her identity as a belle, indicating her difficulties in seeing herself as a wife. On 26 November 1864, for example, she is pleased that a "gentleman" addressed her as "Miss" and that another found her to be "a pretty young lady." As the war complicated her ability to fulfill traditional wifely roles, Bond worked to maintain an effective self-image in spite of an absent husband and frequently ill-humored mother-in-law, and she used her diary to help her do so.

Bond's definition of southern womanhood did not involve becoming a mother; she had no intentions of becoming pregnant.[64] Drew Gilpin Faust has shown that during the Civil War many southern women feared pregnancy. They did not want to face such pain and danger while dealing with the anxieties and material deprivations of war. Nor did they want another person to feed and clothe in the failing economy.[65] Such factors certainly influenced Bond, yet her decision to remain childless seemed to have been made before Howard left for war and before she could imagine the hardships she would encounter. Her poor health likely contributed to and enabled her decision, as her status as an invalid would have allowed her to practice abstinence, the only reliable method of birth control available to her.[66] As a consumptive, however, Bond could have had children. While physicians of the time believed that pregnancy, especially multiple pregnancies, could be dangerous for women with the disease, most did not discourage childbearing, seeing motherhood as women's responsibility, even of those suffering with tuberculosis.[67] Bond's own doctor in Louisiana did not discourage her from becoming pregnant.[68] Bond, however, did not seem willing to take the chance, especially when living with Howard's parents, whom she believed were poor role models for their own children, let alone any she might have.

Bond's diary allows us to witness the process of one woman's redefinition of proper feminine behavior. As she responded to the context of war, Bond gained self-assurance and a greater independence, despite the obstacles she encountered in defining herself as a wife. Her voice strengthens in her writing as she matures, endures hardships, and acts capably in contexts that before the war she would never have anticipated. Historians have explored whether women's wartime responsibil-

---

63. See, for example, entries of 24 January and 23 February 1864.

64. See especially Bond's letter to her mother dated 4 May 1862.

65. Faust, *Mothers of Invention*, 123–34.

66. See Herndl, *Invalid Women*. See especially chap. 1, for a discussion of how nineteenth-century women's illness allowed them to abstain from sex, thus controlling the number of children they had.

67. Rothman, *Living in the Shadow of Death*, 107.

68. See her entry of 24 October 1864.

ities created lasting challenges to nineteenth-century gender ideology. Bond did not survive long enough after the war for us to know if she retained her self-assurance, but the last entries of her diary suggest that, although her behavior changed dramatically in response to the war, her views on gender relationships were not radically altered. Even at the war's end, when she acted outside of tradition by raising her own money, making her own plans to travel to Maryland, and taking off her wedding ring, declaring herself a single woman, she held to the paternalist assumption that a husband's duty was to protect his wife at the cost of his own safety. When she believed that Howard had not returned home in order to protect himself and his political convictions, she felt the right to declare her marriage void; Howard evidently had not fulfilled his end of the paternalist bargain.

A STEADFAST RELIGION

Bond's struggle to define herself as a woman and a wife took place within an evangelical Christian context. Her Christianity shaped her daily activities, her identity, and her self-perception. While historians have found that war's devastation and the Confederacy's eventual defeat caused many southern women to question God's plan, Bond held firm to her faith.[69] Her views provide contrast to those of her contemporaries, such as South Carolina diarist Grace Brown Elmore, who struggled with her faith as the South faced defeat and wrote of her mind's tendency to "question the goodness, the mercy of it's [*sic*] maker."[70] Bond, throughout the war, held to the belief that suffering—both her own and the Confederacy's—was for divine purpose. She voiced the view commonly heard from southern pulpits that the war was punishment for the South's failings and that repentance and reformation were necessary to ensure God's forgiveness.[71] She expressed a very similar belief in regard to her own physical suffering, interpreting her pain as God's way of purifying her from her sinful state.

In Maryland Bond was a member of the Methodist Protestant Church (MPC). She frequently wrote of attending the Watters Meeting House, where the local Methodists held quarterly meetings and where she was converted in 1857. She was a member of the Bel Air Methodist Protestant Church and also visited Episcopal, Presbyterian, and Quaker services. Bond's Methodism, however, was not that of her eighteenth-century predecessors, who preached against slavery and encouraged women's active involvement in the church. As Christine Leigh Heyrman shows, by the early nineteenth century southern churches had "retreated from

69. See Faust, *Mothers of Invention;* and Rable, *Civil Wars.*

70. Elmore, *Heritage of Woe,* 123; entry of 20 June 1865.

71. For more on this view, see Faust, "'Without Pilot or Compass'"; and *Mothers of Invention.*

those promises of liberation and invested their energies in upholding the equality and honor of all white men."[72] The churches began to emphasize dominant cultural ideologies such as strict gender roles, the importance of family, and the "cult of domesticity."[73] Methodists had largely silenced members' antislavery sentiments along with those that challenged the authority of the traditional family in order to attract larger followings and to garner respectability.

The Methodist Protestant Church formed in response to a schism in the Methodist Episcopal Church (MEC) during the 1820s and 1830s as reformers advocated power for laymen and ministers and questioned the authority of bishops. On the issue of slavery, the church passed a resolution stating that slavery was not always sinful although it should be discouraged by the church. The General Conference, however, sidestepped responsibility, claiming that it was not authorized to legislate on the subject of slavery.[74] Thus, in the evangelical churches that Bond attended, ministers would have likely encouraged "Christian" responsibility and treatment of slaves but would not have urged abolition or condemned members of their congregations for holding slaves.

The Methodist church also would have urged women to fulfill their roles as Victorian wives and mothers, actively discouraging them from assuming the role of assertive evangelist that had been open to women in the eighteenth century. Bond would have learned in sermons and Sunday school that her spiritual duty should be confined to the home and family, eventually to teaching her children their religious duty and ensuring that they were converted. As a single woman, her religion prepared her for the sacrifice of leaving home and becoming a wife. During the war, her faith provided explanations for the devastation.

Evangelicalism and Religious Rhetoric

Although her religion did not provide Bond with a public role, it did give shape and meaning to her life. As Cynthia Lyerly explains, one of the "enduring aspects of early Methodism was its expansion of human agency."[75] For Bond religion gave

72. Heyrman, *Southern Cross,* 255. Notably, Henry Watters, descendant of a long line of prominent Methodists and the son of Watters Meeting House founder, owned five slaves. U.S. census, slave schedules, Harford County, Md., Henry G. Watters household; National Archives microfilm publication M653, roll 484.

73. Schneider, *Way of the Cross Leads Home,* xxvii. Schneider argues that with the nineteenth-century Methodist Church's emphasis on home and domesticity, "the once subversive way of the cross was domesticated," and women were relegated to fulfilling their religious duties in the home. See also Lyerly, *Methodism and the Southern Mind.*

74. See Calkin, "Slavery Struggle," 205.

75. Lyerly, *Methodism and the Southern Mind,* 184. For further discussion on how through religion

her a sense of purpose beyond being a belle and then a wife as she worked to improve both her own Christianity and that of her family members. Her diary served as a space in which she attempted to define herself as an evangelical Christian woman, especially before war and marriage became prominent themes in her life and in her writing. Bond saw as vital her role as a Christian example and often wrote about the need to speak the right words at the right time in order to exert her influence over those whose salvation seemed uncertain, including that of her siblings, who were not as religious as she. Her religion required that she speak out, albeit in a limited sphere. Nineteenth-century culture dictated proper outlets for women's speech, but religion provided avenues and even moral imperatives for women to speak. Bond's religion gave her cause to speak out, at times instructing men, including her husband and father-in-law.

Historians also note that, paradoxically, while religion allowed women more room to speak and act, it also reinforced traditional feminine qualities of submission and sacrifice.[76] The tension inherent in this paradox is evident in Bond's writing. She wanted to speak from religious conviction, but to do so she had to reconcile her desire to speak with her culture's tenets that women should be silent. In her diary, she alternately urges herself to speak and to remain silent. She contemplates the appropriate time to speak to friends about their Christianity, laying great importance on her words, believing that they could have everlasting results.[77]

In her struggles to act, speak, and think correctly, she reflects the Methodist doctrine that the faithful, once converted, would begin a long, arduous journey of sanctification, leading ultimately to perfection and freedom from sin.[78] In early diary entries, Bond often expressed her desire to improve as a Christian and her disappointment that her spiritual progress was slow. She used her writing to further internal dialogue between her desires and her religious ideals; in short, through her

nineteenth-century women created for themselves meaningful roles, see Mattingly, *Well-Tempered Women;* and Collins, "Women's Voices and Women's Silence." Mattingly and Collins show how religion allowed women to fashion public roles for themselves. Also Matthews, in *Religion in the Old South,* discusses how evangelical religion provided southern women with a sense of purpose and usefulness.

76. Ruether and Keller develop this argument in *Women and Religion in America,* vol. 1. Edwards, in *Scarlett Doesn't Live Here Anymore,* finds that evangelical religion provided southern women with comfort and peace as they accepted subordinate roles in the social order. Smith-Rosenberg, in "Cross and the Pedestal," clarifies the paradox of revivalism: "Though sanctioning individual women's acts of religious self-assertion . . . revivals instilled in these women a heightened sense of spiritual inferiority, which could then . . . be translated into subordination to same-class men and to the new bourgeois family structure" (154).

77. Two good examples of this are found in the entries on 13 and 15 May 1859.

78. See McLoughlin, *American Evangelicals,* 11, for further explanation of nineteenth-century Methodist doctrine.

diary Bond wrote to herself, trying to decide what actions, words, and thoughts coincided with evangelical Christianity. During the spring of 1859, Bond's health began to decline, and her diary entries became more religious in tone and content as she tried to explain to herself the reasons for her suffering and to persuade herself that her illness was a step in her Christian journey.

Many entries served the function of helping her internalize the doctrines of her religion. Faust, referring to religion during the Civil War, observes that women "invok[ed] religious doctrines and texts almost as incantations in their effort to transcend suffering and grief, to wean themselves from the cares of the world."[79] Such a function is evident in Bond's diary before the Civil War. On 12 May 1859, she writes, "Oh! That I may not live for the applause of the world but entirely for Heaven. Oh, that I may ever endeavor to 'do unto all even as I wish to be done by' and 'love my neighbor as myself.' Oh that I may be enabled through grace to mortify the flesh."[80] The repetition evokes the language of trance, and Bond used such language with the goal of redirecting her desires. By echoing the tone, language, and style of sermons, hymns, and the Bible, Bond worked to create an authoritative voice with which to persuade herself to act, think, and speak according to her faith.

In her early religious entries, she relied on many quotations, interrupting her own words with those from the Bible, hymns, sermons, and published spiritual autobiographies. Sometimes she provided a reference for her quotations, but, more often, she simply inserted quotation marks, sometimes failing to close them. On 16 June 1859, she writes, "O that I may not speak my own words so often or think my own thoughts." Bond's diary was a tool for religious self-instruction as she attempted to replace her own words with those of authority. Her writings indicate how religion was both liberating and oppressive for nineteenth-century women. It provided avenues to speak and act but did not always encourage her to use her own words.

During the war, Bond's church attendance declined, in part because physically getting to church was difficult due to her failing health and the physical distance.[81] Also, Bond did not form a strong attachment to the Protestant churches in Louisiana, as she had in Maryland. Her religion during this time began to serve her differently than it had previously. While religious rhetoric remained part of her discourse and she continued to write prayers, the focus of her religious writing changed. In her Maryland entries, she often chastised herself and urged herself to

79. Faust, "'Without Pilot or Compass,'" 256.

80. Bond continues this entry maintaining the sequence through eleven more sentences.

81. A Catholic church, however, was across the street from Bond's house in Abbeville, and she did occasionally visit, although she considered herself an outsider to the ceremonies.

behave better. When writing in Louisiana, in the context of unfamiliar surround-ings, war, and deprivation, Bond was less severe with herself and more frequently used prayer and religious language to reassure herself of divine comfort and guid-ance. At times her written prayers became substitutes for action. For example, on 28 March 1864, she writes: "I am daily expecting to hear of an attack on Shreve-port. Oh! Father spare my husband. I felt very sad last night about him & I dreamed he was trying to escape from them & I was hiding guns & ammunition. All I can do is to pray for him, & that God will give me grace & strengthen suffi-cient as my day." Although Bond could not physically act to help Howard, as she did in her dream, she acted verbally through prayer.

A Protestant's View of Catholicism

Soon after Bond arrived in Louisiana, she changed her church membership from Methodist to the Presbyterian Church South in order to worship with Howard and his family. While in her letters to her family Bond writes of her regret at switching denominations, the greater change for Bond would have been that the region was predominantly Catholic. In Harford she had been part of a comfort-able majority, with 60 percent of the population being Methodist.[82] Living on her in-laws' plantation, Bond would have been aware of the Catholic influence in the surrounding area; when she moved to Abbeville, as a refugee, she became fully im-mersed in Catholic culture.

In her diary, she recorded some details of Catholic services she observed, ex-pressing disagreement with their traditions and reliance on ceremony. On 21 Jan-uary 1864, for example, she describes her visit to the local Catholic church and her disagreement with a congregation member who criticized her for not kneeling. Bond defended herself by arguing that she would not participate in ceremonies she did not understand. The cultural context of the period, however, would have made it likely that Bond's response to the Catholic Church went beyond criticism of doc-trine. As a devout Protestant, she was surely aware of the distrust felt by many Protestants toward Catholics, a distrust that was touted from many pulpits. As Elizabeth Leonard writes, at the mid-nineteenth century, for many Protestant Americans, "the term 'Catholic' automatically provoked a range of fears."[83] While Protestants objected to the tenets of Catholicism, they were also threatened by cul-tural and political implications of the religion's spread. Certain behaviors, such as drinking and dancing, were not condemned by the Catholic Church, and Protes-tants viewed this as moral corruption. Additionally, some viewed Catholicism as a

82. U.S. Census Bureau, *Statistics of the United States in 1860,* 407.
83. Leonard, "Mary Surratt and the Plot to Assassinate Abraham Lincoln," 296.

threat to the United States, a view that stemmed largely from distrust of Catholic immigrants and fear of the political power of the Catholic Church that for many stood in opposition to the nation's emphasis on freedom. In 1832 Lyman Beecher, the well-known Presbyterian minister, issued *A Plea for the West*, in which he accused the Catholic Church of conspiracy to conquer the West, arguing that the rise of Catholicism in new territories would lead to diminished democratic freedoms. Other Protestants joined Beecher in rallying their congregations against Catholic expansion. The newspaper *Protestant Vindicator*—to which Bond subscribed—was established for such a purpose.[84]

Bond was surely aware of the anti-Catholic sentiments in her home state of Maryland. With large-scale immigration of Irish to Maryland during the potato famine, nativist sentiments increased. During the 1850s, the Know-Nothing Party (renamed the American Party) promoted an anti-immigrant and anti-Catholic platform. In the 1856 presidential election, the party's candidate, Millard Fillmore, carried one state—Maryland. Bond initially defines herself against the Catholics, validating her own religious views by noting their faults. Yet as war and her own poor health increased her dependence on the community, she became more accepting of different religious views, developing a broader definition of Christianity than the one she held when she arrived in Louisiana. She gratefully accepts Catholic prayers for her health and is able to write of a local woman, "I believe she is a good christian, a strict catholic though."[85]

FAILING PATERNALISM: SLAVERY ON THE SUGARCANE PLANTATION AND DURING WAR

When Bond moved to Louisiana, she brought with her ideas about slavery that had been formed in Maryland by farmers who owned relatively small numbers of slaves, by a Dutch American father, and by a Methodist culture, albeit one whose critique of slavery had been largely silenced. Soon after her arrival at Crescent Place, she went with Howard to the sugar house to meet some of the slaves, and she interpreted their greeting to her as that of respect and enthusiasm, seeing their roles and her own through the lens of benevolent paternalism.[86] Even at the outbreak of the Civil War, she assumed that the slaves would perform their work competently and even happily as Howard and his family provided them material goods and security.

84. In a letter to her mother of 27 February 1861, Bond says that she plans to subscribe to the newspaper. For more details on Protestant views of Catholicism, see Yrigoyen, "Methodists and Roman Catholics in Nineteenth Century America."

85. Entry of 2 February 1864.

86. Entry of 23 February 1861.

After only a short time in her new home, however, Bond's unexamined assumptions regarding slavery were directly challenged by the violence she encountered on Josh Bond's sugarcane plantation. Bond's father had foreseen that his daughter would be shocked by slavery as she would find it in southern Louisiana, and largely because of that reason, he had been concerned about her marriage.[87] Louisiana sugar planters had reputations for harsh treatment of slaves, and the hard and unhealthy working conditions on the sugarcane plantations were often topics of abolitionist tracts and speeches. As Joan Cashin notes, "slaveowners in the Southwest became notorious for their harshness and greed."[88] Bond's diary shows how one woman attempted to reconcile firsthand evidence of slavery's abuses with her Christianity and paternalist views that had been fostered in the context of Maryland slavery.

Bond's perspective also provides insight into how the war affected slave/mistress relationships and women's views of slavery. Historians have explored how these complex relationships were affected by war and by gender ideologies; frequently, tension built as slaves sought freedom and mistresses resisted change, at times taking on increasingly racist views as the war ended.[89] Bond's view of slavery was initially challenged not by war but by the form of slavery she encountered on her new family's sugarcane plantation. During the war, however, her personal feelings of benevolence toward slaves diminished as her own security was threatened.

While in Maryland, Bond apparently gave little thought to slavery. She took

87. See the letter dated 14 January 1860.

88. Cashin, *Family Venture*, 113. Genovese challenges the horrific reputation of sugar plantations, arguing that because of movements to improve slavery conditions, by the nineteenth century, "the difference in treatment [of slaves] between the Upper and Lower South became steadily less noteworthy" (*Roll, Jordan, Roll*, 54). Similarly, Malone, *Sweet Chariot*, 52–53, while recognizing the extreme physical demands of sugar production, contends that the high rate of slave death was caused not by long hours and labor but by disease from an unhealthy climate. Nevertheless, the culture of slavery in Terrebonne was in stark contrast to Bond's previous experiences.

89. For more information, see Rable, *Civil Wars*, 114–21. He explains that during the war white women discovered for the first time how few slaves accepted paternalist views. As their world was in crisis, white women sought continuity, refusing to see slaves and former slaves outside of the paternalist vision. When slaves refused to act according to traditional roles, white women's views became increasingly racist. See also, Faust, "'Trying to Do a Man's Business.'" She contends that the difficulties that women had managing slaves contributed to their declining support of the Confederacy. Additionally, Weiner, in *Mistresses and Slaves: Plantation Women in South Carolina*, argues that while the ideology of domesticity created a bond between female slaves and mistresses before the war, this bond deteriorated as the war drew to a close. Weiner also notes that white women desperately longed for continuity as they witnessed the destruction of their lifestyle and sought examples of faithful slaves to serve as psychological comfort.

for granted her household servants' place in the social hierarchy and, at times, reminded herself to fulfill her Christian obligations to them. Her experiences on the Bonds' plantation challenged her to think about slavery but not to question the institution itself. While she criticized the abuses she saw, she penned self-conscious defenses of the institution itself, drawing on the ideology of domestic paternalism that was popular in the South. As Marli Weiner observes, "Most of the women who sympathized with slaves and were sensitive to the practical and moral responsibilities they represented did not want to abandon the institution of slavery."[90] Along with the majority of her contemporaries, Bond was too much a product of her culture for her views to undergo radical change.

In her defense of slavery, she writes a series of entries, beginning on 31 December 1861, in which she paints an "ideal" picture of slavery—describing happy, loyal slaves. She offers an image of the slaves, just finished grinding sugar, marching around the house, carrying the overseer, and waving a Confederate flag that Bond had made and presented to them with ceremony. Similarly, she writes of a slave wedding in which Howard performed the ceremony. Her reason for such description is clearly a defense: she writes, "I wonder what the 'Yankees' would think of it if they had seen how happy they were, in their ball dresses."[91] The descriptions are in sharp contrast to her earlier, less descriptive entries of beatings. As she articulated her defense of slavery, she echoed many of the views found in popular southern novels that defended slavery by answering Harriet Beecher Stowe's abolitionist arguments in *Uncle Tom's Cabin*. Caroline Hentz, in *The Planter's Northern Bride*, drew on southern proslavery theology to argue that freedom came from God, not from institutions. Similarly, Maria McIntosh, in *The Lofty and the Lowly*, responded to Stowe with her story of the Montrose family, in which one daughter marries a wealthy Northern capitalist and spends her days ministering to the poor factory workers, who are paid so little they often go hungry. Images of the poor living and working conditions of industrial workers are contrasted to images of the southern plantation, where the slaves are nursed, loved, and cared for. McIntosh contrasts happy plantation scenes with the ugly poverty of the North.[92]

Bond, on her father-in-law's plantation, encountered a system of slavery that

90. Weiner, *Mistresses and Slaves*, 95.

91. Entry of 4 January 1862.

92. Metta Fuller Victor's novel *Maum Guinea* also portrays an idyllic South with caring relationships between slaves and masters. Other popular southern arguments that color Bond's own arguments include those by John C. Calhoun, who famously argued that slavery was a "positive good." Such arguments used as evidence historically "great" civilizations such as Greece and Rome. For more discussion of such arguments, see, for example, Fox-Genovese, *Within the Plantation Household*; Fox-Genovese and Genovese, "Divine Sanction of Social Order"; Moss, *Domestic Novelists in the Old South*.

matched the horrors described in Stowe's novel. Yet, although initially she criticized parts of slavery, she could not or would not imagine life beyond that portrayed in proslavery propaganda. She did not question the institution, as did some of her fellow wartime diarists, including Dolly Lunt Burge, also a Methodist, who declares that she had "never felt that Slavery was altogether right for it is abused by many."[93] Bond's perspective is also unlike that of the politically astute Mary Chesnut, who questions the morality of slavery and, in her well-known appraisal, calls slavery a "curse" as it compromised morals and encouraged white men's brutality. Unlike Chesnut and Burge, whose experiences led them to make political critiques, Bond did not interpret the abuses she witnessed as evidence against the entire system of slavery. She saw slavery through the lens of relationships, locating the problem within the brutality of a few "unchristian" men—Howard's father and later the foreman. Bond's implied argument is that under Christian influence the institution of slavery is a just one.

Bond initially wanted to improve the lot of the slaves at Crescent Place, but her authority in the home was slight. Weiner notes that southern women were taught that their "benevolent nurturing and caring were supposed to extend to those in need—including slaves" (2). Yet Bond's ability to act as a benevolent mistress was frequently thwarted. In a letter to her mother written after a year in Louisiana, Bond admits that she had given up talking to Josh of "right and wrong."[94] Instead, she expresses her concerns in her diary and pleads with herself to keep her objections silent and to control her speech in order to avoid confrontation. Experiencing the war amid a new family and culture, Bond recognized that she was dependent upon her husband's family to provide her support and shelter. In her diary, Bond chides herself for inappropriate speech and passions and hopes to prevent future mistakes.

In one instance, she writes of speaking out against the harsh treatment of a runaway slave by the slave driver. Cleverly, however, she did not address Josh but Howard; she explains, "I spoke to Howard loud enough for his father to hear."[95] Bond's approach shows her awareness that questioning her father-in-law directly—even on what she sees as a moral issue—was socially unacceptable and could harm her already precarious position in her new family. By addressing her husband, she relied on his role as protector and did not overstep her traditional wifely duty as moral counselor. While Bond does not explicitly comment on how her objections to the conditions on Crescent Place influenced her relationship with

93. Burge, *Diary of Dolly Lunt Burge*, 156. The entry is of 8 November 1864.
94. Weiner, *Mistresses and Slaves*, 2; letter of 4 May 1862.
95. Entry of 22 December 1861.

Howard, we can assume that they created at least some tension, as Bond expected Howard to break from his father's example. Although she despaired of having an influence on Josh, she hoped to influence Howard.[96]

Fissures began to appear in Bond's assumptions regarding her own relationship with slaves when Union troops arrived in Terrebonne.[97] Her unease is apparent as she recounts Howard's request to a slave, "old aunt Patience," that she take charge of his wife while he is in Confederate service. Even as she writes that she believes Patience will be faithful, her very act of reassuring herself indicates her doubt. The rationale for Patience's service, Bond explains, is that Howard promised to buy her and her children after the war. She indicates that Patience will be loyal not because of devotion but because of Howard's promise. What she does not admit, however, is that with the presence of Union troops the offer to purchase a slave family, even away from the violence of Crescent Place, was losing its force as an incentive. Patience perhaps recognized the emptiness of Howard's bargain, as Bond does not mention her again.

By 1863 Bond admits her fear of the slaves; she sees some leave for Union lines and writes that their own slaves are "complaining."[98] Slave uprising was a concern for the women left alone during the war, and such concern was nourished by gossip and by the quick spread of reports when slaves did commit violence. The fear of slave insurrection that gripped the South before 1861 was made only greater by the war. Like most southerners, Bond would have known about slave revolts that had occurred earlier in the century. One of the largest and most notorious occurred in Santo Domingo, when in 1791, rebels initiated a twelve-year endeavor to expel the French, abolish slavery, and gain independence. The revolt was especially violent and bloody, and it caused unease in the United States. This and other slave uprisings were covered widely in the American press and became part of nineteenth-century common knowledge.[99] For Bond, however, that it occurred in Santo Domingo might have caused additional tension, as many of the Santo

96. In her diary entry of 2 September 1861, Bond notes her positive influence over Howard.

97. As historians have noted, other Confederate women also had their illusions about slavery shattered after the arrival of Union troops, as slaves fled for Union lines. See Faust, Glymph, and Rable, "Woman's War," 3.

98. Entries of 22 and 23 October 1863.

99. The revolt in Santo Domingo was so embedded in American culture that references to it appeared widely in literature throughout the century. References appear frequently to Toussaint L'Ouverture, the leader of the Haitian government after the initial rebellion. As late as 1871, riddles appeared about the uprising and assumed that readers held knowledge about the event. For example, one riddle asks, "Why are there no eggs in San Domingo?" The answer: "They banished the whites and cast off their yokes" (*Revolution* [New York], 2 February 1871). I thank Carol Mattingly for providing me with this quotation.

Domingo refugees had settled in southern Louisiana, specifically in New Orleans and neighboring parishes.

Within the United States and also close to Bond's Louisiana home was the 1811 Deslondes slave revolt, which occurred outside of New Orleans. Considered the largest in United States history, it resulted in the deaths of many planters and ended in a bloody revenge as the whites beheaded all surviving participants and displayed their heads on spikes along River Road. Smaller rebellions in the New Orleans area followed in 1811 and 1812. In 1831 Nat Turner's insurrection in Virginia resulted in the deaths of sixty whites, mostly women and children. Within Bond's lifetime John Brown led his 1859 raid at Harpers Ferry, which was intended to stir widespread slave insurrection. Bond refers to Brown's raid, as mentioned earlier, and she later notes his execution. Also, on their journey to Louisiana, Bond and Howard stopped at Harpers Ferry and toured the armory. In the South, political leaders often responded to rebellions by periodically tightening controls on slaves. During the Civil War, south Louisiana lawmakers responded as early as the summer of 1861 to fears of insurrection by increasing restrictions on slaves with new rules and patrols that limited their ability to move beyond their own plantations.[100]

Bond's fears of slave violence were not realized. Nevertheless, as a result of the war and her experience as a refugee, her concern for the slaves and her commitment to benevolent paternalism decreased. In diary entries written when she was a refugee in Abbeville, Bond hints at power struggles with the household slaves. The most obvious conflict is with Amanda (Mandy), who refused to hide her hatred for the Bonds and her support of the Union troops.[101] Bond seems to have no understanding of Mandy's desire for freedom, describing her as an "incubus" and professing relief when Rebecca sells her. Bond's waning benevolence toward slaves is most evident when she records that one of their slave's (Mintty's) "beaus" is assaulted in their kitchen by some local men and brutally shot in the face. Even though she admits seeing no reason for the violence, she does not criticize it. Instead, she offers the men a weak excuse by assuming they were drunk.[102]

Mandy's hatred likely fueled Bond's fear and suspicion as she interacted with the other slaves. Slave/mistress relationships became more uneasy as slaves began to realize and to act upon their freedom and mistresses were realizing their own dependence. As Faust explains, "White women's dependence on their slaves grew simultaneously with slaves' independence of their owners, creating a troubling situation of confusion and ambivalence for mistresses compelled to constantly re-

100. Roland, *Louisiana Sugar Plantations*, 34.
101. Entry of 27 October 1863.
102. Entry of 10 February 1865.

assess, to interrogate, and to revise their assumptions as they struggled to reconcile need with fear."[103] Bond reacted to the slaves' increasing power by asserting her own authority. After Mandy is sold, Bond uses authoritative language when she describes her interactions with Mintty and Betsy. She begins to note in her diary, for example, when she "makes" Mintty work, using command language that had previously been rare in her writing.[104]

In her effort to assert her authority, Bond used her diary to reinforce her own sense of power textually. In her entries, she allows Mintty a voice only when it shows her in an inferior role. In two entries, Bond pens scenes in which she responds calmly to Mintty's fear or confusion. She writes, for example: "About twelve o'clock Mintty rushed in, with her eyes considerably enlarged and says, 'Oh Miss Mitt, Yankees in town.' She looked so frightened I did not feel at all afraid, but sat by the window in my room and watched them passing." Bond contrasts her restraint with Mintty's near-hysteria and emphasizes behaviors that reinforced traditional slave/mistress relationships.[105] In her last mention of Mintty, Bond portrays her as a faithful nurse. Mintty's voice is silent, and Bond, in her own pain and despair, takes comfort in what for her was a familiar relationship between a servant and mistress.

Throughout the war Bond did not question the institution of slavery. As hardships mounted and as she lost her physical strength, she became more dependent upon slaves than she had been before the war. With her own growing dependence, Bond resisted admitting her slaves' independence. Her desire for continuity in racial relationships is evident also in her letters home; in them she imagined her family home as one of domestic tranquility in which the Munnikhuysen' household servants, Charlotte and Betsy, happily performed their duties. Yet Bond's repeated questioning about Charlotte and Betsy indicates the fragility of her ideals.[106] While she wanted to hear about and to encourage their faithfulness, her underlying suspicion must have been that, like Amanda, Charlotte and Betsy would assert their independence when given the opportunity.

103. Faust, *Mothers of Invention*, 61.

104. Entries of 9 May, 22 November, and 27 December 1864.

105. Entries of 28 December 1863; see also 8 December 1864. Bond perhaps also realized that Mintty was an important audience in light of fears and rumors of slave uprisings. Mintty was one of the few household slaves loyal to Bond. Even if Bond did not fear violence from Mintty, she would have been concerned about her leaving the household to claim her freedom since Bond relied on Mintty as a nurse and caregiver during her illness.

106. See letters of 4 May 1862; 2 November and 4 December 1863; 21 September 1864. In her diary, however, including her Maryland entries, Bond seldom mentions Betsy and Charlotte, and when she does, she does not elaborate, seeming to take their presence for granted.

For Bond slavery had been marginal in her thoughts before her marriage. She took for granted racial hierarchy, and her only concern was that she present a Christian example to her servants. Once in Louisiana, her views of slavery as a positive good were challenged, and on her in-laws' plantation, she defended the institution of slavery by attempting to show herself to be a kind mistress who benefited from the loyalty of her slaves. Her criticisms of slavery on Crescent Place had little influence, and as a refugee, Bond no longer criticized slavery or its abuses. She seemed to lose concern for her slaves' spiritual and even physical well-being in the course of her own wartime struggles.

LOVE, FRIENDSHIP, AND POWER: THE WAR'S IMPACT ON RELATIONSHIPS

The war challenged Bond's assumptions regarding relationships—those with slaves as well as gender and family relationships. Such changes in the way she interacted with others impacted Bond's own sense of self, as nineteenth-century women formed the core of their identities through their relationships.[107] They were daughters, mothers, wives, and daughters-in-law, and their sense of self-worth often relied on the success of these relationships. A significant topic for scholars in recent years focuses on the impact of the Civil War upon families; the war shook the structure of the family—the very institution that Confederate rhetoric promised the war would protect.[108] Financially, the war devastated the Bonds.[109] On the level of relationships within the family, the war also had an impact. For Bond the war—with its deprivations and enforced separations—prevented her from comfortably becoming a part of Howard's family. In such a context, she often found developing and maintaining relationships difficult. Her perspective challenges prevailing ideas about nineteenth-century women's networks while clearly illustrating the strong attachment southern women formed to their family of origin.

Female Networks

Carroll Smith-Rosenberg, in her well-known essay "The Female World of Love and Ritual," describes nineteenth-century female relationships as forming "a world

---

107. See Fox-Genovese, "Family and Female Identity," 18–19.

108. Scholarship has focused specifically on how the war affected gender roles within the family; in *Civil War as a Crisis in Gender*, Whites argues that although initially southern women supported the war, believing that it would strengthen the southern family, they eventually realized that the absence of male family members and the economic devastation of war did not protect but, rather, harmed the traditional family structure. As the war dragged on, they began to resist the traditionally masculine roles that the war required them to take. See also Clinton, *Southern Families at War*.

109. The postscript provides further details on the families after the war.

in which hostility and criticism of other women were discouraged, and thus a mi-
lieu in which women could develop a sense of inner security and self-esteem."[110]
Following Rosenberg, other scholars describe women's worlds as dominated by intimate relationships with other women and distant, emotionally starved relationships with men.[111] Even before the war, in her first few diary entries, Bond challenges this view. The world she describes is one of a close, extended family, both
female and male, and bears little resemblance to that described by Smith-Rosenberg. While women family members, especially her mother, are important to her,
so are male family members. For example, her cousin Howard Munnikhuysen is
frequently her confidant; her doctor, George Archer, lends her emotional support.
Another cousin, George Glasgow, is also a close friend. The social world that Bond
depicts is aligned with that described by Jean Friedman: one based on "interde-
pendent kin connections that were reinforced by membership in local evangelical
churches."[112]

Once in Louisiana, Bond looked to both men and women as she created a life
for herself. When she first arrived at Crescent Place, Bond spent most her time
with Howard, occasionally going to his store with him and waiting impatiently for
him when he was away. While she visited local women with her mother-in-law
and cousin Laura, she saw Howard as her closest companion. When living as a
refugee, most of Bond's support came from women; the largely female world that
Bond inhabited was also fraught, however, with discord and disappointment. Lee
Ann Whites, in her study of women in wartime Augusta, Georgia, found that
women "compensate[d] for the absence of men through closer and more tightly
knit relationships among female kin."[113] Bond attempted to see her mother-in-
law, Rebecca, and some of her new female acquaintances as surrogates for her family network in Maryland, yet, in contrast to White's findings, she was not rewarded
with close family connections. Instead, conflict marked many of her relationships
with women in south Louisiana.

Bond often recorded disputes among her female acquaintances. She followed
the turbulent relationship of Mrs. Maxwell and Mrs. Robertson, who often did not
speak, and that of Mrs. Maxwell and Mrs. Nixon (Maxwell's mother), who often
openly disagreed. Bond also recorded conflicts between herself and other women
in Abbeville. She and Mrs. Maxwell, their landlord for a time, argued over rent,
for example, which Bond found too high. Her most contentious relationship, how-

110. Smith-Rosenberg, "Female World of Love and Ritual," 64.

111. See, for example, Theriot, *Mothers and Daughters*, 37, 64, 67; and Stowe, *Intimacy and Power*, 58.

112. Friedman, *Enclosed Garden*, 3.

113. Whites, *Civil War as a Crisis in Gender*, 33.

ever, was with her mother-in-law, Cousin Rebecca. Initially, their relationship seemed to hold promise, but once they set up house in Abbeville without Howard, their interactions became marked by bitterness. Bond explained their arguments by assuming that Rebecca was envious of Howard's affection, but conflict surrounded money and property as well. Rebecca berated Bond for marrying Howard instead of a richer man, clearly indicating to her daughter-in-law that the family wealth was still in the elder Bond's hands, and Bond herself indicated that she incurred expenses while living in Abbeville.[114] She and Rebecca also argued about ownership of Howard's property. To see Rebecca's side of the story, we can only read between the lines. While Bond and her mother often talked about religion and about becoming better Christians, Rebecca did not seem quite as open to such topics and especially not to Bond's advice. Rebecca appeared to favor hierarchical relationships between parents and children and thought Bond was overstepping her role when she offered her advice and moral instruction.

The relationships between women that Bond describes are complex and fraught with difficulty; thus, they complicate Smith-Rosenberg's argument about female networks. The hardships and uncertainties of war created contexts in which such networks were shaken, especially fledgling relationships such as that between Rebecca and Bond. Yet, at the same time, female networks were essential during the Civil War. Bond recounts how she relied on other women as caretakers when she was ill, and she served the same role for others in her circle when they were in need. The war—with its deprivations and mental stresses and the absence of male family members, who had traditionally offered security—redefined female networks as often being necessary for survival but also as sites for conflict.

Male/Female Relationships

During war women's relationships with men also became sites for conflict as, men, both Confederate and Union, no longer adequately filled their traditional roles as southern women's protectors. This change in gender relationships was often first noticed by southern women when they came into contact with Union soldiers. Bond and many other women Civil War diarists chronicle their first encounters with Union soldiers, which frequently illustrated that the status of a "lady" held little influence during war.[115] In 1862 Bond writes of Union soldiers searching their home looking for Howard. She writes in detail of her interactions with the officer

114. See the entry of 1 December 1863.

115. See, for example, the diaries of Dolly Lunt Burge and Grace Brown Elmore. Both Burge and Elmore pen entries that bear comparison to Bond's 29 June 1862 narration of her visit by Union troops. All three diarists emphasize that they behaved appropriately. They were calm, strong, but also ladylike. Their status, behavior, and gender, however, afforded them little protection.

in charge, explaining that, even though she has every reason to be frightened and angry, she does not show weakness, nor does she give reason for offense. She is honest, polite, and "lady-like," and the officer in charge comments as such. Thus, she initially believes that the officer will fulfill his role as protector and gentleman, and she writes him a letter requesting that their property be saved. When she receives no reply, she recognizes that her behavior and role as a lady have little power to protect her, Howard, or their property, even from officers whom she would under different circumstances know as gentlemen.

In addition to noting the failure of Union men to uphold gender norms, Bond soon observed that war affected the reciprocal relationships between southern men and women. As historians have found, women saw men's failure to protect the home as weakness and began to assert their own self-interest.[116] Women acted with strength outside their traditional sphere, and they began to resent their men, who did not seem capable of protecting either the Confederacy or the home. Throughout the war, Confederate newspapers, poems, and songs heralded the strength of southern women, sometimes at the expense of their men. The poet Henry Timrod, for example, urges the faltering soldier to "turn / To some brave maiden's eyes" and "like your women feel, /And in their spirit march." Similarly, George Fitzhugh, in his 1861 article "The Women of the South," credits southern women for supporting the war effort with bravery and sacrifice and argues that they, not southern men, were the first to champion the war. And, close to home for Bond, the fall of New Orleans was frequently seen as a failure of southern men to protect the city.[117]

Once in Abbeville, Bond mentions interactions with men that reflect either their innocent incompetence or their intentional spite. Her doctor, she writes, "left me ill without even coming in my room to see me." Her next doctor often failed to come when called because he was drunk. She describes the men in Abbeville as "the meanest set of men," who "live by gambling and cheating women and children," and she accuses her neighbor, Mr. Wise, a merchant, of "resort[ing] to many mean things to spite us." Similarly, she records an unsuccessful attempt by a Confederate soldier to help her complete a business transaction. The soldier attempted

116. See Faust, "Altars of Sacrifice," "Trying to Do a Man's Business," and *Mothers of Invention*. She argues that this disillusion undermined women's support of the Confederate cause. See also Clinton, *Other Civil War;* and Bleser, *In Joy and in Sorrow,* in which several essays show how the Civil War undermined the traditional male hierarchy. Additionally, Whites, in *Civil War as a Crisis,* shows that "Confederate men found themselves positioned more like their dependents. [And] Confederate women found themselves positioned more like their men" (12).

117. For a detailed discussion of women's reaction to the fall of New Orleans and to Benjamin Butler's rule in the city, see Rable, "'Missing in Action.'"

to help but then left town, and Bond reports, "But he has gone and I have not got my cottonade yet." In spite of the soldier's bravado, the job is not completed.[118] As the patriarchal system failed to protect her, Bond expressed distrust in the men around her, eventually even her husband.

Bond's critique of southern men did not extend, however, to criticism of the Confederacy, as it did for some of her contemporaries, including Grace Brown Elmore and Clara Solomon. Like Bond, Elmore decried the lack of help she received from southern men, but she broadened her criticism to encompass their performance on the battlefield as well, assuming that if they were "unmanly" at home, they were likewise in war. Similarly, Solomon linked her criticism of local businessmen's self-interested dealings to their lack of patriotism.[119] Although the actions of local men required Bond to become more self-sufficient and to lose confidence in traditional gender roles, she did not connect her personal experiences to the political arena.

SICKNESS AND MEDICAL PRACTICES

Bond's health was a frequent topic in her diary, especially after November 1858, when she writes about a prolonged illness accompanied by shoulder and chest pain. Even when Bond did not write about her health directly, it figured in her diary in that her experiences were filtered through her illnesses. Victims of consumption usually declined toward death over four or five years, although the disease was unpredictable. Patients could die suddenly, or their illness could go into remission for up to thirty years.[120] The characteristic signs of the disease included a wracking cough, lethargy, and eventual coughing up of blood as blood vessels burst in the lungs.

In the nineteenth century, tuberculosis was often at an advanced stage before it was diagnosed.[121] In Bond's case, it is not clear when she realized she had the disease. The first specific illness she records is on 4 May 1859, when she writes that she has neuralgia, nerve pain that is usually indicative of feeble health. Bond seemed to suffer mostly from facial neuralgia, one of the more common forms of the disorder, which is marked by sharp or burning pain, with the skin over the affected areas often becoming red, swollen, and tender. The pain associated with neuralgia varies from excruciating to mild tingling. Throughout May until August 1859, Bond was frequently sick and seemed aware that her illness may be chronic.

---

118. See the entries of 3 November 1862; 5 December, 7 December, and 20 December 1863; and 17 September 1864.

119. Elmore, *Heritage of Woe,* esp. 97 and 118; Solomon, *Civil War Diary of Clara Solomon,* 395.

120. Rothman, *Living in the Shadow,* 15.

121. Warboys, *Spreading Germs,* 196.

By the fall of 1859, coughing was a prominent symptom. After August 1859, Bond wrote of feeling sick and tired on occasion but did not record an extended illness again until February 1860, after which time she frequently mentioned that she was confined to bed and prevented from other activities because of her health.

During the years before her marriage, Bond came to see herself as an invalid and described herself as having a "delicate constitution." As Sheila Rothman explains, the designation of consumptives as "invalid" was "as much social as a medical category," and those with the disease "were permitted, even expected, to modify social obligations" in order to improve their condition.[122] Bond's decision to move to Louisiana was influenced by the advice of her doctors to seek warmer weather. Her marriage to Howard, who was medically trained, was also likely seen as advantageous for someone in Bond's health. When she was first settling into her new home, she did not write much about her health and seemed to think that her new lifestyle had benefited her. In a letter to her mother dated 27 February 1861, she reported that she was "not very sick" and was gaining strength. By April or May, however, she was ill again. She did not write in her diary during this period but wrote to her mother about her illness.[123] Soon after her arrival in Abbeville, Bond suffered a serious bout of illness, with pain in her lungs and hemorrhages.[124] In August 1863, she concluded that her disease was not improving, and she began to contemplate death. From the fall of 1863, her health continued to decline; she often wrote that she felt "badly" and that she had pain in her lungs, attributing this to harsh surroundings, lack of medicine, and an unbalanced diet. By February 1864 her consumption was quite advanced. She wrote of weakness and of trouble breathing, eating, and sleeping.

The medical attention she received seems often contradictory. Bond had various doctors, each of whom had slightly different medical opinions. In July 1860, one doctor diagnosed her with a "nervous spell." On 17 November 1863, she writes that her doctor "laughed" and told her to "take a walk," that her throat, not her lungs, was the problem. In May 1864, even as Bond is coughing blood, a doctor advised her that her lungs were improving. Beginning in July 1864, she was frequently bedridden. After three months of serious illness, she seemed to improve in late September.[125] At this time, her doctor decided that she did not have consumption, but by the end of October her condition again worsened, and she was coughing blood. Her doctors' hesitancy to diagnose her condition was not unusual given

122. Rothman, *Living in the Shadows*, 4.

123. See app. 1 for the letter of 19 May 1861.

124. See her entry of 5 July 1863 and her letter to her mother dated 2 November 1863.

125. On 21 September 1864, she wrote to her sister Ann Lee saying that she had been near death. See app. 1.

that the disease bore symptoms common with other, less-deadly conditions until its last stage, at which time the patient became emaciated and debilitated by constant joint pain, uncontrollable diarrhea, and a hollow cough.

As Bond battled the disease, her treatments often caused her great discomfort and varied from large doses of medicine to bleeding. Such remedies were representative of mid-century mainstream medicine, although bleeding and purging— treatments termed "heroic" medicine—were beginning to lose credibility.[126] Bond writes of being cupped, a procedure in which a warm glass was placed over a cut to cause bleeding as the pressure inside the glass dropped. She was treated also by blistering, or the placing of hot plasters or a heated glass onto the skin to raise blisters, which were then drained. When she was not being bled, she was often medicated with calomel, a form of mercury that worked as a laxative and was often used in large doses. In Louisiana she frequently took opium. She also used herbal treatments, such as radish leaves and rhubarb. At times these treatments were prescribed by physicians or by Howard, but at other times Bond decided on her own medication, also a common practice of the period.

In interpreting the impact of Bond's illness on her worldview, we cannot forget that nineteenth-century culture in fact valued images of the sick but desirable woman, images that emphasized women's weakness during a period when women, at least in the North, were arguing for more power.[127] We should also keep in mind Smith-Rosenberg's argument that during the nineteenth century some women might have used their illness as a way to gain control over their lives and as a way to protest or to "opt out" of their traditional roles.[128] We may examine Bond's own poor health through such a cultural lens, arguing that at times her sickness allowed her to excuse herself from social routines and responsibilities, especially when she was depressed or upset. After writing to Howard to deny him her affections, for example, she berated herself for not loving him and then took to bed sick for two weeks. At times her bouts of neuralgia appear to be associated with her reluctance to leave Maryland; tellingly, she took to bed after accepting an engagement ring

126. Cassedy, *Medicine in America,* 29.

127. See, for example, Sontag, *Illness as Metaphor,* in which she notes how the disease of consumption was associated with attributes of delicate beauty and heightened sensitivity. See also Herndl, in *Invalid Women,* who shows that between 1840 and 1890 women were increasingly defined as sick and weak. Also relevant to this discussion is Poovey, *Uneven Developments.* While Poovey focuses on women in England, her arguments are largely valid to women's condition in America.

128. Smith-Rosenberg, "Hysterical Woman," 208. See also Herndl, *Invalid Women,* 28–30. She discusses the benefits that poor health could allow nineteenth-century women as they could claim release from restrictive or unpleasant duties and responsibilities.

from Howard.[129] As mentioned earlier, after hearing from her brother about his experiences in Louisiana, she became sick. Bond's status as an invalid could very well have given her the power to escape from her social responsibilities when she was unhappy or when she needed time to think and to write. It also allowed her to abstain from sex when pregnancy during war and amid a new family would have caused her hardship. But at the same time, in following this line of argument, we must also remember that her disease was a physical reality that finally ended her life.

WAR IN SOUTH LOUISIANA

As early as September 1861, the Civil War's impact surfaces in Bond's writing when she notes the rising price of meat. She felt its devastation, however, in May 1862, when Howard was implicated in an ambush of Union soldiers near Houma, an accusation that resulted in Howard's flight from home, the burning of Crescent Place by Union soldiers, and Bond's move to Abbeville as a refugee. The ambush left two Union soldiers dead and two injured.[130] Citizens of the area refused aid to the wounded soldiers and treated the dead with violence, reportedly stamping their faces with boot heels.[131]

After the ambush, Gen. Benjamin Butler ordered Lt. Col. John Keith, of the Twenty-first Indiana Volunteers, to go to Houma to "arrest and punish" those involved. Keith arrived in Terrebonne Parish on 12 May, arresting locals and threatening them with execution if they did not provide information about the event. He was given a list of names, including those of Howard and his brother, Wilmore (Wellie).[132] As Bond mentions in her diary, a family friend, Dr. J. L. Jennings, was also implicated. The Bonds, along with Jennings, Albert Woods (editor of the *Houma Ceres*), and a former Confederate lieutenant named Morelle, were thought to have led the ambush. On 16 May Colonel Keith ordered that the property of the suspects who had fled be destroyed. The *Ceres* newspaper office was burned, and the parish jail was destroyed because one of the wounded soldiers had been confined there. The Bonds lost "one dwelling house, furniture, and contents; one sugar house, filled with sugar; from 50 to 100 negro houses and other outhouses;

129. For representative examples of such entries, see those of 13 and 15 June and 2 October 1858, 4 May 1859, and 20 November 1860.

130. The event is described in a letter from Federal lieutenant colonel John Keith, of the Twenty-first Indiana Volunteers, written on 22 May 1862, to Gen. Benjamin Butler. See U.S. War Department, *War of the Rebellion*, ser. 1, vol. 15, chap. 27, 450–56.

131. Roland, *Louisiana Sugar Plantations*, 121.

132. Bond describes this event in her diary in an entry from June 1862 and defends Howard, writing that he had no part in the killings.

one steam saw and corn mill; three stables; two corn-houses with contents; one cooper shop and blacksmith shop, with tools and other contents; one store-house, filled with molasses; two buggies and harness; stacks of hay and fodder." They also had livestock, wagons, and farm equipment taken.[133]

The incident of the property burnings in Houma was not the only encounter with war for south Louisiana citizens. Military action in this area has traditionally been overlooked as historians have considered it to have had little importance to the overall war strategy. Yet the Civil War was felt intensely in the area through organized military battles, guerilla warfare, plundering by Union, Confederate, and guerilla soldiers, and shortages of food, medicine, and clothing. In June 1861, a northern blockade closed the mouth of the Mississippi River, stopping goods from coming in as well as making it difficult for sugar planters to transport their produce to markets.

In addition to blockades, south Louisiana endured military action beginning in April 1862, after New Orleans fell to the Union. Some planters in southeastern Louisiana left immediately for Texas to avoid seeing their property invaded. Most waited, however, relying on the protection of a small Confederate force on the bayou. In October 1862, Brig. Gen. Godfrey Weitzel was ordered to take the region and arrived in Donaldsonville accompanied by four thousand Union troops. They began moving down both sides of the Lafourche toward Thibodaux. On 27 October, Confederate forces attempted to stop the advance at Labadieville near Thibodaux but were defeated. After this defeat, many planters who had stayed on their property after the fall of New Orleans chose to leave, and, as a result of Weitzel's campaign, the Lafourche area fell under Union control. Clashes continued into 1863 between Confederate brigadier general Alfred Mouton's troops and Weitzel's. Along with military action of 1862–63, citizens of southern Louisiana suffered with lack of food and other goods and endured pillaging of their personal property by Federal troops and sometimes even by their own troops.[134]

During April and May 1863, the Lafourche district became the site of a new Union effort as Gen. Nathaniel Banks led his army on the Bayou Teche Expedition from Berwick Bay (Brashear City, now Morgan City) to Alexandria, Louisiana, seizing and destroying property along the way. After Banks had moved through the region, Maj. Gen. William Franklin led Federal troops up the Teche from Berwick Bay to New Iberia in the fall and early winter of 1863 with the goal of reaching Texas, engaging in skirmishes as they progressed. Then, in 1864, Banks

133. U.S. War Department, *War of the Rebellion*, ser. 1, vol. 15, chap. 27, 454.
134. Bragg, *Louisiana in the Confederacy*, 131–33.

began the Red River Campaign, an effort to control the central and western portions of the state, and, again, Union troops began moving up the Teche in March of that year.

The marshes and swamps provided an ideal location for the guerilla warfare that began early in the war. Bond writes in her diary about skirmishes in southern Louisiana when Federal forces, often Federal scouting parties, advanced from Brashear City, Baton Rouge, and other areas of Federal concentration. The results of the fighting and occupation color Bond's writing as well. Union troops had burned towns and destroyed property as they passed through. Livestock had been killed for food and for revenge; crops were either eaten or demolished.

In reading Bond's diary entries, we see the gradual effects of the military campaigns and the shortages of food, medicine, and clothing. Perhaps more so than her deprivations of material goods, Bond mourned her separation from her family and her inability to send or receive mail. Bond maintained her loyalty to Maryland, though criticizing her home state's failure to secede.

We also see Bond growing somewhat accustomed, or perhaps numb, to the violence around her. In the early years of the war, she writes of the violence of battle with horror and amazement, noting, for example, the carnage at Manassas and the bloody results of a canon explosion near Thibodaux.[135] As the war drags on, however, she records battles matter-of-factly, dwelling little on their human consequences beyond those of her own family.

FUNCTIONS OF LITERACY AND THE DIARY

Even though Bond's formal education was short, reading and writing were important parts of her life, before and during the Civil War.[136] In Maryland, when entertaining took up much of her time, she looked forward to "quiet Saturday evenings" with her books, papers, and letters. In Louisiana, she continued to make time for reading and writing, even though her new family disapproved. Bond's mother-in-law, it seems, did not share the value that Bond placed on literacy, and this difference could have added to the tensions in their relationship. Nineteenth-century women could be considered selfish for spending time reading alone, with popular conduct books cautioning them against self-interested reading that took

---

135. See her entries of 23 February and 28 August 1861.

136. She mentions only once her school attendance; see the entry of 6 March 1859. Occasionally, she mentions former schoolmates. Most girls of Bond's class received sporadic education, which usually ended completely when they reached their mid-teens. For further detail on southern girls' education, see Edwards, *Scarlett Doesn't Live Here,* 17.

them away from their domestic responsibilities.[137] Bond, more than many of her contemporaries, looked forward to her personal time, in which, in addition to reading and writing in her diary, she wrote poetry, often sentimental verses that expressed her emotional and spiritual views. Ronald and Mary Zboray have found that for antebellum women, reading alone "commonly signified loneliness" and that most "seldom expressed any sense of escape or relief or even desire to read in private if social options presented themselves."[138] For Bond, however, intellectual development was important and was often synonymous with moral growth, both of which required sufficient time alone. Challenging the feminine ideal of self-deprecation in regard to women's intelligence, Bond admitted that she did think of herself as smart;[139] she would likely have seen her intelligence as largely a result of her own dedication to self-improvement.

Bond's literacy acts were imbued with purpose; they were often active experiences serving as means for moral instruction and self-growth.[140] When reading, Bond often interacted with the texts, copying passages into her diary, describing her views of the works, and relating them to her experiences. In an entry on 14 May 1859, for example, she writes about a spiritual autobiography she is reading: "I have been reading a memoir entitled Memoir of Susan Allibone 'A life hid with Christ in God.' It truly is a delightful book. I see so many of my own heart sentiments in it. Oh! if I was such a watchful Christian. But I am such a wicked sinner." In the entry, she continues to ponder her behavior as a Christian, using both her reading and her writing as tools for self-instruction. While she read aloud to friends and to Howard, she seemed to view such reading acts as beneficial for others, whereas reading alone was self-constructive.[141] She drew guidance from various genres, including hymns, autobiography, fiction, poetry, Scripture, and even her own diary.

During the last years of the war, Bond's reading became even more important to her, and its functions changed. She began to value her books because they distracted her from wartime worries and offered her companionship. As Zboray and

137. See Bond's entries of 4 September 1858, 14 May 1859, and 3 January 1864. In the entry of 21 November 1864 Bond records the details of one quarrel in which Rebecca accuses Bond of thinking herself as smart. See also Ashworth, "Susan Warner's *The Wide, Wide World*," 145.

138. Zboray and Zboray, "Books, Reading, and the World of Goods," 601.

139. Entry of 21 November 1864.

140. For further discussion on nineteenth-century women's reading as active and as impacting identify formation, see Kelley, "Reading Women / Women Reading," 401–24. Kelley writes, "Immersing themselves in a variety of ideas and personae, reading women explored a world of possible selves" (415). She also notes the social nature of reading for many women. Likewise, in "Rhetorical Power in the Victorian Parlor," Tonkovich shows that the popular periodical *Godey's Lady's Book* encouraged women to read actively for self-improvement.

141. See, for example, her entries of 12 March 1860 and 6 January 1861.

Zboray note, for nineteenth-century women, books "offered solace, kindled memories, and, in general, helped maintain ties to loved ones."[142] With Howard away,
infrequent mail from her family in Maryland, and growing conflict between herself and Rebecca, she began to take comfort in her books, seeing the books themselves as well as the characters within them as friends. It is during this time that
she began to keep the list of books she read that is found in appendix 2.

Another constant companion for Bond was her diary.[143] Throughout her
courtship, marriage, and then the war, Bond turned to her diary almost as she
would to a friend for advice and understanding. Some diarists named their journals, emphasizing the support they garnered from personal writing and from the
rhetorical space the diary offered. Clara Solomon, for example, called her diary
"Philomen." Although Bond did not name her diary, she clearly valued the acts of
writing, thinking, and reflecting that it allowed her. Bond's journal functioned in
various ways, serving as a tool for self-instruction and self-persuasion. As did many
women of her class, Bond viewed journal writing as a method of improving her
education, her character, and her self-discipline. For these reasons, regular diary
keeping was also a sign of gentility.[144] Her writing also allowed her to exert order
and control over her life during tumultuous times. Noting a similar function in the
diaries of nineteenth-century women on the western frontier, Gayle R. Davis
writes that for these women diary keeping served as a "significant coping mecha-
nism, through which the women adjusted to the hardships, freedom, and challenges of the frontier." Jennifer Sinor also finds such a purpose in the diary of a
woman who homesteaded in the Dakotas in the late nineteenth century. She concludes that through her writing the diarist "creates a fiction of stability" and "order[s] out the unstable." It is not surprising that Bond as she faced the upheavals
of the Civil War and the challenges of a new culture used her writing at times to
cultivate a sense of constancy in her ever-changing world.[145]

The functions of the diary lead to questions of audience. Many well-known diarists, such as Mary Chesnut, Kate Stone, and Sarah Morgan, revisited their diaries before publication. Bond did not do so, lending validity and immediacy to
her account. Although she did not revise her work for publication, she did at times
show concern with word choices and stylistic detail; this is obvious by her strike-

142. Zboray and Zboray, "Books, Reading, and the World of Goods," 587.

143. Some scholars differentiate between the terms *journal* and *diary*, using the first to indicate re-
flective writing and the second to describe a more straightforward recording of events. I have used the
terms interchangeably, agreeing with Bunkers that the distinctions are often artificial. See Bunkers, *Diaries of Girls and Women*, 12.

144. See Gorham, *Victorian Girl and the Feminine Ideal*, 103.

145. See Davis, "Women's Frontier Diaries," 5; Sinor, "Reading the Ordinary Diary," 131–32.

outs, word changes, and spelling corrections. Also, she was concerned with her presentation of factual information, using parenthetical explanatory notes when, for example, she recorded the overseer's proper name but added his position in parenthesis.[146] Along with attention to style and correctness, the diary provides other evidence that Bond anticipated future readers. In her entry of 7 March 1864, Bond lists food and supplies that she has been given and then writes, "Perhaps it is childish to write such things in my journal, but it may be my loved ones at home will not know of the kindnesses their loved one met with in a strange land, amid strangers, and foreigners unless they see it here." She also writes of reading some entries to Cousin Rebecca.[147] While today we associate diaries with privacy, seeing them as books under lock and key, the secrecy associated with diaries was a twentieth-century invention.[148] This is not to say that women shared their diaries freely. It was not unusual, however, for them to show their writing to good friends and close family members as Bond shares some of her entries with Rebecca. Yet Bond also writes of Captain Mouton's request to read her diary, one that she refuses, obviously not deeming him an intimate enough acquaintance.[149]

Often, however, Bond seems to write for herself. She is indeed an audience for her writing, noting in her journal that she periodically rereads earlier entries to herself. In the entry of 29 September 1863, she writes, "I have been reading the first of my journal—& there I speak of having too good an opinion of myself, & being self righteous. *Oh my God* keep me from *all such*. I *know* that is *one* of my *besetting sins*." As she reads religious tracts and spiritual autobiographies for self-instruction and growth, she also reads her own diary.

A number of historians and literary critics have asserted the value of women's historical diaries by arguing that the diaries contain characteristics of texts written for an outside audience and, therefore, that they can be read as public and not simply private documents. Historian Randall Jimerson concludes, for example, that many wartime diarists felt they were making history by writing about their experiences.[150] Similarly, Elizabeth Fox-Genovese observes in her study of women's personal writing during the Civil War that "one after another, they begin implicitly to write for posterity—to write in support of their cause and to justify their ways to God, to each other, to their enemies, and to the world."[151] Classifying most women's diaries, including Bond's, as either public or private, however, simplifies

---

146. Entry of 31 December 1861.

147. In the entry of 25 November 1863, for example.

148. Bunkers, "Diaries and Dysfunctional Families," 221.

149. Entry of 20 February 1865.

150. Jimerson, *Private Civil War,* 56.

151. Fox-Genovese, *Within the Plantation Household,* 346.

the purposes that they served their writer as well as their historical contexts. Many scholars of women's autobiography and personal writing find that women's diaries blur the boundaries between public and private, with Cinthia Gannett suggesting, for example, that "the terms public and private (or personal) don't really account very well for the complex possible relations among diarists, their subjects, and their audiences."[152]

In those diary entries that defy the labels of public and private, and perhaps more so in those in which the diarist seems to write to herself, we gain valuable perspective into the experiences of women during war and understand more fully how they made sense of their worlds during a chaotic and violent time. By extending the concept of audience to the writer herself, we gain insight into how women negotiated wartime dangers by constructing acceptable roles for themselves in their diaries. As Bond wrote about what she should and should not say and about how she appeared to herself and to others, she coached herself to speak and act effectively in her new contexts, whether as a refugee attempting to make a place in a new community or as a young wife facing war with a new extended family but without her husband. Margo Culley explains that sometimes the "pages of the diary might be thought of as a kind of mirror before which the diarist stands assuming this posture or that."[153] For Bond, diary entries indeed served as mirrors, allowing her to assume various rhetorical positions and to rehearse the kind of ethos she should present and the kinds of things she could and could not say. Through self-persuasion, Bond urged herself to fulfill her new roles and to present herself effectively.[154]

By reading and writing, Bond often found temporary escape from wartime troubles, but at the same time, her literacy acts provided strategies for dealing with her circumstances. Comparing entries before and during the Civil War shows not only how war changed Bond but also how the function of the diary changed. At various times it was a tool for self-instruction, self-persuasion, and self-encouragement. It also allowed a space for Bond to communicate her experiences and feelings in writing, alleviating the loneliness of her life away from her Maryland home. During the war, Bond's writing at times takes on a public tone and purpose, but more often, the writing seems personal and private, allowing intimate insight into the life of a nineteenth-century woman and her experiences facing war, illness, and refugee life in south Louisiana.

Bond's diary is valuable for historians of the Civil War, gender studies, and lit-

152. Gannett, *Gender and the Journal,* 129. See also Bunkers and Huff, *Inscribing the Daily.*
153. Culley, "Introduction to a Day at a Time," 219.
154. I further discuss Bond's construction of ethos in "Rhetorical Rehearsals."

eracy and rhetoric. It provides evidence for scholars as they examine the war's impact on southern women and on families. It complicates existing historical arguments relating to women's relationships and provides evidence for rhetorical scholars interested in understanding the functions of rhetoric and writing for women during the nineteenth century. Also, Bond's diary provides a provocative narrative, filled with conflict and tension as well as personal insight into human struggles and sacrifice during wartime.

Editorial Practices

BOND'S DIARY IS WRITTEN in two books. The first is large and covered in green paper; the first page bears the inscription "Mittie P Munnikhuysen's book given to her by Howard Bond of Louisiana May 21st 1858." It is completely filled with entries dated from 21 May 1858 to 17 January 1864. The second, a leather book with a mottled peach and black pattern, is smaller and only half-filled. It contains entries from 19 January 1864 to early July 1865. The journals are in good shape, considering their age, with pages yellowing but intact.

At times Bond's handwriting is extremely difficult to read, especially when she has written in pencil that has now faded. A 1966 transcription of the original diary, undertaken by Bond's relative, Mrs. Hazel McNeal, has been very helpful to me in deciphering Bond's handwriting. Mrs. McNeal also provides details of the Munnikhuysen family tree, copied from the family Bible. Even with the transcription as an aid, I have not been able to decipher some words, usually names, with certainty and have reproduced them to the best of my ability. Bond's handwriting changes throughout the pages of the diary, becoming larger and looser during periods of illness and distress. Her penmanship at times allows insight into her mind-set as she wrote, and, when this is the case, I provide details in the notes.

In editing Bond's diary, I have attempted to keep her voice clear. The entries appear in their entirety, even though some, such as long religious musings, lists of names, and copied poems, are at times tedious for modern readers. Reading the diary in its completion is important, however, when attempting to understand its functions as well as the changes in Bond's outlook and self-perception as she experiences war in south Louisiana. By visiting early entries, readers become acquainted with Bond as a nineteen-year-old young woman and see how she matures during wartime. By presenting the diary in its entirety, I also follow the example of feminist researchers, who suggest that when using excerpts of women's writings instead of presenting their documents in full, we risk appropriating their words and possibly misrepresenting them. We risk excluding information that we deem unimportant but that was exceedingly important for the writer and thus should figure in any historical interpretation of the document.[1]

1. For a full statement of this position, see Kirsch, *Women Writing in the Academy.*

At times Bond's spelling is inconsistent, and her punctuation is scarce. For example, she writes the name of Howard's brother as both *Wellie* and *Welly*. She spells her slave's name as both *Mintty* and *Minttie,* and she has several spellings for her cousin Gerard Gover's first name. She often uses dashes or commas instead of periods. I have left the majority of the prose as she wrote it, changing spelling and punctuation inconsistencies only when they would cause the reader undue confusion. Also, at times it is difficult to decide with certainty exactly how Bond spells a word or if she uses a comma, period, or semicolon. In such cases, I have done my best to present the text as she wrote it. Bond also frequently uses a series of dashes or ellipses at the end of a sentence to indicate a continuing line of thought. I have left these punctuation marks in my edition. Also, I have written *&e,* as she does, to mean "etcetera." Occasionally, Bond makes corrections in her entries, crossing out words or changing spellings. I have indicated in the notes instances when these corrections seem to provide the reader with insight into the entry; otherwise, her corrections stand without comment. For a cleaner appearance, words and phrases that Bond underlines in the diary are italicized here. Also, while Bond does not always begin a new line in her diary when she begins a new entry or divide her entry date from the entry itself, I have done so for consistency.

Further, in order to facilitate reading, I have identified frequently mentioned people and places in a list that follows the introduction. The names listed are also briefly identified in the notes when they first appear in the text. An asterisk (*) in the note tells the reader to look for more information in the introductory list. When possible, I have included in the notes information about people Bond mentions but who are not main characters in her narrative. This information is provided when the names are first mentioned in the diary. I have attempted to identify all main characters in Bond's diary, but some identifications have not been possible. Bond, when writing in Maryland, mentions many members of her extended family, and, although not every name could be identified, I provide basic information about Bond's extended family at the beginning of the introductory list. This information will help the reader better understand Bond's social circle in Maryland. Additionally, I have divided the text into chapters and have headed the chapters with representative quotations from the section. The headings highlight themes and lines of thought in groups of entries.

The letters included in appendix 1 provide a layered dimension to Bond's story. They allow us to see how she presents her experiences to others, in contrast to how she presents them in the more personal space of the diary. (For example, one notable difference is that she refrains from criticizing her mother-in-law in the letters, while she records their arguments in her diary.) Also, the letters fill in some blanks, as some are written during periods in which Bond does not write in her diary. All but one of the letters are from Bond to her family in Maryland. One letter, however, is from Bond's father, John, to his son, William, in which John Munnikhuysen expresses his own reservations about Bond's engagement and about Howard's father, Josh. Appendix 2 includes lists of books that Bond read. A postscript provides details of Bond's life and the lives of her family members after she stops writing in her diary.

TABLE 1

The Munnikhuysen family

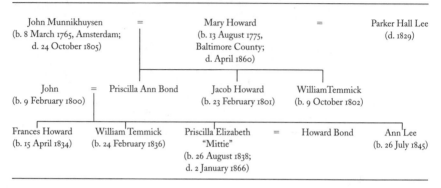

John Munnikhuysen = Mary Howard = Parker Hall Lee
(b. 8 March 1765, Amsterdam; (b. 13 August 1775, (d. 1829)
d. 24 October 1805) Baltimore County;
d. April 1860)

John = Priscilla Ann Bond   Jacob Howard   William Temmick
(b. 9 February 1800)   (b. 23 February 1801)   (b. 9 October 1802)

Frances Howard   William Temmick   Priscilla Elizabeth = Howard Bond   Ann Lee
(b. 15 April 1834)   (b. 24 February 1836)   "Mittie"   (b. 26 July 1845)
(b. 26 August 1838;
d. 2 January 1866)

Note: These charts illustrate only immediate family. The Munnikhuysen diagram does not provide the names of Parker Hall Lee and Mary Howard's children or of John Anthony's brothers' families. Only information on deaths and marriages that occurred before or during Bond's writing is provided here. The postscript to this edition provides details on family deaths and marriages that occurred after Bond's diary ends.

TABLE 2

The Bond family

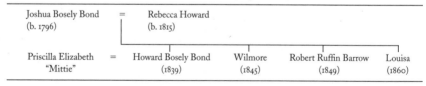

Joshua Bosely Bond = Rebecca Howard
(b. 1796) (b. 1815)

Priscilla Elizabeth = Howard Bosely Bond   Wilmore   Robert Ruffin Barrow   Louisa
"Mittie"   (1839)   (1845)   (1849)   (1860)

Priscilla "Mittie" Bond
Priscilla Munnikhuysen Bond Papers,
Mss. 2155, Louisiana and
Lower Mississippi Valley Collection,
LSU Libraries, Baton Rouge, La.

Howard Bond
Priscilla Munnikhuysen Bond Papers,
Mss. 2155, Louisiana and
Lower Mississippi Valley Collection,
LSU Libraries, Baton Rouge, La.

Principal Friends and Family

MOST OF THE PEOPLE Bond mentions when writing in Harford Country were relatives, however distant. The Lees were paternal relatives. John Munnikhuysen's (Bond's father) stepfather was Parker Hall Lee. The Archers, Dallams, Govers, Moores, Smithsons, and Stumps were related by marriage to the Lees. Also, the Bonds were related to the Munnikhuysens even before Mittie married Howard. Priscilla Ann Munnikhuysen's (Bond's mother) birth name was Bond. The Websters were related to the family through the Bonds.

Archer, Blanche—Originally from Tennessee, she married Stevenson Archer in 1855.[1] She was twenty-three years old in 1858 and was a good friend of Bond's sister Fanny.

Archer, Dr. George—A good friend of Bond. A photograph of Archer is housed with her diaries and shows Archer with long dark hair. An accompanying note states that he began to let his hair grow at the beginning of the Civil War and vowed not to cut it until the Confederates won. Devoted to the Confederacy, Archer left Maryland after the state did not secede. The Archers were a prominent family in Harford County. (See the entry for *Medical Hall* in the list of Frequently Mentioned Places.)

Archer, Stevenson—Stevenson and his wife, Blanche, were friends of the Munnikhuysens. Fannie Munnikhuysen spent much time at their home, Hazel Dell, where the Archers owned seven slaves. Archer was thirty-one years old when Bond

The list is divided by location; the first section focuses on Maryland and the second on Louisiana. Unless otherwise noted, the information in the Maryland list comes from the following census records: 1850 U.S. census, population (free) schedules, Harford and Kent counties, Md., National Archives microfilm publication M432, roll 294; and City of Baltimore, Wards 5–7, M432, roll 283; 1850 U.S. census, slave schedules, Harford County, Md., M432, roll 301; 1860 U.S. census, population (free) schedule, Harford County, Md., National Archives microfilm publication M653, roll 476; 1860 U.S. census, slave schedules, Harford County, Md., M653, roll 484. I provide people's ages based on when they are introduced in the diary.

    1. Hollowak, *Index to Marriages in the Baltimore Sun,* 5.

began her diary. He was the son of Stevenson Archer Sr., a judge and member of the U.S. Congress. Following his father's lead, Archer was a successful lawyer as well as a member of the Maryland state legislature in 1854. After the war, he was a member of the U.S. House of Representatives. From 1886 to 1890, he served as Maryland's state treasurer but was removed from office after pleading guilty to embezzlement.

Bond, Josh—A young preacher and divinity student, of whom Bond was very fond. He is not to be confused with Bond's father-in-law, also named Josh Bond. Likely, he was the brother of Laura Bond, who was visiting in Louisiana when Bond arrived.

Bond, Laura—In Bond's Maryland entries, she mentions Laura only once (on 10 September 1859). When Bond arrived in Louisiana, Laura was there as well. Although Bond seemed to disapprove of Laura (she attends the Catholic church; Bond describes her as selfish), Laura provided a link to Maryland, and Bond was sorry when she left Louisiana. She was likely Josh Bond's sister.

Bond, Mary—Bond's maternal grandmother. When Bond was writing, Mary was widowed and lived in Baltimore. After the war, she moved to Maiden Lane.

Bond, Peggie—A close friend and cousin of Bond. She was a frequent visitor at Maiden Lane and the female witness at Bond's marriage.

Bond, Rebecca (Aunt Rebecca)—Bond's mother's sister, who lived in Baltimore. In 1850 she was living in her family home and was not married. By the late 1850s, however, she lived at the Institute for the Blind in Baltimore, presumably as a teacher. Bond also mentions Rebecca's sisters, Marg and Mary, who also lived in Baltimore. Aunt Rebecca frequently wrote to Bond while she was in Louisiana and is not to be confused with Cousin Rebecca, Howard Bond's mother.

Glasgow, George R.—Bond's cousin, a farmer. When Bond began writing in 1858, George was thirty-six years old. In 1850 he was not married; he owned one slave and claimed real estate valued at seven hundred dollars. Glasgow was a close friend and frequent visitor of Bond. It appears that he had romantic feelings for her; this is most obvious in the entries immediately prior to her wedding. At times Bond seemed pleased by his attention, but she insisted that he was only a dear friend.

Glasgow, James—Bond's cousin, a clerk. In 1858 he was thirty-nine years old, owned real estate worth five thousand dollars, and was single.

Gover, Casander (Cass)—Bond's cousin, whose father, Robert Gover, was a farmer with property worth fifteen hundred dollars. She was fifty-three when Bond began her diary. Bond also mentions Gover's sisters, Priscilla, Mary, and Elizabeth (Bettie). In 1850 she was single.

Gover, George—A banker and cousin of the Munnikhuysens, who in 1858 was forty-eight years old. His wife, Juliet, was also forty-eight. The couple and their four children lived at Woodside, a home that Bond frequently visited. The Govers' oldest daughter, Juliet, was a friend of Bond. Because mother and daughter share a name, it is sometimes difficult to understand to whom Bond refers. Often, however, she refers to her peer as either "Juliet" or "Juliet Gover." She usually refers to George's wife as "Cousin Juliet." The other Gover children were Robert (Bob), Bettie, Mary, and George. In 1860 the family owned real estate worth twelve thousand dollars and had a personal estate valued at five thousand dollars. Bond writes, however, that in November 1860, the family went bankrupt; apparently, this occurred after the census was taken.

Gover, Juliet—The oldest daughter of George and Juliet Gover, of Woodside. She was fifteen or sixteen in 1858.

Howard, Mary (Grandma Lee)—Bond's paternal grandmother. Her first husband was John Munnikhuysen, and her second was Parker Hall Lee. Bond records her death in April 1860.

Lee, Delico H. (Dillie)—Bond's aunt, married to James Lee. In 1858 Dillie was forty-one years old.

Lee, Elizabeth (Lizzie)—A close friend of Bond and a cousin. The daughter of Parker Hall and Mary Lee; she was sixteen in 1858.

Lee, James (Uncle Jim)—Bond's uncle, married to Dillie. James, a farmer, was forty years old in 1858. By 1860 he owned seven slaves and had real estate valued at eight thousand dollars.

Lee, Mary—Bond's aunt, married to Parker Lee. The couple had five children, Elizabeth, Parker Hall, Mary, James, and Bryarly. Bond often mentions their oldest daughter, Elizabeth. Mary was thirty-nine years old in 1858.

Lee, Parker Hall—Likely Bond's father's stepbrother. In 1858 he was forty-six years old and married to Mary. By 1860 he owned seven slaves, real estate worth twenty thousand dollars, and claimed personal property of seven thousand dollars.

Lee, Dr. Richard—Bond's cousin and one of her doctors. His mother, a widow, was Hannah Lee, who in 1850 owned five slaves and claimed property worth two thousand dollars. His brother was Otho Scott, whom Bond mentions occasionally. Richard was thirty-two in 1858. His wife was Mary.

Lee, Sam—Bond's uncle, a farmer. In 1858 Sam was forty-four years old and married to Cassandra; they had five children. He owned real estate valued at eight thousand dollars and personal property of a thousand dollars. Bond, in her diary, mentions that Sam does not visit at her parents' house. It is not clear why.

Maloy, Mr.—A traveling Methodist minister who frequently visited Bond and preached in her local church.

Moores, Fannie—Bond's cousin Fannie (also spelled Fanny) Wyatt Moores was twenty-six in 1858. She was from a family of wealthy Harford farmers, whose property was reportedly worth fifteen thousand dollars in 1850. Bond often mentions Fannie's brothers, John and James (Jimmy), who were twenty-eight and nineteen, respectively, in 1858. She also writes of frequent visits to their home, Mooreland.

Moores, James (Jimmy)—See the entry for Fannie.

Moores, John—See the entry for Fannie.

Munnikhuysen, Ann Lee—Bond's youngest sister, who was thirteen years old in 1858.

Munnikhuysen, Frances (Sister Fanny; also spelled Fannie)—Bond's eldest sister was twenty-four years old when Bond began writing. Bond notes that Fannie was frequently away from home visiting.

Munnikhuysen, Howard—Bond's cousin and good friend; he was a son of William Munnikhuysen (Bond's paternal uncle and her own brother's namesake). During the time Bond wrote her Maryland entries, he attended the University of Virginia.

Munnikhuysen, William—Bond's only brother was twenty-two years old in 1858. He traveled to Louisiana in October 1859, before Bond did, to conduct business with Bond's future father-in-law, Joshua Bond. He stayed less than seven months, returning home unexpectedly on 7 May 1860. Apparently, the venture was not a success, and William did not get along with Joshua Bond. (See the letter to William from his father in app. 1.)

Stump, Herman—A frequent visitor to the Munnikhuysen home. In 1858 he was twenty-four and lived in Bel Air, where he practiced law. His property was worth fifteen thousand dollars. The Stumps, an old Harford family, traced their roots to Prussia. Herman later became president of the Maryland State Senate, a Democrat member of Congress, and commissioner of Immigration.

Valiant, Theodore—The Methodist Protestant minister at Bond's church in Bel Air. She frequently praised his sermons and enjoyed visiting him. While she mentions his wife, the 1860 census does not show him as being married. He owned assets valued at eight hundred dollars.

Watters, Godfrey—A close friend of Bond and her siblings. Bond often mentions Godfrey's father and mother, Henry and Mary, and his siblings, Elizabeth (Lizzie), James (Jimmy), and John (Dr.). They are distantly related to the Munnikhuysens. In 1858 Godfrey was thirty-four. At the time of the 1850 census, Godfrey lived in his father's home and listed his occupation as farmer.

Watters, Henry (Mr. Watters)—Sixty-eight years old in 1858, Henry Watters was married to Mary, who was then sixty-three. They were the parents of Godfrey, Lizzie, Jimmy, and John. The family owned a prosperous farm, valued in 1850 at ten thousand dollars, along with three slaves that year and five ten years later. Henry descended from a line of influential Methodist ministers. His father founded the Watters Meeting House that Bond often mentions.

Watters, James D. (Jimmy)—A friend of Bond and her siblings. He was twenty-four when Bond began her diary. In 1850 he was a student, and he practiced law in St. Louis. During the war he served in the First Virginia Confederate Regiment and in the Maryland Cavalry. He later established the *Harford Democrat* and served as its editor until he was elected judge of the Circuit Court. In 1868 he married Bond's sister Fannie.

Watters, Dr. John—A friend of Bond who was thirty years old in 1859. In 1850 he was studying medicine and was a medical professor in St. Louis when the war began. He enlisted in the Confederate service as a surgeon, a post that he held throughout the war.

Watters, Elizabeth G. (Lizzie)—A close friend of Bond. In 1858 she was thirty-two years old. The 1850 census lists her as single, living in her parents' home.

Wyatt, Louise (Lou)—A frequent visitor to Maiden Lane. She lived in Virginia. Family records housed with Bond's diary show that she later married Bond's brother, William. Lou corresponded with Bond in the early years of the war.

LOUISIANA

Terrebonne Parish

Barrow, Volumnia (Mrs. Barrow)[2]—In Terrebonne Bond mentions frequent visits to and from Mrs. Barrow. In Abbeville she and Rebecca received letters from

---

2. Unless otherwise noted, specific details regarding property and age come from the following census records: 1850 U.S. census, population (free) schedules, Terrebonne Parish, La., National Archives microfilm publication M432, roll 241; 1860 U.S. census, free schedule, Terrebonne Parish, La., M653, roll 425.

Mrs. Barrow, along with encouragement to return to Houma. In 1850 twenty-five-year-old Volumnia married fifty-two-year-old Robert Ruffin Barrow, and by 1860 the couple had two children, Volumnia Roberta (Berta) and Robert Ruffin Jr., seven and two years old, respectively. Barrow's birth name was Washington Hunley.[3]

Barrow, Robert Ruffin (Mr. Barrow)—One of the wealthiest planters in the Terrebonne region, he was a friend and likely business partner of Josh Bond. Barrow owned six Terrebonne plantations, plantations in other parishes and in Texas, and almost four hundred slaves, well above the average for elite planters.[4] He was also a canal operator. Howard's youngest brother, Robert Richard Barrow Bond, was his namesake.

Bond, Joshua Bosley (Cousin Josh)—Bond's father-in-law, originally from Maryland, who owned a large plantation outside of Houma, Louisiana. The Munnikhuysens express reservations about Josh. In a letter to Mittie Bond's brother, her father describes him as "base."[5] Bond herself criticizes her father-in-law, especially his treatment of slaves. After his plantation was burned in 1862, Josh, in ill health, fled to Texas for the remainder of the war. In 1860 he owned personal property valued at $137,400 and real estate worth $52,000. In 1861 Josh was sixty-six years old.

Bond, Laura—(See the entry for Laura in the Maryland section.) After Crescent Place was burned, Laura stayed only briefly in Abbeville. She returned to Terrebonne to stay with Mrs. Barrow and then traveled back to Maryland before the war ended. Although Laura is mentioned frequently in Bond's diary, she is more fully discussed in Bond's letters home.

Bond, Rebecca (Cousin Rebecca)—Bond's mother-in-law, whose birth name was Howard. (Mittie Bond's paternal grandmother was also a Howard.) She was from Maryland and would have been forty-three in 1861. Rebecca and Josh had four children. Howard was the oldest, followed by Wilmore (Wellie), and Robert Richard Barrow (Barrow, named after Robert R. Barrow). The youngest child, Louisa, was called "Sissy."

Bond, Wilmore (Wellie)—Howard Bond's brother. He was fifteen years old when the Civil War began and in school. After Crescent Place was burned, he went with his father and younger brother, Robert, to Texas, where he joined the Fourth Texas Regiment.

3. For more information on the Barrow family, see Becnel, *Barrow Family*.
4. See Menn, *Large Slaveholders*, 414–15.
5. See app. 1.

Campbell, Mrs.—When Bond arrived in Terrebonne, Mrs. Campbell was living at Crescent Place, sharing a room with Laura Bond. It is not clear what Campbell's relationship is to the Bonds. After the family left Crescent Place, Campbell went to the Barrows'. Bond does not mention her when writing from Abbeville.

Helmick, Dr. A. S.—Helmick was one of Bond's doctors in Terrebonne Parish and in Abbeville. He was also a family friend of the Bonds. Both he and his wife, El-neyra Delarand, were originally from Virginia; they were thirty-five and twenty-five years old, respectively, in 1861. Before Howard married, he studied medicine with Dr. Helmick. The Helmicks were also for a short while refugees in Abbeville and temporarily lived with Bond and her mother-in-law. See also Bond's letter to Ann Lee dated 13 April 1862 for further information on the couple (app. 1).

McConnel, Mathern—The Presbyterian minister of the church that Bond joined in Terrebonne Parish. Census records from 1860 show only one Presbyterian church in the area. Mathern was from Ireland and was married to Corrie, from Alabama. They were thirty and twenty-five years old, respectively, in 1861.

Winder, Mrs.—Mrs. V. Winder, a wealthy widow, helped Bond and Howard re-unite after Crescent Place was burned. Bond also mentions her sons, Felix and Johnny.

Abbeville, Vermilion Parish

Abadie, Dr. Jean[6]—One of Bond's doctors in Abbeville, Abadie had emigrated to Vermilion Parish from France. He was married, but his wife's name is not known. Bond also mentions his brother Louis, a merchant, and Louis's wife, Aline, also French immigrants.

Alléman, Pierre (Cousin Pete)—A private in Company B of the Crescent Regiment (Twenty-fourth Regiment), Louisiana Infantry. The regiment played an important part in the Battle of Shiloh. In September 1863 it reported to Gen. Richard Taylor in southern Louisiana.[7] When Alléman began visiting Bond in December 1863, he was likely stationed at Avery Island, slightly southeast of Abbeville. He was also detached as a nurse in New Iberia, Louisiana. He spent time in Abbeville from the winter of 1863 to spring 1864. Bond gave him the nickname "Cousin Pete" and at times spells his name "Aleman" or another variant.

6. Specific details on property and age come from the following census records: 1860 U.S census, free schedule, St. Mary Parish, La., National Archives microfilm publication M653, roll 425; 1860 U.S. census, free schedule, Vermilion Parish, La., M653, roll 426.

7. For details on his war service, see Booth, *Records of Louisiana Confederate Soldiers*, 2:44. Information on the regiment's wartime action is found in Bergeron, *Guide to Louisiana Confederate Military Units*, 132.

Barrett, John, Sr.—An Abbeville saddler, Barrett claimed real estate of $250 and had a personal estate worth $1,000 in the 1860 census. His was fifty-four years old in 1863 and married to Charlotte; the couple had six children. Bond writes that their youngest son, Robert, died of illness while serving in the war.

Barrett, Charlotte (Mrs. or Sister Barrett)—Fifty-two years old in 1863, Barrett was married to John. The Barretts seemed to offer Bond religious support and fellowship.

Beldon, J. K.—Beldon was a lawyer and mayor of Abbeville from 1863 to 1865. He was married to Eliza, and they had six children. Bond occasionally mentions visiting their eldest daughter, Virginia, who was twenty-one in 1864.

Ellis, John—Bond, when writing from Abbeville, often mentions the Ellises, also inhabitants of Vermilion Parish during the last years of the Civil War. John Ellis was a St. Mary Parish sawmill owner who, in 1860, claimed real estate worth six thousand dollars and had a personal estate worth six thousand dollars. He was thirty-five years old in 1863. His wife, Victorine, also from Louisiana, was thirty years old. The couple had four children.

Ellis, Victorine (Mrs.)—See the entry for John Ellis.

Foote, Evelina (Mrs.)—A native of St. Mary Parish, Foote was a refugee in Abbeville. When Bond met her, she was twenty-eight years old and had three children. Her husband, George, was a planter with property valued at fifty thousand dollars; in Abbeville the family rented Mrs. Maxwell's house, the property where Bond and Rebecca lived when they first arrived in the town. Bond mentions frequent visits with Mrs. Foote. (Occasionally she spells her name *Foot.*)

Foote, George—See the entry for Evelina Foote. Foote's parents, brother Henry, and Henry's family were also refugees in Abbeville.

Guegnon, Eugene L.—Lawyer and editor of a French newspaper, *Le Meridional,* in Abbeville. He took over the paper from his father, Judge Eugene I. Guegnon, a native of southern France.[8] His sister Jemimah was married to Dr. Young of Abbeville, whom Bond occasionally mentions. Eugene was forty-five years old in 1863 and owned property valued at twenty-five hundred dollars. He was married to Valerie, and the couple had three children. Bond mentions their son, Eugene, who seemed to have had a flirtation with Laura Bond.

Hall, Sarah (Mrs.)—A resident of Vermilion Parish, Hall was married to James, a farmer. In 1860 their property was worth seven hundred dollars. They had one

8. For further information on Guegnon, see Vermilion Historical Society, *History of Vermilion Parish,* 163.

daughter, Mary, who was twenty-one in 1863. Hall was likely illiterate, as Bond wrote letters for her to her husband, who was stationed with Confederate troops in Arkansas.

Maxwell, Martha (Mrs. Maxwell)—Bond's landlord until September 1863 and a social acquaintance in Abbeville. Maxwell was thirty-five in 1863, originally from Lafayette Parish, Louisiana, and married to Albert G. Maxwell, a Maryland native. Maxwell's family owned a large plantation in Kent County Maryland. In Abbeville Albert, a sugar planter, owned property valued at over twelve thousand dollars.

Nixon, Mrs.—Martha Maxwell's mother, who lived with the Maxwells. Bond writes that Mrs. Nixon and her daughter frequently argued.

Plumlee, Carrie E. (Mrs. Gordy)—Bond's sickly friend with whom she stayed for a month after Crescent Place was burned. Bond describes her as a poet, and she transcribes several of her poems into her own diary. Plumlee was married to John Gordy, a wealthy planter in St. Mary Parish who in 1860 owned real estate worth seventeen thousand dollars and personal property worth seventy thousand. See also Bond's letter of 2 November 1863 as well as the diary entry of 2 January 1864 (app. 1).

Robertson, Mrs.—In her entries written in Abbeville, Bond mentions several Mrs. Robertsons: she writes of Sophia, Susan, Old Mrs. Robertson, Mrs. Murry Robertson, and simply Mrs. Robertson. Often, it is difficult to understand which Mrs. Robertson she means. Old Mrs. Robertson frequently argued with Mrs. Maxwell and often visited Cousin Rebecca. Bond's close friend is the woman she refers to as simply "Mrs. Robertson." She credits her with helping her when she is sick. This Mrs. Robertson is also mentioned in Bond's letter to her mother dated 2 November 1863 and is from the Eastern Shore of Maryland (app. 1). She, her husband, and their young children were refugees in Abbeville. They were relatives of Mrs. Maxwell.

Wise, Fanny and Solomon—While in Abbeville, Bond often mentions Mr. and Mrs. Wise, natives of Poland, whose general store was located next to the house she and Rebecca rented after they left Mrs. Maxwell's. The Wises immigrated to Vermilion Parish in the 1850s and then settled in Abbeville in 1854. Mr. Wise was a courier and scout in the Confederate army. After the war, his business prospered, and he acquired a large sugar plantation and other land. Fanny's birth name was Truskalaski.[9]

9. See *History of Vermilion Parish,* 315, for further detail.

Wren, Mr.—Mr. Wren was the Baptist minister in Abbeville. Vermilion Parish had one Baptist church in 1860. At the time of the 1850 census, the parish did not have a Baptist church; thus, Wren likely was fairly new to the area.

Wright, Mrs.—Bond becomes good friends with Mrs. Wright, even though Wright was in Abbeville only a month. Like many wealthy residents of southern Louisiana, she and her husband left their home in New Orleans for Texas when the Civil War began. After her husband joined the army, Wright made her way back to New Orleans but was delayed in Abbeville because of illness related to her pregnancy. After giving birth, she went back to New Orleans.

Young, Dr. Frances—One of Bond's doctors in Abbeville, Young was a Louisiana native and Abbeville resident. He was twenty-eight years old in 1863, when Bond first mentions him. He was married to Jemimah, who was twenty-nine years old and the sister of Eugene Guegnon, the newspaper editor. The Youngs had one child. In 1860 they claimed property worth fifteen hundred dollars.

Frequently Mentioned Places

CRESCENT PLACE—JOSH AND REBECCA BOND's plantation located on Bayou Black outside of Houma, Louisiana. After marrying Howard Bond, Priscilla "Mittie" Bond lived at Crescent Place with her in-laws, her husband, and his three siblings until the plantation was burned by Union troops in 1862.

Hazel Dell—The home of Munnikhuysen friends Stephenson (Stevy) Archer and his wife, Blanche.

Maiden Lane—Bond's childhood home located on Thomas Run Road in Harford County, Maryland. The two-story house, constructed from stone and logs, sits on one hundred acres of farmland.

Medical Hall—Located near Churchville, Harford County, Medical Hall was one of the first medical schools in Maryland. It was established by Dr. John Archer (Bond's friend George Archer's great-grandfather). When Bond is writing her diary, some members of the Archer family are living there.

Sleepy Hollow—Cousin Casander (Cass) Gover's home, within walking distance of Maiden Lane.

Woodside—The home of George and Juliet Gover, within walking distance of Maiden Lane.

CHURCHES

Bel Air Methodist Church (Methodist Protestant)—Bond and her parents were members of this church. Theodore Valiant was the minister during the years Bond attended.

With the exception of Crescent Place, all of the places identified in this list are in Maryland. Bond shows her familiarity with her birth county through her frequent references to specific place names. In Terrebonne Parish, Louisiana, Bond had little time to establish a sense of community before being displaced by the war. In Abbeville, where she lived as a refugee, she seldom mentions specific place names, likely indicating the nature of the refugee community in which families lived in temporary housing and moved frequently. As a refugee, Bond formed personal attachments in Abbeville but did not seem to develop strong attachment to the place itself. For Bond, Maryland was always home.

Churchville Presbyterian Church—Bond and her family frequently visited this church, located in the town of Churchville, slightly southeast of Maiden Lane. William Finney was the pastor there from 1813 to 1854, and Bond mentions that he preached her friend Helen McGaw's funeral there. The Archers and Glasgows were longtime members of the church.[1]

Protestant Episcopal Trapp Church—An Episcopal church that was so named because of its location near a place called "Trapp."

Rock Springs Church (Christ Church)—An Episcopal church, established in 1805; Bond occasionally attended, but, more frequently, her sister Fannie and brother attended services there. Louise Wyatt, Bond's future sister-in-law, was confirmed there.

Watters Meeting House—The Methodist church that Bond attended was built about 1773. Still standing, it is a small, wood-framed building with a stone exterior that overlooks Thomas Run Valley. Bond, her parents, and her sister Ann Lee were buried in the adjoining cemetery. (See also the entry for *Henry Watters*.)

1. See Preston, *History of Harford County, Maryland,* 176.

PART ONE

CHAPTER ONE

"Friends—Home—and Love, All Are Mine"

21 MAY 1858–10 APRIL 1859

May 21 1858

I received this book from my own Howard Saturday night May 21st 1858. We started from Baltimore that morning between the hours of ten and eleven. I need not say our ride was pleasant for the hours sped by so swiftly. I felt that day as though I loved him enough to be his, and why should I not, does he not love me as no other ever loved me. Why should I not love him in return—he has been very kind to me. We have just returned from a visit to the Eastern shore, Cecil and Kent countys.[1] We spent some happy and sad hours there. The ride we took before we went from Snowden's to Mifflins was sad indeed.[2] Oh! how I grieved his loving heart—for then I told him he must give me up—think only of me as his dearest friend—but how could he when his whold heart is raped up in me. If I had thought I loved him then as I know I love him now, I would have told him so but now it is too late—he has gone—gone. Peace be still poor heart! We got home Baltimore about four o'clock—perhaps five. Found here Fannie Moores, and cousin G. Glasgow.[3] Farewell happy dreams for that day . . . . .[4]

1. Cecil County borders Harford to the east. The Chesapeake Bay separates Harford and Kent, the county directly south of Cecil. The Eastern Shore counties were primarily rural and agricultural in the nineteenth century.

2. Bond refers to Snowden Thomas; Mifflin's surname is not clear.

3. Bond's cousin Fanny Wyatt Moores* was twenty-six when Bond was writing this entry. She was from a Harford planter family that in 1850 owned property worth fifteen thousand dollars. George Glasgow* was thirty-six years old and a farmer. Throughout Bond's Maryland entries, unless noted otherwise, the reference notes that draw upon census information are from the following records: 1850 U.S. Census, free schedule, Harford County, Md., National Archives microfilm publication M432, roll 294; 1850 U.S. census, slave schedule, Harford, M432, roll 301; 1860 U.S. Census, free schedule, Harford, Md., M653, roll 476; 1860 U.S. Census, slave schedule, Harford, Md., M653, roll 484.

4. Until Bond's marriage in 1861, she chronicles details of her and Howard's courtship rituals. She is concerned with testing her love and Howard's affection, weighing whether the relationship is worth leaving Maryland and her family to follow Howard to Louisiana. Her emotions vary from despondency to euphoria as she contemplates her romance. She works to reconcile her emotions with her culture's dictate that she marry well. For more on courtship ritual in the nineteenth century, see the introduction to this work; as well as Rothman, *Hands and Hearts;* and Stowe, *Intimacy and Power in the Old South.*

Sunday 22nd

In the morning sister Fannie and cousin George went to Churchville, to church.[5] Howard and I went to walking first we went up in the woods in front of our house, and gathered flowers for a while; then we came out and walked over in the other wood to our dear tree, where he cut my name and his on it—then we seated ourselves down between two trees close by, and he put his dear arm around my waist and I my head on his shoulder, occasionally kissed each other. Oh! Those happy hours, when shall we spend such happy ones again! After being down there some time a man and woman came along and caught us kissing which made us feel rather bad for a while, at least it did me.

In the afternoon cousin George took sister Fannie in his buggy to church at Watters' Meeting House.[6] Howard took me we heard an excellent sermon by cousin Howard Parrish, after church went to Mr. Watter's met our cousins Martha, Rebecca and James Hale then, also Mr. Parrish. We spend a very pleasant evening, cousin George and I had a long talk in the yard about Howard and myself. We started soon after tea for home as our cousins were coming with us. That ride was a sad happy one. Howard said then, Perhaps this may be the last ride we will ever take together for a long time, and so it was, for he has left me, my poor heart is sad, sad. Oh! how he pressed me to his aching heart and kissed me so fondly, and asked me to be his own true wife, and so I will be in a few long years yet I have not told him so, I want to try my own love and see if it is the right kind or not . . . .

Monday 23rd

Poor Howard he left us this morning for a short while—he will be back to-morrow if nothing happens. How my poor heart has ached today. The company all have left, sister Fannie gone to Mrs. Blanche Archers . . . .[7]

5. The town of Churchville is located slightly southeast of Bond's home. She and her family frequently visited the Churchville Presbyterian Church, which was established in 1825. Also, the Munnikhuysen family friends the Archers and Glasgows attended church there.

6. The Watters Meeting House, a Methodist church, was named after the Watters, a prominent Harford family who trace their roots to William Watters, the first American Methodist itinerant preacher. William's brother Henry was the father of Godfrey Watters, who founded the Watters Meeting House that is often mentioned by Bond. The Mr. Watters* often mentioned by Bond was Godfrey's son Henry Godfrey Watters (1790–1865). He was married to Mary Clendenin. Their children, Godfrey,* Elizabeth (Lizzie),* John (Dr. John), and James (Jimmy),* were friends of the Munnikhuysens.

7. Blanche Archer,* a Tennessee native, was married to Stevenson Archer,* a lawyer who owned property valued at twenty-one thousand dollars. Blanche was twenty-three in 1858 and primarily a friend of Bond's sister Fanny.

Tuesday

It is raining and has been all day. My Howard came this afternoon in all the rain, for O he is going to leave me tomorrow morning—God give me grace to bear this sepperation as I should. This night we were left alone after they went to bed, and I was in the rocking chair, he beside me. When they had all left the room, he threw his arms around me—drew me close to his breast and kissed me so dearly until my heart was nearly bursting. Oh, that night—will I ever forget it? He told me he would give anything in the world if I was going to Louisiana with him. But it could not be. Perhaps I may go the next time he goes. He layed his dear head upon my breast, and raised his eyes to my face. Oh! the love I read there—tongue could not express it.

Wednesday May 25th 1858

This has been the saddest day of my life for I parted with *my own* beloved Howard this morning about 7. He bid all the family good bye in the dining room, then came in the parlor to say that long farewell. I had heard him saying good bye to them and had thrown myself down on the sofa with tears gushing out of my eyes, and when he came in he took me by the arm and raised me up pressed me to his aching breast and said *Pet good bye* do not cry my pet, my Mit—I will see you again in two long years. Kiss me I must go."[8] How could I, my heart was almost broken—how could I give him up for so long . . . . Oh how his heart beat against mine—how the tears rolled down his cheeks—how I clung to him for one more *loved* kiss—but O it must be, taking the last kiss, the long farewell had to be said— I flung my arms around his *dear neck*, pressed my lips to his, and said My Howard God bless you—pray for me, and he replied yes pet—I will . . . . One more kiss and he was gone—yes gone. Oh! how my poor heart ached when I looked out of the window and saw him for the last time. I soon left the room and went to my room where I threw myself down on my bed, and cryed till my brain seemed addled. And now the tears are flowing fast as I pen those lines. I can see the stains where they have fallen. I will have to stop till I am more calm . . . .

Thursday 26th

This morning has been so gloomy as my own sad thoughts. I have been thinking all day of my absent one. And I feel assured he has been thinking of me. I know he has wished more than once he was by my side. Nothing of interest has transpired today. Mr. Evans took tea here . . .

---

8. Here Bond does not fully enclose her quotation in quotation marks, a practice that is not uncommon in her writing.

Friday evening 27th 1858

It has been raining nearly all day until about three when it cleared off, and now the sun is shining very beautifully. Everything looks lovely; even the birds seem to be enjoying the sun shine. We have had much rain this spring, not one 24 hours has passed for weeks but what rain has fallen either in the day time or night. This afternoon Pa & Bob Gover went out to Robertson's place. He lives on the road leading from here to Bel Air. They have just come home.

I got somewhat disappointed this evening. I wanted to take a walk down to Uncle Sam's and was in the act of geting ready but Ma did not want me to go as she wanted me to stay and tend to tea.[9] I am afraid I did not consent in a very amiable mood for I wanted to go much, but after seating my self at my sewing for some time I felt as though I had been most too hasty, in expressing my wish to go. I had thought I had cured myself of those hasty words but satan is ever on the watch to draw one in his net—I hope I maybe careful in future. And may God give me grace to enable me to over come all temptations for Christ-sake . . . .

Saturday night 28th

I have been quite busy all day and how differently employed to what I was last Saturday, for I was then coming up from Baltimore with Howard Bond—but now alas! he is far away from me; on his way to Louisiana. Does not expect to reach home till the last of next or the first of the week after. Peggie Bond came here soon after dinner and is now here staying all night.[10] Cousin George [Glasgow] also spend the evening with me—came from the Post Office; he and I had a long talk together. He is truly a noble man and any woman might be proud to call him husband . . . . .

30th of May

This morning I went to Bel Air to church with Cousin George Glasgow in his new buggy, had a very pleasant drive up. Heard an excellent sermon by the Reverend Mr. Tompson from the First Epistle of John, fourth chap- and part of the eighth verse, "God is Love." I would have enjoyed it much more but he is an Irishman and has a good deal of brogue.

From church we went to John Moores to dinner;[11] we remained till after tea. When we came home we found Fannie had arrived, but had walked up to Woodside for a while. Had not been home long before Dr. George Archer came,[12] he did not stay long . . . . .

9. Sam Lee,* Bond's uncle, was a farmer, who in 1858 was forty-four years old.

10. Peggie* was Bond's friend and cousin.

11. John Moores* was from a prosperous family of planters. He was twenty-eight in 1858.

12. The Archers were a prominent medical family in Harford County. Dr. George Archer* was a relative and a good friend of Bond.

Monday, May 31st

It has been cloudy and rainy all day. Indeed I never saw as much rain at one time as we have had this spring. This evening Cousin George Gover and family moved up to Woodside. I walked up, as soon as I heard they had come to see if could be of any assistance to them, but found I could not, therefore hasten home again. While we were at tea sister Fannie came home (she had been up to Uncle Jim's).[13] When we finished tea we all nearly went out to the swing and enjoyed ourselves till it commenced raining . . . .

June 1st

The "month of roses" has at length come. What changes will it bring forth? As I sit at my window and look out on the beautiful world God has given us, and I think of our unworthiness of so much goodness, I can not help raising my heart up in thankfulness for his long suffering & mercy towards us. As I sit here and watch the clouds, as one by one they roll across the Heavens, methinks I can see little fairies as they were skipping and chasing each other in frolicksome glee till they are lost in the distance . . . The weather today has been warmer and more bright than usually. Nothing has occurred worthy of note, no one was here but cousin Howard P—he took tea with us and then left for Mr. Dallam's in Bel Air, the one who lives where Dr. Wicks taught school . . . . .

Wednesday 2nd

Mr. Valliant and Mr. Thompson spent most of the day here, took dinner and went to Uncle Sam's to tea.[14] They are Methodist Protestant ministers. After supper Fannie, Pa, Ann Lee and myself walked up to Woodside,[15] had not been there long before Peggie and Billie came, so after staying a reasonable time we came home . . . . . .

Thursday 3rd

Today Blanche Archer & Cassie Hall spent the day with us—left after dinner for Henry Archers, soon after they left cousin G[eorge Glasgow] and aunt Dillie came, on their way from Baltimore—he took his horse and came back took Fannie to uncle Parker's where she will stay till Saturday . . . . .[16]

---

13. James Lee.*

14. As Bond explains, Theodore Valiant was a Methodist Protestant clergy in Bel Air. Even though Bond visited many churches, she considered the Reverend Valliant to be her primary minister. In 1860 he claimed property valued at eight hundred dollars.

15. The home of George and Juliet Gover.*

16. Bond often mentions Aunt Dillie, Delico Lee,* whose husband was James Lee (Uncle Jim).* In 1858 Dillie was forty-one years old. Parker Lee* was likely Bond's father's stepbrother. He was forty-six years old in 1858.

Friday June 4th

Nothing of importance has occurred today. Uncle Sam called to see G-ma but would not come in, as he does not visit here . . . . . [17]

Saturday 5th

Today has felt more like June than any we have had yet as it has been very warm. I have been quite busy all the morning—This afternoon Juliet Gover, Bettie & the baby (George Oliver) came down and staied an hour or so.[18] After tea uncle Sam came for Grandma and took a walk with Juliet, Bettie, Bob, Mr. Evans, Brother, and Ann Lee;[19] after I got home Fannie & cousin George came—he did not come in.

Sunday 6th

This morning Fannie & cousin G[eorge] G[lasgow] went to the "Rock's Spring" church, and I went to the "Trap"[20]—in Cousin G. Gover's carriage with Juliet & Bettie, came home to dinner. In the evening Godfrey Watters came[21]— he said he was going to court me hard this summer, as Howard would not be here to molest him . . . . . .

I got a letter from Howard this morning dated from the "Gold House" Louisville, Kentucky. He had a very lonely ride from Baltimore there and wished I had been there to have kept him company—poor fellow, I know his heart ached for one loving heart to beat with his.

Sunday afternoon, June 13

My date is from last Sunday, and not since have I had time to write in my book; but nothing of particular interest has occurred but what I can now remember to give. Monday I was busily engaged while washing; after tea I went up to cousin Juliet's & stayed a short while. Tuesday I spent a delightful day with Aunt Dillie. When I came home I found Mr. Stump & Mr. Moore here.[22] Mr. Moore has engaged me to go to Quaker Meeting with him next sunday.[23] Thursday Cousin Mil-

17. It is not clear why Bond's uncle would not visit the Munnikhuysen home.

18. Bond refers to Juliet Gover* and her siblings. Bettie would have been approximately six years old and George newborn.

19. Grandma is Mary Howard Lee, Bond's grandmother on her father's side. After her first husband's (John Munnikhuysen) death, she married Parker Hall Lee. Lee died in 1829. At the time of the 1850 census, she was living with Bond's aunt and uncle, James and Dillie.

20. Both churches Bond mentions are Episcopal. The Protestant Episcopal Trapp Church was so called because of its location on Deer Creek at a place called Trapp.

21. Godfrey* was thirty-four years old in 1858. He was a farmer.

22. Herman Stump,* twenty-four years old at the time and a lawyer.

23. If Bond attended the Quaker service, she would have heard views on slavery that stood in sharp contrast to those held by her fiancé, Howard, even if the church did not directly call for abolition.

lie Armstrong was here, also Cousin Annie Lee & Clara Lee.[24] Friday Ma went
to Aunt Nancy's and has not got back yet. Saturday afternoon cousin George Glasgow came, stayed very later, and this morning Pa, Ann Lee and myself went to Bel
Air to church, heard a very excellent sermon from Deut. 32 chpt 31st vs by the Rev
Mr. Valliant. The church was quite full. I met many friends there. I was introduced
to Miss Baker of Va.

This day [last] month I was aboard the Champion going from Chesterton to
Baltimore in company with Peggie Bond, Snowden Thomas & Howard Bond. Oh,
how everything rushes up in the halls of memory, even the very looks, the pressure
of the hand of that loved one, all comes as fresh in my mind as though it had just
occurred. The conversation we had on the sofa in the cabin when I told him my
thoughts. Oh! how my heart beat as he talked to me of love. Why can not I love
him best of all? Perhaps I will after a while. Two years will tell whether I love
enough to be his or no. Oh, I hope I will act right in all things . . . .

Sunday afternoon Howard Munnikhuysen came;[25] he & I walked down to Uncle Sam's and remained till after tea; we had strawberries for tea, which was quite
a treat to me. Howard teased me a good deal about Howard Bond, but I do not
care for all their teasing . . . . Monday sister Fannie and Cousin George went to
Mooreland to call on Miss Baker (a lady from Va). She did not get home till the
next morning . . . .

Tuesday 15th

Ma went to Uncle Jim's in the morning in cousin George's buggy; in the evening
H. Parrish came, staid till after tea, then he took me over to Uncle Sam's, where I
remained till next morning. I came home suffering very much with my throat. At
dinner I found it too sore to eat, so I went upstairs & went to bed, where I staied
till after twelve Thursday. I got up then, as we expected company, and put on a
loose dress. It was a little company given to Miss Baker, and there were ten persons here: Miss Baker, Cassie Gover, Lou Wyatt, Mary Lee, Lizzie Watters, Godfrey, George Glasgow, Mr. Moore (from Bel Air), Jimmy Moores,[26] Herman
Stump, and our own family, of course. I did not make my appearance till about
nine, as I did not feel well enough. They left five minutes of 11 o'clock . . . .

Friday, June 18th

I feel much better today; this morning we froze the cream which we had com-

24. Cousin Annie Lee is probably Ann Lee, a widow who lived in Harford County and in 1860
owned a farm valued at ten thousand dollars and three slaves.

25. Howard is Bond's cousin, a son of her father's brother William. John Anthony Munnikhuysen
had three brothers, Jacob, William, and Edward. He also had half-siblings with the surname Lee.

26. Jimmy (James) Moores* was nineteen years old in 1858; Lou (Louise) Wyatt, a native of Virginia, later married Bond's brother.

menced the evening before but could not get it frozen; but this morning we froze it and enjoyed it very much. George Glasgow took Fannie to Mary Lee's this afternoon,[27] as there is to be a company given to Miss Baker. I got a letter from Howard the 17th dated from Donaldsonville,[28] as he had not got home then.

Saturday 19th

This morning I went up to cousin Juliet's to spend a few hours, but had not been there long before Ann Lee came for me, saying company had come, Howard, Jane and Lizzie Munnikhuysen, so I had to come home. After dinner I went down to see Grandma Lee with them. When I came home, found Cousins George and James Glasgow here & soon after Juliet, Bob & Bettie Gover & Cassie Herring from Baltimore. Howard and his sisters left before tea, & directly after tea Cousins James and George left for Mr. Gough's, as they were invited to spend the evening there with Miss Baker. Mr. Henry Watters came soon after they left . . . . . .

Sunday 20th

I did not go to church this morning but remained home & let Ann Lee go in company with Juliet Gover, also Fannie. In the evening Cousin George and James Glasgow came and took tea,[29] also Howard Parrish called for a little while . . . . .

Monday 21st 1858

This evening cousin Howard [Parrish] came, took tea, after which he took sister Fannie over to uncle Parker's, came home and remained all night.

Tuesday 22nd

I went to Uncle Parker's. Ma returned in the carriage. She went then on Saturday evening.

Wednesday 23rd

I came home this evening with Jimmy Moores, and when I got here found uncle Jim [Lee], Aunt Dillie, Dick Webster, and Billie Webster to tea, soon after Juliet, Bettie, Bob Gover and Cassie Herring came. Then Dorsey Gough, Mr. White and Mr. Effinger from Va came, so we had quite a company. They did not leave till five minutes after eleven. Our servant left us to this evening . . . . .[30]

Thursday 24th

It has been extremely warm today. The weather has been & still is fine for the corn crops which are very backward for the season. This evening Mr. Stump and

27. Mary Lee* was Bond's aunt, married to Uncle Parker Lee.*

28. Donaldsonville, La., is located approximately forty miles north of Houma.

29. James* was George Glasgow's brother and was thirty-nine years old when this entry was written.

30. Bond could be referring to the Charity Clark who was in the Munnikhuysen household at the time of the 1850 census but not in 1860.

Mr. Norris took tea with us, and then walked up to cousin George Gover's with sister Fannie. I preferred remaining at home, as I had been very busily engaged all day. When they came back I was sound asleep on my bed, so I had not the pleasure of their company. Well I suppose they cared very little about it . . . . .

Friday June 25

This is the 25th day of the month of June 1858. I am now seated at the back window upstairs & have one of the loveliest views of the "Valley of Thomas Run." As far as the eye can search is seen a beautiful range of "Woodland" and the hills on which it is, look almost mountainous and on the highest hill opposite is Mr. Watters' peaceful dwelling surrounded by many trees; close by stands dear old Watters' Meeting House, it too is a lovely spot and made more so to me by its being the place where my soul was blessed, where my sins were washed away by God's attoning blood. Oh! how I love to worship God there. It is good to be there.

It is cloudy this evening, the sun sits in a bank and I fear we shall have rain ere long, but if we have, God sends it and it is all right. Cousin George took tea here and has taken sister Fannie to Bel Air for Ma's bonnet at Mrs. Hamilton's. Brother has gone to Bel Air . . . . . .

The 26th of June

It has been extremely hot today, & I have been very busy all day, but I have been thinking, well tomorrow will be rest for the weary, as it will be Sunday.

Oh! how cheering it is to be thinking whilst we are here below, There is rest for the weary; when we have done with the trials & temptations of this wicked world and are proven faithful, we shall have rest and happiness . . . .

Sunday 27th

I did not get to church today, but soon after breakfast I walked over to Mr. Hendon's for the papers & letters, expecting a letter for myself but was doomed for disappointment. I came back about ten. After dinner Mr. Evans and Cousin George Gover came and remained till nearly tea time. After which Juliet, Bettie, Bob Gover and Cassie Herring came down;[31] they left pretty late. I was quite sick and soon retired to rest. Sister Fannie went to church with Mr. Stump, did not get home until 11 or 12 o'clock.

Monday 28th 1858

I forgot to mention, I received a letter from Howard dated from Houma, La the 15th of this month, also from Bettie Cage dated the 11th from Tennessee. This evening I spent with Juliet Gover; after tea she & brother took a ride on horseback . . . . .

---

31. Bob (Robert) Gover was cousin Juliet and George Gover's* thirteen-year-old son.

Saturday night, July 10

Several days have passed by forever since I last penned any in this Journal, but my time has been so much engaged since that I have not been able to write any. The Fourth came on Sunday, and the night of the fifth we went up to Cousin Juliet's to witness fireworks, which was quite beautiful indeed; we enjoyed it exceedingly.

Within the last two weeks we have been called to part with our old aunt (aunt Peggie Smithson.) Death has called another. I trust she is as one of the angels of God. We too will have to pass away soon, never to return again. Oh! may we be prepared when ever the messenger comes, and have our lamps trimed & brightly burning. How transitory & fleeting are the moments of life: we are here today & tomorrow gone. Gone! how sad that word sounds, how mournfully it passes upon the ear, touches a cord in the heart which awakes sad memories of the past. There are the friends of our youth, of our girlhood, our playmates that we have enjoyed so many happy hour. Who has not lost a friend, a mother, a father, a brother, a sister, perhaps, or some dear friend. But what a consoling thought, if we all prove faithful we shall meet when parting is no more, when we will never say "our friends our gone," now never mourn, never sigh, no tears are there, no disappointments, there is all harmony of love. Oh! may we prepare to meet them! . . . .

This has been a very warm day. I have been quite busy all day. This morning Howard Munnikhuysen, Lizzie & Fannie brought Ann Lee home, she went up the day before to Bel Air with cousin Howard Parrish to go to a party at Miss Davenports. This afternoon cousin came, took sister Fannie buggie riding. After tea Pink Norris & Juliet Gover walked down. Friday evening Jimmy Watters spent here.[32] He got home the evening before from Pennsylvania where he has been teaching school. Tomorrow will be the Sabbath and it will be the fourth one I have not been to church. Oh, how I should love to go . . . . .

Monday 12th

Yesterday was one of the very loveliest days I ever saw. I was agreeably disappointed in getting to church in the morning, and I heard one of the most elegant sermons I ever listened to from James chpt. 2 vs 22, "Seest thou how faith wrought with his works and by words was faith made perfect," preached by Mr. Valliant in Bel Air. The church was crowded, all the windows were opened and such a delightful breeze came wafting in and the bright sun came in so cheerfully. It looked more like Sunday morning than I have seen for a long time. Everyone seemed to listen so attentively. Indeed it was a lovely sermon. Faith! How much can be said

32. James (Jimmy) Watters* was Godfrey* and Lizzie's* brother, who was twenty-four years old in 1858.

about it. I fear we have very little. Oh, that I had the faith that my forefathers had, for without faith we cannot see God. By faith Abraham, when he was tried, offered up Isaac; and he that received the promises offered up his only begotten son, of whom it was said, "in Isaac shall thy seed be called." Although Abraham loved his son dearly, yet he was willing to sacrifice him to God, as God had commanded. He might have thought—God did not intend I should offer up my son, or why would he say, "in Isaac shall thy seed by called." But he knew God had commanded him so to do, and he had faith. Can we not imagine Abraham with all meekness and fortitude leading his only son Isaac up to the Mount with his servant whom he took with him to help build the alter, and when he completed the alter, his son said, "Now Father, the altar is finished and all things are ready, where is the sacrifice?" Did his faith wax cold? Did he wish he had not done what he had? No! He bound Isaac and placed him on the altar and was about to plunge the knife in the heart of his son: but God saw his faith and caused an angel to stop him. His faith had saved his son's life. God gives us trials to try our faith. Oh, may we all be like Abraham, prove faithful.

I once had a dream which has left a lasting impression on my mind. It was this. I dreamed I was walking along a road leading from our house to one of the neighbors', and I came to a run where I had to cross before I could reach the house I was going to, and when I looked I found there were no stepping stones or any other way of crossing that I could see. But on looking up very far I saw a log, as it were fastened up by bushes, and seeming to be almost entirely suspended in the air. But I thought I had to go, and although the way looked dangerous, I had to cross over. On looking up I beheld our Savior looking down at me with a halo around his head, more like the sun, and as I looked up He said, "have faith in God." It has been several years since I dreamed it, but it is as fresh in the halls of memory as when I dreamed it . . . . .

Friday 16th

Monday evening Cousin George Gover was here. I forgot to mention who was here on sunday evening. Lizzie Holland, Otho Lee,[33] Jimmy Moores, Herman Stump, George Glasgow, Bob Gover and Juliet. Tuesday evening Miss Hannah Archer and Dr. George was here. I never witnessed such a sunset as we had on that evening. It had been rainy and cloudy nearly all day, and just before sunset it cleared off beautifully. The clouds which had been black now looked perfectly bright and beautiful. They first looked like an army arrayed for battle. Some were on horseback, some walking and the flags as it were flying in the breeze. Reminding me of

---

33. Otho Scott Lee, brother of Dr. Richard Lee,* was eighteen years old.

the description of Washington crossing the Delaware. It changed somewhat and looked much like Fort McHenry with the soldiers out drilling and their tents all erected over the island. Then it underwent a complete change. It now represented a City partly in ruins, with some of its palaces and buildings still standing and some had fallen to the ground. It was indeed a very beautiful sight and I only wished I had been an artist that I might have put it on canvas.

Wednesday nothing of interest occurred. I went up to Uncle Sam's expecting to stay only a little while, but rain came up and I was kept all night. Came home Thursday about nine o'clock. In the afternoon Jimmy Watters came and took tea—he seemed to be right sad as he expected to go out West this Fall for good and all. How we will miss him—I will more than the rest I think. Well, the best of friends must part. May his life be happy and his death peaceful is my sincere prayer. Today Mr. and Mrs. Valliant and the three children spent the day, Peggie Bond the evening. Cousin Richard [Lee] called for a short time.[34] After tea Mr. Stump and Pink Norris came, also Howard Parrish.

Tuesday afternoon 20th

On Saturday no one was here excepting the Gover girls and boys and they only for a little time. Sunday morning Juliet and Mr. George Rodgers (from Balto.) were here and Cassie Herring. I expected to have gone to church in the afternoon with cousin Howard P. but when he came by he had a gentleman in his buggy with him, so I was very much disappointed indeed. Dr. Archer and Mr. Stump took tea with us and after tea Cousin H. Parrish, Juliet Gover and Mr. Rodgers came. Howard stayed all night—took sister Fannie to see Peggie, who has been quite sick, has a dreadful cold but is now better, and from there to Uncle Jim's. Aunt Dillie is very sick and she is staying with her. Yesterday I suffered very much with a headache and soon after dinner I laid down and slept till nearly six when Peggie came, soon after Annie Webster & Fred P. came, after tea Juliet and Bettie Gover, after they left I walked up home with Juliet where I enjoyed some music for about an hour, then came home. No one has been here today but the day has not passed yet.

A week has passed since I penned any in this book for my time has been much occupied nearly all the time. Visitors have been coming and I have been visiting some too. Wednesday I walked up in the afternoon to see Aunt Dillie—found her a little better, did not stay long, called to see Peggie a little while, found cousin Richard Lee and Mary there. When I got home found cousin Howard Parrish had been here in my absence. Ma spent the evening with cousin Juliet Gover on that evening. The week passed off very pleasantly with me and seemed quite short. Sat-

34. Richard Lee,* a physician, was thirty-two in 1858.

urday evening I spent at Mr. Watters, with cousin George [Glasgow]. I did not get to church on Sunday, although I wanted to go much, last night cousin George Gover was here and Juliet.

Wednesday, August 11th

Some time has elapsed since I penned any in my journal—circumstances over which I have had no control has prevented me. Today has been exceedingly warm and sultry; and now it has much the appearance of rain. Last thursday we had quite a little company in the evening. The ladies were Lizzie Watters, Bennie and Nellie Lee,[35] Juliet Gover and gentlemen, Godfrey and Jimmy Watters, Mr. Barr, Mr. Stevenson (from Philadelphia) (Mr. B. from Baltimore) George Glasgow, Dr. Archer, Mr. Smith, and Mr. Isaac Evans of Baltimore. They seemed to enjoy themselves very much indeed.

I did not get to church on Sunday but the rest were there and heard a remarkably fine sermon by Mr. Valliant from the 8th Psalm fourth verse. "What is man that thou art mindful of him, and the son of man that thou visited him." Sister Fannie and Aunt Dillie are spending this week with cousin G Glasgow. Tomorrow we are invited there. I would love very much to go, but I scarcely expect to do so.

It is now nine or after at night—all have retired but myself. How calm everything is—not a noise disturbs the stillness of the night except the chirping of the Katydids and singing of the merry Cricket. What a fitted time for meditation. Then the mind which has been harassed with the cares of the day's toil can rest upon divine things. Then the soul can retire from the sinful lusts which surround it and commune with its God. "Retire O my soul from the busy world and employ thyself about that which thou wert created—the contemplation of thy God." Yes, it is when we retire from the busy scenes which have surrounded us throughout the day, that we can pour our sin-sick soul out to God, here we can confess our sins, and with hopes of forgiveness lay our burdens before the Lord; and with Faith we shall receive a full pardon by the Merciful Hearer of prayers. Oh! that each day I may go to him humbly asking forgiveness, asking for his spirit to enable me to fill every duty God has enjoined upon me to do. The good Book says, "Ask and ye shall receive, seek and ye shall find, knock and it shall be opened unto you." So by this we see if we ask God's grace humbly and faith, it will be given us. If we seek him with our whole hearts, we will find him, and if we call upon him in spirit He will hear us, and attend to our cry. O! I pray God to give me more. The Spirit that was in Christ that I may be able to bear patiently the trials and temptations of this life,

---

35. Bond mentions several visits from Bennie Lee. In a later entry, she notes that she is from New York; it seems, however, that she is frequently visiting family in Harford.

that I may be more humble and worthy to be called his child. That I may grow in grace more every day I live and when I'm called be ready.

Monday, August 30th

This day one year I was converted to God at Watters' meeting house. It was a lovely sabbath afternoon, one of the loveliest I ever saw. O! how I can recall even the thoughts that passed through my mind. One year since I was a born again. O have I in that year grown in grace according to the time? I fear not; O God help me, have mercy on me a miserable sinner that I am. I fear I give away too much to my evil passions. Give me grace O my Heavenly Parent to bear with the trials I am constantly beset with, and the temptations in which I find it hard to resist.

It has been some time since I penned in here; but my time has been very much engaged. Aunt Mary, Juliet and Jack (the baby) have been staying some time with us.[36] Also Grandma Bond.[37] The Methodist Episcopals are holding a meeting out in a woods near Robinson's store; it commenced yesterday morning and will continue some time I believe. The weather now is very fine, cloudless and cool. I much enjoy This season of the year. Lovely summer is passing away rappidly and oh! the changes it has made or has been made in those three short months. How many changes has my feelings undergone since this time last year . . . . .

2nd Sept.

The first of autumn—the last rays of the declining sun gives us somber feelings and remind us of the coming winter, when at zenith he stares at us with his big pale face, and tells us he is going to withhold from the world a portion of his heat for a season. There is something peculiar in the atmosphere these days: a sort of mellowness in the shining sun's rays, that makes it delightfully pleasant to be off and bask in them, and think of old times, and old associations. The sun when he rises or sets—he seems to be decorated with flowers and attended by multitudes of ethereal forms, apparently tearing his way through an immense veil of fine delicate lace. He lifts his huge round face across the horizon as if to laugh at the world for such late sleeping, and sinks in the west in a bed of clouds. During this month the air has a smoky appearance, like that of England, and everything in the shape of smoke is magnified to an unlimited extent. This morning it looked very much like rain, but since dinner the clouds have dispersed and things in general look

36. Bond likely refers to her mother's sister Mary (thirty-six years old) and her children. Her married name is not clear. In 1850 she was living in her father's Baltimore home, but, as Bond writes, she is married with children. (See also n. 37.)

37. Bond's grandmother on her mother's side was Mary Bond, a seventy-six-year-old widow. Her husband, Zacheus Onion, had been a bailiff in Baltimore. 1850 U.S. census, free schedule, Baltimore, Md., National Archives microfilm publication M432, roll 283.

pretty bright. I am anticipating a nice ride with Juliet Gover this afternoon but whether I shall enjoy one is more than I can say.

Saturday 4th of Sept.

How delightful, after a tiresome and weary week, to have Saturday evening for quiet. I always look forward to these evenings with pleasure, when we shall get the papers & letters, perhaps hear from a dear absent friend, and receive assurance that we are not forgotten by those we love. I enjoyed a most delightful ride on horseback thursday afternoon, Juliet & I went to Uncle Parker Lee's, from there to Mr. Barron's store, returning in time for tea, after which I went to church, or rather meeting, out in a grove by Mr. Robertson's store, with Dr. Archer; had a very pleasant drive, and heard a very good sermon preached from part of the parable of The Fig Tree by Mr. Gwyn. Yesterday I was at home all day. Juliet came down after tea; we enjoyed a very confidential chat to ourselves. Today such rain has fallen. To-morrow we expect to go to "Bush meeting" if nothing prevents us.

Sunday afternoon, Sept. 26th

It has been some time since I opened this book to write in it. Sometimes I almost despair of ever having time to write again, for someone is always coming to prevent me, or I am otherwise engaged. This month is passing quietly away. This season of the year, is to me, truly delightful, much more so than any other. Autumn is to me a fitting time for contemplation. The foliage is beautiful now—here and there may be seen the yellow and red leaves peeping out among the green ones, which by comparison are lovely. I am always more inclined to wander about through the woods, and view the leaf which has partly faded. On everything seems to be written "passing away." It reminds us of our own bodys. We too are passing away—soon the places which know us now will know us no more. "We fade as the leaf and wither as the grass." I took a walk down the woods this morning and gathered some wild flowers (which I am very fond of.) I thought as I viewed the beautiful scenery, of the surrounding country & watched the water, as it glided so gently off its pebble bed, how could anyone doubt there is a God. Could any man have made such things? Could anyone have formed those lovely clouds as they sail across the blue arch of heaven? Could any but an "all wise God" have formed this earth? No! No! None but our God. And yet there are some who try to believe there is no God. They say the world was made by chance, we were put in by chance, and by chance we go out, I suppose. Well, I think if this is anyone's belief, the "chances" are very much against them. They say they don't believe in the "Bible." Why? Because they don't know any of the people who wrote it, and no one ever saw anyone the Bible speaks of, as they know of. Well, we ought not to believe there ever was such a person as George Washington, because we never saw George Washington. It is all folly for anyone to try to convince me that they don't believe in the Bible.

This is a lovely day. I wished to go to meeting this morning so much but could not; nor this afternoon either. I have been out at the "tent" twice since I wrote, once in the wagon with Mrs. Rodgers, Juliet, Sister Fannie and George (the colored man).[38] We had a jolly ride, broke down both going and coming. Dr. Archer came home with us. One evening I went with Dr. George. I enjoyed the meeting very much indeed. I have been staying several days at Mr. Watters'—went on Sunday evening and returned Tuesday afternoon. Had a very pleasant visit. Lizzie Watters, Bennie and Nellie Lee accompanied me home. After tea Jimmy came and waited on the girls home. The Saturday afterwards they spent the evening with Peggie Bond, and I also. After tea Jimmy waited on me home. But before we started we sat in the carriage a long time and talked. Since then he has been many times. He leaves for the West tomorrow, knows not when he will be back, some five or six years, I suppose. We will miss him very much indeed. I received a letter from La. wednesday—a long one as usual. Oh! how I should love to see the writer this afternoon. It seems like an age since I saw him and yet it will be a much longer time before I have that pleasure. I have been feeling very sad for some time; but this afternoon I do not feel as sad as usual. Why it is I cannot tell . . . . .

Tuesday morning, 28th

This is truly a lovely morning—everything out looks bright and cheerful. Cousin Howard Parrish is here; came yesterday morning. Yesterday morning quite early Jimmy Watters came to bid us farewell for three or perhaps five years. He looked very sad and seemed to feel his departure from us all very deeply; we will all miss him much for he is a great favorite with the family (not me excepted). I went to Uncle Parker's spent the most of the day, had quite a pleasant visit. I called at Uncle Jim's as I was returning home. Before I got to the house I met Cousin George Glasgow coming for me. He turned and came back. I found when I arrived, Mr. Parrish and Dr. Archer here. Dr. Archer had called in the morning to take me to Bel Air but I had left. There is to be seen in the heavens a comet of great brilliancy; every night it is more beautiful.[39] I feel this morning more determined than ever to trust in Providence, for I know God will take care of those who put their trust in him. O! that I could always trust myself fully in him. God help me to do my duty faithfully, that I may be a worthy servant in my master's vineyard.

38. Bond refers to the local camp meeting, the "Bush meeting" that she mentioned in her previous entry. Evangelical camp meetings were marked by emotional worship and an emphasis on community. In her entries Bond notes both the devotional and social purposes of the meetings.

39. Bond refers to Donati's Comet of 1858.

2nd October 1858

Last Wednesday afternoon I went to Aunt Nancy's, walked over there by myself, at least most of the way. When I got there I found Bennie & Nellie Lee. Next morning we all went to spend the day at cousin Sam Lee's. We had a charming day—in the afternoon Dr. Archer & his sister came. After tea we returned to aunt's. I returned home Friday afternoon; just as I was coming out of uncle Jim's gate I met brother & Henry Bond who had a few days since returned from the West. When I got home I found Coz here, who I was very glad to see.

This morning she, Henry, and myself went to uncle Sam's. We had not been there very long before John P. Dallam & Mr. Perryman came—they had called to see me and found we girls were not at home so they came down to see me. I found him exceedingly agreeable. They left before dinner, and we came directly after dinner. Ma accompanied Coz to Bel Air where she expects to stay till tomorrow.

I got a letter from Howard yesterday; he is well, poor fellow, and has not got my last letter yet. When he does how sad it will make him. Why can't I love him? I know he loves me devotedly; and yet he does not seem to be my ideal. Perhaps I may never see the ideal I have pictured to my own imagination. I heard of Henry Forwood's death yesterday, but cannot tell whether it is a true report or not. Miss Annie Walker was married to Mr. Gale Tuesday morning at 8 o' clock.

October 14th

Since writing in this book I have been quite sick, suffering with the neuralgia in my head but now I feel quite well. Last week I spent the most of it with Juliet Gover, as her mother was in Balto. We enjoyed ourselves very much keeping house. Sunday she and Lillie, Mr. Norris, Jimmy Moores, Dr. Archer and Herman Stump were here, but I did not feel well enough to go in to see her. Monday after tea we walked up to Woodside to see her. Tuesday morning she left for school. Tuesday Dr. Archer and cousin Howard were here. Yesterday Louise Wyatt and cousin George Glasgow spent the evening.[40] Lou remained all night in consequence of the rain. This morning cousin George came for her, to go home, soon after they left cousin Richard Lee came.

We are having indeed singular weather. The sun comes out right bright sometimes, and then shortly after it will commence raining. Now it has every appearance of rain. The country now is looking lovely indeed. Cousin George has just come from cousin John Moores, so I will have to stop writing for this morning. I wonder if anyone will come this evening, or not? . . . . .

40. Louise Wyatt, a native of Virginia, later married Bond's brother, William.

16th October

Another week has passed and gone forever, and we are still left to enjoy the blessings of life while many have been called away to answer the deeds done in the body. O! may we (as a family) when called be ready to enter the Kingdom of God. O! that we may have our lamps trimmed and brightly burning when the Master sees fit to call us home. I have been busily thinking today of the passed—how memory loves to wonder back through the dim vistas of the past and view the pictures of scenes, that we have enjoyed in years gone by forever, as they come before us; taking us back, perhaps to our childhood. Methinks I can see the friends of my childhood; those that I loved with that pure childlike love, which knows no deceit. Where are they now? Gone, gone, echo answers—Gone!—"Friends have been scattered like roses in bloom, some at the bridal and some at the tomb." We are nearly always parting with dear ones, here below. And O! how it wrings the heart to sever those ties which bind two loving hearts together. "When parting from the friends we love though sure to meet tomorrow, we still a pang of angwish prove, we feel a touch of sorrow. But O what pen can paint the tears when from those friends we ever are forced to part—for months, for years—to part perhaps forever. But when we are forced to part from those we are sure are gone to the better world—how consoling it is to think—if we hold out faithful to The end, we too shall go to that land, and enjoy the company of those loved ones forever—never to be separated by Death, or any other cause. What a blissful thought? Grant o lord that we may hold out faithful till thou seest best to call us home.

How wild are my thoughts when I think of the past, present and what the future may be. Perhaps it is my lot to go away from those dear ones I have known from my babyhood; to go out among strangers as it were. How sad the thought, Can I leave the dear associates of my girlhood, the dear and familiar objects that all around have greeted my sight since I first opened my eyes on this world? And more than all leave the dear old homestead, where more than 20 summers have smiled on me, the "dearest spot of earth to me"? No! I scarcely think I ever can—how great will have to be that love for the one. I would have to leave all these, and break those ties which are now so dear to my heart of hearts. I will put it in God's hands to do with me as he sees best. O that I may do my part faithfully, is my prayer . . . . . .

Today has been very fine—real fall-like weather; every thing in nature looks lovely. The foliage has under gone a great change, every leaf seems to have changed—We are reminded by this of our own sinful bodies—we "fade as the flower"; we too are passing away. A few short years at most, and "the place that knew us will know us no more," we will be lain in the cold silent tomb—perhaps forgotten by some, who professed to be our friends, and love so much. How very soon the dead are forgotten.

Tuesday morning, October 19th

I did not get to church on sunday as I expected, but remained home all day with the exception of going to uncle Jim's a little while after tea with Howard Munnikhuysen. Mr. Stump, Cousin George & Howard were our sunday visitors. Yesterday morning Howard took me up behind him on horseback. I rode up to the gate. After dinner cousin George Glasgow came and took Fannie to uncle Parker's. They returned after tea. No one else was here excepting the Gover children. This morning has been very foggy but now it is clearing off. When the sun came out everything looked beautiful. "The dew was on the blossom" and the frost on the grass. The sun shining down on it gave it the appearance of silver, and the little dew drops now peeping up out of the grass look like so many diamonds sparkling in the green. How many beautiful things in Nature there are, to remind us of the Supreme Being who has so perfectly formed them, and given them to us, unworthy and unthankful creatures.

November 1st

I have been several days confined to bed but now am able to sit up, though I feel very nervous. I have suffered with a dreadful cold. I see I cannot write now—my hand trembles too much.

Christmas day, 1858

I have been very ill since I penned a line in this book. But now I am a convalescent. This is indeed a lovely day, so calm and still out. How I should love to walk out in the beautiful sunshine. I have not been out of the house for more than eight weeks. But I do not wish to complain, for God has ordered all things for the best; and I only wish to do what will please him the most. Oh! I do want to be thankful for all God's mercies towards me, for his watchful care over me—from the earliest dawn of infancy till the present moment. How many changes has there been since this day one year. How differently was I occupied to what I am now. I was spending the day at cousin John Moores; and it was a very cold disagreeable day—but today it is beautiful.

I have just been downstairs receiving a call from cousin Howard Parrish, he only stayed a few minutes, on his way to his tomorrow's appointment. He seemed very glad to see me going about again. Whilst I was sick he came up and prayed beautifully for me, it did me good, for I had not heard a prayer for so long.

> "As the myrtle whose perfume enriches the bower,
> Is prized far beyond e'en the gaudiest flower;
> So a wife, who a household can skillfully rule,
> Is a jewel of price to all men—save a fool."

Let the fastidious "Lords and Masters" jot down the above lines upon the tablets of their memories.

Wednesday night Feb 16th 1859

Another year has passed and gone forever—one year nearer eternity—How many the changes old year thou has wrought! Blushes have deepen and tears have been wept. Friends have been scattered like roses in blume; Some at the altar, and some at the tomb. This year that has gone has passed swiftly and pleasantly, mostly with me. Oh! how thankful I should be for the many blessings my kind Heavenly Father has allowed me to enjoy—Though affliction has visited me—and been layed on the bed of languishing & pain—yet I feel thankful it is no worse than it is.

I have so many blessings in this life, and we all have so many more than we are thankful for. I am now exiled in my bedroom—by the back window—within is so cheerful & cozy—for my fire is blazing cheerily in the stove snapping & chuckling as it were at the hickory wood. And without is still more beautiful. The Moon is shining so beautifully and bright; whilst all so calm. Jack Frost, I think will scarcely dare venture out under her soft mellow rays, unless he steals a march across the meadows.

I visited "Medical Hall" yesterday[41]—spent a delightful day. It is a very lovely family—Mrs. Archer—Miss William—two children—and Miss Harriet Hays. It was the residence of the late Judge Archer.[42] And a lovely place indeed. Changes are taking place in our neighborhood quite often. Uncle Sam sold his place, not long since, to Gerard Gover—for 35.00. They will move about the 20th of next month. Mr. Barron was married to a lady in Sykesville—he was counted one of the neighborhood beau—Fannie went to Philadelphia the 8th of this month, with *Mr. Stump:* has not got home yet.

Sunday eve Feb 27th 1859

I am all alone this evening. All have gone to meeting to hear Mr. Parrish preach. I am again an invalid, have been confined to my room more than a week, most of the time to my bed. But God has watched over me and given me grace to bear with the pains he has seen proper to afflict me with.

I know it is for some good. I am afflicted, therefore I pray to be enabled grace and patience to bear even *thankfully.* For through tribulations only shall I see God,

41. Medical Hall was one of the first medical schools in Maryland, established by John Archer (1741–1810) in Harford County in the late eighteenth century. Dr. George Archer,* often mentioned by Bond, is a descendant of John Archer.

42. Judge Stevenson Archer, a Democrat, was a member of the Maryland House of Delegates and the U.S. Congress. He later became a judge in the Maryland Court of Appeals. He died in 1848.

and dwell in his Kingdom forever. The Lord has indeed been good, has shown me so many mercies from the earliest dawn of infancy to the present moment. This indeed is a lovely evening. We have had quite a deep snow—it fell on thursday and friday—But the sun has so much power now, that it can not remain on the Earth long; Cousin Howard Parrish, and cousin George Glasgow were both here yesterday in their sleighs; but it could not be very good sleighing.

Oh how I should love to see the absent one now! Hush! I hear a dear little bird singing—How delightful it is to hear *God's* birds singing—For they are his. All things are his. Sending its evening hymn to its Creator. Merry hearted bird sing on—sing some of thy warbling song of Love in my heart—my heart has such a longing for something so far off it seems. O! God make me truly thankful for the many blessings I enjoy—Friends—home—and *Love,* all are mine.

March 4th 1859

This is indeed a lovely day. The sun shines so cheerily, and birds sing so merrily. It really looks like spring out of doors. I am still an invalid. Suffer very much yet with pain. Tuesday March 1st I had a very pretty bunch of flowers sent me; the first of the spring. I love flowers—they were my friends in childhood, in girl hood and now are my friends in womanhood. There is a language about flowers that ever speaks to my heart.

Wednesday evening cousin George [Glasgow] spent here. He brought me some oranges, & some kisses. He is so kind always to me; indeed he seems more like a brother, than any thing else; I got a letter from Louisiana, a short time since. Howard was getting ready for a trip to the "Mexican Gulf," part for the recovery of health, and for the purpose of collecting curiosities for a "Scientific association," in Houma; the village near where he dwells. I feel anxious to hear from him—how he enjoyed the trip, and whether he received any benefit from the voyage.

Sunday morning 6th

I was interrupted whilst writing the above, by Peggie Bond coming—she spent the evening with me. I enjoyed her company very much, as I had been quite lonely the last few days.

This is a charming morning; the sun is shining so beautifully, and the birds are singing so happily—Spring has really come and brought the songsters with it and flowers too—yesterday I received a very lovely bouquet of "spring flowers"; they came from a dear old lady—and I prize them much. It is indeed a pleasant thought to be remembered by those we feel no interest, but to be remembered by dear ones, is doubly sweet—particularly by an old & dear lady friend.

Cousin George Gover & Bob (his son) stayed all of last night with us. I did not see them, only through my window. He brought me some oranges. I have just eaten one. They left quite early this morning. I was down stairs last evening for the first time for more than two weeks; it was quite a treat. How I should love to go to church this morning. We know not the value or privilege of going to meeting 'till we know it is impossible for us to get there. And so with the sinner, he does not feel the importance of preparing for Heaven until he finds it *too late*—he can not get there, then the awfulness of Eternity rises before him; how then he will wish he had made better use of that time allotted him to "prepare to meet his God." Oh! God help *us all* to make that final preparation, that whenever we are called we may have on the wedding garment & *our* lamps *brightly trimmed.*

(Thoughts as they occur) This is a beautiful world—so many beautiful objects in it to make us happy—and yet there is a mysterious sadness sweeps over ones heart sometimes. We scarcely can know what causes it. Perhaps it is *bye-gone recollections,* some were so happy, so bright with scarcely a shadow to darken the brightness. It is a sad happy feeling that dwell on my childhood when I was as free as the air I breathed, as I danced merrily merrily along to the old log school-house. It was a long way for a child of my years to walk twice a day. I was only 7 years old then, and it was three miles around the road, but not quite that through the fields. How I remember the first day I was allowed to go—The first day at school, who ever forgets it? I was with my brother, three years nearly older than I. It was a lovely June morning—our path led mostly through woods, except here & there we crossed an old commons where stray cattle were generally grazing (which was always my terror). I had long begged to be allowed to go to school with brother—and been put off from time to time till my heart had nearly sickend with hope deferred but now the long anticipated time had come, and with book in hand I started off running & jumping till nearly there. How sweet smell the wild flowers that morning, how merrily[43] sang the birds. "The due was on the blossom." It was all sun-shine in the beautiful world for me, my heart was too beat high with joyful anticipation.

At last we reached the school house, how the boys & girls stared at me, some laughed for what reason I don't know. I was dressed as nice, if not nicer than any one there, so it could not be That—perhaps it was my bashfulness, for I was a *very little* girl, with big *black eyes,* and dark hair cut short around my neck. But at dinner time I soon got acquainted with the girls, and very soon with some of the boys, so we all played "hide and seek together &c&c. Oh the merry sunbeams that danced across my path-way then, where have ye flown? Some have been left to widen and grow brighter others have given away to dark shadows. Be it so it is best—we could not appreciate the sunshine if clouds did not arise, and obscure its brightness from our visions.

43. The word *cheerily* was first written but crossed out.

The atmosphere is always more pure[44] after a thunder shower, so it is when God send sorrow to his creatures here—he does it to purify their hearts that they may see with The eye of faith more clearly the "Sun of Rightiousness." As the hymn says—

"God moves in a mysterious way.
    His wonders to perform;
He plants his footsteps in the sea,
    And rides upon the storm.

———— ————

Deep in unfathomable mines,
    Of never failing skill;
He treasures of his bright-designs,
    And works his sovereign will.

———— ————

Ye fearful saints! fresh courage take,
    The clouds ye so much dread;
Is big with mercy, and will break,
    In blessings on your head.

———— ————

Judge not the Lord by feeble sense,
    But trust him for his grace;
Behind a frowning providence,
    He hides a smiling face.

———— ————

His purposes will open fast,
    Unfolding every hour.
The bud may have a bitter taste;
    But sweet will be the flower.

———— ————

Blind unbelief is sure to err
    And leave his work in vain;
God is his own interpreter,
    And he will make it plain.
"Cowper"[45]

———— ————

---

44. The phrase *more pure* is inserted above the line, above a crossed-out *clear.*

45. Poet William Cowper (1731–1800). Bond writes the following sideways beside her transcription: "This hymn is truly beautiful. I love it very very much indeed: *'The bud may have a bitter bitter taste, But sweet will* be *they the flower.'* Mit."

Saturday March the 12th 1859

I have just seen the mail boy go past. I wonder if he has a letter for me; I hope so for I have not got one from La for a long time (four weeks nearly;) I wish he would hurry along—and not gog along as if there was not something *very* important in that mail-bag for some body *I know!* The sun has gone over the Western hills—there is not a cloud to be seen as far as the eye can reach.

All is calm without—From my window I see the beautiful "valley of Thomas Run" and the "mountainous hills of "Deer Creek." The wheat fields are beginning to look quite green and those beside the newly plowed fields are very beautiful indeed. I am quite sick today, not able to be down stairs. Cousin George Glasgow was here this morning, also aunt Mary, and Hall. We heard of Mr. H Carr's death this morning. He died last night about nine o'clock. May he rest in peace.

April 6th

Time has sped by on rapid wings since I opened this book. I have been again ill but thanks be to God I am now much better. I have ridden out but once for seven weeks—that once was with Dr Archer; we went to uncle Parkers, spent the day, when we got home Lizzie Watters, & Bennie Lee were here. They stayed three or four days. I got some beautiful spring flowers the other day—Howard sent me some orange blossoms in a letter, they were indeed very fragrant, the sweetest things I ever smelt. I would love to see them on the trees. I got a letter from H. yesterday, he is studying medicine with Dr. Helmick of Houma—he says he has a very beautiful present for me but wont tell me what it is. I wish I had him here, I guess I'ed *make him tell me.* He says every thing looks so beautiful there: so many beautiful flowers. And wishes for Mit to be there to gather them. Uncle Presbury was staying at his fathers when he wrote, had been there more then a week.

This is a beautiful day—although the wind is blowing a good deal. I am reading now a very interesting work called "Ninevah and Its Remains," by "Layard."[46] It is quite instructive. It tells a good deal about the rivers—Nile & Tigris. As one descends the Tigris, they can from one point see the ruins of "Ninevah," all around the mound are meadows which in April are covered with every variety of flowers, & at least of every hue.

Sunday 10th of April 1859

Again another sabbath has dawned upon us and I am not sufficiently well to attend divine worship. Oh I hope soon to be well enough to enjoy that privilege. This is a very disagreeable day out—It is very cloudy & damp has very much the appearance of rain at every moment.

46. The author, Sir Austen Henry Layard, was an English archaeologist who published popular accounts of his excavations.

Another week has passed away forever, we are seven days nearer *Eternity*. What a solemn thought that word *Eternity,* awakens in our minds, It fills those who are striving for that blissful Home with joy; for then the weary are at rest, then all trials are past, and conflicts over. Oh when shall I reach that happy Land where sighing & tears are no more. Would I exchange my *Hope of Heaven* for all the gold, glitter, and worth of this world. No! No! not for all this, or ten millions of world like it. A *Hope of Heaven,* that Home where angels dwell, where saints sing praises forever to the living God. Where sin is never more known, where all tears are *wiped away—where broken hearts* are healed and bruised spirits cured.

CHAPTER TWO

"Religion in Affliction"

Sunday 1st May

The sun rose clear and bright, shone warm and beautifully all day. I went to aunt Nancy Lee's this day week, spent a delightful week, returned from there this evening. Called at Mr. Watters on my way home, all seemed glad to see me, and wanted me to stay some time. I came home to tea, Cousin George was galantin me.

Monday 2nd

Beautiful day. I feel better after my visit. Uncle Jim was here short time this afternoon. I walked down to Charity's for a little while.[1] Gathered flowers, got a little rose bush from the woods, had it planted in the yard. Felt quite tired when I retired.

Tuesday 3rd

Lovely day, rather cooler than yesterday was—went to uncle Sam's, found all well. Peggie not at home, very sorry. Went with cousin George, took dinner there, after which went over to Mr. Websters[2] to see Lizzie—been sick for a long time. Looks frail but beautiful. Came home to tea. Dr. George was here to tea. Came from Mr. Archers, looked well. Ann Lee gone to aunt Nancy's, sister Fannie at Blanche's [Archer]. Ma and I at home. Feel very weary. This is the anniversary of my visit to Baltimore. I went down the third of May with Howard Bond. How many changes?

Wednesday 4th

I am sitting at my window, looking out on one of the most enchanting spots of dear old Harford, on the beautiful Valley of Thomas Run. The sun is about setting, and everything in Nature looks beautiful. I have a very extensive view of *Woodland*, as it entirely surrounds the hills of "Deer Creek."

---

1. Bond likely refers to Charity Clark, one of the family's former servants. She was either a slave owned by another family and hired by the Munnikhuysens or was free and worked as a house servant. See also Bond's entry of 23 June 1858.

2. Mr. Webster is probably James Webster, a wealthy Harford farmer.

I have been very sad all day, and very sick. Oh when I think that perhaps in one short year we may have to give up our dear old home and go among strangers to seek a *home,* it nearly breaks my heart. Oh Heavenly Father guide us right and that we may see more clearly. Oh, enable us to put our entire trust in Thee, knowing "as our day is so shall our strength be." I am suffering with a pain in my shoulder and head, neuralgia they say. Mr. Henard's son took dinner with us today. He is a Track agent. I did not go down to dinner, was not able. George Hall called this morning. Seemed sorry to hear I had been such an invalid.

Thursday 5th
Beautiful weather; very warm and pleasant. S.M. Lee was here. Uncle Jim after tea. Cousin George Gover called for a little while, just from Baltimore all well at aunt Marg's, saw G Ma day before.

Friday 6th
This day one year I went over on the Eastern Shore with Howard Bond, and cousin Mary Ann Bond. It was not near so pretty a day, as this is—for it rained quite hard before we started which was about ten o'clock in the morning. Went in the Cecil boat to George Town where the carriage met us from cousin Jeams Bond's. My how time flies! It seems like only a few months since then, but alas it has been 12—

Saturday 7th
Beautiful, warm and balmy. Quarterly meeting commenced at Watters today. Many persons have passed by; no one from here went. But I am looking forward to be able to go tomorrow. I took a walk down my favorite woods this afternoon. Gathered some beautiful wild flowers from its mossy bank. Oh! flowers sweet flowers how I love ye. They have a peculiar language that goes right to my heart of hearts. I saw whilst I was taking my walk cousin Jerard Gover—and chatted with him some time.

Sunday 8th
I awoke this morning fearful it would be too damp for me to attend church, but not thinking any thing else would prevent my going. But how my heart sank within me when they told me I could not go on account of using the horses. Tears would come—nor was this all—words of unkindness escaped my lips—but no sooner spoken than I regretted having said them. Oh I pray my Heavenly Father to forgive me, for I am indeed sorry I said and did what I did. Oh that I may be enabled to bear with more patience crosses & trials! Why can I not always put my trust in him; knowing "He doeth all things well." But I was doomed not to be disappointed, for about eleven o'clock Mr. G.R.G. [George Glasgow] came in his buggy and offered to take me to church—How joyfully I dressed and went, with how much self-

ishness too for I left ma alone. I did not think of this when I was grieving over—what I thought then—a disappointment. But I did think of this before I left and received her assurance of not being afraid to be left alone. I fear I did not enjoy the meeting as much as I anticipated for the excitement before leaving home unfitted me for devotional exercises. But I pray God I did, and do—sincerely repent of my former sins, and will live nearer to the Cross. O that I could take up my *Cross* more willingly and cheerfully, and follow after Jesus—God help me to guard my conversation & thoughts that they may not wonder off in unforbidden channels, but be consistent with my *profession*. Came home to dinner, saw Dr. Watters at meeting—came home the evening before. Looks well—but sad. In the afternoon Lizzie Brown & her brother came, did not remain tea. Cousin George spent the evening.

Monday 9th

Very warm today, felt like June. Went with G.R.G. to Mr. Watters, found Mrs. Brown there. I only spent the evening, came home about nine, first time stayed out till after dark, fraid I'll catch cold.

John [Watters] has changed much, looks older, and sadder. Poor fellow he has drank of the bitter cup of sorrow, about two years ago he lost his wife, a bride of some weeks and a few days. How sad, sad. Oh may it prove his spiritual good.

Tuesday 10th May

Very cloudy, raining in the afternoon, cold and disagreeable. Was to have a "Temperance Meeting" held in Bel Air, at the Methodist church, lecturers Revs. Mr. Valliant & Noble. I hope the weather did not prevent a large audience. I should loved so much to have heard it.

Wednesday 11th

I am far from being well today. The weather is not favorable for one of my constitution and disease. It has rained nearly all day. I have been in bed all day till now. I feel better than I did this morning. O I pray that my afflictions may do me good. And I can truly say I have been sustained by the Holy Spirit. It is indeed a pleasant thought to know God watches over and protects *his* sorrowing creatures here in this "Vale of tears." O that my "strength may be as my day is."

Religion, in affliction, is a great consolation. It is then we feel more dependent on God for grace to bear the Crosses of this life, and O he has helped me and will continue if I put my trust in *him* and leave all in his hands. I was this time last year over on the Eastern Shore at Mrs. Thomas's. She had company on this day one year Mrs. Cann & daughter, Mrs. Harris & daughter and Peggie Bond, Howard Bond, Glover Bond & myself—he (the latter Bond) left for home that evening. Oh shall I ever forget that evening. I was truly hurt. Oh I fear I did not treat *one loving heart quite right;* but tis past. Oh! I pray to be guarded in my conversation and guided by My Heavenly Father, in all things.

Thursday, 12th Afternoon.

We have had rain for the last two days. It is now very cloudy and has very much the appearance of rain. The foliage has come out greatly since the fall of rain. And when the sun puts forth its cheering rays Nature will look lovely. So it is, when the cloud of affliction rests upon us and the storm of temptation arises within our bosoms, and if we trust in our kind Heavenly Father and ask *him* to give us strength to bear with them; and make us thankful and grateful for blessings we enjoy, he will send the golden beams of the "Sun of Righteousness" to melt away the clouds; and the storms shall pass away, leaving the atmosphere of our hearts pure.

I have formed some new resolutions within the last day or two. Oh! I pray my Heavenly Father to enable me to act upon them; and that I may be a true follower of the Lamb of God that taketh away the sins of the world. I have fallen into temptation. I have done so many things I should not have done, and left undone so many I ought to have done. I do pray Thee, O merciful Father, to help me in each time of need. And Oh, that I may be willing to give up *all* for *Thee*. "The dearest idol I have known, whate'er that idol be, help me to tear it from thy throne, and worship only Thee." Oh! I do want to be a Christian: a true follower of Jesus! I do pray Thee oh! My Father to take *all* self-righteousness from me; and that I may have a more humble opinion of myself. I do want to be meek and humble. Give me, Oh Father that deep humility of spirit I so much desire! And take away all my pride. For Oh mortal what has thou to be proud of: for thou could not make our hair blacker or whiter. Oh! that I may know myself. Purify my heart. Give me a heart void of offense to God and man. Teach me submission to thy will, Oh! my Father in all things, seen and unseen, all that is, and that is to come. Make me truly thankful for the blessings thou hast vouchsafed to me and my afflictions though severe, may they be my greatest blessing. Oh! that my *heart,* or lips may never complain but that I may bear with cheerfulness each bodily pain, knowing through tribulation *only* shall I see my Father's face.

I am not well today—My Dr was to see me this morning.[3] He says I acted imprudently staying out late at night. I will try and do better, with the assistance from on high. I must try and act with more firmness of character and not be led by temptation by such worldly desires.

My Father, I pray thee to take away all selfish desires from my heart and jealous feelings towards any one. I am sure that is one of my besetting sins. Oh! that

3. Bond writes "Dr. Lee" at the bottom of the page, referring to Richard Lee.*

I may not live for the applause of the world but *entirely* for Heaven. Oh! that I may ever endeavor "to do unto all even as I wish to be done by" and "love my neighbor as myself." Oh! that I may be enabled, through grace, to mortify the flesh. For it is not the outward appearance God looks upon but the appearance of the heart. "Nor he that commendeth himself is approved, but whom the Lord commendeth." Oh, that I may be enabled, by the Holy Spirit, to cast out of my heart all vain imaginations, and every high thing that exalts itself against the knowledge of God. Oh, that I be not envious of others. But let me strive to "gain the mark of the prize of the high calling, which is in Christ Jesus." Worldly things shall have passed away. Enable me my precious Father in Heaven, to come out from among the sinful world; and declare myself more determined to fight manfully under the banner of the Lord's. "None daring to make me afraid." Oh, it is my desire to live nearer to the cross, to sit at its foot, and there bathe my Saviour's feet with my penitent tears. "Oh! that my eyes were a fountain of tears." Oh! that I could pour out with tears, this sinsick heart. O God: renew in me a right spirit and give me a pure heart.

I feel far happier since I penned those above lines and I do pray they are for my spiritual good; and not from my pen alone but from the outpourings of my heart. "My heart is deceitful above all things and desperately wicked." Oh! that I may never be a stumbling-block to any one, but may my greatest wish be, to serve my Master and do his will in all things. Lord strengthen me and give me grace, each day, to bear patiently each *trial,* temptation and difficulty which lies in wait for me. Oh! hear me my Father in Heaven.

Thursday evening 12th

Writing by moonlight. The moon is shining beautifully down on my book. How much to inspire one! But somehow or other I don't feel very much inspired. I hear the croaking of the frogs. It is cheering for it tells us summer is coming. There! Whilst I write, a cloud passes over the moon, but did not rest there long. Oh, I see a little star up there in the blue vault of Heaven, and I would rather be a star, and having companions of stars around me, than that glorious Moon shining "all solitary, and alone." In after years perhaps I will rest my eye upon these few lines, written at my front window, by the light of the moon. When perhaps my eyes have grown dim; and my hand tremulous. I feel a greater determination than ever to be a follower of the "Lord Jesus." And Oh! may I be strengthen and sustained by the Holy Spirit. amen. amen.

Friday night 13th

I have suffered much throughout this day; and I fear I have not been as cheerful and patient as I should have been. I have given up to my imaginations too much here lately. Oh! help me my Father to bring every thought into subjection to thy holy will. I have been too worldly minded and too self-righteous. Oh! Father in Heaven keep me from all such. For what am I to have one vain thought of myself? There is no good thing in me, all is sinfulness. I have not kept near enough to the cross. O, give me grace to overcome all evil desires, and flee from the wrath to come. Oh! may I sacrifice all desires of the flesh that keeps me from taking up my *cross*. I feel as if I had a work to do; a talent to improve. Oh! that I may not be as that slothful servant, that hid his Lord's talent in the earth. O Heavenly Father, send thy Holy Spirit to enable me to improve the allotted time thou has given me here below. Oh! that I may work out my soul's salvation with fear and trembling. I feel I have not done my duty in speaking to those dear and near ones around, and about me, of their souls salvation. Help me to overcome that fearfulness and timidity in speaking a "word in season" to those dear ones, O Father! I want to be more useful in the church, among my relations, intimates and friends. Oh, that I might bring one soul to Christ. Lord help thy unworthy servant! Teach me to will and to *do*. Oh, that I may by thy Holy Spirit, be led to keep thy Sabbath days *Holy* and loving them best of the seven. Give me grace, my Heavenly Father, to bear my pain and sufferings, knowing "whom the Lord loveth he chasteneth."

Strengthen *my Faith*, for I have but little, to what I should have. Make me as a little child, "For unless we become as little children, we cannot see the Kingdom of Heaven." Oh! to be humble, to have the faith Abraham had, when he was directed by the Lord to offer up his son Isaac! Twas faith that brought Daniel out of the lion's den. Now before laying this weary body down, I would ask God to forgive every sinful thought, desire and misspent moment. I know there was many. If, O my Father, thou seeth fit to permit me to see the light of another day, may my first thought be in praise and gratitude to thee, for thy watchful protection over me through the stillness of another night, and to be kept from all sin throughout the day. Help me to overcome all my *besetting sins*. But should thou my Father see fit to call me away from this wicked world, Oh! receive me my Savior into thy arms of love, amen, amen.

Saturday afternoon May 14th

How much I enjoy a quiet Saturday afternoon. When the work and toil of a week has past, I feel more like communing with my heart and being still. I have been reading a "Memoir of Susan Allibone" "A life hid with Christ in God."[4] It truly is a delightful book. I see so many of my own heart sentiments in it. Oh! if I was such a watchful Christian. But I am such a wicked sinner. There is no good

4. The complete title is *A Life Hid with Christ in God, Being a Memoir of Susan Allibone, Chiefly Compiled from Her Diary and Letters,* ed. Alfred Lee (Philadelphia: J. B. Lippincott, 1856). Bond reads this book, as she does many others, for self-improvement and instruction.

thing in me. It is my desire to live entirely to God, but the "flesh warreth against the spirit." I have so many temptations "when I would do good evil is ever present with me." Give me more grace, my Heavenly Parent, to resist the "pomp and vanities of this world." I have indulged in some very wicked thoughts and feelings today. Oh that I may be enabled hereafter to heed the whispering of the spirit of God. Oh Heavenly Father awaken me up to my sinfulness in thy sight. Cause thy light to shine into my heart that I may be healed from all sinfulness. I feel my unworthiness, more each day, for the many, many blessings I enjoy, and my ingratitude to thee "the source of every blessing." Keep my feet from wandering into forbidden paths and my lips from speaking evil. Aid me Holy Father in overcoming my besetting sins. Oh! I have so many. Take all *jealousness* from my heart, *envy*, hatred and *uncharitableness* towards all my fellow creatures. Oh! My Father in Heaven assist me by thy spirit to overcome all the spirit of envy and give me *charity, Faith & Hope.* This morning Sister Fannie came home, after an absence of three weeks, in Bel Air, or rather at Mr. Archers. Ma and Ann Lee went to Bel Air in the carriage that brought sister Fannie home. Quarterly meeting commenced today.

I have had pain in my shoulder, & breast & will try not to complain of my suffering. The Lord knows what is best for me. "Afflictions though they seem worldly oft are sent" and I believe mine were sent in great *mercy*. Oh! that I may *never* complain of their being too great. Give me grace Blessed Saviour.

I hope I shall enjoy a sweet peace in my print devotion this evening. It is my desire precious Jesus to live nearer thee. Oh! that each portion of scripture I read, may be deeply rooted in my heart, and the seed sown in my heart; be enriched by "living water" and "made bring forth precious fruit in due season." I do sincerely desire the society of christian people. But I seldom have that privilege. Why is it, when Christians meet they do not talk more of the Saviour, and Heaven? The ministers do not talk near enough of our religion, particularly to young converts. Oh! help me Father to write whatsoever the spirit may suggest to my heart. I want to write thoughts that are now transpiring in my mind; and my Christian experience now, that I may review in time to come. Oh! that I may grow in grace each hour of my life, and that I may continue more faithfully to crucify the flesh; and sinful lusts thereof. Oh! that the world may soon lose its charms for me, and I can say "I find no pleasures in them." Twilight is closing into night. I will now lay aside my book and pray to my Father "who heareth in secret and will reward me openedly." O Father, incline my heart to do thy will.

Sunday morning 15th

I enjoyed my devotion of last evening more than usual, though was prevented from praying for some time by some one being in my room. I suffered much through the first part of the night—bodily, but had a peaceful mind most of the

time. I regarded an instant that occurred in the morning but I prayed to be forgiven if I acted wrongly and felt greatly relieved by prayer. O why can I not pray
more & "pray without ceasing." I awoke this morning feeling better in body though
far from well, but I thank God felt no disposition to complain but more in spirit
of thankfulness. Though far from being enough so. Oh! that these may not be but
word from the lips and pen but from the abundance of the heart. No one from here
went to church but Pa, that is that was at home. Ma & A.L. are now in Bel Air
and suppose they will be there. Hope they & all may profit by the preaching. Oh!
Holy Spirit touch the hearts of that congregation this day, and throughout this
meeting. Oh! that the whole village may be converted to God. Lord melt their
frozen heart, give them hearts of flesh. I have enjoyed this Sabbath more than any
other for a long time. I know it is because I am trying to keep it *more holy*. Let me,
my Father in Heaven ever "remember the sabbath day to keep it holy." I have so
many temptations on Sunday: we have so much company nearly always. Oh Father, "keep me unspotted from the world." Gard my conversation, that no unclean
thing may come out of my mouth. Oh! that I may praise thee more for the blessed
sabbath and its privileges. And praise thee for the liberty of reading the "Holy
Bible" the "best of all books." O that I may ever remember "Every good gift and
every perfect gift cometh from the Father of life." O Father of light and love, make
me truly thankful for the many, many blessings thou has vouchsafed to me. I know,
I feel, unworthy for even the smallest mercy. O I do hope to grow in grace and the
knowledge thereof and have *faith* enough to believe I will yet "see my Father's face
and in his bosom rest."

I committed a hymn to memory this morning "Oh! for a closer walk with God"
was the hymn. After which, I read it and "Jerusalem my happy home, name ever
dear to me" to Charlotte (our colored servant) also several psalms.[5] I did pray they
might be of benefit to her soul and that the words sink deep in heart, so not to be
forgotten. I tried to read them as impressively as possible. I do hope God will water the seed, that they may take deep root.

Father I pray thee to take all selfishness from me, and O that I may always remember that there is "no good thing in me." But I do pray that thou wilt make me
the instrumentality of winning souls to Christ. Oh! Holy Spirit put words into my
mouth, that I may speak the things most suited to each person I come in contact
with. Help me my God, my God! Many things suggest themselves to my mind, that
I might say, but I fear my faith is too weak just now. If I sin in this, "Good Lord deliver me" and give me faith to believe. "I do believe; help thou my unbelief."

Sunday at twilight. I have just come upstairs from the tea table, to pen a little

---

5. Charlotte was one of two household servants in the Munnikhuysen home at the time of the 1860
U.S. census. She was thirty-four years old in 1859.

in my book. We had a call from cousins Jim & George Glasgow this afternoon and cousin Jim told me he was at "love feast" some time since, heard Josh Bond giving his experience.[6] He was converted last winter. Oh! how happy I was when I heard he had come out on the Lord's side. I really felt more like shouting than I have for a long time. All I could say was, "Bless the Lord O my soul, and I do thank the Lord he is still faithfully serving him. Oh! our Father in Heaven, help him to grow in grace and "press on for the mark of the prize of the high calling as in Christ Jesus." O Lord keep us faithful and prayful. O my dear Savior, I do want to follow thy example, in all things, but flesh is weak. O strengthen me. Give me grace to overcome temptation. Oh! my savior thou knowest me better than I do myself. Thou knowest the temptations with which I am surrounded. O give me grace to bear in times of need! I want to be more humble, more forgiving in my treatment to all around me. Oh! that I may forgive as I wish to be forgiven. O my Heavenly Father thou knowest how I am situated, better than I could tell thee; help me to overcome the flesh and the adversary. I have done many things I should not have done this holy sabbath day. O! forgive them, Father of light and let the "light of thy countenance shine into my heart." The hour of meditation and prayer has come. The sabbath has nearly passed away forever! Quicken me O! Father that I may call upon thy name in spirit, and in heart. Oh! that I may ask for what I need. God thou knowest that I need "Faith" "hope" and "charity." Oh! give me these, and thou shall have all the praise, now and forever, amen.

Monday 16th

I have suffered more pain & been quite sick today; though not more so than I could bear. Oh! I thank thee my Heavenly Father for giving me grace to bear. But I do desire more grace, more fortitude and more faith. I thank thee, for giving me more liberty of speech today. I was enabled to speak to sister F. about attending dancing parties. Oh! I do thank thee O Father for opening my eyes, that I was able to some extent to see myself as a vile sinner. Do thou show me myself more plainly. I feel I have too great an opinion of my self. Oh! my precious Savior, make me more humble, and less self-righteous. I do pray to be kept from all such; and be made to know and feel my own sinfulness. O that I may be kept from respecting God less than man but that I may show to the *world* I respect and love God's *praises* more, double more than man's. Oh! I fear I think oftener of the opinion of my fellow creatures, than my Fathers in Heaven. God keep me from all such *presumptuous* sins. "God is no respector of persons." Let me ever remember this and have the

---

6. At a "love feast" Methodists gathered to recount their religious experiences publicly. The Josh Bond who testified at the gathering was not Howard Bond's father but a young friend and likely distant relative of Bond, upon whom she had a slight romantic crush.

same respect to all, *rich* & *poor;* all; For our good & kind Parent, sends the rain on all, the good & the bad and "no good thing will he withhold from those that love and keep his commandments." My Father, do thou hear my cry, and help me ever to remember them, each and all. Oh! that I may ever "remember my Creator in the days of my youth."

Tuesday afternoon 17th

Rainy, and cloudy all day; has now the appearance of a heavy rain. Dr. Watters, Dr. Archer and pa have gone fishing from here. I think if they don't hurry home, they will get caught in the rain. Sister Fannie has walked down to Cousin Cass Gover's[7] to stay awhile with the children;[8] their parents are in Baltimore. We had quite a controversy today on Christians being inconsistent. I think we all come far from doing our duty, at least the most of Christians. I know I do; but it is my desire to grow in grace, and The knowledge thereof. Lord "help me to watch and pray, and on thyself rely." Keep me from being a stumbling block to anyone. Oh! I feel my weakness. Oh! my Heavenly Father strengthen me, to do thy pleasure. I have been greatly tempted today, and I fear did not resist as I should. Have given a way to my high spirits too much. I do not know if anyone noticed I looked excited; but I felt so for a moment. Lord! "lift up the light of they countenance" so I may see myself. I desire to do thy will, but can do nothing without the aid of thy Holy Spirit. O do thou help me my Savior. I can truly say the Lord is my help, "he maketh me to lie down in green pastures, he leadeth me beside the still waters."

Wednesday 18th of May

It has been raining nearly all day and now is raining quite fast. Sister Fannie and Dr. Archer went down to Mr. Websters to spend the day, but I am under the impression [they] will not get home this evening; as it is nearly dark now.

We are very dissatisfied creatures; When God does not send us rain, we want it, and then if it rains more, or longer than we want it, we complain. Oh! what a merciful Father have we. If he dealt with us accordant to our deserts, where would we be today? I have been led to reflect more lately on being discontented with ones lot, how wrong it is. In whatsoever situation of life I am placed I want to cultivate a disposition of contentment. But I must be prayerful, and watchful. "Help me to watch and pray." They call me to tea, I will not write any more this evening.

Friday afternoon 20th

Yesterday was cloudy & rainy; did not feel well. Had some peaceful thoughts. But O indulged in some very *sinful ones.* I feel each day more my dependence on

7. Casander Gover,* fifty-three years old.

8. It is not clear which children are staying at Cass's, perhaps George and Juliet Gover's.*

my Heavenly Father's guidance. Oh! how weak and sinful I am. There is no good thing in me. We had company most of the day. Sister Fannie and Dr. Archer came home about eleven o'clock. Mr. and Mrs. Rodgers also took dinner here, spent most of the afternoon with us. It is truly delightful to have christians around and about us. But I did feel disappointed she did not talk more on religion. The conversation was so very worldly. Sister Fannie was showing her, her handsome dresses, & presents she got whilst in Philadelphia. And I caught myself wishing some of them were mine; and felt envious too. But when I compared situations, I would not for worlds exchange places. Oh! my precious Savior, enable me to bear with those temptations; knowing "God tempers the wind to the shorn lamb." I am more fully convinced each day that there is no *real* happiness in this world, or the world to come, without *real religion*. Oh! my Father, that I may perceive *this*, enable me to keep thy commandments, that I may *love* thee with all my heart all my might. Help me to put my entire trust in thee and "love my neighbor as myself." Doing good unto all; returning good for evil and doing all to thy glory for Christ sake.

I got a letter from H. He wrote 10 pages nearly, but somewhat different style from what he generally does. I felt very sad and grieved. But I remembered I had asked to be directed from on high, and I believe I have always acted conscientious. I have tryed to act honorably. And I thought perhaps this was for some *wise* purpose I could not see now. I desire O my Father, to be directed in *all things* by thee. And O the "cloud I so much dread may break in blessings on my head." Oh! help me to act towards him as thou wouldst have me, O Holy Spirit. . . . . . .

It is now raining very hard. John Paca Dallam[9] is now in the parlor, Brother & sister Fannie entertaining him. Dr. [Richard] Lee was here to dinner. He has been very attentive and kind since my sickness. (He told me I ought to marry a Dr.) (Perhaps I may, who knows.)

Pa went to Balto this morning. This day one year I was in Balto. It was quite a pretty evening. I went up to the Institution of the Blind; could scarcely get home, had the neuralgia so badly.[10] Cousin G. Glasgow was here yesterday evening.

9. Bond refers to her cousin. Both the Pacas and Dallams were among the founding citizens of Harford and were influential in the community. William Paca signed the Declaration of Independence and was governor of Maryland from 1782 to 1785. John Paca developed the Harford town of Abingdon, of which the Dallams were large landowners. According to Harford historian Walter Preston, Richard Dallam was one of the most prominent men in the county during the Revolution. Preston, *History of Harford County Maryland*, 199.

10. A school for the blind was opened in downtown Baltimore in 1853. It was then called the Maryland Institution for the Instruction of the Blind. Bond's aunt Rebecca Bond* lived there, likely working as a teacher.

Saturday 21st

This day one year Howard B and I came home from Baltimore. Can I ever forget that day? It was one long to be remembered. They do not know what a sad heart I have had today. How many sad memories have come looming over the ocean of time. Oh! many a smile covers a smothered sigh. Many a jest keeps the tears from starting from the eyelid. "Oh! me, I wish I were a merry child again." And yet it is not right for me to brood over those times, that have gone never to return again. I will try and be contented. I have indulged in some sad, sad thoughts on account of not getting what I asked for. Oh! help me, my Father in Heaven to trust thee for all, and in all; knowing the "Lord will provide." I am very unthankful for those blessings that are lavished so bountifully out to me. Oh! that I may praise thee for all thou hast done and trust thee for all that's to come.

I am suffering much with neuralgia all through me. I sometimes wonder if I shall ever be right well again. O I want to be more patient and bearing my cross better, and more Christian like. "Help me to watch and pray" at all times.

Pa came up from Balto this afternoon; brought me a letter. Cousin John Paca has not left yet. He and Ma are sitting in the passage now talking. Billie Webster & Peggie Bond were here for a short while this afternoon.[11] They & Brother have gone to see Dr. Watters. It has partly cleared off, the sun came out beautifully for a while, but clouded up again. This is H[oward's] birthday. O I wish him, all the real happiness that *this* world can contain, not *gilded happiness* of *the pomp* and *vanities* of this world *but real heart-felt religion happiness.*

Sunday afternoon. May 22nd

What an unprofitable sabbath we all have spent, especially I. My conscience has condemned to me so often for my neglect in duty. We have had so much company. It seemed as though I could not draw my mind off from the world. Oh, my Father in Heaven, forgive me for my many sins, for Christ sake!

I am indeed one of thy most unworthy servants. Give me grace to overcome temptation; to resist the adversary in all His forms and fascinations; and cleave to the *cross*. O, how weak and sinful I am. Lord thou art only my help in every good thing! Oh! for more of the spirit that was in Christ Jesus. "Oh! for a closer walk with God." Give me, O, my Father, every Christian virtue, all meekness, humility and gentleness! Take from me the spirit of covetousness, and envy, and that I may put my entire trust, at all times in thee. I have so much to be thankful for, so many blessings. Make me truly thankful, Oh! my Father. *My dear Ma* went to Balto this evening; she has not been there for several years. I do hope she will enjoy her visit.

11. Billie (William) Webster was fifteen years old. His father, John, was a farmer with property valued at ten thousand dollars in 1860.

I felt very sad parting with her, though only for a short time. But I miss ma more than anyone of the other members of our family. Sometimes when I think of her leaving us for good it seems more than I can bear. But I have no doubt she would go in that Heavenly Home prepared for the faithful. Lord bless my dearly loved Ma, keep her from all harm, both spiritually and bodily. And when thou seest fit to call her from those earthly scenes she may be clothed in The robe of immortality. Sister Fannie went to meeting this afternoon with cousin George G. She is going from there to Mr. Watters'. Brother went down to Mr. Websters.[12] I think John Dallam accompanied him, as they left together. Pa, Ann Lee, and I are at home. The clouds have all dispersed, and the sun came out beautifully. The country looks charming indeed. All Nature is lovely! The woods in front of our gate, looks very luxurent. I received a very pretty bouquet from L.W. . . . . . last night.[13] Mr. Stump & Jimmy Moores spent the evening here. Peggie Bond came after tea.

Monday 23rd

This was a beautifully bright day. I went to Belair this afternoon with cousin G.G.[14] [H]ad a delightful drive went to see Dr. Lee's wife, who has been very sick all winter, found her better, looked thin, and like she had suffered much. Also went to see Helen McGaw.[15] She is in deep decline, looks dreadfully, so thin and white. I only was there for a few minutes. Promised to go see her soon again. Oh! how I should love to talk to her about her soul's good. Oh! my Father in Heaven, endow me with the knowledge of leading souls to Christ. Oh! I know and feel my unworthiness to approach thee, and call thee Father, for O I have been so unmindful of my duty to thee. Help me to do better in [the] future, to live nearer thee; to suffer more for thy sake, to endure slights, uncharitableness and everything that wars against the flesh. Oh, that I may subdue by thy grace every unruly passion and disposition to do evil. It is my nature to do evil. There is no good thing in me. But O Father plant within my heart more of the spirit that was in Christ. And O that I may consider it a privilege to suffer for Christ's sake.

Tuesday 24th

Another lovely day has come & gone by. This morning I took a walk up in the woods, gathered some wild flowers. Dr. Archer took dinner with us, after which he and I took a drive. Went to cousin G.R.G.'s, had a pleasant time, came home to tea, found here Mr. Maloy and Reverend Lee, spending the evening. Mr. Maloy is the young preacher in our circuit.

12. Either James or John Webster, both farmers in Harford County. The Websters were another established Harford family with whom the Munnikhuysens associated.

13. L.W. is probably Lizzie Watters.*

14. George Glasgow* (Bond also refers to him as G.R.G.).

15. Helen was twenty-four years old. Her father was a hotel keeper.

Wednesday 25th

Oh dear, shall I ever forget this day one year. This day comes fraught with sad reminiscences of the past. Ah! how sad my poor heart was. And now there is an answering cord in my heart, for that day's sadness. But I must dispel such gloomy thoughts from my mind, and [look] forth on the bright side of the picture. "There is many a cord in The finely strung heart when breathed upon lightly the tear drops will start." Mr. Maloy remained all night with us. He said he wished my path through life might be strewn with many flowers, and all thorns taken away. But I told him, I thought it was not best that it should be, for it takes thornes, sometimes for one to appreciate flowers. And clouds to prize sunshine.

Friday night 27th

I went to uncle Parker's on Wednesday evening with G.R.G. had a very delightful ride, called at the store going, got there while the family were eating supper. Thursday morning, Lizzie Lee,[16] and I took a walk, gathered some moss & wild flowers, had a serious talk about joining church. Hope I was led to impress some serious and important things on her mind. Oh! that I could say *one word* in *season*, Lord help thy unworthy servant. Put words in my mouth, that I may show forth thy praise. Quicken me, that I may know myself.

My faith is weak, Lord help me to believe, and cast all my cares on Jesus, and not forget to pray. I came home this afternoon with G.R.G. Went to the Post Office, found Juliet Gover and two sisters here, very glad to see her.

Saturday 28th

Dr. Archer and Mr. Stump spent the evening. After tea the Dr. and sister Fannie went up to cousin Juliet's.

Sunday 29th

Went to church this morning, heard Mr. Maloy preach from the 42 chap. 18 & 19 verses of Isaiah, "Hear, ye deaf, and look, ye blind, that ye may see. Who is blind, but my servant, or deaf as my messenger that I sent; who is blind as he that is perfect and blind as the Lord's servant." A very excellent discourse it was. Ma came home with us. She came up in the stage on saturday. I was indeed glad to see her. We had class after meeting. It was the first time I have been to class since I joined church. Oh I hope we will have it often, that we may grow in grace. Lord help us. We need more of thy assistance. Oh! we are so cold in heart, pour thy holy spirit out upon us as a people. Came home to dinner.

Afternoon, uncle Parker Lee, cousins George & James Glasgow, Dr. Archer, Jimmy Moores, Herman Stump and Juliet Gover were here, some in the afternoon, and some in the evening. Did not spend a proffitable sabbath. Oh, I have so many

---

16. Elizabeth Lee, daughter of Parker and Mary Lee.*

temptations. Lord help me to overcome them. O, that I may take up my cross daily, and hourly and follow after thee.

Monday 30th

Beautiful morning—sun rose clear and bright, but towards night we had quite a heavy gust. Sister Fannie went to see G-Ma today with uncle Parker. Cousin G[eorge] G[lasgow] called for a short time this morning. This afternoon I walked up to Woodside, had been there about two hours listening to singing and music when brother came for me, Mr. Maloy was here. I came home, felt sorry I had to leave so soon——.

Tuesday morning 31st

Mr. Maloy left early this morning, has appearance of more rain, rather cool for this season of the year. I received a letter from H[oward] B. B[ond] on Saturday, he was well. George Hall and his little son was here this morning, made a call. After dinner cousin G.R.G. brought Fannie home, then took her to Mr. Webster's. Dr. Lee was here. I did not see him, as I was asleep, and he would not let anyone awaken me.

Wednesday first day of June 1859

Cloudy & rainy all day so differently from this day one year. It was beautiful and bright. Juliet [Gover] came after tea, was very lively. Cousin George came for her.

Thursday 2nd

Beautiful warm day. Ma is quite sick, hope not anything serious. I have felt worse today, did not rest very well last night, was very sick. Dr. Archer, and Mr. Stump were here this evening. Mr. S. took sister Fannie up to see Blanche. Brother took aunt Dillie to see Blanche Archer this morning.

Friday 3rd

Another gloomy morning. It rained very hard last night. Dr. A. had to remain with us all night. Left rather early.

Saturday 4th

Very cool weather for this season of the year, the wind blew quite hard in the afternoon, this morning was cloudy, but about ten, I believe it cleared off. Juliet Gover, cousin George Glasgow, and Dr. Archer spent the evening here. Mr. Evans & Bob came after tea. I got a letter from H[oward] B. B[ond] and an essay he had written on "Indian Mounds." It is a sweet thought to be remembered by any one, but how sweet by those dear to us by the tie of relationship!

Sunday 5th

Ma went to The Trap church this morning in cousin G. Gover's carriage. Heard an excellent discourse by Bishop Whittingham.[17] Great many there, some ten or eleven persons confirmed. Lizzie Lee & Mr. & Mrs. Quarles were of the number. Oh pray she may hold out faithful to the end, may grow in grace, and the knowledge thereof. Lord direct her ways, that they may be subject to *thy will* always. John P. Dallam took sister Fannie to the "Trap." In the afternoon Juliet called for me to go to Watters' meeting. We got there when the preacher was about half through his sermon. Going up the hill near the meetinghouse one of the horses commenced bucking, would not pull, the driver jumped out and Mr. Evans undone the door, and Juliet and I jumped out. We were indeed frightened, and I felt thankful we escaped without being hurt. God in his wise providence, saw fit to rescue us. Oh, that we may thank him with our whole hearts, for his mercies and goodness towards us.

Monday 6th

Quite cold. I spent the day at Cousin Cass Gover's. Came home to tea.

Tuesday 7th

Went to Uncle Jim's. Spent the day. When I got home found Mr. Stump & Dr. Archer here. Mr. S. and sister Fannie spent the evening at cousin Jared Gover's. Dr. Archer spent it with me.

Wednesday 8th

Ma & Pa went down to see Grandma Lee, she is quite sick. Sallie Hendon came over this morning to have her dress fitted; while she was here, and we girls were upstairs, we heard some one come up to the door steps. As pa and brother was not at home, we became frightened. I listened and heard them open the parlor door; then I got up and looked over the banisters and who should I see but a man, just in the act of coming up stairs. I called to him, to know who he was, and what he wanted, and told him to go out of the house in the yard to the gentleman of the house. We soon found he wanted something to eat; and gave it to him. My heart beat dreadfully. I scarcely got over it all day. How mysterious is the working of Providence. How he watches over us unworthy creatures, and protects us in the hour of danger. Oh! that my heart may be lifted up in thanksgiving to Him "from whence cometh all good things." Lord teach this unwilling heart submission. O, it is so prone to evil. "Prone to wander, Lord I feel it," "Prone to leave the God it loves." "Oh! take my heart and seal it for thy courts above." Let thy seal of love be

17. William Rollinson Whittingham was an Episcopal bishop in the diocese of Maryland.

so deeply stamped upon it that no sin can erase it. O my Heavenly Father, I feel my unworthiness to be one of thy least disciples. Temptations are thick around and about me; and nothing but thy grace is sufficient to keep me firm on that "Rock of Ages." In my hand no price I bring, simply to the Cross I cling. Thou must save, O my Savior, and thou alone. My God! My God! have mercy on me; pardon my sins, receive me, O despise not this sinful heart-offering. For O my heart is indeed sinful. Keep me from all blood guiltiness. Oh, that I may gain confidence as I advance in Religion. Keep me from *envy* and sin of every kind——

Thursday 9th

Pleasant day, very bright. Brother came home in company with John Dallam. After dinner Uncle Jacob called for a short time;[18] had not seen him for near two years. Ma came home. Grandma little better. Dr. Archer here. Got a letter from H.B.—not well—I felt as though I had seen him, and had a long talk of the future. Oh! I pray to be directed by my Heavenly Father who knowest what is best for his children.

Friday 10th

This was a very pretty morning but this afternoon it clouded up, and rained some, kept so till near sundown. Had pretty sunset. "All thy works praise thee."

Saturday 11th

Another lovely day, very cool—feels like Autumn weather. Walked up to see Cousin Juliet this afternoon. She is so sad, cried very much while I was there. I prayed to be enabled to say something to comfort her. Lord help her by the Holy Spirit, now in this, her affliction, Oh! may the sun of righteousness now arise with healing in its wing—and chase all clouds from her sky. Oh! "thy soul soul-cheering presence renew." Oh, that she may remember that afflictions are sent to try our faith. God tryes us with the fire of affliction. Oh, that we may, when tried, prove finer than the finest of gold.[19]

Sunday morning 12 June

This is a beautiful day. The sky is so clear and blue; and all Nature seems alive, and to give forth praises to the God that made her. O that my heart, as sinful as it is, may be lifted in thanks to the one who created me, who has shown so many

---

18. Jacob Munnikhuysen was Bond's paternal uncle. He was one year younger than John and was a farmer with property worth five thousand dollars in 1860.

19. This is the first indication of the Gover's financial problems, which climaxed in November 1860 when the family declared bankruptcy. The problems were likely related to the economic Panic of 1857 and the resulting depression. As a banker, George Gover would have been vulnerable to the financial upheavals.

mercies, who has brought me out from the mire and the clay, and lit my feet on the Rock, that is higher than I. Establish thou my goings. Lead me by the still waters of faith. O cleanse me from all sin, protect me from all temptation of every kind, O my father in Heaven! I desired very much to go to church today, but was prevented from doing so. Oh! help me to bear patiently—I have been reading a very beautiful prayer in verse which I will write here. There is something so touchingly beautiful in it, something that goes right to the heart. It was written for the "Baltimore Sun."

"A prayer of the Heart."[20]
"Father, I humbly pray to thee, Oh! guide me o'er life's stormy sea;
Help me oh! Father, to forgive. And nearer to Thyself to live,
When human friendships pass away and human loves fade and decay
Oh! let me turn to Thee, Father, the mists of morning falls
Sweet peace is stealing o'er my soul. The storm is hushed my heart's at rest
For then oh! Father, Highest Blest! Hast heard a prayer from *me*.
By Jennie E. Hammell May 28th 1859

Sunday afternoon was spent very unprofitable; we had company and it seemed impossible for me to leave the room, Oh! why is it we have more respect for man than God. God is not a respecter of person, and why should we be? How prone we are to evil. I can truly say my conscience condemned me for the way I spent the sabbath. Oh! my Father in Heaven, when shall I learn to do right, to keep thy commandments. Oh! I see every day there is no good thing in me, no not one. "Pluck me as a branch from the burning. O break this fatal enchantment that holds down my affections to objects which my judgment comparatively despises and let me, at length, come into so happy a state of mind, that I may not be afraid to think of thee and myself. Teach me how to pray, and what I must ask for; teach me submission to thy will, O my Father, for Christ sake.

The visitors on sunday were Cousin George Gover, his two daughters, and son, George & James Glasgow, H. Stump, Roberta Archer, Dr. Archer, Billie Webster, Peggie Bond, aunt Lizzie M, Howard, Jane and Lizzie.

Monday 13th
Cloudy, had a shower about twelve o'clock. Cousin Juliet & George Gover called for a short time. Sallie Gover here for a short time, looked well. Brother waited on her home. After dinner it cleared off for a short time, cousin George Glasgow came, took sister Fannie to uncle Parker's. Dr. Lee was here. Godfrey

20. Only a section of the long poem is included here.

Watters came, spent the evening, had a long talk, told me much of his experience which I hope will benefit me. Strengthen him, Father in each, and every trial!

Tuesday 14th

Beautifully bright, warmer than it has been for some time. Godfrey left this morning, had to stay last night on account of rain. An unpleasant affair took place this morning. I felt like speaking my mind out when I was called upon but thanks to the Holy Spirit who kept my lips from evil speaking. O! I hope I shall be directed at all times, and under every circumstance by that higher power. Tuesday night I spent with Juliet. I went up there in the morning, after dinner got ready for a drive, called at home, found Howard Parrish and Lizzie Brown here; did not stay long; started off again, went to Miss Woolsey's for flowers. Saw such beautiful ones. The garden looked beautifully. Got home to tea, found Dr. Archer here, after tea went up to "Woodside," remained all night.

Wednesday 15th

About half past nine came home from Cousin Juliet's. After dinner, Juliet, Bettie, Brother, and I went to call on Miss Websters.[21] Sallie & Peggie had gone to make calls on horseback. We were hurried home on account of rain coming up very suddenly. We went down to Thomas Run Post Office before we reached home. I was very tired.

Thursday 16th

I was very much fatigued from my ride, did not sleep till near morning so nervous and restless, could not get my mind composed sufficiently for rest. Been very warm today. I am at my window facing the road—many birds are singing their evening songs. They seem to try to rival each other.

The swallows are "Homeward flying," and singing in their strange way. It has clouded up—looks like rain. Not so warm as it was. I have been perplexed in my mind today, about an article of dress. I do not wish to care so much for this worlds goods as to let them distress me, or take my thoughts too much from Heavenly ones. Lord teach me submission, and help me to put my trust in *thee,* knowing from thee, every good thing cometh. Oh, that I may receive them as coming from thee. Oh, that I may not speak my own words so often or, think *my* own thoughts! For there is no good thing in *human flesh.*

Friday 17th

Just one o'clock. Have finished my dinner, dined heartily on lamb, peas & lettuce, also squirrel soup. It has been raining all day—it now is pouring. So cold we

21. John and Susan Webster had three daughters, Mary, Sophia, and Sallie, and two sons, Jacob and William (Billie). Billie is often a visitor at the Munnikhuysen home.

have fire in the dining room and yesterday was very warm. Have been sitting nearly all the time up in my room, sewing—have thought much what my future might be. Oh! I hope I may be directed by "The Higher power."

Yesterday afternoon Juliet & cousin Sallie Gover called for a short while.

Saturday 18th

Beautiful day, rather cold for this season. Dr. A. came, stayed till after dinner when he & sister Fannie went to gather moss for her circle. Juliet spent the evening here, laughed and enjoyed herself much, did not leave till late.

Sunday night, 19th of June.

The Sun rose clear and bright but about ten commenced clouding up and about two commenced raining. I went to Churchville this morning with Juliet, Bettie & Mr. I. Evans. Heard a very excellent discourse by the Rev. Mr. Morrison of Baltimore County. The text was the 3rd chapter of John 16 and 17 verses "For God so loved the world that he gave his only begotten son that whosoever believeth on him, should not perish but have everlasting life" "For God sent not his Son into the world, to condemn the world, but that the world through him might be saved." It was a very plain practical sermon and I hope it touched every heart there. Lord, strengthen our faith. Oh, that I may contemplate, with more gratitude thy wondrous works! Oh! when I look upon the works of thy fingers, "What is man that *thou* art mindful of him, or the son of man that thou visiteth him." "Lord teach us that we number our days, and apply them to wisdom." We have not had any company today. I am truly glad for it is a crying sin, the way we keep the sabbath. O, that I may take up my cross daily and hourly and follow after Thee! Before retiring to rest, I would ask my Father, who is the Shepard of His flock to visit me in the still watches of the night, to guard my pillow, and protect me from all danger both bodily and spiritually. Let my awakening thoughts, if thou, O Eternal King of Heaven, seeth fit to spare me to see the light of another day, be of thee, and how to praise and glorify thy name.

I would beseech a blessing on this household, every member of it. O, that they may taste and *know* that the Lord is good! And O, Father of the Fatherless, do thou bless all my dear and near friends. Feed them with the bread of life. Give them drink out of the fountain of Righteousness. Fill them with peace which passes all knowledge. Those of my near and dear ones, by the ties of *blood* & *love,* who are nearing the borders of the grave, who will o'er long pass into Eternity. Oh! strengthen them by thy Holy Spirit, cause the "Sun of Righteousness" to follow in their paths to light through the dark valley of the shadow of Death. Oh! that they may lean with confidence on thy strong arm. Chase away all dark clouds from their sky, thy soul cheering presence renew. Let the Holy Spirit be upon us now and forever, amen.

Monday night 20th

Have suffered more than usual today, on account, I suppose, of the weather's being damp, as it has been raining nearly all day. It is now thundering, and giving us every proof of a storm. I read today of a little girl who called thunder "God's music." And grand & terrible music it is. It strikes every beholder with awe. What a sublimely grand sight a thunderstorm is! How magnificently the lightning gleams through the black clouds revealing God's power in every flash. "All thy works praise thee." "From the rising of the Sun, till the going down thereof."

How unspeakable are thy mercies towards us! And how ungrateful are we for them! Oh! that we may view thee, O Savior! in the light we should. I am constrained every day, to see my utter inability to do any good thing, unless aided by thy Holy Spirit. Oh, that I may put my trust in my Heavenly Father and be willing to be guarded by *him* in *all things*. Ma and I had a conversation on our unworthiness of being the children of God's, and I trust we were both benefited by it. I made a remark, about a prayer, we often offered up, and asked her if she ever thought of it—she said, she never had! It was to this effect. She remarked, or rather offered up a prayer, thus "O! make us to see ourselves as we are by Nature, and by practice." And when I asked her if she had ever, when asking to know herself, if she thought in what way she was to know herself, was it in affliction, sorrow or any disappointment? And she said "she had never thought of that." I would love oftener to talk on religion. It does me good, makes me reflect and ponder on my growth in grace. Oh! I come so far off from what I should be, so unworthy being a child of God's and yet I have a blissful *Hope* in Heaven that when this mortal frame shall be changed it shall be robed in the robe of Righteousness. "Lord teach me to number my days that I may apply my heart to wisdom."

Oh! that I e'er long may be able to sing the "angel's song," and may it abide ever in my heart of hearts till I shall be an angel in my *Father's* house there to sing it *forever more.*

Tuesday 21st

Mr. John Day was here, bright day, little cool.

Wednesday 22nd

Yesterday went to Mr. Watters' in the afternoon, went on horseback. Came home this morning about half past nine; had a delightful visit. It was only too short. Lizzie came home while I was there, looks badly. I love her so much—she is a lovely character. Found cousin George here, when I got home, took sister Fannie to cousin John Moores.

Thursday, 23rd

Lovely day most of which I have past up in my room. Have felt quite badly, suffered this afternoon dreadfully—had a call at the time, sent word by the servant the ladies were not at home. Have regretted it very much—Indeed I feel now as though I have committed a sin, not only myself but the servant. I was the cause of making her tell a story. Oh! my Heavenly Father, I do sincerely repent of so doing, and by thy grace will try never to fall into the same temptation.

Dr. Archer came to tea, cousin George came afterwards.

Friday night 24th

Heard of Helen McGaw's death—she died about seven this morning.[22] The circumstances of her death I did not hear exactly. I heard she was willing to depart. I hope she is in that "Land of pure delight, where saints eternal rest." O, Father comfort the stricken in heart, let thy Holy Spirit rest upon them! That they may breathe sweetness out of woe. Oh! that we may be reminded that we too are fast hastening to the grave the place that knows us now, will soon know us no more. Oh, that we may ever bear in mind, that now is the expected time, now is the day of salvation. An old schoolmate gone—gone where no traveler returneth. How memory goes back when we girls went to school and vividly my imagination pictures Helen—that smile, that blush—never to return any more. Oh! Death where is thy sting, O grave, where is thy victory? Lord help us in each time of need.

Dr. Archer called here, brought me a nice pan of raspberries, came back after tea. Juliet, Ann Lee & Dr. A. spent the evening at cousin Cass Gover's.

Sunday 26th

Went to Belair to Helen's funeral. It was a very large one. Mr. Finney preached one of the most beautiful sermons I ever listened to, from the first chapt. of Peter, 24 verse.[23] "For all flesh is as grass, and all the glory of man as the flower of grass. The grass withereth and the flower thereof falleth away." How beautifully he spoke to the bereaved parents, to her young companions & friends.

Oh! that it may be a solom warning to them. O I pray she is now, one of the ransom ones in her Father's Kingdom.

Oh! how sad it is to consign to the dark and silent tomb all that is left of a loved one! To look for the last time on that dear face, that has gladdened our eyes for so many years, one we have known from childhood. When they were putting Helen

22. Bond also mentions McGaw in her entry of 23 May 1859.

23. Rev. William Finney was pastor at the Churchville Presbyterian Church from 1813 until 1854, after which date he preached occasionally. See Preston, *History of Harford County*, 180.

in the grave and I thought it was the last time on Earth I should ever see her, and there she was to lay until the last judgment, how my heart ached for those dear ones she has left behind. If I felt sorrow at parting with the clay of my friend, what must be the grief of her parents? Lord strengthen them. Oh! thou dost pity the sorrowing ones.

Mon 27th

Mr. Maloy came this evening after tea.[24]

Tuesday night 28th

Went to aunt Nancy's this morning on horse back with Mr. Maloy—called at the post office—got my two magazines. He left soon after tea. I feel just tired enough to sleep soundly tonight.

Thursday 30th

Lizzie Lee came this afternoon for me to go up to cousin Juliet Gover's with her and soon after she came, Mr. Patterson & John Dallam came; of course we could not go then. Then Dr. Archer came for me to go to Henry's. I did not go. After tea, Sallie Gover, Annie Moores,[25] Juliet Gover & Jimmy Moores came. So I had as much as I well could do to entertain.

Friday 1st

Went to cousin Juliet with Lizzie, took dinner, left Lizzie there, and came home, as we had company (aunt Nancy & Ann M. Watters.)[26] Walked up to Woodside after tea, had a pleasant time.

Saturday 2nd

Lizzie left this morning early. Juliet called this morning, sister Fannie came home with Dr. Archer about ten o'clock, at night. I received a nice long letter from La. tonight.

Sunday 3rd

Went to Churchville this morning with Juliet. Heard an excellent sermon by Rev. Mr. Morrison. Dined with J. and took tea, had cousin George to gallant me home, found Dr. Archer here.

---

24. Maloy is a Methodist circuit minister. In her entry of 30 May 1859 Bond regrets her obligation to leave festivities at Woodside to return home to receive the young minister.

25. Ann L. Moores was the sister of Fannie,* James, and John, who are often mentioned by Bond. She was seventeen years old in 1859.

26. Ann Watters, thirty-two years old, was the daughter of Sarah Watters, a widow. In 1860 the family owned a farm valued at eight thousand dollars.

Monday 4th

Have spent a very quiet day. Do not feel very well.

Tuesday 5th

Very cold, have been sitting by a fire nearly all day, very uncommon accurrence for this season of the year. Mr. Maloy & Mr. Riley took dinner with us. Mr. M. took me to the post office, had a merry ride. After dinner Sallie Gover, Fannie Moores, Aunt Dillie Lee, Lilly Woulford, Pink Lee, Cassie Lee, Laura Lee, Bettie & Mary Gover,[27] Mr. Stump came, after tea Dr. Archer.

Thursday 7th, twilight,

Sitting at my window, have been up to see Juliet off to the party given at Mr. Stevy Archer's.[28] Did I wish to go, I have asked myself that question. My answer is yes & no! My sinful nature would say yes, and conscience says no. It is my nature to be gay and lively and only God's grace can help me overcome temptations my nature would draw me in; my Father, let that be all sufficient! I have been working hard all day to finish sister Fannie's dress for the party. I dressed her head. It looked lovely—braided in wide braids with a wreath of orange blossoms & sprays in it. Her dress was a flounced organdee—blue, brown and white. Bertha of thule, ruches & blue ribben bows. Very elegant set of jewelry—florentine mosaic pin & ear-rings, bracelets, plain gold bands and gold-stone bracelet. Juliet was dressed in a corn colored silk, with very large hoops, and long trail. Bertha of french ruches, white narrow ribben. Jewelry, carbuncle breast pin & bracelet, also gold band, gold chain around her neck & locket. Very wide sash of ribben, white pearl balls in her hair. White kid gloves completed her toilet.

I went down to the store this morning very early, met Lizzie Lee, and went together. John Dallam, Herman Stump, Dr. Archer, & George Glasgow were here this evening—all in their buggys. I beseech a blessing on this disappointment O, my Father! May it show to the world still more I am coming out and being sepperate from them.

Make me *truly* thankful for the grace thou hast given me in this time of especial need.

Friday at twilight, the 8th

I have been sitting here at my window for some time, looking at the magnificent sky. "The work of His hands." All thy works praise thee."

27. Bettie and Mary were forty-three and fifty-eight years old, respectively. They were sisters of Cass* and Priscilla.

28. Stevenson Archer* was thirty-two years old in 1859 and a lawyer. When Bond writes, Stevenson and his family were one of the wealthier families in the Munnikhuysen's social circle. They owned seven slaves in 1860. He was married to Blanche Archer, who was from Tennessee.

How beautifully the clouds look, the purple and gold rolled up together forming one solid bank. How peaceful and quiet it seems. All nature seems falling to
rest! I hear a sweet little wren singing its last evening hymn. Is it not singing praise
to its Maker, before folding its little wings for quiet repose? Oh, what a lesson in
itself sublime, to teach poor mortal man. I have had much to be thankful for
throughout this day. I awoke so thankful I did not go to last evening's entertain-
ment. Though it was a trial—yet *God* has *made* me victor. O! can I praise or thank
him enough? Put the praises thou wouldst have me possess in my heart, O, my
Heavenly Father. Christ was tempted as I, Oh! what a precious thought—we have
a Saviour's sympathy. He is acquainted with our grieves, our troubles and our temptations and pities us. "He *was* a man of sorrow and acquainted with grief." When
they were talking of the party, they said the lights were so brilliant and what a beautiful sight when they drove up. How I wished then I could have seen them. But
since I have been thinking of it, I have thought it was only to be seen for one
night—for a few hours. But that beautiful city, set upon a hill, which shall greet
our sight, when this earthly tabernacle is dissolved, can anything earthly compare
to it? Shall we not behold it and rejoice? Oh! how beautiful, how grand, when the
pearly gates are opened for *our* entrance, will be the *home* prepared for the faithful!
Oh! methinks I can see those that have passed from death into life, standing 'gazing with unclouded vision on the splendors of that land and exclaiming half has
never yet been told.' Oh! how rapt in joy and wonder we will be viewing the "Rainbow circled throne." And the entrancing music gushing forth from harps of a
"thousand strings." Is this not enough to inspire us to push on to the "mark of the
prize, of the high calling?" Lord give us grace to be as we should be. We are very
weak and sinful but thy grace is sufficient. I heard a lady remark some time since
"She could never understand why people, when they were good say "O! how bad I
am—there is nothing but sin in me." I think I understand why they do. They examine their hearts, and the more they do, the more they see of their corrupt nature to detest, for there is no good thing in us . . . . Peggie was here this evening,
took tea. Howard Parrish here this morning for a short while.

Saturday 9th
    Beautiful day, very pleasant. Nice weather for the harvesters, to get in their
grain. Mr. Hoskins was thrown from a horse today, and very badly hurt. It is not
know exactly how he became so much so. When they first found him, he was in-
sensible and after he came to, he could not remember anything at first but now he
remembers something about how it took place. Oh! that it may prove a blessing.
His belief is, I believe, that Christ was no more than a very good man, no better
than Moses. O, that his eyes my be opened to his real sinful state! and that he may

believe on Christ, our savior, and turn, and make his vows unto the Lord our God, who rulest in the Heavens.

Josh Bond, & Mr. Spencer Davidson came here, from Balto this evening. It is the first time I have seen Josh since his conversion. I was very glad to see him. O Lord keep him faithful to the end of life! He told me he had received a letter from H- a few days ago and he said that he was going to join the Presbyterian church. Oh! I am so glad. Encourage him in *The* good work—O my Father. That he may not faint or fall by the way.

Make thy truths plain to his mind that he may read and profit by Them! make him a true Christian, Oh! that he may be the cause of winning souls—those precious ones around him—those dearest to him, by the ties of blood, and love, to Christ, and that the family joined on Earth may be reunited in Heaven.

Sunday 10th

Went to Belair, to meeting with Mr. Davidson in the buggy. Heard an excellent sermon from Lamentations, third chapter, 40 & 41st verses. "Let us search and try our ways, and turn again unto the Lord." "Let us lift up our hearts with our hands unto God in the Heavens." Josh and his friend left this afternoon for Uncle Lane's and Mr. Websters.

Cousin George Glasgow, Dr. Archer, Jimmy & John Moores, & Mr. Stump were here this evening. Oh! what an unprofitable way to spend the sabbath. Oh that I may be constrained by thy Holy Spirit to keep thy commandments all!

Monday 11th

I went to Mr. Gough's today, spent the evening, went with Cousin George, had a very pleasant time. Met Mr. & Mrs. Jarrett there.

Tuesday 12th

Very warm day—Mr. Stump & sister Fannie spent the evening at cousin Juliet's. Dr. Archer and his sister here.

Wednesday 13th

Beautifully warm day. Sister Fannie and Cousin George went to uncle Sam's, to spend the day, very warm for visiting. I am suffering very much with a pain in my breast, and shoulder. Have just sealed a letter for Howard, & his mother. They get it next thursday or friday week.

Thursday 14th

Last evening we had a thunderstorm. It lightened for a long time, before we could hear the thunder. I was sitting at the back window, watching the vivid flashes of lightening which was perfectly grand, when Juliet commenced playing. I thought

I had never seen such beautiful flashes, and heard such exquisit music. The hour was twilight, deepening into night and altogether, the sky presented a magnificent appearance.

It blew very hard, had very little rain. Today has been warm. It is twilight now, the most lovely part of the day. It is at this time the mind is released from the cares and toils of the day, and thought let loose, runs through its channel with rappidaty incomprehensible. How it sweeps down "memory's halls" disturbing many things, many recolections of the past and some brighten, others are dimmed by time's trick. This is the most fitted time for contemplation. I will lay aside my book for the present, and try to drive worldly thoughts from my mind.

Friday 15th

Today has been entirely different from yesterday; it has been very cool and pleasant. This afternoon it commenced raining about three o'clock, and has been at it till now. Cousin George Glasgow called this morning. . . . I have just been listening to a little child's saying her prayer before retiring to rest. Oh! that she may understand what is meant by "our Father in Heaven." Let thy kingdom come to every heart and thy will be done on Earth as it is done in Heaven. Oh, if thy will was done on Earth, as in Heaven, what a paradise this world would be! Lord teach me to number my days that I may apply my heart to wisdom! I feel more than ever the need of *thy* quickening, grace in my heart. My heart is indeed very sinful. O! lead me to the "Rock" that is higher than *I*.

"Hide me under the shadow of thy wing." Oh! my Heavenly Parent, help me to over come temptation. Take *all* deceit out of my heart and all envy & hatred. My heart is sick with sin!

Saturday 16th

Rainy, & disagreeable—after dinner it partly cleared off. Lizzie Watters, Godfrey & Bennie Lee came, Bennie stayed, and the others with sister Fannie went up to Mrs. Archers. Juliet & Lilly spent the evening.

Sunday 17th

Beautiful day—sun rose most beautifully. Bennie Lee remained with us all night—she is now lying by me, on the bed, looks think and badly. I expect to go home with her this evening if nothing happens to prevent.

Monday 18th

Spent the evening at Dr. Archer's—good many there. Cousin George took us back to Mr. Watters'.

Tuesday 19th

Sister Fannie, Mr. H. Stump, cousin G. Glasgow, Dr. Archer, spent the evening here. I got a letter from Howard on Monday.

Wednesday 20th

Warm and quite pleasant. Walked down to the store, for a letter, did not get any—was in company with Bennie Lee, and Miss Fannie Wilmore. Had a pleasant walk. Heard Jimmy Cole was at "Maiden Lane" yesterday. Came to see me, sorry I was not at home, have not seen him for a long time, been many changes since we've met. Phoebe & Annie Webster, John Dallam and Fred Patterson also were here.

Thursday night 21st[29]

Came home from Mr. Watters' last evening after all had done with tea, with Dr. Archer. We took a long ride before reaching home, went about eleven miles. Was at Hop's mill. Came by the Hickory. Had a very pleasant visit at "Willow Hill."

Friday July 22nd

Had company all afternoon; left soon after tea. Cousin S. Archer, Glasgow (her son) & Aunt Dillie.[30] Sister Fannie went up to Mrs. Archer's this morning with Dr. Archer. This is now Saturday afternoon. I expect to take a ride on horseback.

Thursday August 4

On last Wednesday evening week, I went to "Mooreland." Cousin Aphia Moores & cousin Fannie,[31] spent the evening here, & took me home. Thursday, Mary Gough & Mrs. Crompton spent the evening there. Friday, Lou & I went into Belair,[32] spent the day with Cousin Lili Lee, saw Mr. & Mrs. Valliant.[33] Sunday, we went, in the morning, to St. Mary's, heard an excellent sermon by Rev. Mr. Brand on Confirmation. Something funny occurred after church. When we got home found cousin George Glasgow there.

29. Bond places this entry immediately after the one from Sunday, 17 July. Apparently, she did not write the next three days, when she was away from home visiting, and added these entries after writing on 21 July. I have placed the entries in chronological order.

30. Bond refers to Susannah Archer and her son James Glasgow Archer. Susannah was married to Thomas Archer, a farmer who claimed assets of eleven thousand dollars in 1860.

31. Aphia Moores, fifty-four years old, was the mother of Fannie,* Jimmy, and John, often mentioned by Bond.

32. Lou is Louise Wyatt.*

33. Bond refers to her Methodist minister and his wife.

After dinner, he took me to hear Mr. Valliant preach beautiful sermon; good many there. After church we took a drive down the Abbington road. Got home in time for tea. Monday, Lou, cousin Sallie & I went into Belair. Lou & I called on Bessie Doan. She is a lovely girl. Called at Mr. Jarrett's & Mary Lee's.[34] In the evening, Lou & I went to aunt Hannah's.[35] I had not been there for about six years. Met Mrs. Johnson there. Tuesday morning came home. Had invited company to dinner. Mrs. B[lanche] Archer, her baby & nurse, aunt Lizzie M[unnikhuysen], Bessie Doan, Frank D. & Howard M. In the afternoon Mrs. Williams, Mrs. John Archer, Stevy Williams, Juliet Gover & Dr. Archer.

Wednesday August 10th

Time has sped by. I have not written in here for a week. Have been very sick—dreadful cough, had to be cupped quite deeply. I still have a bad cough. My breast very sore, & painful. I often ask myself the question, why am I sick? And the answer is most frequently "to know thyself." Yes, for our kind Father seeth what is best for us. I must be brought under the "rod." Oh! that I may kiss it, thankfully. "Whom the Lord Loveth, He chasenteth," is of great comfort to me. I feel He is carrying on the good work *He* commenced in my heart. Lord help me to improve this time of affliction! I was very much refreshed the other evening in my private devotions. Lord increase thy work. O, that I could always be so filled with thy grace and Love for Christ. I was thinking this evening of Heaven, of what a theme for contemplation. I was pondering in my mind, what Heaven *would be* when the earth was destroyed, would *it* be let down on this earth? I know Earth will have to undergo a change. "All things will pass away," and the Heaven's roll back, as a scroll. I wish I could see Heaven in a clearer light. I could imagine more about it. I know no tongue could express the grandeur, the magnificence of *that* "*City*" Heaven. What a *world* of meaning expressed in a word! "The Home of God's People." A City of pearly-gates, of golden streets, of *living waters*. Throne of pearl & sapphire with the "Rainbow of promise" circling it. Then God—our Savior—on this "Throne" with the holy angels, the blood-washed-throng worshipping the living God. Drinking of the pure waters of *eternal life*. Not for a day will this be, but Eternity through. "Oh! what must it be to be there." Lord, "help *me* to work out my soul's salvation, with fear and trembling." Be with me this day, and teach me what to say.

Thursday 11th

I feel sad this morning, depressed in spirit. Why this mysterious feeling of sadness? I ask myself, but no answer can I find. I feel as though I could weep and why

34. Mary Lee* was Bond's aunt.
35. Bond probably refers to Hannah Lee, Dr. Richard Lee's* mother.

weep, why feel so sorrowful: Have not I the blessed assurance *God* careth for me, *me*, poor miserable creature! "What is man that thou art mindful of him, and the son of man, that thou visiteth him." It is cloudy and damp today—perhaps, the weather may have some affect on my spirits. "Help me to watch and pray."

Friday 12th

Have not been well today, had the neuralgia in my head badly. Much company been here today.

This morning cousin Josh, Mrs. Jarrett & Annie Lee, came after dinner, they left, and Lizzie Lee & Hall, Miss Susie Bryley came and two Miss Websters, Miss Webster from Baltimore, Dillie Webster, two Miss Downings, Mr. Downing, Mr. Wilson, Dr. Archer & Mr. Stump. It rained and four has to stay all night.

Saturday 13th

I rode out this morning, went to the post office—did not get a letter, felt *disappointed.* Received, yesterday, a very handsome birthday gift from Howard.

Sunday 14th

Brother & sister Fannie have gone to Calvary Meeting, all day meeting.

Tuesday 16th

Was a beautiful day. I felt much better. Went to cousin Juliet's in the evening, met there Lizzie & Godfrey Watters, Bennie Lee, Mary & Lillie Gough, John Holland, George Glasgow. Sister Fannie, brother & I, were the other visitors. Spent a very delightful evening, danced, my conscience did not condemn me, only perhaps some might think it was a regular dancing party.

Wednesday Aug 17th

We were invited to aunt Nancy's this evening. Brother & Sister Fannie went. I had no way. Fannie stayed at Mr. Watters' all night—did not come home till next evening after tea.

Friday 19th

I went to uncle Sam's this evening with cousin George, stayed all night, did not get home till Saturday 20th. Had a pleasant time. Cousin George brought me home. When I got here found Howard M- & Frank Doan here also Wake Munnikhuysen.[36]

---

36. Wake Munnikhuysen was a farmer and doctor. He was married to Elizabeth and would have been fifty-five in 1859. He is Bond's paternal relative, but the exact relationship is not clear. It is likely that he did not live near Bond's family until 1870, when he is listed in the census records from Harford County. 1870 U.S. census, population schedule, Harford County, Md., National Archives microfilm publication M593, roll 588.

Sunday 21st

Morning—went to hear Mr. Valliant in the church which has been just finished, very sweet and lovely it looked. Heard a very excellent sermon. Many persons there, large collection 200.47$. Came home to dinner. No one here in the evening. I *was glad.*

Monday 22nd

Cousin George & I started about nine o'clock on a long talked of trip. Went to Aberdeen first, remained there about an hour and a half. Started off to Havre de Grace,[37] met a man on the road playing with his monkey—we stopped and witnessed some *of its feats.* Drove on, through the principle streets in H[avre de Grace], then went to the United States Hotel—dined, refreshed ourselves, with a lie down, and about half past three, started for Gover Hill. Got there, found both the girls absent. Cousins Jeams & Betsy glad to see us. They teased me about _____[38] said he was a great favorite with them. Told me I must bring him down to see them. We walked up on the "Hill." I never saw such a grand view of the bay,[39] and Havre de Grace. It is perfectly lovely. The Bay looked magnificent indeed. H[avre de Grace] is much prettier looking down on it, than riding through. It is a very irregular place. Has a very handsome Methodist meeting house. Coming home, we passed Com. Rodger's house.[40] Very pretty place. Got home about seven, found Lizi Holland here. She stayed until nearly eleven. I was truly tired. I had to be entertainer, as brother & sister Fannie went up to cousin Juliet's to meet some company.

Tuesday 23rd

Rained nearly all day. Peggie, Bennie Lee & G. Watters came. Peggie left about five. Godfrey about twelve. Bennie is still here. I got a letter from H- this morning. It has made me *sad. Can* I, *Oh! can* I *leave* my home for one so far away! May my Father in Heaven direct me in this important matter, as well as others. Let me be directed by thee, O my Father.

Wednesday 24th

Raining & cloudy nearly all day. Mary Gough & cousin George spent the evening, stayed all night.

---

37. Havre de Grace, in Harford County, is approximately twenty miles from Baltimore.

38. Bond leaves a blank space here, but we can assume she is referring to Howard.

39. Chesapeake Bay.

40. Bond likely refers to John Rodgers, a naval officer born in Harford County in 1771. Rodgers participated in subduing the slave revolts in Santo Domingo (see the introduction for more information on the revolts). He also defended Fort McHenry against British attack. Bond mentions the fort twice in her journal, in entries on 16 July 1858 and 12 September 1859.

Thursday 25th

Mary left early this morning, sent her love to H-. I must not forget to give it to him when I write. Grand temperance meeting out at the "Tent"—Mrs. Green (a woman, or lady) from North lectured, and some man, name unknown. George Glasgow took tea, Godfrey Watters dined here. Dr. Archer came after tea. Bennie Lee was taken so sick had to send for Dr. Archer. Is better now.

CHAPTER THREE

"Can I Do a Wife's Duty?"

26 AUGUST 1859–31 MAY 1860

Friday night, August 26th 1859

This was my 21st birthday. 21, how time flies! Growing old—what will another year bring? I often ask myself. Shall I be here in the old "homestead." Or will it be my lot to give up my dear ones here, and go among strangers in a *strange land.*

Oh! guide me Father, let thy protecting arm be ever around me. In whatever land I roam, I know the same watchful eye is upon me. It will be a thought to soothe my troubled heart, when far away—that I have the *same* kind indulging Father to go to. He is never so far but the needy's prayer can be heard. Oh grant that I may live nearer to thee through this year that I have just entered upon! Bennie Lee & Godfrey took dinner here. Bennie & I took a walk down the road—Gathered some wild flowers. Got home, found G. here. She left soon after dinner. Sister Fannie, and cousin George have gone to Dr. Archer's to spend the evening. Raining very hard, don't think they will get home tonight. Long looked for came at last, in the shape of Ma's barrel of sugar, and my box. How sweet it is to be remembered by those *we love,* dear good Howard.

Saturday 27th

Very much surprised by aunts Rebecca and Marg coming[1]—did not expect them. Came up on the stage, Mr. Stump brought aunt Marg out. Great meeting commenced at the "Tent" today. Aunts, Pa, sister Fannie, brother & Ann Lee have gone to Woodside.

Sunday 28th

Rainy nearly all day, cleared off in the afternoon. Did not go to meeting. Aunts went to uncle Sam's in cousin George Gover's carriage. Cousin G. Glasgow took Fannie to meeting. Jimmy Moores & Otho Lee & George Glasgow came to tea. Dr. Archer afterwards. I received a very pretty portfolio for birthday present.

---

1. Bond's mother's sisters.

Monday 29th

Beautiful day, cool—went and spent the evening with aunt Dillie Lee, aunt R- & M- in company, had a pleasant time, came home found we had company during the evening—Miss Lewis from Philadelphia, Mr. Jarrrett, Mrs. & Mr. Archer, baby and Dr. Archer.

Tuesday afternoon 30th

They (my aunts, Ma & brother) have gone to uncle Parker's. We were at Woodside this morning. I have been busy preparing to go to Balto tomorrow in the stage. Going to Belair this evening.

Wednesday

I came to Baltimore in the stage, with thirteen passengers inside and one out.[2] Very pleasant day, quite cool. Felt very tired. Found all well—grandma[3] so glad to see me.

Thursday 1st Sept.

In the house nearly all day—Mr. Everest called to me.

Friday 2nd

Went to market this morning. Wished for some money to buy grandma something nice but what was the use of wishing. Miss Fuller spent the evening here. Dr. Goldsboro called after tea. I was very glad to see him. He wanted me to go out home with him.

Saturday the third.

Went up to the Blind Institute in the afternoon, took tea, spent a very pleasant evening. After tea, aunt Rebecca and I went to cousin Millie's. I stayed all night.

Sunday 4th

Went to Charles St. church, heard a very beautiful sermon by Rev. Mr. Deshiels from Paul's epistle to the Corinthians, 3d chapter and 8th verse "Think of These Things," were the words of his text.

After dinner I took a nap, felt much refreshed. Then went over to Dr. Fuller's church to the "Young men's christian association," I enjoyed it very much indeed. Those meetings I think are doing an amount of good. I felt as though the Lord was there.

2. Bond travels to Baltimore with her aunts Marg and Rebecca* when they end their visit to Maiden Lane. Bond's visit lasts until 27 September.

3. Bond's maternal grandmother, Mary Bond.

I went in the morning with cousin Priscilla Lee,[4] in the afternoon with cousin Millie Armstrong. Came home, Cassie Wilson came soon after, Lillie, Cass and I went after tea to Utaw to meeting, heard Mr. Brook preach. Cassie stayed all night.

Monday 5th

A very rainy and disagreeable day out, but very pleasant indoors. We laughed all day. I mimicked cousin Millie talking to her *hubby*. I thought she would have hurt herself laughing. I wrote to Josh to come see us[5]—quite an urgent letter. He came, looked *lovely*. So agreeable. Cassie and I both *half* if not whole in love with him, stayed half past 11 o'clock. I do not know when I spent such an agreeable day as last Monday.

Tuesday 6th

Lovely morning. We got our breakfast about 8, started off soon after from home (downtown). Did some shopping. Cass, Millie, and I, got home about half past 11. Last night the two Mr. Ellis' were here.

Wednesday 7th

Beautiful day—sun rose clear and bright. Feel pretty well excepting the headache.

Thursday 8th

Miss Lydia Forman was here, spent the evening.

Saturday 10th

Was very much surprised at breakfast at seeing Lawrence. Looks thin, has been sick, seemed very glad to *see me*, stayed till after ten. Cousin Josh, Laura & Vergie Bond came. The girls stayed all night. I went shopping with Laura; had lots of fun, forgot to pay for everything till coming out of the store, when they asked me for the money. Lawrence & Mrs. R. called after tea.

Sunday 11th

I went to Charles St. church in the morning with Lawrence. Heard a beautiful sermon from 11 chpt. 6th verse of St. Matthew, delivered by Rev. Mr. Jackson. Oh! it was so lovely. He used the 26 Psalm and 1st Chap. of Paul's epistle to the Corinthians. Josh came home with us, took dinner, left for sunday school about three.

4. A daughter of cousin Ann Lee, Priscilla would have been thirty-one years old.

5. Bond is still referring to Josh Bond,* the recently converted young preacher.

Monday 12th

The military turned out today to celebrate the battle at fort McHenry.[6] Lovely day—quite warm. Lawrence came whilst I was eating my breakfast, stayed till about 11. Came back about half-past three, took tea, left soon after. I went to meeting at Charles St. with Josh, heard an excellent discourse by Rev. Mr. Coopman, from the text "The night cometh, wherein no man can work."

Oh! it was so beautifully delivered—he spoke so lovely to the young. There's a work to be done for us—for *me* to do, Lord help me to perform my duty cheerfully and Christianly. I feel I'm weak and sinful, but Jesus cares for me. Give me grace, and put words in my mouth, that I may be enabled to speak a word in season and out of season.

Tuesday morning 13th

Poor dear little Zach is very ill this morning.[7] Night—I was much surprised and delighted to see brother this evening. I expected to have gone to see Mrs. Anderson this afternoon with Lawrence but the rain prevented. I spent a very pleasant evening at home. O, I hope my words to Lawrence will prove beneficial! how I wish he was a good christian. He told me he wished he was himself. Lord put words in my mouth.

Wednesday 14th

I felt sad most of the day, did not feel well, had the neuralgia in my face badly. Brother and Lawrence left. I got disappointed in going to Kent, went to St. Michaels, had a pleasant trip, got back about six, was surprised to see them, thought they had gone to Kent.[8] Spent another agreeable evening with Lawrence. He said I was the only one who ever talked to him about religion. Oh! that my words may cause him to ponder and reflect.

Thursday 15

They left for Kent again this morning. Pretty day, not very well.

Friday 16

Very stormy and rainy. Saturday also stormy, driving rain.

6. During the attack on Baltimore in the War of 1812, American troops at Fort McHenry held off British forces. After failing to bombard the fort, the British army left Chesapeake Bay.

7. Probably Bond's aunt Marg's son, named after his grandfather, Zacheus.

8. Kent County is located across the Chesapeake Bay from Baltimore, on the Eastern Shore. St. Michaels, a waterfront village, is also on the Eastern Shore, south of Kent.

Sunday 18th

Beautiful day, agreeable surprised to see the sun this morning when I awoke—for I had come to the conclusion it was going to be a settle rain.

Went to Fayett Street to church this morning, heard Rev. Augustus Webster preach a most excellent sermon from Hebrews 6th chap. 6 verse "If they shall fall away, to renew them again unto repentance; seeing they crucify to themselves the Son of God afresh, and put *him* to an open shame." I was much pleased with the explanation. The church was reopened. Rev. E.G. Reese preached at night from Romans[9]—

It was the first time I ever saw him, I was much pleased—Sunday afternoon Josh was here. He is so good, I love to listen to him. Mr. Simson waited on me to church at night.

Monday

[A]nother pretty morning but cloudy in the evening. I got a letter from Ma and one from Peggie. Brother came—glad to welcome him. Oh! how soon he will leave us! It makes me sad, sad when I think of it.[10] Lord answer my prayers. Oh! how fervently I pray for him—I was praying for him when he came.

Tuesday 20th[11]

This morning, Tuesday 20th is very disagreeable, raining hard—brother has left for home. I am quite sick—feel as though I wanted to be at home now.——

Forgot to say Mr. Richardson called to see me last night—also Mrs. Peats, her sister and child. Wednesday, Thursday and Friday rainy days. Passed pleasantly indoors.

Saturday 24th

Bright. I took care of Zach while aunt Marg went to see aunt Rebecca, in the morning. In the afternoon Mr. Drinkhouse and Mrs. Roby called to see me. I took a walk with Mary Cass.

Sunday 25th

Was ready to go to church with aunt R-, when it commenced raining, and continued, sunshine, & showers till one o'clock. Afternoon clear, Josh came down, stayed till church time, ½ past 7.

---

9. Bond leaves three dashes here, perhaps intending to fill in the specific chapter and verse, as she usually does when mentioning sermons.

10. Bond's brother is planning a trip to Louisiana, to work with Howard's father.

11. Bond does not provide a dated heading for this section. I have included one here for clarity. Also, she mistakes the dates in her entries, correcting herself above the line.

Monday 26th

Beautiful bright day. The odd fellows and orphan children turned out. Six chariots with the children, drawn by six horses each. It was a very interesting sight. A sad pleasantry, to see those orphans dressed prettily, and seated in those beautiful white chariots. In the afternoon Pa came down, for me. Mary Cass, Mr. J. Ellis waited on me up town. Mary & I went to see Josh. I had my likeness taken for brother.

After tea the two Mr. Ellis' came, also cousin Josh, and Harris.

Tuesday 27th

I came home, found all at home, Peggie [Bond] here to welcome me, soon after I got home, Godfrey [Watters], Billie Lee,[12] Juliet Gover, Jimmy Moores & Dr. Archer. I felt tired, *very tired.*

Sunday 9th 1859

A rainy & disagreeable day. Cousin George came to take me to church—rained too much; he stayed till nine at night.

Monday 10th

Beautiful day, cold. Brother went to bid his friends goodbye.

Tuesday 11th

Lovely day. Brother and Fannie went to Mr. Websters this morning to make a call. I went chestnut-hunting. Mr. Stump and uncle Jim spent the evening here. Our hearts are sad, sad.

Wednesday 12th

Dear brother left us this morning for Balto. on his way to La. O how our hearts are sadden by this parting. I shall miss him so much. Poor fellow, he was indeed grieved leaving his dear old home. But it is a great consolation the same God watches over us all, to protect his creatures from evil.

Thursday 13th

Jane and Wake [Munnikhuysen] came out this afternoon. Jane intends staying several days. Mr. Stump took Fannie to the Presbyterian meeting in Belair tonight. The Presbytery meets there.

Friday 14th

Went out chestnut hunting this afternoon, Pa, Jane, Ann Lee and I; got home in time to escape the rain. Cousin George Glasgow came soon after. Mr. S[tump]

12. Probably she refers to Uncle Sam Lee's* young son.

and sister Fannie got home to tea. Cousin G. and I had a long talk in the passage about religion. I think he is serious. O I hope God will aid him with "His Holy Spirit." Cause him to turn from his worldly ways and put his trust in a higher power. O that the words I was constrained to speak, be seed sown in due season. May they bring fourth meats fit for repentance.

Saturday 15th

Morning—Jane, Fannie, Ann Lee and I walked down to the post office, that is the two former went as far as the "Run."[13] Ann Lee and I went on. I got two letters, one from Bettie Cage and one from Mary Cass Linville. I was very tired when I got home. Ate my dinner, lay down, took a rest.

Sunday morning 16th

Pa, Ma & I went to Belair, also sister Fannie and cousin George. Heard Mr. Maloy, preached from 3rd chap. 5th ver. of Thessalonians "And the Lord direct your hearts into the love of God, and into the patient waiting for Christ." It was a very beautiful sermon. Some said he preached particularly for me. All I took. Came home to dinner, after which I walked up to see cousin Juliet. When I got back, cousin G. and Jimmy Moores was here. Dr. Archer and Mr. Maloy came to tea. After which Ma, Jane, Mr. Maloy and Ann Lee went to meeting in the carriage, I with cousin George. The protracted meeting is going on at Watters' meeting house. Heard Mr. Gwyn preach from 2nd Kings 5th chap. part of the 6 verse "Let him come now to me, and he shall know that there is a prophet in Israel." Mr. Maloy stayed all night with us.

Monday 17th

Cloudy, appearance of rain. Jane left this morning, also Mr. Maloy. This afternoon it commenced raining.

Tuesday Oct 18th

Cleared off about 12—very windy in the afternoon. Ann Lee out hunting chestnuts.

Wednesday 19th

Beautiful morning, cool, Sister Fannie went to Baltimore this morning with cousin Jared Gover. Dr. Gance was married this morning at the catholic church to Miss Caroline Richardson of Belair. I spent the day with cousin Cass Gover, cousin Priscilla Gover was there.[14] Pa met me coming home, told me of the persecution at Harpers' Ferry with the blacks and abolishioners. Mr. Stump was here in the afternoon.

13. Bond refers to the Thomas Run Valley.
14. Priscilla and Cass (Casander)* were sisters.

Thursday 20th

A letter from La. stating cousin Rebecca was very sick.[15]

Friday 21st

Juliet Gover was here in the afternoon.

Saturday 22nd

Pretty morning, rained at night. Sister Fannie got home at eight in the evening.

Sunday 23rd

Cool—windy. I thought of walking up to meeting in the afternoon. But thought Mr. Mendanhall was going to preach; did not go. Walked up to see aunt Dillie with Betsy (black girl), was overtaken coming home by Godfrey who accompanied me.[16] Mr. Stump here in the morning.

Monday 24th

Bright, pleasant. Fannie & Ann Lee walked to the store, Lou Wyatt,[17] John Moores spent the evening here.

Tuesday 25th

Mr. S. took Fannie to Mrs. Archer's. I got a letter from La.

Wednesday 26th

Frank Bond was married at eight o'clock this evening to Miss Sandie Webster. Cool and disagreeable day. Godfrey brought me a letter from Cass.

Thursday 27th

It snowed, & rained last night. This morning the sun has come out and trees, fences and ground look perfectly magnificent. Like sheets of silver, and the sun's rays are melting the ice, causing it to look like raining of silver.

I never, as I sit at my window, viewed such a sight in my life. The trees, before

15. Howard Bond's mother.

16. When Bond mentions Betsy, she usually identifies her through a parenthetical note. Perhaps she wants her meaning to be clear for a future audience; more likely, she is making a note for herself. From census records it seems that Betsy, being only eight years old, had not been with the Munnikhuysens for long. Therefore, Bond, a frequent reader of her own writings, might have feared she would not remember Betsy when she later reread her own diary. This action would support the findings of historians who point out that slaves (and in Maryland free black servants), despite their work and daily presence, remained peripheral to many white southerners' perspectives. As noted by Stowe, in *Intimacy and Power*, there are very few references to black people in white southerners' accounts of their daily lives and rituals (253).

17. Bond refers to Louise Wyatt* of Virginia.

the ice came were of every color, and now those many colors are covered with ice. The flowers are frozen stiff.

8th of Nov

Not one line have we heard from brother since he left. Oh how sad my heart is. Where is the wanderer this morning? Four weeks tomorrow since he left us. Peggie and Mifflin came down on Sunday evening. Left yesterday evening. On Saturday evening last Mrs. Glasgow and I took a ride on horseback. Went to the store and to William Watters', made a call early; we were on horseback. I called at the office coming home, got a letter from Howard. Brother had not arrived on the 26th. Poor fellow! God protect him from all evil.

I was sick in bed all day Sunday. Neuralgia in my head. Got up just before tea. Godfrey called for a little while. Yesterday was a beautiful day. Sister Fannie got home from Blanches [Archer]. Mifflin and Peggie left after tea. The moon shone lovely. This morning is foggy and gloomy. I too feel sad and gloomy and why should I? I ask myself often. He loves me with all the devotion of his noble heart. And I am his *promised* wife. Do I love him to leave father, brother, all dear and near ones for one? Can I do a wife's duty? Oh! my Heavenly Father look down from Heaven and bless thy poor sinful child. I have no power to do good unless thou givest it me. Do thou choose the path wherein I am to walk all the rest of my days. If it be right, O my Father, that we would go hand and hand over the hill of life, fit us for the responsibility. Give us grace to bear with each other's failings. Oh my Father in Heaven, guide *me* in this important matter. May I choose well. I do with all the sincerity of my heart, ask a blessing on my action. May I do thy will.

Nov. 17th 1859

Has been cloudy nearly all day, rather cold. Sister Fannie gone to Mrs. Blanche Archer's. Ann Lee to the post office & Betsy, Ma & I at home. Heard from brother. Ma & Pa got a letter, and I got one. Still on the river, so sick and lonely, poor fellow, how I sympathize with him.

My letter was so sad. I did not let anyone know I had received it but sister Fannie. I knew it would nearly break Ma's heart to know her son was still sick and alone. God bless my dear brother is my daily prayer.

Sunday I went to hear Mr. Maloy preach a most beautiful sermon. It was from Hebrews 4th chap. 1st verse. Rain came up, and I had to stay at Mr. Valiant's. I had a very pleasant visit. It was the first time I ever spent an evening at a parsonage. An evening at a parsonage! Who ever spent one there but what it left a bright spot in memory. So calm, so sweet the hours sped by. We had a lovely sunset. Next morning was beautiful but so cold. I called to see Mary Lee. Met Mrs. Glasgow there. Mr. Maloy brought me home in the buggy, about 11. He remained til near night, then left. Dr. Archer came, spent the evening.

Tuesday sister Fannie went to Medical Hall. Dr. Lee came. Wednesday—yesterday—was a beautiful day, very pleasant. Dr. Archer & Fannie went to Blanche's. I took a walk with Betsy. After tea Dr. Lee went up to "Woodside." Juliet came down in the evening, stayed a little while. This evening I am looking for a letter from my own—The country begins to look dreary and lonesome. The foliage has nearly all fallen off the trees, which gives them a naked appearance.

30th Nov.

Last Sunday week I went to hear Mr. Finney preach. Cousin George Glasgow took me in the morning to hear him, and in the afternoon to hear Mr. Britten. He preached a very plain and practical sermon from "Lord increase our Faith." After tea Mr. G.P. Gover and Mr. Oliver Evans came. Last Thursday cousin George and I spent the evening with Juliet. Friday evening cousin Lizzie Watters, Godfrey and Lou Wyatt spent the evening here. Lou stayed all night. Saturday morning Lou and I spent an hour or two with Juliet. After dinner she, Juliet, Ann Lee and myself, made a call at cousin Cass Gover's, then went to the post office. Were disappointed not getting a letter from brother and H-. Came home, found cousin John Moores here. Lou left. Sunday went to hear Rev. Mr. Valiant, preached from "Let us lay aside the weight and sin, &c &c-. In the evening cousin Fannie & Jimmy Moores came, also Dr. Archer and sister Fannie, cousin Juliet and cousin George Gover. Monday Juliet, Lillie Gough and myself went to uncle Parkers, spent the evening. I stayed all night at "Woodside." Came home noon yesterday morning. Today Blanche, the baby, Mrs. Williams & her daughter took dinner. Juliet, Lillie Gough, Martha and Mr. Bouldin spent the evening. It is raining a little. Ma is quite sick, has gone to bed. Tomorrow night Mr. E.G. Reese delivers a lecture in our church, on "Home and its influences," I hope I shall get there. Cousin Howard Parrish is to be married tomorrow morning at 9 o'clock in the Madison Avenue church in Baltimore, to Miss Lizzie Brown. Mr. Jim Anderson is to be married to Miss Susan Fulton in the Presbyterian church at Churchville.—

Thursday Dec 1, 1859

Today has been beautiful, and warm, I have spent altogether a very agreeable day. This morning Ann Lee started to school, in Belair, to Miss Davenport, sister Fannie went to Mrs. Archers. This afternoon cousin George Glasgow and I went to see the marriage at Churchville. Mr. Finney married them. Many were there. It was quite a novelty to see a marriage take place at four o'clock in a *country church*—from there we went to Mr. Gough's, expecting to get tea, but found no one at home.

Went into Belair—got tea at Dr. Lee's and then went to a lecture on "Home," by Rev. E. G. Reese, It was beautiful. The church (M.P. church) was full. "Home is where the heart is." He is a beautiful lecturer. I wish I could remember all he said.[18] Coming home I stopped at the store (Mr. Robertson's). Cousin George gave me a box of figs. I am very fond of them. When I got home found a letter from H- and one from brother, and one for pa & ma, from H- asking of them the hand of their daughter.[19]

It made me feel sad. For I know not whether I shall be happy *so far* from my *own dear home*. Lord direct me in the way I should go. Oh! I do wish to do the Lord's bidden. "Lord increase my faith." Brother had arrived on the 22nd. He was well and our gloomy fears were driven away.

Friday 2nd

This is a perfect love of a day. Like a May day—so warm and balmy. What I should imagine *Southern weather's like in Winter.* Mrs. Judge Archer and Miss H. Hays called for ma, this morning, to take her to Mr. Watters. I am housekeeper today. Betsy and I are the only occupants of the house—excepting in the kitchen. Pa is out in the field.

I have an engagement at "Woodside" this evening, to meet some company. Do not know whether I can go.

"Brown," the "Insurrectionist" was to be hung today. . . . I went to Cousin Juliet's. I enjoyed myself much, was rather quiet though. Had dancing but by the grace from above resisted. Dick Boulden galanted me home, Lizzie Lee and Susan Briarley came home with me, Jimmy Moores waited on them here.

Saturday 3rd

Raining cold, the girls left this morning. Mr. M. Evans came, made a call.

Sunday 4th

Still raining, very disagreeable. Cousin George Gover was here short time this afternoon.

Wednesday 7th

Has been raining since Saturday and at it yet. Looks very gloomy out. Though I am the only child at home, I am not lonesome. Have felt very well contented and thankful I have such a good home; and so many many kind and loved ones. I received, last night, a letter from Bettie Cage (who will soon be Mrs. []).[20] She will

18. Reese is first mentioned in Bond's entry of 18 September 1859. His sermon is indicative of nineteenth-century religion's general domestic emphasis. See the introduction for further discussion.

19. See also app. 1 for Bond's father's letter of 14 January 1860 to his son regarding Howard's request.

20. The name is unclear.

be married the 8th tomorrow. May she be directed by the almighty and be faithful
to the vows she will speak at the Bridal Altar. I wrote a long letter yesterday to H-.
One also enclosed to brother. O that he may be directed and guided from all temptation of the evil one. Lord throw thy arm of protection around him. Overshadow
him with thy shield of mercy. I hear J.B.B. [Josh Bond] is going to study divinity—I am so glad. I hope he may be the means of bringing many to the Cross of
Christ. Oh grant Heavenly Father he may point out, to many of his irreligious relations, the path that leadeth to Everlasting life. Oh! that we may pray more for
our relations and friends and enemies, if we have any.

Thursday 8th
    Rather cloudy. Bettie married at 10. Many blessings on thy head, dear one. Thou
hast taken an important step. May you discharge every *christian* duty!

Friday 9th
    Pa left for Balto this morning. It is very cold—clear though.

Saturday 10th
    Pa returned this afternoon. Juliet here for a short time. Sallie Gover, and Pink
Norris came after tea, sit an hour or so. Looks well.

Sunday 11th
    Did not go to church today. Stayed home & let Pa & Ma go. Was here by my-
self till eleven when Betsy came (the little colored girl). Did not feel at all afraid.
Spent a quiet time most of the day. Dr. Archer came, spent the evening. He is so
agreeable, so sensible.

Monday Dec. 12th
    I walked up to "Woodside" this afternoon, had not been there long before Ma
sent for me; Mr. Maloy had come (the preacher). He seemed very glad to see me.
Calls me "Pretty Mittie." Speaking of our country and of Washington, he said
"God's blessing rested upon all Washington did for his country" and he thought it
still would be upon it and our country would be kept from war that now threatened it. It is in great commotion. They are discussing a disunion, North and South.
Mr. Maloy is a sensible man, quite young.

Tuesday 13th
    He left this morning. Cold and cloudy. I spent several hours with cousin Cass
Gover this afternoon. She and I had a long talk on religion. I hope I was enabled
by the spirit to say some good things. She thinks she is a great sinner. Lord en-
lighten our darkened minds and make us see ourselves, what we are by nature and
by practice. When I came home found two letters, welcome messengers of love,

one from brother, and one from Howard, both made my heart *sad, sad.* I pray to be guarded from all evil. Oh my Father in Heaven remember not former iniquities but purge our hearts from *all sin* for thy Son's sake. Oh! that I may not act from any *worldly* gain, and do nothing displeasing in thy sight. Teach me to pray more—and with a more *fervent spirit,* asking with faith, believing thou will hear—and answer my poor petitions.

Wednesday 14th

Not well today, did not breakfast till after ten. Snowy & cold—not enough to sleigh, though. Wrote to brother today. I do sincerely ask God's blessing on it. O Father give me faith, to believe thou will bless it. Guide my brother from all evil, into the path of peace and righteousness.[21]

Thursday 15th

The anniversary of ma's & pa's marriage. Married 30 years. How many the changes! Oh if it is my lot to be a wife—may I be as meek and gentle kind affectionate, and forbearing. 30 years of *smiles, frowns,* and *tears!* No one but a wife knows the trials of a wife and mother. Oh! that I may help bear my parents burdens. This is a very lovely morning, quite cold. The snow is melting fast. How many blessings I have, how many comforts of life, so many more than I fear I am thankful for. Grant me thy blessing, o Father through out this day. Night, I went to Mrs. Gough's, spent the evening and there met Mrs. Dallam & Mr. Dallam. Left directly after tea for Belair. Heard Rev. Mr. Valliant deliver a beautifully learned lecture on the "Influence of Christianity, its progresses and developments in Patriotism." Many there. Got home between and ten and eleven. Cousin George Glasgow was my escourt.

Friday 16th

Another lovely day, cousin George and I took dinner at aunt Hannah Lee's. Alice not at home. Reverend Day wants cousin George to speak a good word for him to me. Came to Richard Lee's for tea. Went over to Mr. Moore's store with Jimmy Moores, sister Fannie with cousin George. After tea came home, found all gone to bed.

Saturday 17th

Very stormy day—rain and windy, blew very hard.

21. As she fears Howard's father's influence over Howard, she also fears his impact on her brother. Moreover, she was likely concerned about William's contact with the culture on the sugar plantation, one that would have given him power over many slaves and license to exercise it freely. See the introduction for more on the contrast between the established Seaboard culture and that of the southern frontier.

Sunday 18th

Cloudy, disagreeable. I was engaged to go to church at Churchville with cousin George. He came 'twas too late, went to aunt Dillie's to dinner, from there to Meeting at Watters, heard Mr. Britten preach an excellent sermon from Psalm 6 chpt. 19 verse. Came home to tea. Godfrey took tea with us. I got a letter from Howard M[unnikhuysen] from the U.V. [University of Virginia], seemed like *old times* to be getting *letters* from there.

Monday 19th

Cloudy this morning. I went to uncle Parker's in the carryall. Cleared off after dinner—clouded up before tea. Had a Christmas gift from Grandma (*four dollars*). Came home after tea, on horseback, one of the servant boys came with me, took the horse back.[22] Have had quite a pleasant day.

Oh Father of mercies, make me thankful for *all* the privileges I enjoy, all the mercies and blessings. . . . .

Tuesday 20th

Cloudy, rainy all day. Cousin George came in the afternoon to let me know he could not go to Baltimore tomorrow. I have been quite busy, have had pleasant thoughts.

Wednesday 21st

I spent several pleasant hours at "Woodside" this morning. Came home to dinner, soon after, walked down to cousin Cass Gover's. Got some sage for ma. Met there cousin Sallie Wilson. She has a step-son in Louisiana. It was quite cold and cloudy this morn, but this afternoon it partly cleared off and now the stars are shining brightly.

I am anticipating a trip to Baltimore tomorrow to see some of my dear friends. I hope if it is right I may go. But should weather, or anything else prevent, I hope I may feel thankful and see an all wise Providence in it.

Oh! that I could see the Lord's doings in all things I have no control over. Another year has nearly gone! Have I or have I not improved, grown in grace? Not as much as I should have done. If thou should spare my unprofitable life My Father, O that thou may grant me more grace, to overcome more temptations and sacrifice more worldly enjoyments. Oh! that I may live nearer the Holy Cross. Give me grace "my Father" to bear patiently with the *aged ones* thou has given me to *love* & *respect*—To give up to *them*, who are older and wiser than I. Make us love one another even as thou lovest us. . . . . . .

22. In 1860 Parker Lee owned three slaves, one of whom Bond likely mentions here.

Wednesday Dec. 28th 1859

One week since I penned in my journal. I went to Balto as I anticipated, on Thursday. Had a very agreeable drive, was not much cold. Stoped to warm on the road. Got there about two; all charmed to see such an unexpected guest. Spent a delightful time. Received several very handsome presents. A very handsome writing desk, a pretty book, pair of sleeve buttons, another gold button, a very pretty dress, several others. Cousin George and I made a call at Mr. Rodgers, and from there out to Balto. Street. Had a very pleasant promenade. We returned home Saturday. Cousin G. would make a noble husband for any woman. I was told I was very much in love with him. But I love him only as my intimate friend. Christmas day was beautiful, quite pleasant. Cousin Jeams Hall came to dinner from the church dedication out at Robinson's, stayed all night. Left Monday. I spent the morning (26th) at cousin Juliet's took dinner, came home, found Howard M[unnikhuysen] here. Looks very well, just home from the University of Virginia. Cousin George came for me to go to a large company given at Mooreland. We went—enjoyed ourselves much. Stayed all night. I met there an *old* beau, he renewed his suit said he would come see me this week. But I have an answer for him. I came home yesterday morning *soon*. Was in bed with sick headache all afternoon. Peggie came before tea, stayed all night. Howard, and Wake M- [Munnikhuysen] came a while ago. H. took Peggie to the post office, will be back to dinner. It is snowing very fast—looks like we were going to have sleighing. I hope I shall get a letter today.

Thursday 29th

Cold snowy day. Peggie left this morning, aunt Nancy came, also cousin Charles Lee & Dr. Lee. Yesterday got a letter from brother. Friday clear and cold, the ice and snow looks magnificent. Dr. Archer called for a short time. Howard Parish & his bride made us a fashionable call. She looked quite pretty. Howard [Munnikhuysen], Wake & their two sisters came this evening. Howard took me sleighing, wanted to know if I was engaged. Aunt Nancy left this afternoon.

Saturday 31st

Alice Lee and Otha called this morning.[23] Ann Lee and pa went to the office, brought me a package from H-, a beautiful Christmas gift in the shape of a gold thimble. I walked up to Woodside after dinner. Stayed till dark.

Sunday 1st of January 1860

This, the commencement of another New Year, should be the time to make new resolutions and pray for more grace to help us bear the burdens of life with more

23. Hannah Lee's children and Dr. Lee's* siblings. Alice was twenty-two and Otho twenty years old.

gentleness of spirit. Keep us, O Father, under the shadow of thy wing. Robert Gover drove me to Belair this afternoon in the sleigh. I heard a beautiful sermon by Mr. Gwyn from the 10 chap. of Romans, 1, 2, 3, 4 verses. Coming home the horse ran off, kicked himself loose from the sleigh with the shares following him, started off for home. We were in trouble sure enough then. We started back for Belair, was met by Mr. Rodgers who brought me home. Robert rode the horse back; someone caught it before he got very far. My feet were nearly frozen, had to put them in cold water.

Monday Jan 2nd

Very cold, cousin George came for me to go to Belair, did not go till after tea. Went to Dr. Lee's, got home about ten. Moon shone perfectly lovely.

Tuesday 3rd

After tea cousin George & I went to Mr. Harry Webster's; found all at home. Lizzie [Watters] reached home week before. Looks better. She is a lovely Christian. I wish I was more like her. So patient, gentle and resigned. Returned home just at eleven, found nice hot fire, my dear Ma's forethought.

Oh! wont I miss her, when I leave my home, for another's, my southern home! Will he always love me? Will I always love him? Will I ever wish I had never left my pa's house? Will I be kindly & *affectionately* received as their son's wife? Are the questions I am ever debating in my mind.

O, Father if there is a sincere prayer in my heart, it is, that I may be directed by Thee. Not my will but thine be done. Do not leave me to my own desires but guide me by thy council.

Wednesday 4th

Pa & I went in the sleigh to cousin Cass Gover's, made only a call, from there to uncle Jim's, did not get out, as neither were at home. Snow very fast before we got home. Snowed till night.

Thursday 5th

Charming morning. Juliet Gover came about ten. Mr. John Rodgers came in his two horse sleigh whilst we were eating dinner which was after two.[24] We found him quite agreeable. He came to take me out sleighing. Of course I would not go and leave Juliet. So sent her off in my place. They came back to tea, after which Mr. R. insisted on my going. The moon was shining bewitchingly. I could not resist, so off we started, went as far as cousin Cass Gover's, found Peggie was not

---

24. Bond could be referring to John Rodgers, a Harford native, naval officer, and son of the Commander Rodgers she mentions in her entry of 22 August 1859. John Rodgers would have been forty-eight years old in 1860.

there; turned and went to Churchville. The roads were very fine, the sleighing delightful. I was not feeling very well, was quite cold too. He left about ten. Juliet remains with me tonight. She has been trying to find out if H & I are engaged but I will not satisfy her curiosity.

Friday 6th

Lovely day. Dr. & Mary Lee & child called for a while. Juliet remained till after dinner when her mother sent for her to go home. I have felt quite sick all day. Did hope no one would come, as I felt too sick to entertain company. After dinner I lay down on the lounge in the dining room, got a little nap, when I got up my head felt better. Dr. & Mrs. Archer came (his mother) spent the evening. Cousin George came to take me sleighing. Did not go till after tea, after they left. Went to see Grandma Lee, who I heard was quite sick, had a very pleasant drive, lovely night. He is *one dear friend.* Made an engagement to go to "Hazle Dell" tomorrow evening.

Sunday 8th

Commenced raining yesterday very soon after dinner. I was greatly disappointed as I had not been able to see Blanche for more than two years. It continued raining till some time in the night, and now the sun is struggling through the mist. I received last night a letter from Howard. I went to pa and asked if any letters came; he said "no." I came in the house with a sad heart, though I commenced singing. After being in the room a while, pa came and gave me my letter; no letters had come, but one letter had. It is a nice long letter, breathing devoted love till death. Says he can never love any one as he does me. O if it is my lot to be his wife, I may be all that a true wife should be. Guide me my Heavenly Father in the path that it is right for me to go in.

Dr. Lee has come. I must run down stairs and see him.

Tuesday night 10, 1860

Sunday evening Dr. George came, took tea, after which Lou Wyatt, John Moores, H-. Stump & Godfrey Watters came. I wrote to Howard this evening.

Monday Pa went to Baltimore, as far as "Churchville" in the sleigh, took the stage for "Perrymanville" and then the cars for Balto. Godfrey Watters came after tea, stayed all night. Tuesday was very foggy, warm & close. John Dallam brought pa home in his buggy from "Perrymanville." Left before tea. Had not seen him for a long time. I heard of the illness of our President of the M.P. Church. Hope he is better now. Lord be with him, in the hour of distress.

Wednesday 11th

Warm, cloudy, snow going fast. Miserable roads. Jimmy Hendon here for a short while. Several called today. Pa went to uncle Parkers this morning; this afternoon I persuaded Ma to go up to "Woodside" she did so, went on horse back. I received a *dear long* letter from H-. this evening, pa brought it from the office. Has been cloudy nearly all day, rained a short time this afternoon. . . . . Home! O! home, shall I be here this time next year! I often think of the future. Will I be happy in my *new home* if I should go! I often ponder on it. How many changes this year will bring. Letest thy servant, our Father, be directed by thy will, for if we were let go by our own inclinations, we should come very far from doing right. But thou art willing to guide us if we will harken to thy precepts.

O inspire me with a knowledge of right towards my fellow men, that I may do unto all (every one) as I would they would do unto me. That I may treat *servants*, or *those* not my equals, by birth, with all kindness, and consideration, knowing as I do, they are creatures of feelings and have souls to save. That I may never treat any one with contempt. For if *I* treat others with contempt, how will my Father in Heaven treat me? Could I expect Him to look with kindness, and love, down upon *me?* How could I dare to ask his blessing upon me! I heard Josh [Bond] preached his first sermon last Wednesday night (5th). The Lord help him and give him grace to overcome temptation.

Thursday 12th

Hailing and raining. Very disagreeable, warm though. Dreamed I was in La. last night. Been reading lately the "life of a blind girl, Miss Mary Day."[25] Poor thing, she went through many trials. May her last days be her best. Am reading now "Marmion," a Tale by Sir Walter Scott. These lines are very beautiful

> O Woman! in our hours of ease,
> Uncertain, coy and hard to please,
> And variable as the shade
> By the light quivering aspen made;
> When pain and anguish wring the brow,
> A ministering angel thou!"

We went up to "Woodside," spent the evening with cousin Juliet. I received a letter from Howard in La.

Friday 13th

Peggie was here for a little while this morning. Mr. Valliant called, he & I took dinner at "Woodside." In the afternoon Dr. Archer called, took me to "Hazle Dell." Had not been there for more than two years. Got there to tea—all glad to see me, stayed all night—sister F-. & I sat up till two talking. Rained all day, very sleety.

25. The full title of the book is *Incidents in the Life of a Blind Girl: Mary L. Day, a Graduate of the Maryland Institution for the Blind,* published in 1859.

Saturday.

Spent pleasant day.

Sunday 15th

Dr. & I came home right early this morning. Everything looked beautiful with ice covering them. The woods was perfectly grand. It was like riding through fairyland. Each spray was silvered over and seemed studded with pearls & diamonds. Ma went to Watters' meeting in the afternoon.

Monday 16th 1860

Beautiful weather—warm & bright. Juliet B- & Bettie spent the day. Jimmy Cole spent the evening with me. I had not seen him for a long time; was very glad to have that pleasure. He is a very good young man. Is home from Princeton spending the holidays. Did not leave till about ten.

Tuesday 17th

I arose very early this morning to attend Victoria Billingslea's wedding. I went with Lizzie Watters. She married a gentleman from the E[astern] S[hore] of Maryland. She was dressed in white satten, low neck & short sleeves, long veil hung to her feet. Orange blossoms in her hair. I never saw a prettier bride. The bridesmaids were Sallie Webster, Carrie Coats. They wore corn colored dresses, looked lovely. It was a very pleasant affair. The groom (Mr. John Palmer) looked so happy. He is not handsome. I liked his looks though. Lizzie Watters returned home with me; stayed all night. Mrs. Kitty Richardson was buried this morning at 11 o'clock. She was quite an old lady and very much beloved.

Wednesday 18th

Cloudy but pleasant afternoon. I do not feel very well. Lizzie remained till this afternoon. Godfrey came for her. I sent him over to cousin Cassie's for Peggie. Dr. Lee called just as we were done dinner. Grandma Lee very ill. Ma went down to see her. Cousin Juliet came down to spend the evening, found Ma not at home, stayed till sundown, went home. Peggie stayed all night. I received a letter from Bettie Seay, this evening.

Thursday 19th

Cloudy, cooler than has been this week. Peggie left this morning. Virginia Richardson is to be married tonight. I was invited. Juliet went down to go to it. She is to be married to Mr. Read of Baltimore. Sister Fannie came home this morning after an absence of seven or eight weeks.

Friday 20th

Pretty day, warm. Fannie went to cousin Cass Gover's. Dr. Lee called. Dr. Archer spent the evening.

Saturday 21st

Like spring, so pleasant. Ann Lee came home from school. I went to uncle Parker's. Grandma [Lee] very sick. I stayed till Monday morning, 23rd. Spent a pleasant sunday, hope a profitable one. Monday afternoon Pa, Ma, cousin Juliet, sister Fannie went out in the carriage to make calls. Left me to keep house. I wrote a letter to Howard M[unnikhuysen], just finished when Dr. Archer and his sister came. Spent the evening. Cousin George Glasgow also spent the evening with me. Ma, Pa, returned to tea. Fannie did not come with them. Will come tomorrow. I heard of the death of Mrs. Patterson. She was an old lady and she intended celebrating the anniversary of her fiftieth year of marriage. But alas she has gone, in a few weeks she would have been married 50 years. She was buried yesterday.

Tuesday 24th Jan.

Lovely day. Roads very messy.

Wednesday 26th

I rode down to cousin Cass Gover's on horseback; whilst there cousin George came here, found I was not at home, went down there; he accompanied me home. Whilst riding along my saddle turned, had to sit on the fence till Cousin George fixed it. Got home about twelve o'clock.

Got a letter from brother & Howard this evening. Dr. Archer waited on sister Fannie home, he did not come in.

Thursday 26th

We were very much startled this morning hearing of the death of cousin Betsy Wilson who has been spending the winter with cousin Cass Gover. She had been sick about two weeks. She died at 8 o'clock, this morning. Sent a dispatch for cousin Gerard Gover. Sister Fannie & Peggie helped to lay her out. Has been snowing nearly all the evening, not very cold though.

Friday 27th

Ma & cousin Juliet went down to cousin Cass' this morning. The ground is covered with snow. Looks like we might have some more snow before long. . . .

Saturday 28th 1860

Cousin Betsy was buried this morning at the "Rock Spring." Sermon preached from 14 chap. of St. John first four verses by the Rev. Mr. Keech.[26] I did not go. I have not been so well as usual for a week or two. Cousin G. Glasgow spent the evening here. Charlotte had a party tonight.[27] I received a letter from H- La.

26. John R. Keech, a Protestant Episcopal minister, was sixty years old and in 1850 claimed property worth fifteen thousand dollars. In 1860 he also owned two slaves. His wife was named Susan.

27. Charlotte was one of the Munnikhuysens' house servants. See Bond's entry of 15 May 1859.

Sunday 29th

Beautiful day. None of us went to church, had no way, roads bad too. Peggie, Dr. Archer and Jimmy Moores spent the evening. P- will stay all night.

Monday 30th[28]

Peggie left the neighborhood this morning and Aunt Betsy came down to stay with cousin Cass. Sister Fannie spent the day there ("Sleepy Hollow").

31st

Cloudy, cousin Richard Lee and Mr. Stump here this evening. Night, snowing fast.

Feb. 1st

Ground covered with snow, drifted much. Dr. Archer spent the evening here.

2nd

Dr. Archer and I took a sleigh drive soon after dinner, called at his house, from there to aunt Nancy's and from there to Uncle P. Lee's, took tea. I received three letters today, one from cousin M.A. Bond, one from L.A.L. and one from M.C.L.[29]

Friday 3rd

Another cloudless day. Mr. Maloy came this morning, took dinner, after which we took a sleighride. Had quite an agreeable one. He left before tea.

Saturday 4th

Cloudy morning. I feel quite sick, and weak this morning, have had a bad cold. Ma & Pa have bad colds—Ma spent the day at uncle Parker's. Dr. Archer took her. Sister Fannie came home after tea with Dr. Archer. Cousin Richard & Clarence Lee were here. I got a *long* letter from *poor* H-. . . .

Sunday

Dr. A- took sister Fannie to church. I was quite sick all day. Lou Wyatt & cousin George, cousin Richard, sister Fannie and Dr. Archer took tea.

Monday 6th

Pa went down to see Grandma Lee—she is very ill, can not last long. Aunt Lizzie & Wake Munnikhuysen called—also uncle Jacob M.

---

28. The entries for 30 and 31 January were written as one entry, likely at the same time. Bond apparently had little time to write with her social engagements yet felt compelled to leave at least a brief account of her day.

29. The initials probably refer to some of Bond's paternal cousins (Lees).

Tuesday 7th[30]

=   =   =   =

Wednesday 8th

Pa & I went down to see Grandma, found her something better. Got home to dinner. Juliet Gover here, took dinner. After which Josh Bond came. I enjoyed his company very much indeed. Juliet left before tea. After tea Josh & I walked up to "Woodside," spent some very agreeable hours listening to Juliet's *sweet songs*. Got home at nine. He had prayers. The first time I have every heard him pray. Oh, it did me much good. I *felt happy*. Will the Lord look with love upon him and make him an instrument whereby souls may be converted.

Thursday 9th

The sun rose most beautifully this morning, not a cloud to be seen. Josh & I started off on horseback about nine o'clock. We went to Uncle Parker's. Grandma no better—looked dreadfully. Called at "Sleepy Hollow" on our way back.[31] Got home at twelve, found Sallie Davidson here, Josh remained till after dinner, Sallie remained till sun set. I received a letter from the University of Virginia. Pa received one from brother. I feel so sad tonight. Heavenly Father thou sendst all things, knowest all things, will thou direct all my ways, Let me have grace to help me in such time of need. Josh read last night for prayers the 5 chap of Thessalonians. This is pa's birthday; he is 60 today. I wonder if I shall live to be that aged!

Friday 10th

This is a very bright day but very windy like March weather.

Monday 20th Feb. 1860

I was taken sick to my bed saturday evening 11th. I have passed a week of suffering. Tuesday all day & night I was *ill*, no one knows the suffering I experienced. I am still in bed as I pen these lines, but feel much better. Lizzie Watters—dear friend—stayed with me last week, she is a dear and true friend, and nurse. I hope the Lord will reward her for her kindness to me. I feel thankful to my Heavenly Father for the many blessings he has allowed me to enjoy. Oh! Father give me more faith to believe the "Lord will provide" for all who put their trust in *him*. O, that my faith may be strengthen! May the *cloud* I so much dread break in blessings on my head. *Thou* knowest the evilness of the human heart. Father, do thou cleanse mine from all filthiness. My trust is in thee. "Lead me to the *Rock* that is higher than I."

30. For this entry Bond writes a series of double lines.
31. Cass Gover's* house.

Wed 22nd Feb.

Washington's birthday. Oh, may many of the sons of America imitate his example, be good and wise men not ashamed to own their Maker. It is raining today. Clearing off the snow which has been on the ground for some time. Had elegant sleighing several days and quite good for a week. I am sitting up today but feel far from being well. I will try and feel thankful that it is as well with me as it is. I have numerous blessings to give thanks for. Oh! that my heart may be filled with thanksgiving. I have been enjoying some nice oysters which a dear friend brought me yesterday. They really seemed to do me good. I was much amused whilst eating them; the little colored girl who waits on me stood watching me enjoy them;[32] and exclaimed "Miss Mit, your *kind* beau brought you them." But he is not a beau, only a *friend.*[33]

I have been writing to H- of La. today—hope I may be prevented from saying all I should not say and say that which is right for me to say. O that my writings may prove a blessing and not a curse! Many kind friends have been to see me since my illness, and have brought me so many nice things. The old saying and a very true one, is "*affliction* proves friends." And I have found more than I flattered myself I had.

Thursday 23rd

This is a lovely day. So warm and still out. But I can only enjoy it from my windows, as I am still in my room. Dr. Archer called this morning. He has been very attentive to me since my sickness. He and Dr. Lee attended me; he stayed all night one night and I felt so glad, for I was very ill that night. Ma & cousin Lizzie Watters sit up with me all night.

Friday 24th

This is brother's birthday—24. How time flies! I hope he will enjoy it with good Health, and God's blessing. I hope his life may be as bright as this morning.

Night, Juliet Gover spent the day with me. Cousin Cass Gover called to see me this morning, sat awhile. Cousin George Glasgow called this afternoon to see how I was. He brought me while sick a large can of oysters. I enjoyed them so much. The first I was permitted to eat. Betsy brought and stood watching me eat them. When she said "Miss Mit your kind *beau* brought you *them.*" I could not help smiling, but he is only my *friend.* Oh, *a true one.*

32. Bond refers to Betsy.

33. Bond again mentions this scene in her entry of 24 February. From these entries, it is not clear when George Glasgow gave her the oysters. Her repetition, however, indicates her feelings for her cousin, whether they were indeed platonic, as she insists, or romantic, as her friends and Betsy seem to think.

Ann Lee came home this evening. Mr. Stump brought her. Juliet called for a short while.

Sat. Feb 25th

Beautiful day. Mr. Monk a young man who professed religion at the same meeting I did, three of the number who bowed themselves before the mercy seat—have passed away. He was out in the woods cutting wood, when the lim of a tree fell on his head—killing him directly. He was a good young man. Fannie & George Archer came to tea.

Sunday 26th

Such a lovely day! no one of us to go to church. Cousin George & cousin Juliet Gover spent the afternoon.

Monday 27th

Another pretty day—so warm and bright. Lizzie Lee spent the morning. Aunt Nancy Lee came—Ma has been very sick all day.

Tuesday 28th

Beautiful Day, Aunt still with us—ma something better.

Cousin George Glasgow, Cassie Gover & Juliet called to see me; and cousin G expressed much pleasure seeing me downstairs again. I received a letter from Betty Seay.

Wednesday 29th

Spent a very pleasant day—reading, sewing and talking. Aunt Nancy left us this evening. Dr. A. took her. Juliet here for several hours.

Thursday March 1st

The first of the budding months! Lovely afternoon, very cloudy this morning. I was sick in bed till after dinner. Did not go downstairs all day. Dr. Archer took sister Fannie to Uncle Parkers. He was going to take me riding but I was not well enough to leave my room. Sallie Hendon spent the night with me. I have been reading a very interesting book called "The Methodist."[34] It is very entertaining.

Friday 2nd

Just like a spring day, so warm and bright. Dr. Lee called for a short while. Uncle Jacob and Mary came this evening. Mary is still here.[35] She will stay all night with me. She is very much like dear brother.

34. Bond refers to Miriam Fletcher's *The Methodist; or, Incidents and Characters from Life in the Baltimore Conference*, 2 vols. (New York: Derby and Jackson, 1859). The work is set in Virginia and Baltimore, Md., and is a fictional narrative of the early history of Methodism.

35. Jacob Munnikhuysen and his daughter Mary (b. 1846).

Saturday 3rd

This morning was cloudy and sunshiny, but now it is raining. Sister Fannie came home this morning. Night—I received several papers and a letter from H tonight.

Sunday 4th

Lovely day. Pa went to hear Mr. Valliant, Ma and I at home. Dr. A. called for a short time about one. Cousin George Glasgow spent the evening with me. Godfrey [Watters] and Dr. Archer here to tea. Dr. brought sister Fannie from Mrs. Archer's, she went up the evening before.

Monday 5th

A real March day, very bright, clear and windy. Cousin G. Glasgow called this morning, brought me some nice apples. Mr. Thomas Roberson here to dinner. Uncle Jim [Lee] spent the evening. I wrote to brother today. I have been thinking why it was the wind blows always so hard in March and have come to the conclusion it is because it breaks off the dead twigs and limbs of the trees and bushes, sweeps off the dead grass and so the new can sprout out better, for if we keep a rose bush trimmed up and all the decayed parts cut off it will grow and be more healthy. I think it is a very reasonable idea. It blows for some wise purpose; we all know, or the Ever Wise would not cause it to be.

Tuesday March 6 1860

Again another lovely day has dawned upon us and we are still left to enjoy the good things of life. Ma & pa have gone down this morning to see Grandma Lee, who is still lingering over the grave.

I hear the little songsters caroling their lays to the great and glorious Being who has inspired them with such musical talents. May my poor heart be lifted up, giving thanks and rejoicing for the many blessings I enjoy. How unthankful is my heart. O teach me to be thankful, my Heavenly Father.

Monday, March 12 1860

My last penning in here was Tuesday 6th. That afternoon Cousin George Glasgow came in his buggy and took me to Mr. Watters. It was the first time I had been out of the house since the 9th of Feb. We remained there till nearly five, called at the office; did not get a letter. Was quite disappointed, called at home and then went up to "Woodside," to stay all night. Remained till sunday morning. The weather was so I could not venture out of doors. Had a very pleasant visit—all so kind. I read to them "the Methodist—" Though I had read it before, I was willing to entertain others by reading it over again. Cassie Gover was there when I got there tuesday,[36] left after tea. Oh, how delightful it is to visit kind friends—and those whom we have every reason to believe love us! The book alluded to above, there are two characters, Susan & Rose. I am led to believe there are many Roses but few, very few Susans.[37]

We have had some real March weather, sunshine, thunder showers and snow storms have been its characteristics. Yesterday was quite pretty, pa went to Belair in the afternoon, heard Mr. Valliant preach to quite a full house. This morn is quite cloudy, has been raining some, quite cold.

I had a beautiful little pink given me Tuesday by Mrs. Watters, my dear friend, one who loves me next her own children, I believe.

Wednesday 14th

This is a beautiful day though the wind is blowing quite hard. Juliet R. Evans came down this morning. I had an invitation to go to Belair this afternoon but could not venture out. Lou Wyatt called for a short time; she had been to see grandma. I wrote to H.M. [Howard Munnikhuysen] and H.B. [Howard Bond] today sent the letters to Belair by Juliet Gover.

Thursday 15th

Lovely day. I have been wishing to go out of doors all day. I received some papers and a letter today from La. Mr. Hendon came after tea, set 'till bed time.

Friday March 16th

Cloudy but colder. I had an invitation to go to Mr. Watters this morning but shall have to decline, as the weather will not permit and I am not so well today.

Saturday 17th

St. Patrick's day. Very pretty and warm. Mrs. Hendon spent the evening. Mr. H. took tea; sister Fannie & Dr. Archer came after tea.

I felt so disappointed I did not get a letter from dear H- this evening.

Sunday 18th March

Sister quite sick—I'm far from well—Juliet, Bettie, Mary, & George Gover, also Juliet Evans here this morn. Pa went to Churchville to church. Fannie, John

---

36. Bond is not referring to Cousin Cass; it is not clear who this Cassie is, but likely she is a cousin.

37. In *The Methodist* Susan Allington is modest and kind. A devout Methodist, she values goodness in others and seeks to be a Christian example. Educated at home, Susan benefited from the example of her mother and developed moral and mental discipline. In contrast, Rose Carter attended a prestigious boarding school but because she did not have the advantage of a mother's example, developed little discipline. While physically beautiful, she is thoughtless and pleasure seeking.

& Edie Moores called this afternoon. Uncle Jacob M[unnikhuysen] and Peggie (his daughter) came to tea. Peggie is going to stay several days. She is very *green*.

Dr. Archer took tea.

Mon. 19th

Rainy, disagreeable day. Fannie sick abed. I laughing at Peggie's *greenness*.

I hope I feel more thankful than ever, I was brought up surrounded by christian people and had *christian parents*. What a blessing I have enjoyed all my life! Give me a thankful heart, Oh, Father in Heaven!

Tuesday 20th 1860

Bright, windy and rather warm has been the characteristics of today.

Wednesday 21

I sick abed, cold and windy. Peggie left this morning. Uncle Henry took her home. Sister Fannie went to Uncle Parkers. Yesterday I received a very nice book from Howard. How kind of him to send it to me.

Thursday

I have been sitting up today. Received two letters from the *two H's*,[38] of course I read *H.B.'s first*.

Fri. 23rd

Pretty day. Mrs. Archer, Mrs. Williams and her son made a call this afternoon. Soon after they left Cassie and Juliet came, sit til dark.

Sun. 25th

Windy; no one went from here to church. Cousin George Gover called in the morning. Cousin George Glasgow spent the evening.

Monday

I was much surprised when I woke this morning to find the ground white with snow and it snowed till about 10 o'clock.

Tuesday 27th[39]

Ma went to uncle Parker's with cousin Juliet who sent for me—but I'm not well enough to venture out, so ma went in my place. Cousin Richard [Lee] & Dr. Archer called—Ma got home about three—had not been to dinner.

---

38. Howard Bond and Munnikhuysen.

39. Bond misdates the entry as 25 March. I have corrected it here.

Wednesday 28th

Beautiful bright day, windy tho'.

Thurs. 29th

Ann Lee came home from school with Dr. Archer.

Fri. 30th

This afternoon Mr. & Mrs. Stevy Archer, & Mr. H. Stump called. Then they, Ma, pa, sister Fannie went up to Woodside to spend the evening. I was invited, but could not go—I felt very much disappointed. Wrote a letter to H-B-

Sat 31st

Lovely day. Sister Fannie & Ma went to uncle Parker's. In the afternoon Dr. Archer came, took me riding, went to the office and to uncle Parker's. Got home to tea. I enjoyed the drive very much. I had not taken one for a long while before.

Sun. 1st of April

Ma & Pa went to Belair to church—heard Mr. Greenfield preach. I have not been to church for three months today. Rained little this evening. "*April showers will bring forth May flowers.*"

Monday 2nd

Juliet spent the afternoon with me; tried to teach her how to make tatten. But could not.

Tuesday 3rd

Busy all this morning writing to the *two Howards.* Ma spent the day at uncle Parker's. Cousin Betsy worse. Grandma about the same. I feel very badly have the Neuralgia in my head, in fact all through my body.

Wednesday 4th

I was quite sick this morning, dreadful headache, feel better this afternoon. It is now four o'clock and raining. I am glad to see it for the grain needed it badly to sprout. The fields commence to look a little green. I have some wild flowers of the forest. I have sent to the office, hope I shall get a letter from H-B- Mrs. Hendon took tea here. Did not get any letters.

Thursday 5th

Clear, bright and windy. Juliet spent the afternoon. Was trying to finish a collar before she went home. Teasing me about Howard, called me Mrs. Howard Bond.

Friday 6th

I have felt sad nearly all day—Why, I cannot tell. Ma & pa went to uncle P-'s a little while this afternoon. Ann Lee up at cousin Juliet's, I home by myself. I do love my home! How hard it will be to part with all those dear objects, which has greeted my vision for nearly 22 years. Will the good Lord direct my steps that I may not wander in the forbidden paths? Leave me not to my own desires, but my will be thine, O my Father in Heaven!

Saturday 7th April

Lovely day—quite cool tho. Ma & Ann Lee have gone to uncle Jim's—will take dinner and come home to tea. I been planting out some bushes this afternoon—Charles [Lee] and I. Did not get any letter—*felt so* disappointed.[40]

Sunday 8th

Rained all the morning, real April weather, cloudy and sunshiny. Pa went to see grandma this afternoon. She's about the same.

Monday 9th

Rained nearly all this morning. Juliet sent for me to go stay while her mother is in Baltimore. But I felt too sick to go—sent the pony back. Will go up this afternoon if able. Looks like it might rain soon.

Wed. 11th

I went up to Woodside on monday afternoon as I promised. Tuesday it rained all day. I felt so very sad; the wind whistled so mournfully around the house and seemed to forebode something sad. Several times I said to Juliet, the wind whistled right through my heart. That evening Juliet received a letter from her father stating the death of aunt Mary Blanche, which took place Monday 6 o'clock in the morning, April 9, 1860. It was the greatest shock I ever had. She leaves three little helpless babes and a husband to mourn her loss. I understand she died very happy, leaving her children in the hands of God. May the good Lord watch over those orphaned ones. He for some wise purpose has seen best to call their mother away from them, will take care of them. "God moves in mysterious ways His wonders to perform." May it prove a blessing to others. She was buried tuesday afternoon at "Lowden Park," Balto. Today has been a rainy one, until about four. It cleared off beautifully.

---

40. Bond pays close attention to the frequency of Howard's letters. As Stowe in his study of southern courtship explains, "the number and timing of letters preoccupied the lovers. How frequently letters should be written, and who owed what to whom, became an index to other, less tangible obligations" (*Intimacy and Power*, 91).

Dr. Archer came for me. I came home soon after tea. Peggie Bond was here. I came in and nearly the first thing I asked was "how's grandma?" The answer was "She has *gone.*" Although I had been expecting it hourly, yet it was a sad reality. She suffered till the last.

Was more than willing, was *anxious.*[41]

Thursday 12th

Peggie stayed all night with me. Beautiful day. I walked to the gate this morning. I received a letter from brother tonight, one also from Howard.

Friday 13th

I followed the mortal remains of dear grandma to her last resting place. She had selected the text of 119 Psalm 75 ver. I know O Lord that thy judgments are right and that thou in faithfulness has afflicted me. Mr. Keech preached. Mr. Jones, the pastor at the "Trap" church read part of the service at the house. Poor uncle Henry, I pitied him; he has truly lost his best friend and I may say only one. It was quite a large funeral.[42]

Sunday 15th

Very cold, really wintry weather. Lovely day. Sister Fannie's birthday (26). Pa, Ann Lee and I went to Belair this morning. Heard Rev. Mr. Valiant preach a beautiful sermon from Exodus 20 chap. 8–11 verse. Many were there. First time I have been to meeting since New Year afternoon. Many seemed glad to see me out again. Godfrey Watters came home to dinner with us. Peggie, cousin George Gover, cousin George Glasgow and Dr. Archer, Juliet, Bob and Mary Gover came. Not all stayed to tea. Cousin George Glasgow said he often thought seriously of the good things I had said to him, and I really believe he wished to be a christian. Oh! Heavenly Father remove the obstacle, whatever it may be, which keeps him from Thee. O, that I may be constrained by thy Holy Spirit to say some words in season. "A word in season, how good it is."

Monday 16th

Disagreeable rainy day. Not well—neither one of us well.

Tuesday 17th

Cleared off about 8 this morning. Mrs. Judge Archer and George Vanbiber spent several hours with us. Dear old lady, what a dear friend she has been to us.

41. Bond is writing about her paternal grandmother, Mary Howard Lee.

42. The service was held at the Episcopal church. Bond's Uncle Henry Lee was forty-six years old and unmarried. After his mother's death, he moved in with his younger brother, James Lee, a farmer, and his wife, Delia.

May the Lord reward her in the next world. Lovely afternoon. Sister Fannie sick abed. We are now seated in our room upstairs, sister F- being in bed, Ma seated near sewing. I am sitting at the front window, my favorite place. I have seen the mailboy go up. Hope he has some letters for me. Night—Dr. came about five and took me riding. I enjoyed it very much. He remained till after 9 o'clock.

Wednesday 18th

Lovely day—Juliet here for a while this morn. Fannie Moores & Laura Moores spent the day.[43] Aunt Dillie here this morning. I fitted a dress for her.

Thursday 19th

George Vanbiber called this morning, Mary and Delia Archer, Peggie Bond & Dr. Archer spent the evening. Dr. A. took sister Fannie riding. Rained after supper.

Friday morning 20th

Very cloudy and disagreeable. Mr. Stump called this afternoon. Dr. Archer brought sister Fannie home from uncle Jim's.

Saturday 21st

I am very sick today, have a bad cold and cough. Lovely day. Cousin George called for a short time this morn. Dr. Archer took sister Fannie to uncle Parker's home to dinner. Cousin George took her to John Moores—spent the evening. Peggie and Gerard Gover here little while this afternoon. I fully expected letter from H. this evening, was disappointed. I will trust all in the hands of a Wise Parent. He will not leave me or forsake me.

Sunday 22nd

Cloudy, rained some. Fannie & cousin G- went to churchville, heard Mr. Hicks. Up to Watters in the afternoon, heard Mr. Fergerson—liked him much. Went to cousin Gerards to tea. Heard Bennie Lee had joined church—the first of April. Glad to hear the good news. May the Holy spirit be with her at all times, In affliction, and trials and keep her *faithful* to the end.

Monday 23rd

Cloudy—looks like rain. Pa went to Balto in the cars this morn—sister with cousin George Gover, in his carriage. I still am suffering. Have a bad cold, my breast—hurts me very much. This afternoon Pink Norris & Mr. Hooks of Towsentown called. I was far from being well, I did not see them, so they left and went up to Woodside.

---

43. Laura is Fannie's* fifteen-year-old sister.

Tuesday 24th

Fannie and pa came this evening in the cars. Cousin George brought her from Churchville home. She then went to Uncle Jim's to tea. The "evening star" was attached to the Moon. Very singular and beautiful sight. I received a very pretty dress for a present tonight.

Wednesday 25th

Dr. Archer came, spent the evening, also Phoebe Webster and H. Stump. We had quite a severe snow storm tonight. It is very cold. Dr. A. is going to stay all night. I received a letter from H-, which had been missent to Boston.

Tuesday 26th

Very pretty day. I spent the day at Woodside. Was treated coolly. Peggie [Bond] and Lizzie Watters came over this afternoon. Peggie went up to Woodside for me. Had a pleasant walk down through the woods. She said she is going to tell Howard what would cure me. I reckon she won't.

Friday 27th

Lovely day, cold. Lizzie and Peggie left afternoon. Sister Fannie went with P-, stayed all night.

Saturday 28th

Cloudy morning, something warmer than yesterday. Mr. Stump called this afternoon, sister Fannie took tea at Woodside. Mr. Isaac Evans came home with her. I received a letter from H[oward] M[unnikhuysen] tonight.

Sunday 29th

I wanted to go to church very much. Was not able—pa went, liked Mr. Strayer very much. George Archer, Peggie and cousin John Moores took tea here. We are having beautiful nights. How much I want to see somebody. O Father thy will be done. O that I may put my entire trust in Thee.

Monday Apr 30th

Lovely day, rather cool. I was digging in the yard this morning. Walked up Woodside this afternoon to see the little children. Dear little Zach and Juliet are there now.[44] Juliet Gover went to town today.

Tuesday May 1st 1860

Very cloudy disagreeable morning. I feel quite badly the weather is against me. I have just finished a letter to Howard Bond.

---

44. The children of Mary Blanche, whose death Bond records on 11 April.

Wednesday evening, 2nd May

Cousin George Glasgow called yesterday morning, commenced raining before he left, continued all day and night and all this day—is still at it. John Peca Dallam came yesterday about five, is still here. I have been quite sick all day, have been in bed till now. I am now seated at my window fronting the road. The lane is nearly covered with water. The apple tree in the yard looks perfectly lovely, covered with so many pink blossoms. I hear the little chicks crying in the yard. How wet they must be. I hear sister Fannie's voice and John P's in the parlor. I wonder what she has found interesting to talk to him about all day.

I wish I had some dear friend up here to have a confidential chat with. How nice it would be. I feel like talking over the things lies nearest my heart. I have been thinking much today of the past. How it swept across my mind. Sometimes hurriedly, till I would have to stop and recall my thoughts, to make them of sense. And then again scenes which have long sped by would rise up before my mind's eye, pass slowly on like a moving panorama. O those happy visions of the past, of early girlhood, can ye ever be erased from memory's tablet? No never. I was thinking today of the changes since this time last year, of the friends and dear ones I had been called upon to relinquish. About one year since Helen was consigned to the cold silent grave, there to sleep till that Great Resurrection Morn. One year, resident of the tomb. And I am one year nearer Eternity.

How oft do I think perhaps before another year I too shall be sleeping under the green turf. But not dead, only sleeping, my poor body shall only rest in that narrow house, my spirit, shall it not be with the blessed? God grant that when this earthly tenement shall be dissolved—I may have a house not made with hands but dwell in the mansion prepared for me. My prayers have been answered, my faith is stronger. O, that it may be my constant prayer, "Lord increase my faith." When I get to thinking of things of a perplexing nature, and I find my thoughts debating how shall I do—what will be the consequence of such & such things that I now can understand, I try to pray for more faith—that the Great Being who seest all things, knowest all things will direct all right. O that I could act with more faith, could put my trust more explicitly in His love. "Let not your heart be troubled, ye believe in me, believe also in him who sent me."

This portion of scripture is often forcibly brought to my mind and this also. "They that put their trust in the Lord shall be as Mount Zion." Oh! that my prayers may be with stronger faith.

May 7th

Cousin Josh left Thursday morning, cleared off. In the afternoon Ma rode up to "Woodside." Dr. Archer and cousin George spent the evening. I got several letters and a paper from the office. One stating brother had left La. Lovely night. Friday beautifully warm. I was out in the yard nearly all the morning fixing up the bushes. Mrs. B[lanche] Archer made a call, cousin George took sister Fannie to "Hazle Dell."

I walked down to "Sleepy Hollow," found Miss Adie Allen there, stayed all night—next day at dinner, Anne Smithson & Nattie Chues came, I came home late in the afternoon, found aunt Dillie & *brother* here. He had come home unexpectedly, of course *we* were *so* glad to see him. Jimmy Watters sent me a little present—*a rabbit*. How my heart ached that night. Oh! Father in Heaven, not my will but thine be done.[45]

Sunday

Splendid day—warm & clear, brother went to Churchville to church, took dinner at uncle Jim's. Mr. Archer brought sister Fannie home, took ma up to go in the stage this morning, aunt Nancy Lee called—Dr. Archer spent the evening. Ann Lee went to school this morning. It is lovely out—so warm—the bees & birds are seeming to enjoy themselves.

I shall go to uncle Jim's today if nothing happens. I feel sick & sad. Oh! for more *true faith*, Lord increase my faith.

Wednesday 9th

Mr. Stump called monday morning & Otha Lee. Brother took me to uncle Jim's after he came back from Belair. Got there to dinner. I spent a very pleasant afternoon. I suffered a good deal with neuralgia at night. I hope I spoke *some* encouraging words to aunt Dillie. She was so kind and sympathizing. She allowed me to sleep as long in the morning as I chose. I was helping her about a dress. She gave me a present which was very acceptable. May the Good Lord reward her!

I came home from Uncle Jim's yesterday evening. Walked. Met cousin Cass Gover, stopped, had a chat, went on up to Woodside, set a little while, came home to tea. This morning is very disagreeable, foggy and cloudy. Cousin George and sister Fannie have gone to the "Rock Spring" today to confirmation; several are to be confirmed—Lou Wyatt and Annie and Fannie Moores, Alice Lee and others. I miss Ma very much indeed. I feel very sad, have felt so for a long time. Why is it? Will the good Lord direct my ways and make me his. I often think it would be a great privilege to die, to lay this poor weary body down to sleep in the quiet grave.

45. Likely Bond is upset after hearing William's tales of Louisiana and of life with the Bond family. His experiences only make her more hesitant to leave Maryland. For more discussion on this topic, see also the introduction and John Munnikhuysen's letter to William in app. 1.

For O, I am so weary. This life has very little attraction for me. What is there in the world worth living for? But I pray to be contented to remain till *my Father* see fit to take me *Home,* Sweet Home. A home in Heaven, the *thought* is bliss; what must be the reality.

I often think the sands of my life is nearly run out—that I shall soon be released from the trials and temptations of this evil world, and then again I think perhaps there is a field in the Lord's vineyard for me to cultivate my talents. Oh! Father, thou who seeth the secret workings of my heart, knoweth all the evil of it, guide me, let me never be left to my own sinful desires but rather cleave to thy precepts. I know my afflictions are for my own good, that every pain and ache are intended for my especial good. Oh! that I may have grace to help bear them with even thanksgiving. For the Lord loveth those he chasteneth.

Thursday 10th
Raining very hard. Mr. Evans here for a short while.

Friday 11th
Still raining, has been since Wednesday. Mr. Evans called for a little while this morning. I made a bonnet for myself, which I think very pretty and very becoming.

Saturday May 12th
Another rainy and disagreeable day has passed away. Our single preacher, Mr. Stayer came this evening, will remain over night. I like him very much. He reminds me of Lawrence Thomas. I received a letter from New York and one from La. this evening.[46]

Sunday 13th
Cleared off about dinner time. Mr. Stayer left for his appointment about nine. This afternoon we had one of the most severe storms we've had for a long time. Our lane looked most like rowing a boat down it. Dr. Archer & Godfrey [Watters] spent the evening here. Sister Fannie went up to "Hazle Dell" this evening and I fear she got caught in the rain.

Monday 14th
This is a right pretty day. It clouds up some times and I fear for more rain. H- writes it is very dry in Louisiana. I am housekeeper now. Cousin Juliet took little Zach back to Balto. this morning—poor little *motherless children.* Uncle Jim, Mr. Evans & Robert came after tea—had a pleasant chat together.

---

46. The letter from New York was perhaps from Jimmy Cole, who was studying at Princeton and whom Bond mentions on 16 January 1860.

Tuesday 15th

Lovely day, rather cool for the season. Betsy & I went up in the woods this morning—got some dirt for my border. I fixed it—dug a circle for flowering beans & planted them and sowed my flower seed. Ma came home this afternoon from Balto, *sad & tired*. She did not enjoy her visit as she anticipated. Mr. Stump brought her from Belair. I was truly glad to see her. I missed her so much—no one to talk with.

Wednesday 16th

Beautiful day—Mr. E[vans] came down for a short while this morning.

Thursday 17th

Annie Smithson spent yesterday afternoon here. I was suffering with a terrible sick headache. I had to leave the tea table and go to bed. Dr. Archer called this morning. Brother and I were invited to Sleepy Hollow to spend this evening. I did not feel well enough to go, brother went. I received a letter from H[oward]M[unnikhuysen]. It is quite delightful to receive his letters, just as though he was talking to me—so full of humor and still, sober sense.

Friday 18th[47]

Looked very much like rain this morning—afternoon, has cleared off, birds singing gaily. I am not well.

Saturday 19th

Pleasant cool day, clear. Dr. Lee took dinner, looks badly. Dr. Archer, uncle Jim, Mr. Evans & Bob called. This afternoon I walked up to Woodside for a while. Mr. Isaac Evans there. Felt very tired when I got home.

Sunday 20th

Beautiful sunshiny day. I was sick in bed till after dinner. Juliet came down this morning for a while. Willie Smithson,[48] cousin Jim and George Glasgow and cousin Sallie Lee, Mary Lee and Clarence spent the evening here. Cousin George Gover, Mr. I. Evans and Bob called after tea; also Dr. Archer.

Monday 21st

This has been a beautiful day till near sunset when it clouded up, looks gusty. I have felt badly all day.

47. Bond initially headed the entry as "Wednesday" but corrected herself above the line.

48. William Smithson, twenty-two years old, was the son of a Harford farmer who in 1860 owned property valued at eleven thousand dollars. In a later entry, Bond says that he is deaf and dumb. She also mentions several Smithsons, likely Willie's relatives. She does not, however, mention his sisters, Louisa and Juliana. The Smithsons are Bond's paternal relatives.

Tuesday 22nd

This is Howard's birthday—21. He is a man in years now. May the Lord watch over and shield him from temptations he is surrounded with. I promised to pray for him today, more than ever. My mind has been, and is now distressed about his going to his father's to live.[49] I fear if he does he will be ruined—for oh, his father does not respect God's holy commands, no not even the sabbath is allowed to be kept. Lord open thou the eyes of the blind that they may see themselves as they are by nature, and by practice.

My Heavenly Father thou knowest all things—what is best for *us,* direct us in *all things,* for thy name sake. Juliet Gover and Willie Smithson spent the evening with me. He is deaf and dum. What blessings we enjoy! Blessed with speech, hearing and sight! We cannot be half thankful for those mercies. I got a letter and paper from La.

Wednesday 23rd

Another lovely day has passed—so pleasantly too. I spent most of the morning with ma—talking—may I profit by her gentle councils and advice! Willie called for a little while this morning. Mr. & Mrs. Watters, Bettie & July Beck took tea. Fannie & John Moores called. I got a dear letter from my old grandma. I prize her letters very much indeed. The weather has been so fine, the sky so clear and bright today.

Friday 25th

Quite cool but pleasant. I took tea at Woodside. Juliet walked home with me, found Mary Lee and Ann Lee here, come home from school.

Saturday 26th

Had very much the appearance of rain this morning—did not till in the afternoon. Had magnificent sunset. Pa came from Balto & brought some nice *strawberries.*

Sunday 27th

Cloudy morning, I went to Belair with Pa & Ma—heard 'our young' preacher preach a very excellent sermon—from John's first epistle & 28 verse. "Behold the Lamb of God who taketh away the sin of the world." Came home to dinner after which Jimmy Moores brought sister Fannie home; & Lou Wyatt came with cousin George. Dr. Archer also took tea here. Rained & Jimmy had to stay all night.

---

49. Howard had been living in a boardinghouse in Houma, the largest town near his father's plantation.

Monday 28th

Lovely day. Dr. Cadden, came we went—that is Lou, sister Fannie, *Cadden*, and myself—drove out to Miss Woolsey's—got some flowers—had a charming time, met there Mrs. Williams. Godfrey & Dr. Archer called, took tea, just from the fishing party at the mouth of Deer Creek.

Tuesday 29th

Another exquisite day—Lou, Dr. Cadden & I took a walk directly after breakfast, enjoyed it very much. He left directly after. I took a *Colt* and prepared to go to Mr. Watters. Lou and cousin George went in a buggy, Dr. Archer and Fannie in one also. I on horseback—perfectly *independent*. I enjoyed my ride very much indeed—all seemed so glad to see me there. Took dinner and then a nap—went over to Dr. Archer's, spent a very pleasant *evening*. Dr. A. brought me home then went back after sister Fannie.

Wednesday 30th

Cloudy most of the day—rained near night—slightly. Lou & I took a walk up in the wood. Lou, Fannie, George Glasgow, Dr. A., brother & myself took dinner at uncle Jim's, went to "Oak Spring" to tea, all excepting Dr. A. Sally Gover is staying there. I remained all night. Cousin Sallie and I talked after we retired till very late.

Thursday 31st

Beautiful morning. Lou, Sister F., Dr. A., cousin George, went to Mr. Thomas Archer's, took dinner, went to Uncle Parker's to tea. I walked up to Woodside for a little while. Cousin Juliet came down this afternoon, sit about an hour. Bob brought me a letter and a box of cake all the way from *Louisiana*. (He brought it from the office.) It was a piece of H–'s birthday cake. I enjoyed it very much. Oh, how my heart has been saddened this evening. My heart aches—what shall I do? I must not write the words in my heart. Oh! what a sinner I am. How filthy my heart is! Will I ever be what I should be! Sure enough—will a man ever be benefited by me. "Bless the man I get"—"he better tie a stone around his neck, and jump into the river." Perhaps he had—no, he better never marry *me*. Am I then *really so bad?* Can I make *one* happy? The question remains to be answered.[50] The last few days have been pleasant—but I feel so *hurt*, so *sad*, I can not look forward to a happy tomorrow. And what originated such feelings? A few flowers—*my pets*—flowers I love and feel they are at *least* my friends.

---

50. In the nineteenth century, single women frequently had doubts about living up to their future husbands' expectations. They feared that after marriage, their husbands would be disappointed if they could not uphold the idealized image of a wife. See Rothman, *Hands and Hearts*, 98–99.

CHAPTER FOUR

"I Have Released Him"

Friday 1st June

We went to the mouth of "Deer Creek" to fish—Lou, sister Fannie, myself, Dr. A, cousin George, Mr. Stump, Jimmy Moores, and Archer Jarrett. Had a very pleasant time. I went with the Dr., stopped at Mr. Archer's to see a patient. The scenery along the Creek is magnificent. So picturesque—so many beautiful little wild flowers.

Saturday 2nd

Beautiful day. Lou and brother took a drive. Juliet here for a little while. Mr. Stump called. Lou, sister Fannie, brother and Dr. Archer went to Mr. Webster's, spent the evening.

Sunday 3rd

Brother was the only one went to church. He heard Stevy Archer from the south, preach. . . . . Lou Wyatt left this evening.[1]

Mon. 4th

Miss Hannah Archer and Dr. spent the evening, had to remain all night—it rained.

Tuesday.

He took sister Fannie up to Mooreland to go to Balto next day. Friday Emma Valliant, Laura Moores and Ann Lee come from school.[2] Saturday. They spent the afternoon with Aunt Dillie; went up to Woodside after tea. Sunday—lovely morning. I expect to go to church in Belair, from there to cousin Rachel Wilson's.[3]

---

1. The ellipses here could indicate that Bond is leaving out information about her brother and Lou Wyatt's relationship. They would later marry.

2. Ann Lee's school friends are the daughters, respectively, of the Methodist minister, Reverend Valliant and cousin Aphia Moores. Laura Moores was fifteen years old.

3. In 1860 Rachel Wilson, sixty-four years old, was single, lived alone, and owned property worth ten thousand dollars.

June 10th

I went to cousin Rachel's as expected. Had a very pleasant visit. It was a beautiful cool day. Hallie Wilson spent the day with us. I walked part of the way home with her.

Tuesday 12th

Was a beautiful day. I took a walk to the post office—from there to St. Mary's church. Walked through the grave yard—was very much frightened at the scream of a peacock. I did not get over the fright for some time. In the afternoon cousin and I called at Mrs. Stevy Archer's—she was not at home, called at Charles Lee's, then at Dr. Lee's, then came on home.

Wed. 13th[4]

Beautiful. I received a note from Mr. Ralph Wilson to take a drive. I was engaged and could not go. Cousin & I went to Aberdeen in the evening, from there around to Dr. Wilson's—had a pleasant drive, did not get out at the Dr.'s. Aunt Mary Evans' little Blanche died today.[5] Dear little thing, it is better off.

Thursday

I walked out after breakfast—around the road towards Mrs. McGovern's, gathered some wild flowers, throwed them over the fence to Mr. W. but he did not find them.[6] Dr. Culligan spent the evening with us.

Friday

Mr. R. Wilson came over, asked me if I was engaged for the evening. I was not, so about four we started, drove down to Otta Point—beautiful drive—some parts of the road we saw the Bay distinctly, even the boats sailing gracefully over it. I went to Dr. Wilson's to tea. Met Mr. Brand, the Episcopal minister there—liked him. It was so late and damp I remained all night. Cousin Annie Lee got there some time in the night. Next day we concluded to spend the day there, and then go to cousin R's in the evening, but rain came up, continued it till near sunset. Cousin Annie went over after tea. I remained all night—as it was too damp.

Next morning Ralph drove me on. I went with Cousin R- to Abington, heard Mr. Strayer preach a good sermon—returned to dinner, after which cousin Annie, Cassie, Dr. Wilson, Mr. Fred Morrison, and Phill Lettager spent the evening. I

---

4. This and the following two entries are written in one entry and likely at the same time.

5. Bond possibly refers to her mother's sister, whom she usually calls "Aunt Mary," without indicating her married name.

6. Here she likely refers to Ralph Wilson, who is mentioned in her previous and subsequent entries.

liked Mr. Morrison, very much. I saw in the Sun the marriage of aunt Mary Lennele to Mr. L. Bridge on the 10th. On the 14th her daughter Mary Cass was married to Mr. Ellers—a very worthy young man. Two marriages and a death in the family in one week.

Monday 18th

I came home this morning in cousin Rachel's carriage with Ann Lee. Was very tired when I got here. Sister Fannie as usual away from home. This evening Rev. Mr. Keech brought cousin Betsy Moores.[7] She spent the evening, he stayed a little while. Lizzie & Jimmy Lee took tea, Lizzie stayed with me.[8] We walked up to Woodside for a while. Mrs. Rodgers and children are there. Mr. Evans walked home with me.

Tuesday June 19th

Has been raining nearly all day. Lizzie had to stay another night. Very heavy gust tonight, such vivid lightening, wind blew very hard before tea, and I expect hail fell, as the air is considerably cooler than it was. I received a letter from H. stating he could not come on this summer. It is all his father's doings, I know. He cannot leave his mother alone. Oh! how my heart aches. I knew it would never be. I have acted wrong. I deserve more than this, much more. But I do hope I shall be enabled to act better in the future. Strengthen my weak faith, O my Heavenly father! I will free him from this engagement. He *shall* at least *feel free*. I did not know until now how much I loved him, how much I wanted to see him—how much I trusted him. But the dream is past, I am awakening to the *sad reality*—we must be only friends.

He shall not know how much I suffer—Perhaps it may teach us both *good lessons*. Lord grant we may be more devoted christians. It is a great struggle—a great trial but I see *now* it is a *duty*. I will try and perform it to the best of my ability. Lord assist me! Oh! my poor heart—why beat so sadly—hope thou in God.[9]

Wednesday 20th

Another day to be thankful for. Lizzie left early this morn—uncle Parker came for her. They wanted me to go home with them. I am too sad, too sick—I am suffering terrible this morning with my shoulders. But I want to suffer if it will pu-

7. Elizabeth Moores was sixty-one years old.

8. Jimmy was Lizzie's* thirteen-year-old brother.

9. When Howard left for Louisiana on 25 May 1858, he promised Bond that he would return to Maryland in two years. Bond's reaction to his failure to keep this promise echoes the findings of Stowe that deception (perceived or real) was the stumbling block of many courtships. In her entry on 21 June she explicitly states her belief that Howard deceived her. Bond's plan to hide her feelings from Howard also supports Stowe's observation that letters written in response to a lover's deception were marked by an aloof tone and sought to "make personal injury into a moral lesson" (*Intimacy and Power*, 66).

rify me for Heaven. Night. O! my sad sad heart. I have wept & prayed for strength—for guidance—to do all right—to act as a christian. Oh! my Heavenly Father, leave me not to my own sinful lusts.

Thursday 21st

It has been very cold today—enough so for a fire—rained too. Housecleaning. Cousin Lee Hall from St. Louis, and Henry Hall, paid us a visit this morning. I had not seen cousin Lee since I was a little child. I have been suffering all day. Not only my body's sick, but my heart. O, how it throbs, and aches! The words "Howard has deceived me" rings continuously in my ears. I trusted so—I could not doubt him. When others would say "he is not a-coming," "I know his father will not let him come," I laughed, I knew he would. I never for one moment doubted his word. For had he not for two long years promised he would this spring, if he was alive. Did I not know if he lived he would be to see me this June. How vain! O my sad, sad heart was all *thy trust!* I am *deceived!* Those bitter words—they sting and pierce my heart through and through. But I must bear it—the world must not—shall not know anything of this. O! that I could cover him from blame entirely. O, the pleasant anticipations I have enjoyed—I would say to myself—Howard will accompany me now—He will admire this dress—I shall read this book to him, We will enjoy such walks together. He will admire those flowers in my plot—H will enjoy the same sermons I do. And so many other pleasures. And now, vain hopes where have ye gone! Fled—left this heart mangled & torn by fates adverse winds. "He tempers the wind to the shorn lamb." Oh! that I may "breath sweetness out of woe." I feel it has been for my own good. I have been chastened by the Lord, so may I bear it without sin, "Lord thou art my helper." Oh how the promises of our blessed Lord comes as "peace branches from above to cheer our sinsick and sorrowful hearts!" "Help us to number our days that we may apply our hearts unto wisdom." "Lo! I am with you always, even unto the end of the world."

Friday 22nd

Very beautiful day, very cool. Ann Lee came home this evening.

Saturday 23rd

Cool, but bright. I have been suffering all day with Neuralgia. My heart still so sad. The very birds seem to mock me with their joyful songs. Things have lost their interest to me. O! that I may see all things work together for good.

Sunday 24th

All have gone to church excepting Ann Lee and myself. I am suffering too much to go. Godfrey called at the gate for me to go with them. This is a lovely morning. It is quite cold though for this season of the year. I feel so sad. There is such a weight on my heart when I get up in the morning. It seems as though I could not go through another day. Howard is the first and last thought I have. It seems like a dreadful dream; and yet I know it is a reality. I believe it has happened for *good*. Oh that I may have grace to bear it patiently!

I asked direction from above; and I want to have faith to believe God has directed all things well. Night—I walked up to Woodside with Ann Lee for a short while, came back to tea found Dr. Archer here—then soon after John Rodgers came—stayed till after ten. Rev. Mr. Poysel preached in Belair this morning—a young man—nephew of the Rev. Poysel of the M-E- church. Say he preached an excellent sermon, his third one, I believe.[10]

Monday 25th

Beautiful day—very pleasant. Pa took Ann Lee back to school very early this morn—I went also—got Dr. Daner to draw two teeth for me. Suffered good deal afterwards with my face—the gums bled all day. In the afternoon Ralph Wilson called to see me—wanted to take me home with him. But it did not suit me to leave just now.

Tuesday 26th

Cousins Cass & Sallie Gover called this morning, sit for a little while. I got my magazine. How pleasant "Harper" is after a busy day, to sit down and be so agreeably entertained is a treat these warm days. For the weather is quite warm now.

Wednesday 27th

Juliet and cousin Sallie called in the carriage to take me a riding. We went to Miss Woolsey's first to get some flowers—got some lovely ones. Went to Robersons store—from there to Churchville. Got a letter from Mifflin. Then to cousin Cass Lee's, found her better. She has been very ill. Called at uncle Parker's. Juliet invited Lizzie to come to a little company she had after tea. I got home just as they finished dinner, found Lizzie Watters here. Glad to see her. It rained towards night. Dr. Archer came to tea. Lizzie Lee came soon after tea, she, cousin Lizzie & brother, walked up to Woodside, Dr. took me in his buggy. Spent quite a pleasant evening. I danced three sets. I do not feel that I have committed any sin by it. If I have I pray for forgiveness and a sense of my wrong. Got home between one & two.

Thursday 28th

Very warm day—Lizzie Lee left soon after breakfast. I have been suffering with headache nearly all day.

10. John Poisal, likely the young preacher Bond mentions, became chaplain of the U.S. House of Representatives in 1877.

I finished a letter to H- telling him he was free. O! I hope I've done right. Father direct me in *all things*. Mr. Watters took tea, then took Lizzie home. I do love her dearly, she is such a lovely character.

Friday 29th

Another warm day—Dr. Archer called this afternoon for me to go to Mrs. Archer's. I could not leave. He & I paid our party call at Woodside. After tea Ma rode up there and sit awhile—brother went for her. I was all alone. How I wished for H- what a nice walk we could have had. My how long it has been since we had a long talk! More than *two long years*. How long will it be before we do. But I have released him.

Saturday 30th

This is a lovely night—Ma & I have been seated in the parlor for some time enjoying delightful breezed and magnificent moon light. Dr. A. brought sister Fannie home about ten tonight. I was invited to Dr. Parker's, did not go, too warm to ride on horseback. Did not get a letter tonight, was much disappointed, but why? I ask myself. I have given up *all* claims.

Sunday 1st of July 1860

Rained part of the day—cousin George Glasgow came this morning—would have taken me to church but it rained. After dinner he took me to Watters' meeting—got there too soon—went up to Mr. Wattters, stayed till time for preaching. Mr. Britten was there—told us about old Jimmy Stevenson getting married. He has his *fifth wife*. Married Miss Rutledge, only been acquainted seven weeks and two days from the time he went to see her till the day they were married. Mr. Britten preached from 12 ch Math, 42 ver. After church we went to uncle Jim's to tea.

Monday 2nd

Rained part of the day—sister Fannie & Dr. A- went up to Mrs. L. Archer's. Quite pleasant today.

Tuesday 3rd

Howard M[unnikhuysen] came just as we were finishing dinner—he is such a nice fellow. I love him dearly. He and I took a nice walk down to "my tree." Had a nice chat together about old school times. He and brother walked up to Woodside after tea. I remained home. No letter again this evening. What can it mean—I'm very sad—"why why my heart is sadness."

Wednesday 4th

Raining some this morning. Fishing and Rocks parties today. I took a ride on horseback this evening, went to the post office, did not get any letters. Was very tired when I returned. Had not been on a horse for some time. I enjoyed a feast of good things tonight. About 9 o'clock I was attracted towards the west by a comet. It is not very bright yet but still approaching earth. It is, I believe, said to be the Charles the fifth comet. In the North was to be seen beautiful "Northern Lights" and at Mr. Brown's (over the Creek) and at cousin George Gover's beautiful fireworks and moon rising at the same time. It was indeed grand.

Thursday 5th

How differently has this day been spent to what this day last year—and great difference in the weather too. It was so cold the 5th of July 1859 we had to have a fire in the parlor.[11] Today has been very warm tho a delightful breeze blowing most of the time. I started from home about half-past nine on horse back—went to uncle Parker's took dinner—about five Lizzie Lee, uncle Jim [Lee] & myself started off—called to see cousin Cass Lee—sit a while, then to cousin George Glasgow's. I got some wine to drink which made me sick. I feel now very sick. Uncle Jim waited on me home, took tea. I am very fond of riding on horseback.

July 6th

Mrs. Evans & the two children spent the day with us. I received a letter from *Howard* this morn. I've felt so sad all day, partly owing perhaps to my indisposition.

Saturday 7th

Sick a bed most of the day—feel very bad.

Sunday

Sick still but would not allow ma to remain from church on my account—she & pa went, also brother. Dr. A. came after tea. Aunt Nancy Lee very ill this morning, little easier this eve—Dr. left to sit up with her—cousin George Gover also here for a while.

Monday 9th

I am very sick today—Dr. Lee to see me this morning. Said it was a nervous spell—Oh, he doesn't know what my feelings have been the last two or three weeks. No wonder I'm sick. My heart has been for along time. O that I may say in truth "Not my will O Lord but thine be done." He said I ought to go to the springs—yes to cure a diseased heart & mind—no that will not cure me. I have been lying in my bed today reading "old letters." What changes have been wrought since they were penned! I have laid aside one, to make a note of it in my next let-

11. This entry shows Bond as a reader of her own diary. Before writing, she read her entry from the same date, one year earlier. Her previous entry established the topic for this one, in which she contrasts her present circumstance to that of one year ago.

ter to H-. I received a very beautiful bouquette from Sallie Webster this morning—How pleasant it is to be remembered when one is sick! And especially kind
words, O they sooth the heart and whisper "Peace be still."

> How softly on the bruised breast
>   A word of kindness falls,
> And to the dry and parched soul
>   The moistening tear-drops calls;
> O, if they knew, who tread the earth,
>   Mid sorrow, grief and pain,
> The power a word of kindness hath,
>   'Twas paradise again.
> The weakest and the poorest may
>   The simple pittance give,
> And bid delight to withered hearts
>   Return again and live.
> Oh, what is life, if love be lost!
>   If man's unkind to man—
> Or what the heaven that wofts beyond
>   This brief and mortal span!
> As stars upon the tranquil sea
>   In mirrored glory shine;
> So words of kindness in the heart
>   Reflect the source divine;
> Oh then be kind, whoe'er thou art
>   That breathest mortal breath,
> And it shall brighten all thy life
>   And sweeten even death.

Tuesday 10th

Beautiful day—I feel better, was downstairs little while. I have much to be
thankful for. So many mercies—so many blessings.

Wednesday 11th

I feel very weak, my eyes are very painful.[12] Cousin Cass Gover spent the
evening here. H- Munnikhuysen & Jimmy Moores called—then went to uncle
Parker's to take tea. Cousin Juliet & Mr. Evans came after tea—poor cousin, how
she grieves at the loss of her "dear George."[13] Lord comfort and help her to bear
this trial.

12. Bond's neuralgia caused pain in her facial muscles.
13. Bond refers to the death of Juliet Gover's infant son.

Thursday 12th

Mr. George Rodgers' baby died at Woodside this morning early—Ma went upstairs till near dinner time. Mr. & Mrs. Valiant & children took dinner here. Mr. Valiant took his family home in the afternoon, came back to stay all night, as he has to go to Woodside early tomorrow morning to speak before the corpse starts for Balto. It rained this evening towards night.

Friday 13th

Mr. V., Pa & Ma went up to Gover's. Mr. Valiant made some beautiful remarks, ma says. Has gone home. This is a lovely day. I do not feel very well.

Saturday 14th

Lovely day. Ma went to aunt Nancy's to stay all night. Dr. Archer came about 4 o'clock. He & I took a ride on horseback, had quite a chapter of adventures. Got down to Mrs. Booth's. Had a delightful ride, got home to supper. He left about 10.

Sunday 15th

Beautiful sabbath. I was very glad to see Josh Bond, who came just after we had finished dinner. He put his horse in our carriage and took Ann Lee & myself to Watters' meeting.[14] He preached. It was the first sermon I ever heard him deliver. Oh, the many emotions of my heart whilst listening to him! How wild he used to be—the dances and frolics we've had together! All rushed through my mind and there stood he, who had been the participant of all those scenes; preaching God's holy gospel, with all the zeal of a true hearted christian. I do not think I shall ever forget that sermon. His text was the tenth chapter of John, first verse. Verily, verily, I say unto you, He that entereth not by the door into the sheep-fold, but climbeth up some other way, the same is a thief and a robber. He said some said Christ was only a *good man* but was not God's son. But if he was not Christ, he was not even a good man but the greatest hypocrite that ever was—for did he not make himself out to be God's son. And if he was not the Christ then Paul, John, and all the disciples were hypocrites, vile ones at that. Then speaking of persons saying, "they looked at some, who professed to be christians, how did they act, and they blamed the church." "Now if because there are some wolves in sheep clothing, that don't stand to reason all are wolves. If our governor was a reprobate, it is not the fault of our government & our state." He & Jimmy Moores took tea here.

Monday 16th

Howard Munnikhuysen came out this evening, is staying all night here.

14. Bond writes *carriage* over the word *buggy*.

Tuesday 17th

Howard & Juliet took a ride on horse back this morn—I called on Miss Laura Evans, liked her very much. She is a cousin of Juliet Gover's from Philadelphia. H. took dinner here. Dr. Archer came to tea, after which he and I went to Hazle Dell, stayed all night, found Mrs. Archer, and the baby very sick.

Wednesday 18th

Beautiful day—had an eclipse of the sun this morning. Dr. and I got home about half past five. Jimmy & Annie Moores took tea here. Brother got a letter from poor Howard—There are *two* sad *sad hearts* in the world! Heavenly Father give *him* grace to bear patiently. I hope *all* is for the best. I have tried to act right, but I know I have not in all things.

Thursday 19th

Very warm today—I rode down to "Oak Spring" this morn—took dinner intending staying all night. But about five ma sent for me. Came home, found Mrs. S. Archer, Glasgow A.[15] and aunt Dillie Lee. They left soon after tea.

Friday 20th

Lovely day—very warm. I feel so sad. My heart is heavy indeed. O, Father, I do want to be as a *little child*, to look up to thee, and with child-like faith expect a blessing, and guidance in these affairs which harass my mind and heart so much. Give me judgment—how to act. Let not my own sinful nature over rule my actions; for O, Father thou art acquainted with all my weaknesses better than I am myself—He writes brother he is going to *Europe*—poor fellow—how my heart aches! Howard, dear Howard, you don't know my heart, if you think *I* don't feel. No one knows the sorrow in my breast. I laugh and *seem* to be cheerful, but O, how many smiles hide a heart-felt sigh. Yes, and God knows my heart. "He sees my fears—and counts and treasures up my tears." Many times when my eyes are not weeping tears, my heart's weeping blood. And while I write those lines, both are weeping. The opposite page is blotted with burning tears. Oh! my heart, my heart is sad today. What would I not give to see him just now—Two long—long years & two months have passed since I saw him——This has been the saddest day of my life. Oh! my heart has seemed near breaking.

Dear ma has sympathized with me so much. O, what a blessing a *Mother* is. I do want to be very thankful for *that* blessing. I often think what would I do if I had no ma to comfort me in my afflictions—but I know the Lord would strengthen me as my day is. Oh, how good He has been to me, ever since my eyes were unclosed in this world. Lizzie Lee & Sallie Hendon called this evening.

15. She refers to Susannah Archer and her eighteen-year-old son, James Glasgow Archer.

Monday 23rd

Ma's birthday—49—How old she is getting—O, may she long be spared to us! Lovely day. I walked up to Woodside—did not return till after tea. Mr. Mabury Evans came home with me. I have been too sad all day, to laugh and talk. I expect they thought me very quite, and disagreeable, but when my heart is so sad, I can't exert myself, away from home especially. Why have I not received an answer to my letter?

Tuesday 24th

Beautiful day—so pleasant. It is the experience of every heart to know its own sorrow. Thank God I am wonderfully strengthened. My faith seems stronger, and more firm.

Wednesday 25th

Ma is very sick. I have been nursing her and housekeeping—brother left for uncle Parker's. I am the only child at home. May I discharge *every duty*, revolving upon me! Mrs. Hendon, Mr. Evans and his children spent the evening. I am very tired. Lovely night, O, how lovely the moon shines. How I should love to have some *one* to sit down by me and enjoy it. Moonlight nearly always calms my soul—fills my heart with inexpressible feelings of thankfulness, and love. The heavens are the work of Thy fingers—Oh! what mystery is contained in those stars! Look at those constellations, what volumes they speak—what lessons they teach. In every twinkle they utter—"there is a God."—

Thursday 26th

Foggy this morn'—Cousin Rachel Wilson called brought me a vinegar plant—to make vinegar with. Ma is still very sick. But I have much to be thankful for. O, Father cause my heart to be truly thankful. Dr. Archer came after tea. It is a lovely night.

Friday 27th

Dr. A. spent the evening—after tea took me riding—went round to "Medical Hall"—from there to the office, where I met many of my friends. Ma still continues sick in bed. I got a letter from Bennie Lee.

Sunday 29th

Did not feel very well this morn—cousin G. came to take me to meeting—Ma persuaded me to go—went to churchville, heard Mr. Vicker. Godfrey came to tea.

Monday 30th

Lovely day. Mr. Evans here this morn—afternoon Dr. A. and Glasgow Archer called—Dr. and I had quite a romp over a bouquet. Ma got a letter from dear aunt

Rebecca—I also got a note from her. Grandma is sick. I am so sad tonight. Moonlight always makes me feel sad. O, how I wished for Howard tonight, so we could talk over our affairs. I have not received a line from him since I wrote and released him from our engagement. What is the reason, I can not tell.

Tuesday July 31st

Has been a beautiful day. I was very much surprised to have a visit from Mary Cass Elhers this morning. She and Billie Bond came about 12 o'clock, had only two hours to stay. We did lots of talking. It is the first time I've seen her since her marriage. She is about 18, young and inexperienced wife, but so gay and happy—not a thought to mar the future. May she always be so. Sister Fannie and Mr. Stump came, spent the evening. Howard Munnikhuysen came to tea, whilst taking tea Lizzie Watters and Godfrey came, soon after, Juliet Gover and Laura Evans came. H- walked up with the girls. I was soon left to enjoy the moonlight *alone*. H- came back about half past 10 oc. Magnificent night. Oh! if I knew *he* was well—what what the reason *he* don't write—but thought after thought of why & wherefore rushes through my mind. This suspense is killing me. If I don't get a letter soon—I don't know what I will do. Lord *help* me to bear with patience *all*.[16]

Wednesday 1st[17]

Not very well—so sad—with the feelings of a rebellious heart troubling my conscience. Take from me *all* envy—give me a heart void of offence. That I may receive all the slights for thy sake, O, my Father. It is all done to move me from this world. My heart has had some bitter feelings. Grant thy holy spirit, to enable me to overcome them. For thou, O Father knoweth I can do no good thing within my own power.[18] Lovely day. Want rain badly—everything parching for it. God will send it in his own good time. May we trust Him more, and fear less! Howard has gone to Uncle Jim's. I am going to take a ride on horseback pretty soon. I hope I shall get a letter this morn.——

Thursday 2nd

Splendid day. Ma worse today, sent for the Dr. Sallie Hendon, sister Fannie, Josh Bond and cousin Richard Lee took tea here. Fannie and Josh left soon after tea. I left to my own sad thoughts. No letter. O what can be the reason! Give me faith, O Father! I have tried to trust all to His care, who never slumbers, or sleeps. There is such a dark cloud hanging over my heart—it has hid from sight the star of Hope & Faith. O, that it may be fraught with blessings!

16. *All* is underlined with a double line.

17. Bond misdates this and the following seven entries. She notes the errors in her entry of Thursday, 9 August. I have used the correct dates to prevent confusion.

18. Bond initially writes *ability* but crosses it out and writes in *power.*

Friday 3rd

Another pretty day, without rain: been so long since we have had a good rain. Every thing parching for the want of it. I've been quite sick, with a dreadful headache all day—in fact had it nearly all the week.

They say I'm looking better—But if they could see in my heart—how sore and bruised it is, they would know if I feel any better. A sick heart is worse than a sick body—and I have both. But I'm *convinced* all is done for the best. Give me an eye of faith! It is said Hope's our guiding star, shining brightest in the darkest hour, and peoples the gloom with the fairy forms of its own creation; like a beacon to the storm-tossed mariner, it speaks of rest and joy after the bitter present shall have passed away; and while the parting voice still lingers on the ear, cheers us through the long perspective of coming years with the prospect of the returning spring. . . .

Saturday 4th

We had a *gentle* shower early this morn—let us be truly thankful for that. Dinner time Dr. Lee & Ann Lee came. Ma still sick.

Sunday 5th

I was greatly disappointed did not get to hear Mr. Valiant this morn. Expected to have gone with cousin Cass Gover. Brother taken very sick; pa went to see him. Sister Fannie came home this evening after an absence of several weeks. Uncle Jim Lee took tea with us.

Monday 6th 1860

Annie Webster and Evans Rodgers called this morning. I liked him very much. I said to him, I did not believe in old men and widowers getting married. I forgot he was a widower. But he said he thought they were the very ones that should marry.

Tuesday 7th

Beautiful day. Very warm though. Annie Moores came with cousin Richard—made a call. In the afternoon Dr. Archer came about four oc, stayed till late. Cousin Cass Lee & Mr. Robert Armstrong took tea here. Mr. A- is from Balto. Mr. H-Stump also called. No letter from H- O, what is the reason he does not write.

Wednesday 8th

Oh, so warm today! Had a delightful rain in the evening, looks like it might rain more tonight. I prayed whilst the rain fell for a good shower. O, that may strengthen my faith. It needs strengthening. I wrote a letter to cousin R-. I don't know whether to send it or not. I fear she will think I wish to renew the engagement. But I want to be on friendly terms with H-. I hope I have acted right. I have done it for the best. May the Lord direct me, is my constant prayer. Oh! give me faith to see thy hand in this work.

Thursday 9th

I have been making mistakes in the date of my journal; today's the 9th. Beautiful one. Oh! How sad I am. I received a letter from Howard, dated Houma, mailed from Balto. How came it there? Why was it put in there is the mystery! Can it be he sent it to his father?[19] If so then indeed I am despised. I hardly think he would do such a thing, but how strange it should be in Baltimore. I will write him once more, and ask his forgiveness, for wronging him, accusing him falsely of deceiving me. I can do no more than acknowledge my faults. He says he still loves me dearly. He don't know how much I love him. I did not know it would be so hard to give him up. He says he is going to Europe this fall and does not know whether he'll come see me or not. Oh! if he does not come I shall die nearly. My brain seems to be on fire. I scarcely know how to act. Lord direct me. I am blind to doing right. Give me the eye of faith to see my way clear. O, father in Heaven! Mr. Stump took dinner here. Cousin George Glasgow came after tea. Bettie Gover, Juliet Evans, & Zach spent the evening.

Friday 10th _____[20]

Saturday 11th

Annie Moores & Smith Norris called this afternoon, sister Fannie went to the office on horseback.

Sunday 12th

Twelfth of August—three years ago I went to a large Pic Nic in Belair.[21] O, how I enjoyed it. How many changes since then! I was greatly disappointed I did not get to church today. I wanted to go much. Cousin George Glasgow took dinner with us.

Monday 13th

Pleasant day—

Tuesday 14th

Rained—I was invited to Dr. Archer's—did not go—cousin Cass Gover called for me—she & Miss Caroline Hall, sister Fannie went.

19. Howard's father is likely in Baltimore to oversee the construction of a house, one that Bond mentions in her entry of 20 November 1860.

20. She pens only a blank line for this entry.

21. To remember such detail, Bond obviously read her diary from 1857, one that no longer exists.

Wednesday 15th

Lovely day—George Glasgow took sister Fannie to Belair this morn and to Mr. Watters' this afternoon. I was at Woodside this morn—spent very pleasant time, went to Mr. Watters, with Dr. Archer, stayed all night. Met there Miss Henrietta & Ann Stump, Miss Hannah Archer—spent a delightful evening.

Thursday 16th

Went on a fishing pic nic to the mouth of Dear Creek with Godfrey, 14 of us. I did not catch any fish. Dr. Brumble came there for Mrs. Joe Evans. They are believed to be engaged. Coming home we drove up to the "Rock Run" house, went on the hill above the house, saw a beautiful view of the river—It reminds one of the scenery on the Hudson.[22]

Friday 17th

Camp meeting commenced today near Aberdeen. Had visitors. Party in Belair tonight—brother went with Herman Stump.

Saturday 18th

Had great deal of company this evening. This Miss S[tump] and brother, Miss Hannah A[rcher] and Dr. A[rcher]., Lizzie & Godfrey [Watters], Fannie Willman, Juliet Gover, H. Stump, George Glasgow, Bob Archer, & Willie Smithson. Did not leave till near twelve.

Sunday 19th

Did not go to Camp today—fraid I'd break the sabbath. Laura Moores took tea, John Evans came after tea.

Monday 20th

Went to Camp—never enjoyed a camp so much—heard nearly two sermons. John Brown preached in the afternoon, very good sermon—from "what is your light." Cousin George Glasgow took me. Got home about seven. Saw very few I knew. Josh was there. I was so glad to see Mr. *Hicks*, he *seemed* glad to see me.

Tuesday 21st

Cousin Betsy Jarrett is to be buried this morning at Mrs. Jacobs. She died very suddenly sunday evening with heart disease. Eat a hearty dinner and died soon after.

Mr. Stump took Sister Fannie to the funeral, then to Camp—aunts Rebecca & Mary came from uncle Sam's this evening. So glad to see them. Mr. Stump had to stay all night, as it rained.

---

22. The Rock Run House was owned by the Archer family and is a fourteen-room stone mansion located in the Susquehanna River Valley (now a state park).

Wednesday 22nd

Dr. A. & the two Miss Stumps called this morn. Pa took dinner, brother took him to Camp—Mr. Stump came to tea, brought an invitation to Mrs. Scott's party. Did not go.

Thursday 23rd

I expected to have gone to Camp this morn with George Glasgow—did not get off till in the afternoon. Got home after ten. Aunts spent the evening at Woodside.

Friday 24th

Aunts & Sister Fannie went up to grandpa's place—spent such a pleasant day, Henrietta Stump & Dr. Archer came to pay a call this morn, but rain came up, had to stay till nearly six o'clock. Howard Munnikhuysen came as we were drinking tea; stayed the night.

Saturday 25th

Ma & aunts R[ebecca] & M[ary] went to uncle P—spent the day. Brother drove, from there they went to Aunt Nancy Lee's, stayed all night. Dr. Archer came to tea.

Sunday 26th

My birthday—Lovely one.[23] How many changes since the last 26 of August. My life has been checkered with joys and sorrows. I have had much to be truly thankful for. Took a walk this morn—ma and all came home to dinner, after which aunt Dillie came. Just before tea cousin George Gover, then Dr. A- who had taken sister Fannie to Belair, heard Mr. Valiant preach. While we were eating, Jimmy Moores, and cousin Juliet came. I received a very pretty bouquet.

Monday 27th

Lovely day, aunt R. and Mary started for Balto in the stage.

Tuesday 28th

Had a visit this morning from old Dr. Wilson—he is such as pleasant old gentleman. Gave us an account of his visit to the "Great Eastern." A very large boat built in England. I went to cousin Cass Govers after the Dr. left—spent the day—cousin Cass had gone to Balto. Cousin Priss Webster, cousin Cass Lee & children, & Margarett Smithson were there. I stayed all night, and came home the next evening (29th) Got a letter from Howard wishing our engagement renewed. I have not answered it yet; I scarcely know how to do so.

23. She turns twenty-two.

Thursday 30th

Dr. Archer came for me, and took me to aunt Nancy's, found cousins Annie & Callie at home. I stayed all night—all the next day; had a charming time.

Friday 31st

Cousin George Glasgow spent the evening there, had a very merry time.

Saturday 1st Sept.

Lovely day. Dr. Archer came for me and brought me home to tea. Found M- Smithson here & Mary Gover. Our wood's meeting commenced today, at Hoop- man's chapple. Jimmy Watters & I met with quite a little adventure down there two years since.

Sunday 2nd

I did not go to meeting today. Sister Fannie, Mr. Stump & brother went.

Monday 3rd

Dr. Archer called to take me to Mr. S. Archer's, could not go, sister F. away.

Tuesday 4th

Beautiful day. Jimmy Moores & Dr. A. took dinner here, after which, Jimmy & I went to uncle Parker's, in the buggy, sister Fannie came home to tea.

Wednesday 5th

Dr. Archer took Fannie to "Medical Hall."

Thursday 6th

Cloudy day. Cousin Richard here this morn. Uncle Parker took tea. Looks very much like rain. The world seems alive with bugs tonight.

Monday 10th

I went to Belair this morn with brother & Ann Lee, intend staying here some time. Staying at Dr. Lee's. Beautiful day.

Tuesday 11th

Spent the evening at uncle William's—had a pleasant visit. Howard waited on me home. Dr., Laura Moores, Ann Lee, and myself went to Moores store. He gave me a medal, a Breckenridge medal.

Wednesday 12th

Spent the evening at cousin Charles Lee's. He was very much intoxicated. Coming home another intoxicated man got after us. I was very much frightened indeed.

Thursday 13th.

I went out to Mooreland, took dinner. Annie and I went to Mr. Gough's spent the evening. I remained all night. Annie called for me this morning, Friday 14th, came to Dr. Lee's to dinner after which we went to the court house to make wreaths for the "Grand Mass Meeting" to be held there tomorrow. Had a pleasant time. Mr. & Mrs. Archer came in for me. I came out to their house to tea, and here I am now.

Saturday 15th

Beautiful day for the "Meeting." We went into Belair about two o c'. Mrs. Williams & Minnie Turpin with us. Mr. Bradford delivered the first address.[24] I did not get to hear him. I was sorry as I had heard him so highly spoken of. Dr. Archer brought me out to tea, after which we went back—sister Fannie & Mr. Stump also came to tea. The fire works were the most beautiful I ever saw, and the music was elegant, a band from Baltimore. Mr. Dennis spoak beautiful. Hon. Edward Webster gave us a lovely little speech. Spoke very prettily to the ladies and then the meeting was brought to a close.

Sunday 16th

I was not able to go to church. Met Mrs. Scott & C Watson from La.[25] Sister Fannie left this evening.

Sunday 23rd

I came from Mr. Archer's yesterday. Dr. Archer brought me. I spent a very pleasant week, visited Mrs. Scotts, got some beautiful flowers. Annie Webster & Mrs. Webster called. I caught a dreadful cold at the political meeting, still have it. Did not get to church again today. Could not leave home; all the rest went but Betsy & I. John Moores and Mr. Baker from Va. spent the evening here—also cousin George Glasgow and Dr. Archer took tea.

Monday 24th

Cousin George took me to Mr. Watters' spent the evening. Bennie Lee staying there from New York. I got a letter from Howard. O what a letter it is. How shall I answer it? He says he will never be happy unless I'm his wife. I believe I shall never find one I love as well, and who will love me as he does.

O Father direct us in all our ways. I wish to do thy will whatever it may be. Help me to see thy way and thy doings in all things.

24. She is likely referring to Augustus W. Bradford, a Harford native, who would be governor of Maryland from 1862 to 1866.

25. Watson's first name is not clear.

Tuesday 25th

Howard M[unnikhuysen] took dinner here. Mrs. Herring & cousin Juliet Gover took tea. Laura Smithson called this afternoon. It commenced to feel real fall like now and the foliage is changing quite fast. Winter is fast approaching.

Wednesday 26th

Lovely morning, cool—I do not feel well today. Ma is not well either.

Friday 28th

Ann Lee came home from school today, it's her vacation. I doubt whether she will return again this winter. Laura Smithson spent the evening here; she, Ann Lee & I walked down to the Beach tree. Mr. Authur is building a dwelling house and Blacksmith shop on the hill this side. All my pleasant walks down there, I must bid adieu.

Saturday 29th

I spent a delightful day at Uncle Jim's. Beautiful day, rather cool.——

Sunday 30th

It has every appearance of rain all day, consequently did not venture out to church. I was truly disappointed for I was very anxious to hear Mr. Valiant today. Our sabbaths are not spent as they were when I was a child. Why is this! I often ask myself. I remember when we would scarcely cook any thing and now some times our greatest dinners are on sunday. This should not be. I wish I could prevent it. I do not like having company on sunday but it is a great day for visiting. Lord help us to take up our cross, each & every day, that we may follow after thee more closely. O, for more of the christian love shed abroad in our hearts. Let us love one another, even as thou lovest us.

Monday 1st

One month of fall has gone! How quickly passes away time! How near is Eternity! Eternity. Who can fathom it? What a world of meaning there is in it. A world of endless joy or eternal misery. It has been raining nearly all day.

Tuesday 2nd

Mr. Archer came this morning for sister Fannie, his little boy is very ill. May their affliction be their souls salvation.

Thursday 4th 1860

Rev. Mr. Boulton (the Bible agent) came just before dinner. He went up to Woodside, but returned to tea. He is a very good and agreeable old gentleman.[26] Dr. Archer called on his way to Mr. A. It is raining tonight.

26. Mr. Boulton was likely an agent of one of the state societies for Bible distribution, such as the

Friday 5th

I have just heard the sad intelligence of little Annfield's death. Dear little angel, has left this world of sin for the bright and glorious land, where no sin or sorrow, pain or death are felt, or feared no more. He died near ten o'clock yester morning the 4th. O how deeply I feel for those bereaved ones.[27] Sanctify this, O Lord to their hearts. May Heaven seem nearer to them.

Three precious lambs they have there, to welcome them to that better land. His funeral will take place this afternoon at three o'clock at his father's residence. Mr. Boulton left here this morning. All I had I gave him which was only 50 cts. May it do much good. O Lord let not that mite be lost but let at least one soul be saved. May I ever give ungrudgingly—for the Lord loveth a cheerful giver.

Thou indeed did constrain me to give it. To thee all honor, and glory be given. It still continues to be gloomy and cloudy, a sad day to many hearts.

Saturday 3rd of Nov 1860

Nearly one month has gone since I penned in my journal, during which time some very important things have occurred. We have had much company, some staying with us, Bennie Lee several days. I spent nearly a week with her at Mr. Watters. I have been also to uncle Sam's. The road so long and stony, felt like I had gone the other side of Baltimore. So glad to see them all, seemed like a long time since we all been together, cousin Cass Gover took me there in her splendid new carriage, on the 18th of Oct.—stayed only one night. Came to cousin Cass's Thursday, stayed all night, got acquainted with "Miss Brooke." Jimmy Moores came next morning for me. We called at Woodside. Last Wednesday week, Mr. Watters' people called for me to go to Mr. Henry Webster's. I did not feel well enough, did not go. Bennie came here that night, stayed till last Sunday afternoon.

Friday Godfrey called, took Lizzie, Bennie & I to Churchville—Protracted meeting going on. Heard a beautiful sermon from those beautiful words "Thy ways are ways of pleasantness, and thy paths are peace" by Rev. Mr. Valiant, our pastor.

Went from church to Thomas Archer's to dinner, stayed till after tea, after which we went again to church—heard Mr. Visher preach from "Almost thou persuadeth me to become a Christian." Lovely night, got home about nine. Saturday morning Lillie Gough, Juliet Gover, Miss Brooke & May Gover called. After dinner I went with Juliet to Belair to the Democratic meeting held in the court-house

---

Maryland Bible Society. The Baltimore Conference of the Methodist Church would appoint traveling ministers to serve as agents with these societies. See Apsley, "Educational Concerns, 1816–1861," 145–46.

27. Annfield was likely Stephenson and Blanche Archer's child. If so, the couple did eventually have five children. (See entry 2 October.)

yard. I got one of the wreaths from off the stand which was very beautiful. Otho Scott spoke—and two others, Mr. Richie from Baltimore and a gentleman from "Cecle."[28] I stayed all night at Dr. Lee's. Went next morning to hear Mr. Valiant. Such a prayer I never heard. Text from Phillipians 1st chap 9 verse. The Lord's supper was then administered. Give me resolution, O, Father, to live in Charity with *all.* Archer Jarrett brought me home after dinner. Jimmy & Laura Moores & Godfrey here. I wish we never had company on sunday. Has been raining all this week. Mr. Stump spent wednesday evening here. Dr. Archer here yesterday to dinner. Sister F. went to Mr. Watters monday, stayed till thursday, then went to Hazle Dell. Ann Lee went to Mooreland sunday, is there yet, brother & I are the only children at home. George & Gerard Gover broke on tuesday last. I don't suppose they are worth a dollar in the world. O I hope it may cause them to lay up their treasures above. We heard George Gover was dead and was much distressed, but it was a false report. I'm anxious to hear more particularly about it. It is raining now very hard. When will it clear off!

Sunday 4th

Sister Fannie came home last night. Dr. A- brought her. This is a lovely day—after such a gloomy week how we appreciate the glorious sunshine. A good omen for those sad hearts at "Woodside." Cousins George & Juliet came here this morning. Cousin Juliet said she believed she would go crazy if she did not open her heart to some kind friend.[29]

I never witnessed such grief in my life. Every cent taken from, or rather they have given up every cent, and everything to their creditors. Poor grieved ones, how I do sympathize with you all. Fannie Moores & children & Laura Moores took dinner with us. Jimmy brought A- Lee home. Mr. Stump called. Billie Webster took sister F. to Watters meeting. I went to see Juliet for a little while this eve.

Monday 5th

Spent the day with Juliet,[30] found her very sad indeed—she bears it beautifully. O may she be comforted by God's grace. I tried to say words of comfort. I hope I did not fail of offering some inspired words. Dr. Archer took tea here.

28. Otho Scott was a state senator from Harford County from 1838 to 1843. In 1860 he owned six slaves.

29. See also Bond's entry of 11 June 1859, in which she indicates problems at the Govers' home. She writes of comforting her cousin Juliet, perhaps indicating that the family's financial troubles had existed for some time.

30. Bond refers to cousin Juliet's daughter, who would have been seventeen years old at the time.

Tuesday 6th

Election day. The Whig candidates are "Bell" & "Everett." Democrats "Breck-enridge" & "Lane" & "Douglas" & "Houston" and Black Republic "Lincon."[31]
Cousin George G- called this afternoon and took me as far as "Mooreland," on his
way to Belair—spent a pleasant evening. Mrs. Glasgow, Martha Gough, Godfrey
Watters, brother & I were there to tea. Got home before ten.

Wednesday 7th

Lovely day—housecleaning—took a walk—overtook Sallie Gover, went down
to cousin Cass' stayed all night. Cousin Henry Smithson there. All very sad.

Thursday

Came from there this morn—with cousin Priscilla Gover, went up to Wood-side—stayed little while—got some lovely flowers. Clouded up—looks like rain.

Friday 9th

Got a letter from Peggie from Chestertown. Wants me to come over. Mifflin
going to be married 27th.[32] Raining.

31. In the 1860 presidential election, Whig candidates were John Bell (for president) and Edward
Everett (vice president). Lincoln, of course, was the Republican candidate. As Bond indicates, the
Democratic Party had two sets of candidates, as the party was split over the issue of slavery. The dele-
gations of eight southern states met in their own convention and nominated presidential and vice presidential candidates John C. Breckinridge and Joseph Lane on a platform supporting slavery in the territories. The "Douglas Democrats" nominated Stephen A. Douglas and Herschel V. Johnson.

32. Bond mentions visiting Mifflin on the Eastern Shore of Maryland in her first diary entry.

CHAPTER FIVE

"The Greatest Trial of My Life"

12 NOVEMBER 1860–2 APRIL 1861

Monday 12th

Went up to uncle Jim's—met Dr. Archer on the road. Came home soon after dinner. Ma went to Woodside—spent the evening. Mr. Hendon came after tea. While we were all seated around the table, who should walk in but Howard Bond. He looked in and saw us all seated there. I had my back to the window, had a red net on my head, and he said he thought to himself "well there is a red-headed girl." I was *delighted* to see him of *course*. It was such a surprise. He has improved much, looks much better than when he left. Why do I not love him as he loves me. O for more faith. Lord direct me and cause me to act rightly in all things. Forgive me for my past offenses.

Tuesday 13th

Had much company this evening. Mrs. Glasgow, Mrs. Dallam, uncle Parker, and Aunt Mary, Dorsey Gough and Lillie, Annie Moores, Aunt Dillie called.

Wednesday 14th

Howard and I went up to Woodside little while this morning. Bennie Lee came to dinner, after which Dr. Archer and his sister, Bob Archer and Mr. Smith called. The others spent the evening. Bennie remained.

Thursday 15th

Lovely morning. Went to Baltimore with Howard. O what a talk we had. We explained all to each to other and then our hearts felt lighter. Started between nine & ten, got there about three, found all well & glad to see me.

Friday 16th

Howard, Mary Cass & I went up to the Institute of the Blind to see aunt Rebecca. Saw Mrs. Poisle and Sterling Thomas there. Coming home Mary Cass got sepperated from us, and could not find her. So we went to Butchers and got our dinner. Had fried & stewed oysters. Howard made me a present of a very handsome pair of gloves. Brother came down after tea, he Howard and I went to see Professor Anderson perform. He was quite entertaining.

Saturday 17th

I was busy all day making my bonnet.

Sunday 18th

It rained the day before—pavements very damp—did not go to church in the morning. Howard went. He & I went at night, heard a very good sermon by Rev. Mr. Sherman. Protracted meeting going on at Fayett Street. It seems to be doing great deal of good.

Monday 19th

This afternoon Howard & I went up to Barnums to see Mrs. Archer.[1] She seemed very glad to see me. At night we went to The "Maryland Institute" to a Concert given by The Blind. I liked it very much indeed.

Tuesday 20th

This afternoon Howard and I went out to his father's place on Charles Street avenue. Went all through the house. It is a very handsome house, not quite finished.

We were in the third story, standing by the window, and he put the ring on my finger, we *were engaged.* I felt then as though I loved him well enough to be his—but now sometimes I fear I don't. It makes me *right sad*—for I don't wish to flirt with him but he loves me so devotedly, and is willing to try still to win my heart. I cannot turn him away. He says he will be perfectly miserable without me, that life will be a drag—that he will not have energy to be of use to himself or any one else. And when I think can I give him up forever, I find I can't. Oh what must I do—Lord direct me, put words in my *mouth,* that I *may say what I should.* Came home to tea. Went to another concert by the blind.

Thursday 22nd

Howard & I went and had our likenesses taken. Saw the parade. I got cold, felt very sick. Howard got me some medicine to take.

Friday 23rd

I was sick abed nearly all day. Lawrence Thomas came to see me, looked well. Howard so kind, O I should love him so much.

Saturday 24th

H- started over to Cecil but so windy the boat came back. Juliet Gover came to see me, also Carrie Hendon. Howard went out to Mr. Bradford's stayed all night.

---

1. Barnum's was a luxurious Baltimore hotel.

Sunday 25th

Aunt R- came down, went to church—took dinner at Mr. Evans, came soon after dinner. Dr. Goldsborough & Miss Day spent the evening. Mr. Evans and Mr. Herring called to see me. I did not get to church today. It was too cold, and blustery. Dr. G- said I must take good care of myself. Howard got me a plaster for my back.

Monday 26th

Rained.

Wednesday 28th

It rained—cleared off about three, Howard & I took a walk up Baltimore street—he bought grandma a turkey for her thanksgiving dinner.

Thursday 29th

Howard and I came home, had a pleasant ride up. Got home about 6 o'clock, started about 12 o'c, found pa sick abed, all the others complaining. This is Thanksgiving day, and Lovely one it is.

Saturday 1st Dec.

Very cold—windy. George Bond came this afternoon. Had lots of fun mesmerizing.

Sunday 2nd

Very cold—wind blowing. Not able to go to church. Howard took sister Fannie to Churchville—afternoon George Bond took her to Watters' meeting house in Howard's buggy. When he came back, he & H- went down to cousin Tom's. Mr. Furgason, Jimmy Moores and cousin George Glasgow came. After all left but cousin George, he, sister Fannie, brother, Ann Lee and myself were in the parlor enjoying ourselves. Shall I forget this evening——

Christmas day, 25 Dec. 1860

How many changes has the last few days brought forth? Howard and sister Fannie went to Balto last week. Whilst there, H- got a letter from his mother, saying, she & his father wished him to marry me while here, and bring me on with him. I have been very ill. Two Drs. attending me. I feel little like it now. I did not expect to be married for at least two years, and it has unnerved me so I can scarcely think. My Dr. thinks it better for me to marry now, as my health is very bad, and this climate is killing me. I have promised if the Lord sees best, I will be his wife—so I expect to be married in a few weeks.

It nearly breaks my heart to leave my old home, and especially my dear ma, Oh, God watch over her—and grant that we may be permitted again to meet. Give me strength, & grace to bear up under this heavy trial.[2] And that *we* may so love each other, as to live happily together, looking to *Thee*, as *our help* in every hour of need. O, Father I try to put my trust in *thee*. Let me not be afraid. But give me *faith* to believe all will work together *right*. Oh! make us christians! Howard and sister Fannie gone to cousin John Moores, are going to take tea, old Mr. Evans here for a little while.

Wednesday 26th

Lovely day, cold and clear. Howard Munnikhuysen came. Dr. Lee to dinner, says I *must* go south. Howard went to Mr. Watters and Dr. Archers. Brother dined at John Dallam's with a small party. Lizzie and Godfrey [Watters] took tea and Howard B. Lizzie stayed all night. I told her of my intending marriage. Mr. Stump took sister Fannie to John Moores to a party. We spent a delightful evening at home, Lizzie, Howard & myself. Juliet [Gover], Cassie Herring & Ann Lee went to the party in the same carriage. Ann Lee's *first party*.

Thursday 27th

Howard & sister Fannie went to Baltimore this morning. Lizzie & Godfrey took dinner with us. I felt very sad, Ma talked a long time with me. Oh! what a trial to have to leave her. But I will hope to see her dear face soon. My Father in Heaven prepare me for this important step I'm about to take.—

Friday 28th

Pretty day—aunt Dillie came in the afternoon, she & Uncle Jim took tea with us. She seemed glad to think I was going to get such a good husband. I really believe I have some as true & warm friends as ever lived.

Saturday 29th

Cousin Cass Gover took dinner here. Mr. Hendon here for some time in the morning. Brother went to uncle William's to a company, enjoyed it very much, met there Parker Moores & his wife. Was charmed with her.

Sunday 30th

Rained all day. Godfrey came in the afternoon, stayed till after nine. Had a very pleasant evening. Got a very sweet note from Lizzie Watters, dear Lizzie, how I do love her. I sung hymns after tea with ma & Ann Lee. Sung brother's favorite "When I can read my title clear." We were a very happy family group.

2. Bond's reluctance to leave her mother was not uncommon. Historians including Nancy Theriot and Caroll Smith Rosenberg have pointed out the closeness of mother-daughter relationships in the nineteenth century. Stowe, in *Intimacy and Power,* found that women delayed their marriages in order to remain home with their mothers (104).

Monday 31st

Last night good deal of snow fell. I was surprised to see snow on the ground when I looked out this morning. Beautiful day—cold very—about ten, Dr. Archer & Miss P- Stump came. I did not know she was in the neighborhood. She is a very lovely girl. Nearly 12 when sister Fannie & Howard came. They came from Balto Saturday night to Mr. Archer's—stayed all night, and [there] was a storm, stayed sunday. Howard was nearly perished when he got here. Sister Fannie went down to get my *wedding fixens*. I am well pleased with all she got. Mr. Stump here this afternoon. Howard asked him to wait on him. He said he would with pleasure. He is to wait with sister Fannie & Peggie with brother. I am to be married on the morning of the 15th of January 1861. If nothing occurs to prevent. I have put my trust in a higher power, to be directed in all things, and I believe He will, and has. Howard seems so happy, & I am, I feel as though I had directed by my Heavenly Father. It is all for the best.

Oh! that I may have some good influence over those who are unsafe as regards their souls welfare. Lord help me, is my prayer.

Tuesday 1st Jan.

The first day of the year. It is a lovely morning. The snow glistens in the sunlight. It is very cold. Cousin George Gover came whilst I was eating my breakfast. Godfrey took dinner here. Went down to Mr. Websters, Lizzie very ill, not expected to live.

Jan. 2nd

Sister Fannie & brother went down to Mr. Websters. Lizzie just as ill as she can be. Came back after dinner, she & Howard gone to Mr. Archer's. It is now raining. I wish he would come. I want to see him. Ann Lee & I seated up stairs, Ma & Pa down, brother gone to uncle Jim's to spend the evening with several—Miss Stump included. Howard returned. I trimmed Ann Lee my fall bonnet for spring. It will save the expense of getting one for her.

Thursday 3rd

Brother & Howard went to Balto this morning. Looks like rain. Cousin George Gover here for a while. Ma & Ann Lee at home, cousin George Glasgow came, spent the evening. Said he would miss me very much. I shall miss him too.

Can I remember how we all sat in the dining room this evening. Ann Lee knitting me mats for my wash-stand. A letter from Bettie Leary saying she had a fine daughter, called her Ella.

Friday 4th

This day is set apart as a fast day throughout the U-S- and prayer should be in every heart—for our country stands in need of it more now than ever.[3] Lord preserve us and give the "Heads" of our *country* knowledge to act right. Put it in their hearts, to act just in all the affairs of The nation.——

Saturday 5th

Beautiful day—Lizzie Watters & Godfrey came yesterday evening. Lizzie stayed all night. Cousin Cass Gover also was here for a little while. Bennie Lee came this morning, spent the day. Sister Fannie came home this morn. Mr. Stump brought her. Annie Moores & cousin John [Moores] spent the evening[4]—also George Archer. Howard & brother came home from Balto this evening. Ma, Howard & I were up stairs, when we heard Annie Moores coming up we sent H. in his room 'till after she left, when he came back we had such a laugh. Dear Ma how I shall miss seeing her dear sweet face. O, how shall I be able to give her up.

Sunday 6th

Beautiful day. None of us went to church. After dinner I sat down stairs to read to Howard & all, a book called "Memoirs of Miss Alibone."[5] Godfrey came, took sister Fannie down to see Lizzie Webster, so ill could not let her see her. Howard & I sitting up in my room. They came home to tea.

Monday 7th

Busy writing the invitations to our wedding—this morning looks very much like rain. Mr. Stump came, after dinner, George Archer came to write invitations. Cousin George Glasgow spent the evening here. He & I had a long *old fashion talk*. He told me he had felt so sad since he heard of my going to be married—he could not laugh & talk as he once did. That no one could not know how much he would miss me. But I was getting a man after his own heart. I told him no, he was one after *my own heart.* Howard went to Belair this afternoon. Dr. Archer has been so kind, also Godfrey Watters is doing every thing to oblige me.

Tuesday 8th

One week from today I expect to be a bride. O, who knows the emotions of my heart. This has been a sad gloomy morning. Aunt Dillie came sit for awhile. She

3. South Carolina had seceded on 20 December 1860, and Mississippi, Florida, and Alabama would follow only days after the national fast.

4. Annie is John's* nineteen-year-old sister.

5. Bond mentions reading this also in her entry of 14 May 1859.

seems sorry I'm going to live so far from home: but glad I'm getting such a good husband. Peggie came down to wait on me, with brother, sister Fannie and Mr. Stump. Mr. Watters came this afternoon to bid me "goodbye." That good old word "goodbye." Howard came from Belair this evening, brought my dresses. We all were sitting up in "our room," that is sister Fannie, brother, Peggie, Ann Lee, Howard & myself. We were all seated in a group. Peggie & sister Fannie sang the "Bride." "O take her & be faithful still." I felt very sad. Howard had his arm around me, and my hand in his. I felt *he would be faithful.* We spent altogether a very *merry evening.*

Wednesday 9th

Snowing—Peggie & sister Fannie went down to cousin Cass Gover's in Howard's buggy, uncle Jim came. He came up stairs—had such hearty laughs. We have been so busy getting ready. Dr. Archer came to take sister Fannie to Mr. Webster's but did not go. Brother went to the [post] office. Ma came up stairs and sit with us. Peggie, sister Fannie, Ann Lee and myself are sitting around the little stand, Ma standing up by the bedstead. They are telling yarns. I must stop.

Thursday 10th

Cold and disagreeable morning. Pa went to Balto with cousin Gerard Gover. Cousin Cass came this far with him. Ma, she and I had a long confab upstairs. After they went downstairs, cousin Cass and I had a long talk on Religion, as we always have when we get together. She thinks that the state of the nation is a judgment on the wickedness of our land. So think I.[6] After dinner, in fact it was nearly dark, Mr. H- Stump & Howard came. Howard came up in our room, sit with me some time. After tea, we all adjourned to the parlor, and commenced practicing how to get married. We wanted Peggie Bond & Mr. Stump to act as bride & groom but brother was decidedly opposed to them getting married—even in *fun.* So she and Howard got married, then Mr. Stump & I. He said he would have me, and I said *no.* So he said he felt very badly.

I felt very sad, Howard & I talked—up in my room for a long time—I told him it was the greatest trial of my life to leave home, and O, when I think about it my heart *grows sick*, O, shall I be satisfied out there! My Heavenly Father guide me in

6. Much of the Christian South believed that the war was a result of their forsaking Christian principles and embracing what they saw as the "northern" vices of materialism and greed. Neglectful treatment of slaves was often cited as a cause for God's displeasure and was associated with the South's desire for material gain at the expense of their moral duties. See Royster, *Destructive War,* 183. In their diaries, many women explained the war as a result of the South's misdeeds, and they urged the Confederacy—and themselves—toward reformation. See, for example, Bond's later entries of 26 August 1861, 20 July and 16 October 1863, and 2 February and 6 March 1864.

every thing. I have tryed to put my trust in *thee*. I believe I have acted right—I feel misgivens—but O, I suppose all feel so when they are about to take such an important step. Fit & prepare me for each and every trial. Give me grace to bear up under this heavy, heavy trial.

Friday 11th

Cloudy—looked very much like snow. Godfrey [Watters] called after dinner, on his way to Mr. Webster's. Cousin Betsy Moores and Hall Lee came this afternoon.[7] She seemed very much distressed parting with me, she said "Mitt you are leaving great many friends behind you—those who love you very much." When she bid me goodbye, she clung to me, and wept over me. O, my heart felt as though it would burst. After I came down stairs we all had a good family cry. I could not help but cling around *my* dear ma's neck. Can I, O can I, leave that dear face so far behind! Cousin George Glasgow spent the evening—He seemed so *very sad*, he could not talk. He wanted me to tell him what my "bridal present" should be. I told him, whatever his good taste & judgment dictated. Godfrey came after tea. The girls were very lively, but I could not be.

Saturday 12th

This has been a very changeable day, sometimes sunshining and sometimes snowing—I was quite busy down stairs this morning, for some time, when I went up stairs, found Peggie & sister Fannie cleaning out my closet & drawer, burning up everything I did not want, to keep ma from seeing them after I leave. Ma & I had a long, serious talk—shed precious tears. O, my God help me to remember her good *advice*. For she has passed through deep waters. Mr. Stump called just before dinner, brought me a beautiful butter knife, jelly spoon and pickle fork, in a case for a bridal present. After dinner Sallie Hendon came sit awhile with me. Peggie & cousin George went to Mr. Webster's—made a call. Sister Fannie got the present of a very handsome set of fur. Brother & Dr. Archer spent the morning at Stevy Archer's. Cousin Juliet & cousin George Gover spent the evening here, also George Glasgow took tea.

Cousin Juliet seemed sorry I was going so far—but was very cheerful. I felt very sad. I bid them good night and came up stairs. O they don't know how my heart aches.

Sunday 13th

The last sunday at home. The sun has been shining so beautiful all day. I hope tuesday will be as pretty. Though it is bitter cold. Protracted Meeting commenced

7. Hall Lee is probably Uncle Parker and Aunt Mary Lee's* seventeen-year-old son, Parker Hall.

yesterday at Watters meeting house. Mr. Sargent preached there yesterday and to-day. None of the family sent to church from here. Where shall I be this time next sunday, or two from now? I try and feel cheerful, and believe it's all for the best. O I look at ma and think, can I leave *her*, will I ever be happy without her, as delicate as I am. My heart feels so heavy—and sad. Direct me, O "Father of Light" in this affair. Not my will but thine be done. It seems hard to give all up, perhaps never again to see them all again. But I am leaving them for *one* worthy the name of *husband*, one who has promised to love me and even to sacrifice his pleasures for mine. May I prove to be a good wife, not only in name but *indeed*. It is a very important step, one for life. Give me, O, Father every christian virtue to enable me to do all for *thy glory!*

I am now seated up in "our room," Peggie, Sister Fannie & Betsy (little black girl) and myself in here, sister Fannie copying a piece of poetry, Peggie holding the ink, I asked her how to spell *Phthisis,*[8] she could not spell it. Ma has just come in—talking to Betsy. (Night) Cousin George Glasgow & Dr. G. Archer took tea here. I felt very sad this evening. Peggie and brother went to meeting tonight, sister Fannie and I had a hearty cry upstairs sitting by the stove. O how my heart ached thinking of how shall I bid adieu to those *loved ones,* especially *one.*[9] God give me grace—help me to "watch & pray, and on thyself rely." Dear ma talks to me so cheerfully, and all the time, I know her heart aches dreadfully. I have been singing hymns with sister Fannie and Peggie. How oft have Ma and I sang those sweet verses together on sunday evening. "How happy every child of grace, Who knows his sins forgiven."

Monday 14th

Only one day more at home. My head aches very badly, and my heart's very sad. It seems as though my heart will break when I bid adieu to my *own* dear *Ma.* It has been snowing all the morning and it is now twenty-five minutes of 12 o'c. It is snowing very fine. I would not be surprised if we had a deep snow. The earth is clothing herself in her bridal attire, preparatory to mine. By this time tomorrow I shall be a bride. Be Mrs. Mittie Bond. How my heart throbs when I think what is before me, a mingling of bitter & sweet. But so it is in this life! Every heart has its sorrows, be they at home or a broad. As thy day is, so thy strength shall be. As Howard said to me a short time since, when I was grieving about the affairs of our country being in such a state and my leaving home at such a time.

He said, "Pet, we have trusted in God so far, can we not trust Him yet farther?"

8. *Phthisis,* from the Greek word for "wasting," is a term that was used interchangeably with *con-sumption.*

9. Bond underlines *one* with three lines, likely referring to her mother.

I will try and put my trust in that "Good Father" who reigns above and "who sees my fears and counts, and treasures up my tears."

I have been writing some advice in Ann Lee's Album. I hope she may profit by it. I will try now and write sister Fannie something. O direct my pen, My Father.[10] Lizzie Watters & Godfrey have come, busy squeezing lemons in the dining room. I just received a beautiful letter from Howard Munnikhuysen. It is *perfectly beautiful*. O! Father strengthen me for the trials of *tomorrow*. Thy grace is sufficient. Uncle Jim came to tea, teased me a good deal, just as we finished supper, Mr. Stump & Howard came. We went into the parlor to practice getting married, sister Fannie fixed the bride's cake. It had a beautiful bride on it, which I gave to ma.———

Tuesday, Jan 15, 1861

This morning about 15 minutes to ten o'clock, I gave my heart & hand to Howard. Mr. Valiant performed the ceremony. Mr. Stump, & sister F[annie], Peggie & brother, waited together. There were between 60 & 70 persons there. I felt very much frightened, and nervous half hour before I went down stairs, but I knelt down before God, and beseeched His blessing on us. That He would give me grace to overcome all such feelings, and He did. I felt the weight of leaving home taken off my mind. I of course felt sad—but it was different from what I had felt. I received several beautiful little presents from friends this morning and good many before. We came down to Balto in a hack. It rained soon after we left home and is still at it. Many persons came to the wedding in sleighs. I felt tired tonight but went down to supper, But retired soon after. Had several calls, did not see anyone.

Wednesday 16th

Still raining—I did not mention where we stopped. It is at Barnums, sister Fannie & Mr. Stump is with us. Went down to see grandma, all well—and glad to see me.

Thursday 17th

Went out this morning to have our ambrotypes taken, Howard and I had ours taken for sister Fannie, and hers for me. When we got back from the artist to the Hotel, found the Miss Bradfords here to see H. & me. Very pleasant girls. I liked them very much indeed. Had many other calls. Cleared off before sun set.

Friday 18th

Another rainy day. Drove down to aunt Marys.[11] Spent a very pleasant hour, got back—dressed for dinner, took it at five. Had some calls.

10. See her letter to Fannie in app. 1.

11. Bond's mother's sister.

Saturday 19th

Left Balto this morning about 8, sister Fannie & Mr. Stump went to the depot with us. We parted in the Cars. I felt indeed sad, but soon brightened up and tryed to be cheerful for Howard's sake. It was the first ride I ever took in a Steam car. I like them exceedingly.

The scenery on this road is beautiful. We stopped at Harper's Ferry short while. H. & I got out, and looked at the "Armory." It is a beautifully grand place. So wild, and picturesque in its appearance. But the grandest sight I enjoyed was the "Point of Rocks." It is perfectly beautiful. I wish I had time to describe it here. We traveled 178 miles today. I am now in Cumberland.

"As the mountains are around Jerusalem," so are the mountains around Cumberland. The town is completely hemmed in by mountains. We are stopping at the "Revere House." It is on Balto street, and is an excellent house. I felt very tired.

Sunday 20th

This has been a lovely sabbath day. I felt as though God had favored us. The first sabbath of *our* married life. Howard & I went to the M.E.C.[12] heard Rev. Mr. Creamer preach, an excellent sermon. I did not hear the text—but from the discourse I believe it was this. The spirit beareth witness in us, we are heirs of God, and joint heirs with Christ. Very neat and pretty church. I looked around and over that church full of people to see if I could see any one resembling any one I knew, but alas! there was not one. A stranger in a strange land! This afternoon one of the ladies in this house buried her little boy, about two years old, she was very much affected and cryed bitterly, when she kissed it goodbye, before consigning it to the cold grave. When she kissed it, she exclaimed, "Oh my dear little Jessie, can I let you go, never to see you again!" The minister spoke beautifully to the bereaved mother. I wrote a long letter home to ma, after which Howard and I took along walk around town. The scenery here is beautiful, but the Town is very irregular— and very dirty. The sun was setting, or rather sinking behind the mountains, when we were above the town surveying its beauties. The golden clouds rolled up above the distant peaks—looking so lovely in comparison with the dark blue out lines of the mountain. Tomorrow we again will be on the wing, I know not where we will stop.

Monday 21st

Started off this morning after 11 oc, passed through some of the most magnificent scenery I ever beheld. The Blue Ridge nearly is covered with snow. Down

12. They visited a Methodist Episcopal Church; Bond usually attended the Methodist Protestant Church.

many of the mounts are to be seen immense rocks jutting out, covered with sprays of ice,[13] as it had frozen in its downward progress. It surely was magnificent. In some places the frozen spray looked like marble statues. We traveled from Cumberland to Wheeling, and will remain here at night, are putting up at the "Maclure House."[14]

Tuesday 22nd

Got up at five o'clock this morning to go to Cincinnati. Crossed over on the far-famed suspension bridge. It surely is something grand, and is wonderful how human hands could have constructed it. When we crossed the Ohio River on the bridge—we were then in Ohio state. We took the cars and came to a little town called Belair, stopped for another train, then started off. The sun rose beautifully over the distant mountains, bathing the river with its crimson rays. I enjoyed the setting of the sun, this evening too, very much. We were traveling along a creek when the sun sank in the West, casting lovely pink reflections on the stream. There was a beautiful growth of trees on each side, which were beautifully reflected on the water. Soon after the moon arose. We traveled yesterday 201 miles. Today 256. I have a dreadful headache—did not go down to supper. Howard had it sent up to my room. We are putting up at the "Burnet House." It is a beautiful building—painted to represent granite. Much larger Hotel than Barnum's in Balto.

Wednesday 23rd

Raining. Howard would not let me go today. I suffered with sick headache so much last night, says I must rest, so as to be able to go tomorrow. I did not get up till near twelve. Had my breakfast in bed. I have got one of the best, and kindest husbands in the world. I wrote to sister Fannie this evening, Howard to his mother. Cincinnatti is a very pretty city. The streets are clean and wide. I regreted it rained—for we intended to have driven around town.

Thursday 24th

Started off soon this morning—arrived about sun-set in Vincense in Illinois. Very poor accommodations. Feel tired, and home sick. Ohio has some very pretty scenery, but Indiana is one of the roughest states I ever was in. Illinois can not boast of its highly cultivated soil.

Friday 25th

Arose bright and early—did not get my breakfast till arrived at the depot, got a cup of coffee. Came on to Cairo. Traveled 192 miles yesterday. Crossed the

13. She replaces the word *sheets* with *sprays.*
14. They are staying in Virginia.

Wabash this morning after leaving "Vincense." This has been a lovely day—but cold. I noticed snow very near this place. We are stopping tonight at a very nice House—called the "St. Charles." Can see from the window the Mississippi, the Missouri & the Ohio Rivers. I saw the sun rise this morning, and set this evening. Howard and I went shopping in Cairo, got some Crackers & cheese, and ribbon. I really feel like I was going south now.

Saturday 26th

Got up before five, took the steam boat, breakfasted on it, went down the Mississippi about 20 miles to Columbus Tennessee. Got on the cars, got to Jackson—a very pretty town—about half-past 11 am, stayed there till six p.m. Took a walk around town with Howard.

The southerners were holding a convention here to day. The Court House seemed full. It is quite a pretty building. I expect to have to travel all tonight.———

Jackson City Jan 27th 1861

Traveled all of last night, and part of today. Did not like the thoughts of so doing—but seemed could not avoid it. Did not get here till half-past one o'clock. Passed by some large fields of cotton. Saw much moss hanging on the trees. Some snow here on the sides of the roads, which I was surprised to see. Jefferson City is the capital of this state and is a very pretty place. We are staying at the "Bowman House" the best here. The capitol is just opposite, and is quite a handsome building. The sun has just set. Everything looks calm & lovely. There is not a cloud to be seen, not one as large as my hand. I am sitting in my room. Howard lieing on the bed sleeping. We do not expect to leave here till tomorrow afternoon; so I'm in hopes will get to see something of the town.

How I would love to peep in at them at Maiden Lane, this evening! Company there of course. I expect it is very cold there, as it is so cold here.

Monday 28th

Lovely day—soon after breakfast Howard and I started off for a walk, went over to the Capitol, met with general "Allcorn" of the *army*,[15] who made himself very agreeable, and conducted us through most of the building. We visited the "House of Representatives," I got some ribbon the secessionists had, and two or three envelopes. We then went into the "Senate Chambers." He told me he had had a seat there 8 years—pointed the seat out to me. He was from Kentucky, but resided in Miss- now. We could not get into the Cabinet, as the gentleman who had the key

15. Bond originally wrote *Longcorn* for *Allcorn* but corrects herself above the line. A Mississippi politician before the war and general in the Confederate army, James L. Alcorn became Republican governor of Mississippi during Reconstruction and later served in the U.S. Senate.

was not there, which we regretted very much. From there we walked down one of the principle streets. Saw some of the loveliest places. One in particular took my eye as being perfectly beautiful. It belongs to a widow lady whose name I learned— but have forgotten. Jackson is a beautiful place. There are few houses together, mostly like country residences, with beautifully laid out yards. I saw some flowers—some hyacinths, & violets, those flowers we have in Maryland about the last of April, or first of May. I gathered some lovely moss which I intend to send Dr. Archer, and some beautiful little pebbles. I enjoyed my walk very much indeed. It is a perfect morning—like *our* autumn weather. The birds singing merrily, and the air smelling so sweet. We expect to leave here about one oc this afternoon, for New Orleans.

Tuesday 29th

Arrived in New Orleans last night about twelve oc, very tired, and sick, suffering with headache & sore throat. Cousin Josh here,[16] came yesterday evening. Mrs. Barrow call to see me this morning.[17] I got acquainted with Mrs. Armfield—like her exceedingly, she's so agreeable. Dick Bond called to see me too,[18] a little changed, for the better though. Staying at the St. Charles. It is a magnificent building. So much wealth, and fashion. The ladies dress so much, they seem to think that's their life, to dress, and flirt.

Wednesday 30th

Got up with a dreadful sore throat—feel better tonight. Howard gone out to make some purchases. I'm sitting in my room. Dined at five o,c. Dick and his wife called on me this morning. I like her very much. Mrs. Armfield and I took a nice walk this morning to see the sights. And lots of beautiful things we saw.

Thursday 31st

Rained—Cousin Josh, Howard & I eat breakfast about seven, started off for the boat, crossed the Mississippi to Algiers, took the cars there, got to the depot— found carriage waiting for us. Arrived at Crescent Place about two o,c. All seemed glad to see me.

I do pray I shall be directed to act right in *all* things. O, Father let the prayers of thy people be heard. And put it in my heart to do good to others. I know "O Lord thy judgments are true and thou in righteousness has afflicted me." Those

16. She refers to Howard's father. See the introduction for more information about Howard's family.

17. Volumnia Barrow* was married to Robert Ruffin Barrow,* a leading sugar planter and canal operator in Terrebonne and Lafourche parishes.

18. She refers to Richard C. Bond.

words came in my mind just now and I wrote them almost without thinking. Laura Bond is here, she is lively & pleasant. I like her with all her faults.[19] I spent a very pleasant evening. O, I do hope we will live happily together.

Friday 1st of Feb.

Cloudy & drizzling, sent for our trunks—busy unpacking—cousin Rebecca & I out in the garden gathering flowers.

Saturday 2nd

Howard had his furniture brought over from Houma, our room fixed very nicely—looks quite cozy.[20] Beautiful day—cool.

Sunday 3rd

Very cold—ground frozen; looks as though it would snow. Howard & Barrow went to church,[21] Laura to the Catholic Church. Cousin Rebecca & I had a long chat. Dr. Good came home with H-, took dinner, I liked him very much. I could scarcely keep warm.

Monday 4th

Beautiful day—cold—Laura & I been laughing nearly all day. I feel sad at times but hope ere long to be more happy. I have put my trust in a Higher Power, in "One" who will not forsake me.

Tuesday 5th

Lovely weather. Had several to spend the day, Mr. & Mrs. Sample, Miss Sample, & Mrs. Good. I liked them very much, particularly Mrs. Good, she seemed so motherly. But I see none to come up to my own dear ma. They left about five o,c. Howard & I in the parlor on the sofa, I talking of home, and distressing him by *crying*. He says he can always tell when I'm thinking of home. There's a sadness over my face. Well, I must think of dear old Maiden Lane, there's no two ways about it.

Wednesday 6th

About 11 o,c Howard came home from Houma to take us (that's Laura & I) to Mrs. Good's. But after we got in town we concluded not to go there, so we stayed in Howard's store till after the Mail was opened, then drove out past Mr. Barrow's, and back home again.

Got here, found cousin Josh with palpitation of the heart. O, if I might but say

---

19. Bond mentioned Laura* once in her Maryland entries.

20. Houma is the parish seat of Terrebonne and where Howard, as a bachelor, had been living.

21. Barrow is Howard's youngest brother, Robert Richard Barrow Bond. He was twelve years old at the time.

a word in the spirit of God, so it would touch *his* heart. Lord incline my heart to do thy will. Give me grace to overcome every temptation, to cleave to thee—and take up my cross and follow after thee. I forgot to mention, on Monday the Presbyterian minister, & his lady called on me. Their names are McConnell. I liked him exceedingly. He is an "*Irish gentleman.*"[22] I also met him in Howard's store. Got acquainted with Miss Mary Robinson. Was disappointed did not get a letter from home. Perhaps will next mail day for be it known only have tri-weekly mail.

Thursday 7th

One week since I arrived here. Had a sad scene this morning. Dear Cousin Rebecca's feelings were so hurt. I deeply sympathize with her. Lord grant it may never be my lot to suffer as she had done. O! that I may have spoken words in due season. I find I've a heart to love me and one open to *my love*. O, that I may be a true daughter to her, and comfort her in her trials. Put words in my mouth, O, Father. I thank thee, O, my father, for speaking through me this morning, for I am sure the words I spoke were inspired by thy spirit. Let me not be self-righteous but knowing and believing that there is no good thing in me except thou help me. O Father let me not be so mean a vessel but what I may be filled with thy precious spirit and thine shall be the honor, the power, and the praise forever, and ever, Amen.

Howard left early this morning for the store, has not returned, and it is nearly half-past five o,c. I am looking for him. This is a lovely evening. Every thing looks beautiful. The flowers are in bloom, and the trees budding out. I like the south very much—and if my people were here, I would like much to live here. As it is, I will try and be contented. This is a very pretty place, the house stands facing west. The sun is slowly descending behind the western horizon, making all nature look so beautiful.

Friday 8th

Lovely day. Miss Sue Woods & Mr. Con Woods called this morning.[23] She took Laura in Houma, to go to a supprise party, at Mr. Albert Woods. I liked her exceedingly, she is so modest & unassuming in her manners.

Spent a very pleasant evening in chat with dear cousin Rebecca.

22. Mathern McConnel* was from Ireland and was thirty years old in 1861. His wife, Corrie, was from Alabama and was twenty-five years old. Unless noted otherwise, specific information regarding Bond's Terrebonne acquaintances' ages and wealth comes from the 1850 U.S. census, free schedule, Terrebonne Parish, La.; National Archive microfilm publication M432, roll 241; and the 1860 U.S. census, free schedule, Terrebonne Parish, La., M653, roll 425.

23. Susanna Woods, thirty-three years old and from Mississippi, was living with Mrs. Phoebe Pierce, a planter, at the time of the 1860 census.

Saturday 9th

Mrs. Dr. Jennings & Mrs. Acock call on me this afternoon.[24] Laura came home this morning. Acted *very strangely*. Clouded up this afternoon.

Sunday 10th

Had a very heavy rain this morning, thundered & lighteninged very much. Cleared off about three, Lovely sunset, a rival to *Italy's far famed sunsets*. Howard & I upstairs all the afternoon, Laura in her room.—

Monday 11th

Rode in to Houma with Howard this morning in the buggy, purchased some things, several dresses & lace. After dinner, got a letter from home. Laura & I went into Houma, I drove—Fred out-rider. Left Laura at Mr. Woods, to stay several days. Howard took me short drive down the bayou. Lovely evening.

Tuesday 12th

Beautiful day. Dr. & Mrs. Helmick spent the afternoon with us, she is a very pleasant lady.[25] After they left, Howard took me riding, stopped at the bake-house as we came back, saw how they baked bread.

Wednesday 13th

Went into Town this morn with Howard, ordered some things from New Orleans. Had the headache nearly all day. Blew up rain this afternoon, heavy rain & thunder storm. Got a letter from sister Fannie. How glad was it welcomed!

Thursday 14th

Lovely day, I do not feel very well. This afternoon Mrs. Tenant & her little Mary called, stayed till after sun down. Cousin Rebecca and I were very busy cutting out work—no she was ironing—I cutting—when she came. Had a good deal of fun after Howard came home. This is St. Valentine's day. I got one yesterday. I know Howard sent it. It is called *"Vain Mother."*

---

24. Rebecca Lewis was married to Dr. James Jennings.

25. A. S. Helmick* and his wife, Elneyra Delarand, originally from Virginia, were thirty-five and twenty-five years old, respectively. In her diary entry of 6 April 1859, Bond writes that Howard had been studying medicine with Dr. Helmick. See Bond's letter to Ann Lee dated 13 April 1862 for further information on the couple.

Friday 15th

Another lovely day. Been writing home, wrote to brother, Peggie & coz, feel tired.

Feb 23rd

Saturday last I went up to Houma with cousin Josh and sis, in the carriage, to see the presentment of a flag to the Terrebonne Rifle Company.[26] Miss Susannah Woods presented it. Mr. Bunn delivered an address. There was quite a turnout. We call on Mrs. McConnell. Got acquainted with Mrs. Albert Cage,[27] she is beautiful. Mrs. Pearce, Miss Sue Woods & Laura came home, stayed all night with us. Sunday morning I went to the presbyterian church—heard Mr. McConnell preach a very biblical sermon, came home to dinner, after which Howard & I went down to the sugar house, got acquainted with some of The Blacks, several delivered quite an adress to their *young missus,* as they termed me.

Monday afternoon, Mrs. Dunn & her mother, Mrs. Fuqua, called on me. Wednesday, cousin R, Laura & I went into Houma shopping—paid two calls, no one home, consequently left our cards.

Friday 22nd, Howard left home about six in the morning, to join the company at Houma to go to Thibodaux, got about a mile and a half from there, when they stopped to fire the canon off—when it went off before the ones who were attending to it thought it would, and shot two men, pitched them about ten feet, shot off arms fingers—out eyes, set them on fire.[28] O I never heard of any thing so dreadful. How thankful we should be that Providence watched over & protected Howard. He offered to set it off and walked up to do so, but some one told him others were already appointed to do it, one died last night—was buried this morning in Houma—his name is James Hagers. The other David Phips—

Howard left early this morning to put the mail up. It has been very warm, rained this evening. The birds are singing merrily—There seem to be a great many french mocking birds . . .

April 1st 1861

Some time has slipped by, since I penned in this book. The weather is very fine & warm—Looks like *Northern June.* Roses out & flowers of various hues. The air

26. "Sis" is Howard's sister Louisa's nickname. She was seven years old in 1861.

27. Bond refers to Elvira Cage, who was married to Albert G. Cage, a Terrebonne planter who in 1860 owned over one hundred slaves and approximately seventeen hundred acres of land (Menn, *Large Slaveholders of Louisiana,* 414–15).

28. Thibodaux was the second largest town in the Lafourche district, with approximately one thousand inhabitants. The district state militia established its headquarters in Thibodaux during the summer of 1862.

is greatly perfumed with the China tree blossoms. We've had sunshine & showers, pretty much as first of last April. How I remember it. I april-fooled my Dr. I got a letter from dear aunt Rebecca today. One characteristic of herself.

2nd

Lovely day. Mr. McConnell call on us this morning—spent several hours. He gave me two tracts to read—I think of joining his church next sunday.

CHAPTER SIX

"War Is upon Us"

4 JULY 1861–27 JULY 1862

July 4th 1861

Three months have passed since I have opened this book, to write one line. Many have been the revelations in political affairs. War! Civil War! is upon us, in all its horrors. Lincoln has waged war against the southern Confederacy. Virginia has joined us, also Tenn since April. Sumpter has been taken by Gen Beauregard,[1] a battle at great Bethel was fought in June,[2] Southerners *victorious*. May they always be so. All mails are stopped between the United States and Confederacy.[3] I can not hear from home. I am trying to bear it bravely. Nor do I know when I will be able. O, for one more letter.

How many the changes since this time last year. How differently I have been occupied today. Howard sick in bed—I nursing him. Billious attack. About this time in the evening last fourth, I was on horse back. I remember it well. I wonder what they have been doing at home to day! The ladies of Terrbonne have been very patriotic. They have formed a sewing society to have clothes made up for the "Grivot Guards" of this parish.[4] They are now in Va.[5] The ladies propose holding a concert on next wednesday night, in Houma for the benefit of the G-G's. Had

1. The Confederate army, under command of Gen. Pierre G. T. Beauregard, attacked Fort Sumter on 12 April 1861, firing the first shot in the Civil War.

2. Bond is referring to Big Bethel, the first land battle in Virginia, which took place on 10 June 1861.

3. The Confederate Postal Service was established on 21 February 1861. In March Jefferson Davis named John H. Reagan postmaster-general of the Confederate States. In May 1861 Reagan issued a statement that he would assume control of the Confederate Postal Service on 1 June. In response, Montgomery Blair, the postmaster appointed by Lincoln, ordered the cessation of United States mail service in the South. Confederate mail service was sporadic, due to factors including blockades and scarcity of postage stamps.

4. Bond mentions the sewing society in her letter to her mother dated 19 May 1861 (see app. 1).

5. The Grivot Guards of Terrebonne was an infantry unit led first by F. S. Goode and then, after his resignation, by J. B. Dunn. In Virginia its members, along with other Louisiana companies, were organized as the First Louisiana Infantry Battalion. By mid-1861, twenty-three hundred Confederate soldiers from Louisiana were in Virginia. Louisiana outfits in Virginia led by General Beauregard played a large role at the Battle of Bull Run in July 1861. See Bergeron, *Guide to Louisiana*, 148.

the appearance of rain early this morning but is now clear & beautiful. Cousin Josh has gone to Mr. Barrows.[6] I am seated in my room at the north east window. Howard in bed. Laura in the next room. The rest on the gallery.

July 5th

Rained very hard this morning. I was greatly rejoiced getting letters from home, two from sister Fannie. O, how thankful I should be. I have been permitted to hear again from the loved ones. I feel very sad indeed. Home seems so far off. O, My Father in Heaven, give me grace to bear up under the trials of this life, keep me for Christ sake. Bless all my dear ones, and shield them from all evil. There is a very large comet to be seen now.[7]

July 7th

Lovely morning—Cousin Josh left for the city this morning, with Mr. Aycock. Howard still sick. Mrs. Barrow, Berta, & Mrs. Henly called this evening.[8] Howard much worse. Sent for the Dr. No one went to church from here today.

Monday 8th

Howard was very ill last night, has had dumb chills & fevers.

Better today. Cousin R & I sat up last night. Very warm today. I did not go down stairs till near tea time.

Tuesday 9th

Expected cousin Josh home, did not come. Howard better. Rained very hard. This is the "Rainy Season."

Wednesday 10th

Howard able to come down stairs. Cousin Josh came home today.

Thursday 11th

I feel very sad today. Had my feelings hurt so badly. O! my dear old home, how I have longed to see you today. I can scarcely realize even now, my being so far from home. And War in the land, in our once happy country. The Confederate troops are concentrated in Va. Winchester & Martinsburg are the principle places. But Richmond is the seat of war & the Capital of the "C.S.A."[9]

6. Robert Ruffin Barrow* was one of the region's leading sugarcane planters and also a successful canal operator.

7. Bond refers to the Great Comet of 1861, visible from the end of June to early July.

8. Berta is Mrs. Barrow's daughter, Volumnia Roberta, who was eight years old in 1861. Mrs. Henly's identity is unknown.

9. The Confederate capital was moved from Montgomery, Ala., to Richmond, Va., in May 1861.

Friday 12th

Another beautiful day! And very warm. Yesterday was real cool. I had to put on more clothen. This climate is very changeable. But I do not take cold so easily as I did in Maryland, but, old Maryland still for me!

Saturday 13th

Beautiful day. I have been thinking much of *home* today. O, could I see them *all* again. O, Father stay the avenger's hand.

Sunday 14th

Went to church this morning in the carriage with Mother,[10] Mrs. Campbell, sis & Howard, heard a beautiful sermon by Rev Mr. Carter of the M[ethodist] E[piscopal] church, from Malachi 3 chap 8 verse. "Will a man rob God? Yet ye have robbed me. But ye say wherein have we robbed thee? In tithes & offerings." We rob God of his praise, was one of the principle points. He dwelled on avarice. Mr. McConnell has not returned from Galveston, where he went two weeks since to see his wife who then was supposed to be dieing. Have not heard from her yet. Laura has been staying at Mrs. Barrow's since last Sunday, suppose she will be home today. . . . .

August 26th

Another birthday I have been permitted to see.[11] As bright as the last one, so far. How vividly it rises before me. Here I am I La and my last birthday I was at Maiden Lane.

Many changes has transpired since I wrote here. War, war is the theme. There was a glorious victory gained by the Southerners at Bull's Run, and Manasses,[12] the former the 21st and the latter the 27th of July. Other battles have been fought in Mo. One at Springfield.[13] We are daily expecting to hear of a battle in Maryland. Our troops are progressing slowly towards the Potomac. O, Father look in mercy on my dear ones. Hasten the time when war shall be no more. Peace may be declaimed. Forgive our past sins of omission and commission. Keep us from erring in the future. I heard from home two weeks since. My dear ma was sick. I do pray she is now well. Keep her as the apple of thy eye. Hide her under the

10. This is the first and only time that Bond refers to her mother-in-law, Cousin Rebecca, as "mother."

11. She turns twenty-three.

12. Bond confuses the one battle, the Battle of Bull Run, also called Manassas, for two. The battle was won by the Confederates on 21 July 1861.

13. Bond probably refers to the Battle of Wilson's Creek, fought on 10 August 1861, about ten miles southwest of Springfield, Mo. The battle was a Confederate victory.

shadow of thy wing. Safe into thy harbor guide. O receive her soul at last. The sun is shining beautiful now, but I hear murmuring thunder, indication of a storm. It has rained every day, but two or three for weeks. It is what's called the 'Rainy season.'

O, how my ears have been stressed today by the cry of the distressed! How bestial it is to whip the negro so severely. God will not wink at such cruelty! Mr. McConnell & family came home yesterday.

Tuesday 27th

I feel sad—more whipping going on. One poor old man is the sufferer of *man's* passions. Thank God my husband is not so heartless. It is indeed hard to bear to be compelled to stay where such is carried on daily. All are not like him here. He is the father of my husband, but I can never love him as such. I have no respect for him. He is too mean for anything. I wish he was not Howard's father. Yester day's papers stated no more letters were to be sent by Adam's Express.[14] O, shall I not again hear from my dear home. Father grant me that privilege. O to be so far away without the way of communicating with the loved ones at home.

Wednesday 28th

Rained this morning—The sun comes out with fits & starts. I feel sad today. "Why O, why my heart is sadness." This is a pretty piece of poetry, and true too

> "*Solace in Sorrow*"
> "There's not a hearth, however rude,
> But hath some little flower
> To brighten up its solitude
> and scent the evening hour.
>
> There's not a heart however cast
> By grief and sorrow down,
> But hath some memory of the past
> To love and call its own."
> Mittie Bond

I received a dear nice letter from Lou Wyatt. She lives in Winchester Va. She says the battlefield (Manassus) was perfectly awful. The Yankees fled & left their wounded & dead on the field. The southerners buried all they could, before the stench got so sickening, they could not stand it. And a week after the battle some

14. The Adams Express Company delivered paychecks for both Union and Confederate armies until, after receiving complaints, it established a separate company, Southern Express, to handle southern deliveries.

were seen crawling about "just gasping for breath." Capt. Frank Bond & Otho Lee are stationed at the "Junction."[15] We are daily expecting exciting news from the seat of war.

Thursday 29th

Busy most of the day making mango pickles. Mrs. Eastern call about 12 out of the rain, did not see her as she did not ask for me. Do not feel well at all. Got bad pain in my back, feel so sad about my poor dear ma. Lou tells me Sallie Gover wrote her Ma was quite sick. O, how I want to see her. But I must be patient. I have much to feel thankful for. Many dear blessings. The best of husbands. I was sitting late this evening at my window up in my room feeling very sad, tears trickling down my cheeks when Howard came up, seemed to feel for me so, says I must not be alone so much. I get to thinking too much about home.

Friday 30th

Mrs. Campbell quite sick. I feel sorry she & I can not agree, she is a very singular woman—very proud & haughty.[16]

I have tryed to live in peace with her but she appears to prefer the opposite.[17] She & Laura has not spoken for two months, & room together. I have been reading the life of Queen Elizabeth today, she called herself the Maiden Queen. She had one of her *two thousand* dresses woven with eyes, ears & snakes on it. She was said to be the vainest woman in the world. I'm glad I went in to see Mrs. C. this evening. It was a struggle, but the good angel conquered.

We had a very severe thunder storm this evening. Howard was at the shop with others, he was very much stunned. It was a merciful dispensation of Providence he was saved.

O, Father in Heaven grant that this open act of mercy towards us may be felt & appreciated in a proper light, *by us all.* Do thou give me a heart full of gratitude to thee, the guider of all things good.

Saturday August 31st 1861

Raining—when will it stop! We have had rain four or five weeks. I had such a singular & bad dream last night. I'm not inclined to be superstitious, but I can't

15. Frank Bond, from Baltimore, was married to Landie Webster. Otho Lee, from Harford, was sergeant major in Johnson's Battalion Stuart's Horse Artillery. After the war, he studied law with Henry Archer and later became president of the Farmers and Merchants National Bank of Belair, Md. See MacKenzie, *Colonial Families of the United States of America,* 2:439.

16. Mrs. Campbell's* identity is not clear. When Bond arrived in Louisiana, she was staying with the Bonds, but she is not listed as a member of their household in any census record.

17. Bond crosses out the word *like* and adds *prefer.*

help thinking all's not right at my dear old home. Oh! could I know all were well there. My dear Ma I know is sicker than the rest will let on to me. Spare her O, my God still many years to us. She is a priceless gift. My mother, O, my mother, what melody in these words.

Sunday 1st Sept

Rained most of the day. Did not go to church—felt very anxious to hear Mr. McC- cousin Josh went.

Monday 2nd

Cousin Rebecca got a letter from Mrs. Barrow (who is now in the city) asking her if she did not want a seamstress, as there was a very decent woman there who would come out in the country for four months just for her board. It was a case of charity, but he would not take her. Why is it money makes people *so mean!* Ah me. I want to be rich, to do good. I do hope I would do so. O, Father, I had cause to thank thee yesterday for the effects of some advice I had given Howard previously about being kind to the servants & encouraging them. Do thou O, Father help him to do what is right and me also. We are weak & sinful, not able to do any good thing within ourselves. Keep my lips from evil speaking & my thoughts from thinking guile.

Friday 6th

It has rained every day this week. The roads are in a dreadful state. Yesterday I was grieved to learn the demise of our esteemed friend Mrs. Wm. Bisland.[18] She was in Houma on a visit Monday, got caught in the rain going home & died yesterday morning about one. It is a warning, "be ye always ready, for ye know not the day or hour the son of man cometh." Howard has gone with some 70 soldiers today down Grand C. They are going to build a fort there.[19] Miss Joe Dorsey sent the carriage for Laura today, she has gone.

Saturday 21st

Howard & I rode up to Houma, to see Mr. McConnell. I gave him my certificate from the Methodist church in Belair Harford County Maryland. I now am a member of the Presbyterian church south.[20] Got home about dinner time—found Dr. Helmick here, sis is very sick, taken in the night. Cousin Josh came home from the city, this afternoon.

18. Mrs. Bisland's husband, William A. Bisland, was a Terrebonne planter from Mississippi who in 1860 owned ninety-two slaves and approximately twenty-five hundred acres of land.

19. Fort Quitman was built on Grand Caillou Bayou.

20. In her letters of 27 February and 5 June 1861, Bond writes to her mother about her decision to join the Presbyterian Church South.

Sunday 22nd

Magnificent day, real fall like. Looks like a Maryland day. Did not go to church—roads so bad.

Monday 23rd

Sis very ill last night—delirious, sent for the Dr. about midnight, something better today. Dr. here this morning again. Been busy getting Howard ready to go for beeves tomorrow.

Tuesday 24th

Howard & Wellie left after breakfast for New Iberia La. to purchase beeves[21]— pork can not be had unless paying 40$ per barrel. They went on horse back. It is the other side of Berwick's Bay. Expect them back saturday. Another lovely day. Hope they will have as fine weather all the time.

Wednesday 25th

Heard whilst at breakfast Mr. Delahoussey had shot & killed Frederick a tailor in Houma.[22] Have not heard the particulars. Mrs. Campbell & I had a spat *again* this morning on persons carrying weapons on their persons.

Sunday 29th

Lovely day. I felt so anxious to go to church—but Howard & Wellie have not come home yet. I would have walked (as they have the carriage horses) but I was taken quite sick soon after breakfast. I feel better now. I have felt so sad all day. So long since I heard from home. Oh! when shall I be able to get a letter. My Father do thou watch over & protect them from all evil, and O, hasten the time when peace shall be declared & we a happy & free nation again.

What would I not give to be at home this evening. I can well imagine how things look there. O, for a loving kiss from those loved ones! My ma, how I *do* want to see you. It seems like two years since we parted. It has been most nine months.

I miss Howard so much. I wish he would come home. Gov Moor has issued a proclamation that all the militia shall be drilled & those from 18 to 45 are subject to be called for service, those over 45 & upward for home guard.[23] It makes my heart ache to think of this war. Lord protect us! I must be brave—be a "*true*

21. Wilmore Nichols Bond,* Howard's brother, was fifteen years old in 1861. In going to New Iberia, the brothers were traveling approximately sixty miles northwest of Houma.

22. The gunman was probably Octave Delahoussey, a wealthy planter who was married and had five children. He was sixty-seven years old in 1861. Bond would have found strange the frontier culture in which men carried guns and often used them freely.

23. On 28 September 1861, Louisiana governor Thomas Moore decreed that all citizens between the ages of eighteen and forty-five were subject to militia duty.

woman." O, how oft those words have rung in my ears! "Be a true woman Mit."
They are my mothers words.

Monday October 7th

I was suffering much with neuralgia most of last week. In bed all friday. Got a
letter from Howard from New Iberia, saying he would be home in five or six days.
So he came that night. I was *so* glad to see him. He had made some narrow escapes
with wild cattle whilst driving them. Got his eye badly bruised. Saturday Mrs. Barrow called, brought Berta to spend the day with sis. Laura sent home with Berta
in the evening.

Sunday 6th I joined church. Received the sacraments with Howard for the first
time [since] I joined. O, how my thoughts went back to when I joined church before. Nearly four years since I joined the Methodist church.

This morning Howard went to Thibodaux.[24] Very windy & cool—real fall like.
I imagine I see the beautiful foliage in dear old Harford. O, if kind providence will
permit me to get a letter from home soon!

Tuesday 8th

Harry horse died last night. Howard drove him yesterday, & he had not been
home but a few minutes before he dropped dead. I felt so sorry.

Thursday 10th

Cousin Rebecca, Mrs. Campbell, sis & myself spent the day at Mrs. Barrows,
had a very nice time. Mrs. Barrow sent the carriage for us. Laura came home
with us.

Saturday 19th

Laura, Barrow and I walked to Houma to see the soldiers drill, called to see
Mrs. Good, took dinner at Dr. Helmick's.[25] Met there Mrs. Banks and the two
Miss Calhoun's. Miss Laura Banks, Laura & I went out shopping. Got home about
sun down.

Sunday 13th

Howard took me to church in the buggy. I joined the Bible class. Lovely day.

Tuesday 15th

I was very much surprised & grieved to heard of Mrs. Albert Cage's death.[26]
She has been sick for about a month, but did not apprehend any thing serious. We

24. The town is located approximately fifteen miles north of Houma.

25. Barrow, Howard's youngest brother, was named after Josh Bond's business partner, Robert Ruffin Barrow.

26. In her diary entry of 23 February 1861, Bond mentions meeting Mrs. Elvira Cage.

attended her funeral, a very large one, about 40 carriages in procession. She was buried in Houma about half past three. Mr. Cage did not arrive till the evening before she died. He was in Va. She leaves a little babe a few hours old, and several other children, she left them to Mr. & Mrs. Duncan Cage's care.[27] Mr. Mc-Connell's remarks were beautiful at the house. He prayed so beautiful for the motherless children. O, that *we all* may profit by her example.

Wednesday 16th

Cloudy, I feel so sad. O, Heavenly Father direct me in all things. Keep my lips from evil speaking and my thoughts from thinking guile.

I forgot to mention, we had a brush at the Passes on saturday 12—with Lincoln's fleet, our little fleet, whiped. We have one vesel we call Manasses, built in New Orleans. She is of iron, she sunk one of their vesels.[28] We are looking daily for news from the Potomac. I hope it will be good news when it comes. A good Conundrum—Why is a bee-hive like a spect potato? Because a bee-hive is a beholder, and a beholder is spectator and a spectator is a bad potato. If you were compelled to swallow a man, whom would you prefer to swallow? A little London porter. When does the farmer act with rudeness towards his corn? When he pulls its ears.

Got a letter from Dr. George Archer dated 8th and mailed from Winchester. He had made his escape across the Potomac the 6th. Soon after he arrived in "Dixie" he wrote me of my dear loved ones. O, Father in Heaven I thank thee for that privilege of hearing from home. My poor ma is still sick but slowly recovering. O Father spare my dear parents that I may behold their faces once more on Earth. Dr. wrote me dear aunt Magg Bridge died in July, of Typhoid fever after a weeks illness. We are parted now but O, may we meet where parting is no more. I was sorrow stricken to hear of her death.

Monday 21st

I answered the Dr's letter today. Cousin Josh commenced grinding sugar yesterday (sunday). O, is there any hope for his soul? Does he ever think there is a time to die, & a place to be punished? Open thou his eyes, ere it be too late O Father! . . . .[29]

Wednesday, December 18

What a long time has passed since I penned a line in here. Why do I not write oftener in my journal? I believe it is because my thoughts are so often sad ones. I

27. Duncan Cage, Albert Cage's brother, was also a planter and was married to Sarah Jane Cage.

28. Bond refers to a Confederate naval attack on Union forces on the Mississippi River. The Confederate ram *Manassas* struck the USS *Richmond* and forced it aground.

29. Bond separates the October and December entries with a line of dots.

have been gliding along pretty much at the usual rate. I received a letter from dear Aunt Rebecca Bond last week dated Balto Nov 27, mailed from Norfolk, Va. She told me my dear Ma was in Balto the week before, looking well & happy as possible. O, how I thank God for permitting me to hear from her (my precious ma) once more & to hear all were well. My Father in heaven, make me *truly thankful.* I have been taking a retrospective view of the past year.

What sad changes have occurred! "As my day is so shall my strength be." O, Father help me to number my days, that I may apply myself unto wisdom.

Thursday 19th

Grand Picnic at Fort Butler, on Grand Cailleu or rather Inauguration of the Fort. Washington Marks, Cap. "Twiggs Rifles" B.[30] I was invited—but did not go. Laura went to Mr. Col. Robinson's to go with the girls. Wellie went to Mr. Pierce's to go. It is about 25 miles from here. Glorious news in today's paper. England demands Mason & Slidell (our commissioners to England). They were taken off of the British steamer "Trent" by Capt. Wilks of the "San Jacinto," & taken to New York & from there to Boston, placed in "Fort Warren." England now demands a surrender of they & their secretaries Eustice & McFarland. They I suppose (that's Lincoln)[31] will not give them up—and of course a war with England is inevitable.[32] O, when will this horrid war terminate?

Saturday 21st

Busy most of the day making cake. This day one year, I was looking for Howard & sister Fannie from Baltimore, they came after dark. He gave me his mother's letter, saying that his father wished him to marry me & bring me home, and here I am. What changes! What struggles I had before I could make up my mind to leave *my precious home.*

Sunday 22nd

Raining. Howard gone to church. I'm not very well, got the headache. Did not get much rest last night. Wellie caught a runaway in the kitchen last night. Had

30. Fort Butler was located near Donaldsonville on Bayou Lafourche. Washington Marks was commander of Company H, Twiggs Rifles Company B, of the Twenty-third Infantry Regiment. The company was assigned to Fort Quitman on Grand Caillou Bayou. Marks was promoted to major in 1863.

31. Initially, Bond wrote "that's the Northerners" but adds Lincoln's name above the line.

32. Bond refers to the Trent Affair. On 8 November 1861, Confederate commissioners James M. Mason and John Slidell were en route to England on the British steamer *Trent* when the U.S. warship *San Jacinto,* under the command of Capt. Charles Wilkes, stopped the steamer. Mason and Slidell, along with their secretaries Eustis and McFarland, were forcibly removed and imprisoned in Fort Warren (Boston). The event led to talk of war in Britain and a demand for the prisoners' release. Secretary of State William H. Seward ordered their release on 26 December and thus avoided further trouble with Britain.

the whole house aroused. . . . . . Had quite a scene this afternoon. Howard object-
ing to the way the runaway was treated by *Nace* (the driver) I spoke to H- loud
enough of his father to hear & said, Howard, if you are going to have a black master over you—it is more than I'm willing to have. Cousin Josh thinks more of Nace
than any one of his children; he will believe him sooner than he will his children.

Monday 23rd
Busy making cake most of the day.[33]

Tuesday 24th
Very cold yesterday & today—moderated a good deal before dinner. Grand
Tableaux Vivante tonight at the Academy, followed by a splendid supper, after
which to break up with a "Ball."

Christmas day 25th 1861
. This time one year I was in my own precious home—we all dined together.
When shall we dine together again? O, how often has my thoughts traveled back
to my childhood's home, & I feel assured they were thinking of me, & wishing I
was there.

I attended the Tableau last night—great many there. Every body seemed to be
pleased. The first scene was Queen Esther in the presence of King Ashuarus. Miss
Mary Robertson was queen, Mr. John Bisland, king.[34] Laura was Caucasian slave,
she looked very well. I made part of her dress. The last Tableau was the Confederate States, with Maryland kneeling before them—her arms chained and hands
clasped—Laura Bond represented Maryland, she was dressed in a crimson dress
with a black scarf, on it "Maryland" printed with silver letters. After the curtain
was drawn, Maryland threw her chains off & arose and sang "God Save the South."
It was beautiful. We spent a very pleasant evening. Cousin Josh Barrow,[35] sis,
Laura, & myself dined at Mr. Barrows. I got a pretty bouquet. Christmas here isn't
like it is at *home*. I was so in hopes of getting a letter from home.

Thursday 26th
Not feeling very well today, thoughts will travel back to *that loved spot, home*—
O, that I might hear from home.

33. Bond initially wrote "Got up & made two spunge cakes before breakfast." She crossed this sentence through and replaced it with the one here.

34. The queen and king were, respectively, a daughter of F. E. Robertson, a Terrebonne planter originally from Virginia, and John Bisland, a Terrebonne planter from Mississippi who in 1860 owned 130
slaves. See Menn, *Large Slaveholders*, 416–17. Bisland became a Confederate colonel and was one of the
citizens arrested by Union Colonel Keith in the investigation that led to the burning of the Bonds' plantation.

35. Josh Barrow is a cousin of Mrs. Barrows and likely Laura Bond's suitor whom Bond mentions
in her letter to Ann Lee dated 13 April 1862.

Sunday 29th

Went to sunday school early this morning with Howard.

Monday 30th

Mrs. Calhoun, Miss May, Miss Emma, & Cortland Calhoun spent the day also Miss Lee Beaufort & Miss Alice Baker. I made the negroes a Confederate flag. They finished cutting cane. I presented it to them & told them they must not let the Yankees get a'hold of it.

Tuesday 31st 1861

Miss Mary & Miss Emma, & Mr. George Calhoun came out this morning & spent the day. The girls are staying all night. Old Mr. Calhoun, Mrs. Helmick, & Fannie made a call this afternoon.

The negroes finished grinding sugar today, & marched up & a round the house, under *their Confederate flag.* They carried Mr. Board (the Overseer) part of the way.[36]

Howard, Cousin Rebecca & myself had such a pleasant chat in the parlor this evening after the rest of the family had retired.

Wednesday 1st of January 1862

The Lord has again permitted me to see another New Year. It does not seem like winter here. It is so warm, winter clothes are too warm. This day one year, at home, it was very cold and beautiful. Mrs. Col. Robertson & Mrs. Lannent called this morning.[37] I went to Houma early this morn with Howard.

Thursday 2nd

Beautiful day. Jokey Goode was married last night to Miss Fannie Holden. They will come home today; are going to live with old Mrs. Goode in Houma. There has been several weddings this week. Buck Wright & Sarah Fields were married monday evening.

Friday 3rd

Laura went to a party at Col. Robertson's tonight. Been busy all day preparing a dress to wear.

36. In this and the previous entry, Bond describes slave work at the end of the sugar harvest, or "rolling season." The harvest usually began in middle to late October and continued for two months. Some slaves worked in the fields, cutting cane and collecting it to be transferred to the mill. Those who worked in the mill ensured that the cane was fed into the mill rollers to extract the juice. It was then purified by boiling it in large kettles and finally granulated. The work was strenuous and constant. Still, as Rodrigue, in *Reconstruction in the Cane Fields,* explains, slaves "viewed the rolling season as a festive occasion that provided a change from the routine drudgery of everyday life" (17).

37. She perhaps refers to Mary Robertson, the wife of Frances Epes Robertson, a Terrebonne planter from Virginia.

Saturday 4th

Had a wedding here tonight; two of the servants got married. Howard performed the ceremony. The bride looked quite nice dressed in white. I made her turban of white swiss—pink tarlatan & orange blossoms. They were married at the gallery. The moon shone beautifully. They afterwards adjourned to the "hospital," where they enjoyed a "Ball." I wonder what the "Yankees" would think of it if they had seen, how happy they were, dressed in their *ball dresses*. The groom had on a suit of black, white gloves & tall *beaver*. The bride dressed in white swiss, pink trimmings & white gloves. The brides-maid & groom's man dress to correspond.

Sunday 5th

Have not felt well today, did not get up till after twelve. Howard & his father went to church. Sis sick today, had a chill. Rained last night and blew quite hard. The sun is shining beautifully now and it seems more like spring weather than winter; the birds & crickets are singing merrily. What kind of weather are they having at home! and what are they doing! How my heart yearns for "the loved ones at home." Do they miss me at home do they miss me, would be an assurance most dear to know that this moment some loved one was saying *I wish she were here.*

Monday 6th

Lovely day—Mr. & Mrs. McConnell called this afternoon. Miss Alice Baker & Laura came home this evening, walked. We visited the Quarters—went into uncle Bob's cabin, had lots of fun, he said he had the advantage over all the rest of the darkeys—for having the most fun from the white folks during the holidays. (They have had a week holiday.)[38]

Wednesday 8th

The anniversary of the battle of New Orleans in 1814. Rained all day. Miss Alice still here. Howard mesmerized Jeff tonight—stuck pins in his ear, and through the skin of his hand—and he never felt it. Had a heap of fun.

Thursday 9th

Had quite a thunder storm last night. Rained most of the morning. Miss Alice went home this evening, sent me an orange by Barrow.[39] I got such a sweet letter from Lou Wyatt yesterday.

---

38. Slave Christmas and New Year holidays ranged in length from three days to a week. They were marked by many parties, drinking, and present giving. Josh could be considered generous as he allowed a weeklong holiday. Judging by his leniency, we can assume that the sugar harvest at Crescent Place was profitable that year. For more detail on slave holidays, see Genovese, *Roll, Jordon, Roll,* 573–84.

39. She refers to Howard's youngest brother.

Sunday 12th

Warm—most like a summer day. Howard & I went to church today. Had communion, many persons there. Thoughts often traveled homeward today. The last sunday at home, how I remember it!

Monday 13th

Rained quite fast this morning, but cleared off about ten o'clock. Miss Mamie Skudy & Miss Alice Baker came, going to remain till tomorrow.

Tuesday 14th

This day one year, and about this time I was *at home* (*my own dear home*) writing in this book. I have been living over the day, today. Yes, I feel as though they were thinking of me. O, if I now felt but one of their dear kisses upon my brow. My ma! My ma! do you know how much I want to see you? This pen can not paint my many emotions of grief at being separated from my 'loved ones.' Very cold today, some thing like this time last year, only it was snowing. The last time I saw it snow the day before my marriage.

Jan 15, 1862

This is the anniversary of our marriage day. One year since I left home—one year since I saw ma—that sweet face. O! those good byes, those tears & God bless you—when shall I hear them again! Give me grace O Father in Heaven, to bear up under this heavy trial—Separation from home.

This time last year, I was on my way to Balto. It has been much such a day as last 15th of Jan—raining. Does this betoken another year of tearful separation! O Father forgive this unthankful heart, keep me from mesmerizing. May my entire trust be in thee. Keep my lips from speaking evil, and my thoughts from all guile.[40] O, how I picture them at home. My ma in her chair thinking of me—her eyes filling every few minutes—her prayers breathing to Heaven for the welfare of her children here—O, that they may be answered! Dear pa too is thinking of his absent child—his head bowed down—till his chin is buried in his bosom, his eyes are closed—while his mind's eye perhaps is taking a retrospective view of the events of today a year ago. Ah! yes kind & loving brother & sisters are thinking of their sister, far away from home—sighing for her return around the fireside. That

40. Bond also writes of mesmerism in her entries of 1 December 1860 and 8 January 1862. She was obviously aware that established Christianity objected to mesmerism, seeing it as a threat and as related to occult healing. Howard could have learned to mesmerize when he studied medicine with a local doctor. While many doctors did not take mesmerism seriously, some were curious about it, especially its anesthetic effects. For more information on mesmerism in the South, see McCandless, "Mesmirism and Phrenology in Antebellum Charleston."

fireside has been vacant a *year,* twelve months has that chair at the table been un-occupied. O, let me ever remember that day. Its cherished scenes are pictured faith-fully in memories halls—time can not obliterate them they are indelibly traced—never to be effaced by time or distance. My mother's face, how I should love to be an artist to paint her angelic face, as I saw it last. It were as though an angel had fan'd her face with its angelic wing—sweeping away every cloud and leaving there the bright silver light of its own face.

> My Childhood's Home
> Home of my youth! still fondly I love you,
> Though years may elapse ere I see thee again!
> The dear ones I loved may all be departed,
> And the last link be broken in friendship's ernest chain.

Sunday 19th

We had quite a scene here last night, between Patience, Nace, cousin Josh & Rebecca. We sat up till nearly two o'clock. It unfit me for church—I did not go. Why is it *he* is so wrapped up in *that vilain Nace!* I felt so nervous all today.[41] Mrs. Lennant brought Laura home this afternoon, she went there last evening. Lovely day & lovely weather. Took a walk down to the quarters this eve.

Monday 20th

Had several visitors this evening—Mrs. John Bysland, Miss Cassie Bride, Miss Mary Roberson, and Miss Susannah Woods. They came on a begging expedition, didn't get any thing tho.[42]

So warm today. Went out fishing this evening. Fred caught a shoepick (or mud fish), they are very nice fish. Written to aunt Rebecca—going to send it via Fortress Monroe, tomorrow.

Sunday did not go to church today, was not feeling very well—besides have no way of going unless walking, or driving cousin Josh's horses—do not care about being under such obligation to *him.* I wish I had better feelings towards *him.* There is no affinity between *us.* We are oil & water. He is the *strangest man I ever saw,* and hope ever to see again. O, I wish he was not Howard's father. I hope I'm not committing any sin by so doing.

Monday 27th

Got a nice long letter from my old Maryland friend, Dr. G.W. Archer, also a piece of original poetry, "A Dirge for Maryland" written before leaving that state.

41. Patience was a slave in the Bond household.

42. For information on John Bisland, see n. 34. The women were likely collecting money or sup-plies for soldiers. It is not clear why the Bonds did not contribute to their collection.

Poor fellow, he feels, like me, what it is to be separated from *loved ones*. He had heard from home & my home too, Ma better—joyful news—sister Fannie been sick—but well again.—

Wednesday 29th

Howard been gone all day on business—I feel lonely when he goes even for a day, I'm looking for him every minute.

I wrote home Monday evening sent it via Norfolk-flag of truce. I do hope it will reach them safely. God bless them all is my daily prayer.

I have been purchasing some oranges today—how I wish those *at home* could have them. Ma would enjoy them so much—dear ma, how oft do I call up her lovely face as I saw it last. O! *Father* shall I ever behold it again. *God grant.*

April 23rd 1862[43]

Howard, dear Howard came home this eve—will remain several days, then, I shall accompany him back. O, I feel so glad & thankful to have him once more with me—he looks so well & handsome—his mustache so becoming.

May 10th 1862[44]

Three months & more have passed away. O! the changes they have brought forth. War—war, still raging in our land. We have had many defeats & some victories. Fort Donelson has been taken by the Federalists, Nashville occupied by Buells army. McCook is king there. Island No. 10 has been evacuated by our men, and I believe Fort Pillow. There was also a battle near Winchester in March I believe. General Stone Wall Jackson engaged the enemy. General J- had to retreat because he was overpowered by overwhelming numbers. But we had a glorious victory the 6th or 7 of April at Corinth Miss. General Albert S. Johnson was killed—we took large numbers of prisoners, amongst the number General Prentiss.[45] But

43. In Bond's diary, this entry is placed between July entries; it is the only entry that Bond wrote during April, a period of frequent military activity in southern Louisiana. When she wrote the entry, she had obviously skipped pages in her diary, planning to go back and recount what had happened from 29 January to 23 April. During this time, Howard likely was participating in skirmishes and was often away from home. While she did fill the pages with entries from the summer of 1862, she never fulfilled her plan to narrate the events from the winter and spring.

44. In this and the following entry, Bond's handwriting is larger, with words widely spaced and slanted more than usual. The style of her handwriting seems to indicate her emotion and perhaps shows that she is writing quickly, with little time to spend on the diary entry. For more insight into her life during the months she did not keep her diary, see her letter to her mother of 4 May 1862 (app. 1).

45. Bond reports military activity that took place in Kentucky and Tennessee during the winter and spring of 1862. Fort Donelson surrendered to Ulysses S. Grant on 16 February 1862. The defeat led to the Confederate retreat from Kentucky and the evacuation of Nashville on 25 February. Island Num-

sad to relate, the Yankees have New Orleans. Yes, they (Picayune Butler's Fleet) fought nearly two weeks at the Forts (Jackson & St. Phillips), then several of their iron clad gunboats passed the fort & went up to the City—demand a surrender of the Forts of General Duncan before they went to the city, but he positively refused. They then went up to the city—shelled the banks of the river all the way to the city. General Farragut then demanded a surrender of the city of Mayor Monroe— but he told him he would not surrender—he would not resist him, as the Military had all left the city & if he tore down our flag it would be by brutal force. They took possession, & have since come out on the railroad—taken possession of all the road leading from the city to Berwick's Bay & have been in Thibodaux search- ing for arms.[46] I suppose they will be in Houma too, hunting for arms. Howard has given me in charge of old aunt Patience (a negro woman). She has promised faithfully to take charge of me. I believe she will be faithful. He promised her, he would buy she & her children after the war is over. Troubles have come thick & fast upon us. Cousin Josh has been confined to the house nearly three months with paralysis, is now in bed.[47] Oh! it is so awful to hear him blaspheming the name of God & we do not know but it may be his last word. Lord, look with mercy upon him, cause him to turn ere it be too late. I forgot to mention, whilst the Yankees were bombing the Forts, our governor called for a thousand men to board their boats. Howard with a party of gentlemen from Houma started down. O, what

---

ber Ten was captured by Union troops on 7–8 April 1862. The island, located on the Tennessee-Ken- tucky border, was an important Confederate stronghold on the Mississippi River. Fort Pillow, Ten- nessee, was not evacuated until 4 June. At the end of the paragraph Bond refers to the Battle of Shiloh and repeats erroneous information about a Confederate victory. After the Confederates surrendered Is- land Number Ten, Grant's army marched from Corinth, Mississippi, over the Tennessee border. The Confederates attacked, nearly defeating Union forces. Bond refers to Benjamin Prentiss, who surren- dered to the Confederates on 6 June. The direction of the battle changed, however, as Union rein- forcements arrived during the night of the sixth. The next evening Confederate forces withdrew to Corinth. The battle was particularly bloody, with more than seventeen hundred men killed and eight thousand wounded on each side. Confederate General Beauregard evacuated Corinth on 30 May, re- treating to Tupelo. The General J. to whom Bond refers in the middle of the paragraph is Albert Sid- ney Johnston, Confederate commander of the Western Department, who, as Bond reports, was killed at Shiloh.

46. In April 1862, Capt. David G. Farragut led the naval attack on New Orleans. As Bond states, two masonry forts located below New Orleans, Forts Jackson and St. Philip, were first attacked. When they did not surrender, Farragut ran his ships past the forts and on to New Orleans on 24 April. The militia fled and civic authorities surrendered the city the following day. On 1 May Union troops under Gen. Benjamin F. Butler occupied New Orleans.

47. In 1862 Josh was sixty-seven years old and apparently a victim of a stroke. See Bond's letters dated 13 April and 4 May 1862 for more details of Josh's illness. In her diary, Bond previously mentioned Josh's health problems on 6 February 1861.

agony was I in. I felt sure Howard would be killed by scalding water, or some other dreadful way—

May 13th

I have been in intense excitement for nearly a week. The Yankees are in our Parish—they are even in our town—my husband & his brother have fled their lives—are *exiles from home.* God only knows what the consequences will be. In Thy hands O God I place them—take him under the shadow of thy wing. We are look-ing for the Yankees every moment—such suspense—such agony of mind—I look at myself and can scarcely realize it is me. I am calm & have shed few tears. God is my helper in every hour of need, Lord to thee I look. Keep us from *all* danger seen & unseen. Look with tender compassion upon us. Grant us thy protection. No white persons on the place but cousins Josh & Rebecca (& the former not able to leave the room) Barrow & self—Laura & sis are away. The negros are fright-ened nearly to death—they are as afraid of the *Yankees* as we are & more so too. I hear two are dead———

It is so beautiful outdoors—nature seems mocking our misery & woe.

June 29th 1862

Some time has elapsed since I penned in this book—frought with many changes. The Federals visited Houma on the 12th of May, about 2:00. It was the 21st Indiana Reg—commanded by Liet Conl Keith. It seems we had a steamer—(the Fox) to come in Grand Caillou from Cuba, a few days before & the Yankees heard of it through some of *our traitors* & sent a body of the 21st Reg- to take pos-session of it. Those men came down on the Rail Road, got Mrs. Tanner's wagons & negroes & passed through Houma Friday 9th of May at night but one or two persons seen them as it was about one, or two o'clock in the morning. The alarm spread like wild fire next day—a meeting was held in the town—some were for going & trying to retake the steamers, others against it—finally a party of men consisting of 13 or 14 started down the road thinking the enemy would be coming back to get reinforcements & stationed them selves some where in the road. The wagons came driving a long, thinking they were filled with soldiers, they fired upon them, killing two & wounding two—only being four in the wagons[48]—Howard was one that declined going & stayed in Houma all day—attending to his store.

48. A small force of Butler's men had occupied areas on the west of the Mississippi River since May. Shortly after the troops arrived, armed citizens ambushed a wagon carrying four men on the way to Houma. Two of the soldiers were killed, the other two wounded. The Federal army responded to the event immediately, sending four hundred soldiers to Houma. Citizens were arrested, property seized, and houses burned. The one plantation burned was Crescent Place. As Bond notes, the home of Dr. Jennings was also burned. (See the introduction for more detail about this event.)

Mr. McConnell says he will swear to it—for he was talking to him when the messenger came riding into town stating they were fighting down below. Then Howard & several others got into a buggy & went above the town about four miles—to burn a bridge if they saw the Yankees acoming & prevent their passing, to give notice, so we could retake the steamer. He not knowing the number of men they had attacked, nor did not until he returned to town about ten or 11 oclock at night—he then came directly on home—had not had any supper. I got it ready & took it in the parlor myself, gave it him—he was too tired to go get it himself. He did not know when or where the Yankees were buried, for I asked him & he said they were not buried when he left town. Next day (sunday), he with a company of others started down towards grand Caillou to take the boat—but before getting there learned the little boat & cannon which was to help them was sunk, they then abandoned their project & returned home.

Monday the 12th Howard walked into Houma, & after he got there was told the Yankees were already in the town—had search Mr. Calhoun's house, & had his & Wellie's names as being the head of the murder (as they termed it) of their men—and they intended to hang him if he could be found. Whereupon Howard hasten home & he, Wellie & Mr. Henry got on their horses & left. We did not know where nor did not until the following Sunday—(after the Yankees had left).

Tuesday 13th in the afternoon, the Coul & Lieut Carruth with a number of men on horse back came & surrounded the place—The Coul & Lieut came in. They were invited in politely—asked to be seated & treated with the greatest politeness but nothing more. He (the Coul) stated he had been informed we were harboring some of those men who had *murdered their men* & that the "Young Bonds" were participants in the *murder.* We assured him they were not, & we had no one concealed, that the "Bonds" had left before he came—He did not believe one word we said—and said he would have to make a search—whereupon I got all the keys & Barrow went with us—I galant'd them up in my room—The Coul did not seem disposed to make a very close examination around the room—I insisted he should look *under* the *bed,* & in the armoire, he declined—I conducted them all of the house—thro every house in the yard & wished them to go to the sugar house & quarters—but he would not—he remarked "it was a very unpleasant business to him & knew it was to me." I told him no it was not, it was rather a pleasure for me, as I wished to convince him what we had said (that we had no one or anything hid here) was true. He assured me, he believed what I said was so, and assured me, us & our property should not be disturbed. He seemed anxious to know what my name was before I was married—but I told him I did not think it prudent to give names these times.

When he was about to leave, he thanked me for my *lady like deportment.* They left & we felt somewhat secure, but late that same evening they came & drove all the cattle, sheep, mules & ten or twelve negroes up to Houma.

About two o'clock the next morning, about 50 men with an officer came & searched the house & whole plantation. The officer asked me who I supposed they were looking for, I told him I did not know—for it had not entered into my head they were expecting Howard and Welly here—he said, "we are searching for The Mr. Bonds, & are determined to have one of them any how, & if we get him we will *hang* him." I very calmly asked "which one"—"the oldest—*Howard-*" O, how I wish I had been a rattle-snake & could have bit him then! I assured him he would not find him or anyone else concealed on the place. They remain'd about the premises til sun up- & then left. I wrote Coul Keith, a letter stating facts & wishing to know if he (as a gentleman of honor) intended to keep his promises—that we & our property should be respected. I did not get a reply from him as he was out of town but got one from Capt. Roy (the same that afterwards burnt our house). Every night after they were around the house & place. I never spent such a week & hope never to spend such another—What must my feelings have been—when from 50 & 100 Yankees hunting my husband like he was a wild beast, night & day—& he just as innocent as he could be. But just because some villains who were enemies to his father & our country told them a pack of lies—they did all that & were so rabid after the "*Young Bonds.*"[49]

Thursday, Lieut Connelly with a wagon of men came & took forage to feed the stock—he too told us if they caught Howard he would be hung—that was the only time I felt my hopes failing—& as I look'd out of the door, every thing began to grow dizzy & turn around, I soon however checked my feelings—for he should not note one pang he caused me—Since then our men have taken him prisoner & say he is to be hung for the destruction of this property. He is at Camp Prat.[50] Friday morning, 16th, about half past four, we were awakened by the cry of "soldiers around the house"—sprang up & was informed we had 20 minutes to dress & take a change of clothes, then the "order" was to set fire to the house—I dressed as soon as possible, hurried up stairs in my room, threw my clothes in spreads & sheets & tied them up. The negroes worked faithfully doing all they could to save all they could, tho' they were constantly being warned not to carry any more out—still they rushed in and saved all they could. We managed to get the most of the clothing & saved one bedstead, then was ordered out in the yard there in the hot sun we stayed till two o'clock. They reserved a house with two rooms for us to live in—only a quart of clabber & as much hominy, was saved for *all* to eat. Everything eatable

49. Bond does not break the paragraph here; I have done so for readability.
50. Camp Pratt was near New Iberia.

was burnt, or taken away by them. About twelve one negro woman who has been afflicted for several years—cooked a chicken, some eggs, & baked a pan of bread & sent us. How thoughtful of her! her house had been burnt down, she driven down the fields, & then in the sun, cooked us some thing to eat. Our neighbors were very kind, so many came & offered to do any thing for us in their power. Some even offered me a home—O, how my heart long'd for the loved ones at home! And my poor husband, where was he—I did not know. About two weeks afterwards, Mr. W- came for me & took me to his house on Lafourche[51]—there I met Howard—spent one day & a night with him—Poor fellow! I did not know him when I saw him, so changed—. All there were strangers to me—but so kind I can never forget their kindness—God bless them, is my prayer.[52]

Four weeks after that I got a letter from Howard to meet him at Thibodaux, as he with cavalry would be stationed at Lafourche Crossing. Mrs. Winder sent Johnny with the letter.[53] I went up with him after dinner (20th) stopped at his mother's a short while—met there Mr. Holden who had come there to get me to stay at his house. Mrs. Winder had gone to "Camp" to take some mosquito "bars," & had not returned—so I got in Mr. H-'s buggy & started off for Thibodaux, met Howard on the road coming in search of me—before getting in the town, we met Mrs. W- who insisted on our turning back, but Mr. H- out-generaled her & drove on. I was met by Miss Emma Holden, his sister, with the greatest kindness—of which I hope never to forget—& be able to return some of their kindnesses one day. I stayed there & with Mrs. Winder til tuesday morning—I visited the Camp three times but did not meet Howard either time.

Sunday the Cavalry had a skirmish near Raceland with the enemy.[54] Howard was not there at the time—but got there 15 minutes after.[55] We killed a good many—three was left on the track & the rest were carried away in the cars. Three

---

51. Mr. W. is probably a son of Mrs. Van Perkins Winder, a widow and large Terrebonne landowner and planter who in the 1860 census owned 202 slaves and 4,550 acres of land. The large Bayou Lafourche is located slightly west of Houma.

52. Bond does not break this or the following paragraph.

53. Mrs. Winder's son Johnny was fifteen years old in 1862.

54. Raceland is approximately ten miles northeast of Houma, on Bayou Lafourche.

55. From what Bond tells us, Howard was likely fighting with the Tenth (Yellow Jacket) Battalion, which conducted operations between Brashear City and New Orleans during June and July 1862. As Bond reports, on 22 June the battalion had a skirmish near Raceland. It is not clear how long Howard participated in this battalion; military records list him as a private in the Twenty-sixth Louisiana Infantry, of which the Bonds' acquaintance and fellow Terrebonne planter Duncan Cage was a colonel. See Booth, *Records of Louisiana Confederate Soldiers*, 30. During the summer of 1862 the Twenty-sixth regiment was in Mississippi. For information on the regiments' operations, see Bergeron, *Guide to Louisiana Confederate Military Units*, 163, 135, respectively.

of our men were wounded. (I forgot to say the Yankees left Houma the 17th of May, after destroying a great deal of property. Dr. Jennings' was burnt, the Jail torn down, & other houses destroyed.[56] Howard's store lost, was about 1500$. They pillaged & destroyed most all the valuables in it.)[57]

Tuesday the 24th I came to Houma (Johnny W. bringing me) supported by two bodies of Cavalry, one in front, & one in the rear, Howard & Wellie being with them—we took dinner at Dr. Hemlick's, where cousin Josh has been staying several weeks.[58] It was quite affecting to see H. & his father meet. Howard *kissed* him. About four o'clock in the afternoon our bonnie blue flag was raised in Houma. The Yankee *one* had previously been torn down by Capt. Coons & some of his men— & carried off, it with the rope which the vandals had hung on a tree to hang our men they had taken when there—to get them to confess who had *done the crime.*

Howard & Welly came home & stayed two nights, left for New Iberia thursday the 26th about daylight.[59] O, how I do hate to give him up. I suppose I have to be martyr during this war. Reports are England, France & Spain has recognized our Independence. But I don't believe one word of it. I've head such too long. The Militia of Terrebonne & Lafourche are to be ordered out this week—a good order———

July 4th[60]

The militia went in Camp today—they have a rainy day to commence Camp life—I have been quite sick for several days. Heard from Howard tuesday—well.

Tuesday night 8th

Welly got home bout half-past nine oc. I got a dear letter from my husband. O, how I want to see him! It seems hard people who can live happily together have to separate, & those who are not happy have to live with each other. I have felt so homesick most of today. O, how I want to see them all there.

Wednesday 9th

Rained this morning—I wrote to ma this afternoon. Got a letter from Miss Susanna Woods.

56. James L. Jennings, a physician from Kentucky, was married to Rebecca Lewis, a teacher from Massachusetts.

57. See the introduction for further details about the property destroyed.

58. On 17 May, Dr. Helmick was one of several Houma residents taken prisoner by Lieutenant Colonel Keith.

59. The Yellow Jacket Battalion drilled at Camp Pratt near New Iberia.

60. Until 27 July, it is not clear from where Bond writes. She is likely at Crescent Place, living in property that was not burned.

Saturday 12th

Mrs. Campbell & Berta [Barrow] spent the day. Berta staying all night. Wellie left early for New Iberia.

Lovely day—but exceedingly warm—I wrote home & sent it by Col Soulakowski to the city to be put in the Yankee mail for the north.

Sunday 13th

Mrs. Barrow, Miss Joe & Laura call'd late this eve—did not go to church, have not for some time—

Tuesday 15th

Spent the day at Mrs. B's. Cousin R. & I had a pleasant visit, met Miss Sue & Lizzie, also Col Fisher—Rained quite hard—

Thursday 17th

Had glorious news today. Miss Stuart brought it. That European powers have intervened—*Peace* will soon be declared between *our* Confederacy & U.S. Mr. & Mrs. McConnell here this eve—

Sunday 20th

Mrs. Pierce & Lizzie took dinner here.[61]

Tuesday 22nd

Cousin Rebecca & I spent the day at Mrs. Pierce's today, met Mrs. Barrow, two children, Miss Joe Dorsey, Laura, Miss Carrie Pride, Mr. & Mrs. McConnell & child. Mr. James McC & Mrs. Col Bisland.[62] Had a very pleasant day—but a very warm one.

Friday 25th

Lovely day—I'm feeling very sad—O, this constant anxiety will kill me by inches—My poor dear husband—I wonder if we shall ever live together again for any length of time.

Dear Savior take charge of him, preserve him from *all* danger—& save him for Christ's sake. Last night I cried so bitterly after I went to bed. My heart was so sad. O what a comfort to know there's a *God* to pour out the sin sick soul to. Make me watchful & prayerful, O Father.

Saturday 26th

This is Ann Lee's birth day. O how I should love to see her. May the good Lord keep & bless her on this her 17th birth day. And my dear Ma's birthday was the

61. Mrs. Phoebe Pierce was a Terrebonne plantation owner from South Carolina.

62. James McCullough was of the Second Louisiana Regiment, and William Bisland was commander of the Grivot Guards Company B. Bond records his wife's death on 6 September 1861. If this is the Colonel Bisland to whom she refers here, then he had quickly remarried.

23rd. Dear Ma—how I should love to see her. I wrote sometime since—when sick & sad a few verses to my Mother.

> Are you thinking of me Mother
>   Are you thinking of your child?
> We have not seen each other
>   For a very long, long while
>
> My heart aches badly mother
>   To hear your gentle voice;
> To feel thy loving kiss, mother,
>   That makes my heart rejoice.
>
> Oh! that I were near thee mother
>   Close kneeling by thy side;
> My faults are very many, mother
>   And I wish you, me to chide
>
> Oft I think of that sad morning
>   When I bid you all adieu
> The sky was dark & lowering
>   And my joys very few.
>
> I'm happier far dear mother
>   Than when I gave you my hand;
> To leave *you all* my mother,
>   For this strange and distant land.
>
> My husband's kind and true mother,
>   As one could be to me;
> But in all the world, there's no other,
>   I love *like* I love thee.
> Mittie P. Bond.

July 27th[63]

Howard gone up to Houma—looks like rain. Monday 28—Howard spent the day at Mrs. Barrows. Tuesday 29th, he & I spent the day at Mrs. Pierce's, met James McConnell & Miss Lou Winder there. Called at Dr. Hemlick's coming home. Cousin Josh fill'd me with horrors. Quite a ludicrous scene occurred yesterday morning with Howard & myself—Mrs. Dank & Miss Laura—

---

63. Bond heads the page with her location—Berwicks Bay, St. Mary Parish, approximately fifty miles east of Houma.

CHAPTER SEVEN

"We Fled Our Home"

Friday 1st

Left home this morn about nine—got to Mrs. Winders at 12—found Van very ill.[1] Howard doctored him & was soon better. Rained this eve—had visitors however, Mr. Chamberland & Mrs. Fulton of Thibodaux.

Saturday 2nd

Went to the depot to go to Berwick's Bay but no cars leaving—had to return to Mrs. Winders. Spent a very pleasant day. Lizzie Pierce & Lou came home.

Sunday 4th

Left early in the cars—had a disagreeably slow ride. Got to Brashear City about two oc, put up at Mrs. Daly's hotel, the last in creation! Such accommodations I never saw! Met there Cap- & Mrs. Allen—very agreeable friends. Stayed until Monday 5th & left in the "Red Chief," was very sick on board. Mrs. Allen made me a cup of coffee—so kind, & good. The scenery down the Teche is perfectly grand—I enjoyed in exceedingly.

Some of the residences are magnificently grand. Got in New Iberia Tuesday to breakfast. Mrs. Allen & the Capt stopped at Franklin, about 50 miles from here, a pretty place—but this place is not—but larger than Franklin.

August 8th

This is July 8th.[2] I've been here since tuesday. I don't think much of the place— I have formed some pleasant acquaintances. Mrs. Thomas & Mrs. Donjeun & their husbands are very pleasant. Mr. D- & his lady took me riding the other evening—I enjoyed it very much. Yesterday Howard & I walked out to the Foundry—saw them mounting canon—quite interesting scene.

---

1. Van is one of Mrs. Winder's sons. In her last entry, Bond was in St. Mary Parish, but here she is back in Terrebonne, although, as she states in her next entry, she is planning to return to St. Mary on her way eventually to Abbeville.

2. Bond mistakenly notes the month as July. She writes from New Iberia, La., on the Bayou Teche. Although the town's name was officially New Iberia by 1860, it was still called New Town by many English-speaking residents, including Bond in her following entry.

Capt Allen & his lady came this morning. I'm so glad to see her. (She turned out to be a Yankee spy.)[3]

July 5, 1863 Abbeville, Vermillion Parish[4]

One year has passed since I penned in this book—O! the changes it has brought. I spent two months in New Town (where I was when I wrote last here.) I met with a Mrs. Gordy of Bayou Sale, who took a fancy to me & I to her.[5] She gave me such a pressing invitation to visit her I could not resist; so after leaving the Hotel I went to see her, & remained four weeks, she was very sick most of the time. I sit up at nights, the most of a week. She is a Poetess! a rare & gifted woman— but unfortunately, as is mostly the case with such gifted women, married to a very narrow-minded and uncongenial man. I pittied her.

After being at home (Crescent Place) about two weeks, the Yankees made an- other raid on Terrebonne, we fled from our home & traveled night & day till we were out of the reach of the vandals—

On Oct. Tuesday 28th, we left Terrebonne—stayed all night at Mr. Morrison's, met with a little adventure with General Lewis and his aide-de-camp.[6] Laura & I enjoyed it very much, much to cousin Josh's dismay (*old folks will be old fogies*). It was about one o'c at night, the Genl & his aides were I suppose quietly sleeping, when we drove up. We brought news, in regard to his army (as we passed through the camp). The genl got up, when he found ladies had arrived & wished accom- modations, & slipped into another room.[7] We were invited in a room where cheer- ful fire was burning, & in which two beds were with their bars drawn, supposing they were intended for us. After a while Genl Lewis came in, half-dressed, in the act of finishing his toilet & talked awhile, asked questions in regard to his men. Then he turned to one of the beds—put his head under the bar & forthwith is- sued mysterious sounds. At last I caught the words, "*How can we, ladies are in the*

---

3. Bond inserts this information at a later date; it is written in different ink.

4. Southern Louisiana, west of the Mississippi, saw increased Union presence during autumn 1862 as Federal troops attempted to free the region of southern troops. Interestingly, Bond does not write during this period, only recounting events at a later date. Abbeville is approximately eighty miles slightly north and west of Houma.

5. Mrs. Gordy's birth name was Carrie E. Plumlee,* and she was twenty-one years old in 1863. Bayou Sale is in St. Mary Parish. Census information for Bond's acquaintances in the subsequent entries comes from the following records: 1860 U.S census, free schedule, St. Mary Parish, La., National Archives microfilm publication M653, roll 425; and 1860 U.S. census, free schedule, Vermilion Parish, La., publication M653, roll 426.

6. Maj. Gen. John L. Lewis was commander of the state militia.

7. The handwriting from this point becomes very small, as if Bond is trying to fit all the details of her trip on a single page.

room." Pretty soon after, two pairs of pants & coats were thrown under the bar, & in the course of events two spruce young aides hopped out & skedaddled into the next room. Laura and I were tickled nearly to death. I never wanted to laugh as badly, but a grunt from cousin Josh & a look from cousin R- kept it in.[8]

We left there the morning of the 29th—Stayed all day at Dr. Robert's plantation on Lake Palmid and the Boeuf, a beautiful spot. Crossed over the Boeuf at night in a flatboat, the moon shining beautifully—quite romantic. Stayed at Mr. Cooke's place, nine in one room—*Pennsylvania style!* Got plenty of oranges.

Thursday 30th traveled all day without meeting with any adventures, arrived at Brashear City about sunset, stayed all night at Captain Carr's. I was very kindly treated by a lady there. "Little acts of kindness" are often more appreciated than the actor thinks, sometimes. 31st. Crossed the Bay, stayed all day in Berwick City, left at five o'clock. Stayed at night at Mrs. Stanley's plantation in the overseer's house—found *fleas* rather plentiful.

Nov. 1st Sad day to me. I never had my heart so torn. Cousin Josh said "he wished I had never come to Louisiana he never was willing I should." Many words passed between us, and all from a little simple thing—he went on so far, & saw he had said too much; he apologized, & we shook hands and made up—but could he heal the gash in my heart! I don't believe he ever has forgiven himself entirely for what he said. Ate dinner at Mrs. Flemming's place, under two large spreading oaks. Washed my *feet in the Teche.* Slept that night at Madame Fuselier's on a marble floor.[9]

Sunday 2nd Lovely day—beautiful plantations on the Teche. Mrs. Porter's & Bethel's places are magnificently laid out, marble statues of fishes & fountain girls, fish ponds.[10] Took dinner under the live oaks at Mt. Olivier, six or eight miles from New Iberia, at which place we arrived about five o'clock. Met Coul Robinson & family at the Confederate Hotel.[11] Came out about a mile from the town. Eat our supper in the woods under the most beautiful oaks I ever saw, had large campfires built in different directions for us and negroes. The moon too was shining lovely. It was quite a picturesque scene—it was a "real gypsy scene." Was kindly offered

8. I have added the paragraph breaks in the remainder of the entry.

9. Two prominent landowners with the surname Fuselier lived in St. Mary Parish. It is not clear with which family Bond stayed.

10. Bond refers to Mrs. James Porter and to one of the two Mrs. Bethels who were married to large plantation owners in St. Mary Parish.

11. Bond likely met Confederate colonel J. B. Robinson, a Houma native. Before burning Crescent Place, the Union troops sent to find Howard and Wellie Bond also sought Robinson but found that he had fled the area. Bond notes later in her entry that the Robinson family had been in Abbeville for a month.

beds at Mr. Hopkins, treated very kindly by the old gent and lady—had *biscuits & coffee—memorable!*

Monday 3rd Went in to town to make calls & shop—call on Mrs. Montgomery—Laura delighted with her—spent a pleasant evening at Mr. H- Left Tuesday 4th and arrived in Abbeville about sun down truly worn out, took tea at Conl Robinson's who had, with his family, been staying here a month. The girls were truly tired of the place & moved off to Texas third day after we came—we were left in a place knowing no one, & known by no one. Sickness soon laid its hand upon us & brought us friends. We have received many kindnesses from Mrs. Maxwell & Mrs. Nixon (her ma), also Mrs. Robertson.[12]

We had not been more than three or four days in Abbeville, before cousin Rebecca was taken ill (also several of the blacks).[13] She continued so for two weeks, we did not expect her to live, but God has spared her to her children.[14] What should *I* have done without her good nursing? O! my Heavenly Father, reward her for all her goodness & kindness to me. I suppose the fatigue of running away from the Yankees & sitting up with the sick was too much for my delicate constitution, as soon as cousin Rebecca was well enough to go about the house I was taken with Pneumonia.[15] Dr. Helmick and his wife and daughter were staying with us (and he did not attend to me right.) The cold fell on my lungs. After many weeks of suffering, and whilst still confined to my bed, I had a hemorrhage. I was taken with it wednesday evening and had them twice a day till sunday, at which time I had a very severe one—had three Drs.—Dr. Helmick, Young, & Abadie. It was a long time before I was able to go about. I rode out as soon as I could.

In March I took cold by some unaccountable way & was sadly neglected by our former doctor (tho' he was always staying at our house) & left me ill, without even coming in my room to see me. I was persuaded by Mrs. Nixon to send for Dr. Abadie—he came, did all he could, I had more hemorrhages.[16] The Dr. despaired

---

12. Mrs. Maxwell,* formerly Martha Nixon of Lafayette Parish, La., was married to Albert G. Maxwell, a Maryland native and Vermilion Parish sugarcane planter. In 1860 Mrs. Nixon, Martha Maxwell's mother, lived with the Maxwells. Mrs. Maxwell was thirty-five in 1863. While no census information is available for Mrs. Robertson,* possibly indicating her refugee status, Bond writes in her letters that she is originally from Maryland.

13. Several household slaves stayed in Abbeville with Bond, Cousin Rebecca, and sis. They included Amanda (Mandy) and Mintty. It is not clear when Josh, Wellie, and Barrow left Abbeville for Texas; however, it seems that they did not stay in Abbeville long. As Bond reports later in this entry, Laura left Abbeville with Mrs. Maxwell, intending to go to Maryland. Howard seemed to spend most of the time from November 1862 to April 1863 in Abbeville with Bond, his mother, and young sister.

14. Bond's handwriting becomes larger here as she begins a new page in her diary.

15. Bond also describes her sickness in a letter to her mother dated 2 November 1863.

16. Jean Abadie* had emigrated to Vermilion Parish from France.

of saving my life. I too felt there was little hope, but God has willed it otherwise. I did pray God to spare my unprofitable life, if it was his will, that I might get well, & live many happy days with my devoted husband.

God has answered my prayer so far. I'm spared yet, my health is better but still *very critical.* The Dr. does not allow me to sew, read or talk much. My noble & good Howard did all in his power to aid my comfort—he nursed me as though I was an infant. How oft was my thoughts lifted up in thanksgiving for *such* a *husband,* & such kind friends. Heavenly Father reward them, for Christ's sake. The Yankees out-numbered our men by far on the Teche & our men were compelled to retreat after several days hard and brave fighting. This was in April 12 or 15.[17] Howard had to bring me from the house where we were living to Mr. Maxwell's, where cousin R., sis & myself & three servants are now. Poor Howard—brought me in a little wagon on a bed (I was not able to use my hands even) & the next day he had to leave me, for the Ordnance Department where he has been ever since.[18] I have been looking for him for about a month, & has not come. But the Lord has been my support & helper—I feel so trustful in God's power—I will trust him in all things. Not my will but thine O, Lord be done. I think these are the *true* sentiments of my heart. Laura came here with us. But Mrs. Maxwell wished to follow her husband, who she had reason to believe had gone to Md. (Mr. Maxwell had killed a man, & had to leave) & Laura thought she would go to. So they got their pass ports to New Orleans from the Yankees—for they had this part of the country then; and Mrs. Nixon was left to attend to affairs. She is a different kind of woman from what I took her to be at first. I thought her a dear old lady & a pious christian—but she has a very unhappy disposition, & has made many enemies—& has tried hard for cousin R & I to be her enemies—because we won't be at enmity with her supposed ones. Oh! Father, grant I may act right. For I'm but a creature of the moment. I do try to do what is right, & thou knowest it, but the flesh warreth against the spirit.

Our soldiers have driven the Yankees out of Terrebonne, or rather captured them and & the negroes whom they were drilling to fight against their masters.[19]

17. Bond writes of battles that occurred as part of Union general Banks's drive up Bayou Teche. The Battle of Bisland, or Bethel's Place, ended on 13 April, with the Confederate command under General Taylor abandoning Bisland. On 14 April the Battle of Irish Bend, or Nerson's Woods, ended as Taylor's forces escaped initially unnoticed by General Grover.

18. Howard's post took him over two hundred miles from his wife, to Shreveport, in northwestern Louisiana.

19. For a brief period in the summer of 1863, Confederate troops recaptured the region around Bayou Lafourche.

The Yankees have been whipped severely at Port Hudson & Vicksburg, & in Va we have gained several battles.[20] I hope this war will soon be over.

I have learned Mrs. Maxwell did not succeed in getting off to Md. Laura is staying at Mr. Barrows, & Mrs. M- since our men got the Bay has crossed over & staying at Franklin—at Mrs. Carson's. Mrs. Nixon sent for her Thursday—we are looking for her every hour—she was sick—I expect to learn much news from our Terrebonne friends.

Wednesday 8th

Mrs. Maxwell arrived Sunday afternoon, very ill, she is better this morning. She was in the battle of "Berwick's Bay."[21] I had letters from dear home there. I suppose all are lost. Oh! what unspeakable pleasure would they have given me. Perhaps it is all for the best. If it is right I hope I'll get them yet.

My beloved husband came this morning—I had just started out to take a walk, when I spied him riding up. Oh! that was a happy meeting. God has answered our prayers—It should strengthen our faith. O! grant that it may, My Father.

Thursday 9th

H- & I took a walk before breakfast on the bridge. I got a letter from Laura yesterday from Terrebonne. The "Rebels" have indeed got possession of our country again. I hope they may whip the detested Yankees from New Orleans—that is their intention. There were battles fought at Thibodaux & Lafourche crossing.[22] I understand they burnt Donaldsonville & retreated towards the city.[23] Rumor states so many falsities we know not when to believe her.

20. The siege of Port Hudson lasted forty-five days. The first assault was on 27 May, and the Federals were pushed back and suffered heavy losses. In July, however, Confederate forces met with defeat: Lee was beaten at Gettysburg on 3 July, Pemberton surrendered Vicksburg the next day (see Bond's entry of 20 July), and General Gardner surrendered Port Hudson on 9 July. With the fall of Vicksburg and Port Hudson, the Confederates lost control of the Mississippi and Red rivers. Bond mistakenly writes of Confederate victories at Vicksburg, likely having heard news of battles on 19 and 22 May, when Confederate troops successfully resisted Grant's attacks.

21. On the morning of 23 June, Brig. Gen. Thomas Green led a bombardment on Union troops from the west bank of Berwick Bay. Green's attack distracted Union troops from Confederate action that resulted in Sherod Hunter's defeat of Union forces at Brashear.

22. On 20 June, Confederate troops attacked Thibodaux, which was then under Federal control. The surprised Union troops fled to Lafourche Crossing, four miles away. The following evening the Confederates attacked Lafourche Crossing but were repelled and forced to abandon Thibodeaux, which was briefly reoccupied by Federal troops. Upon hearing, however, that a large Confederate cavalry was to attack Thibodaux and Lafourche, Union forces retreated to Algiers, La., outside of New Orleans.

23. Much of Donaldsonville was destroyed on 9 August 1862 by Union gunboats under command of General Farragut. In this entry, Bond may refer to the Confederate attempt to take Fort Butler at Donaldsonville on 28 June.

Friday 10th 1863

I have spent a delightful day with my husband. O! what a blessing God has given me in my good husband. We took a long walk, walked over the bayou. One might suppose Howard my lover, from the way he treats me. So lover-like.

Saturday

Howard left for Terrebonne this afternoon. I hated to part with him even for a short time. He has gone down to see if it is prudent for us to go home. I scarcely know when to expect him back. I hope he'll not get in any trouble, with the enemy. God keep & bless him! I went over to Mrs. Robertson's a little while this afternoon, also called to see Mrs. Wise.[24]

Howard told me of the death of Felix Winder, he died at Vicksburg, was killed in the third days battle, he was a Captain of a company.[25]

Sunday July 12

I'm feeling quite badly today. My cough hurts me very much. I coughed most of last night. I miss being petted by my good husband. God bless him for being good & kind to me.

Sunday, July 20th

A week passed without my writing in here. I have learned bad news—I hope not true. Our soldiers retreating from Lafourche country—Yankees in strong force.

My dear husband, I know not what has become of him—perhaps taken prisoner. Oh! father in thy good hands do I place him. Bring him safely to me! I hear the Yankees took Vicksburg on the 4th & Port Hudson on the 8th. I also hear we have captured Washington D.C. & 60,000 men[26]—When will this horrible war be at an end! Grant O Lord soon!

---

24. Fanny Wise was married to Solomon Wise,* and the couple owned a general store in downtown Abbeville. Bond's friendliness toward the Wises diminishes as the war progresses, as supplies dwindle and as prices soar. Being merchants, they were likely suspected by the community of profiting from wartime inflation—of profiting by others' misery. For more analysis on merchants' roles during the Civil War, see Whites, *Civil War as a Crisis in Gender*, 65–71.

25. Felix Winder was the eldest son of Mrs. Van Perkins Winder, with whom Bond stayed after Crescent Place was burned. Winder was killed on 19 May 1863, the first day of the Battle of Vicksburg. He belonged to the Twenty-sixth Infantry Regiment (the regiment to which Howard Bond also belonged) and was captain of Company K, Terrebonne Pickett Guards. He was twenty-four years old.

26. Gen. John C. Pemberton surrendered Vicksburg to Grant on 4 July 1863, after a six-week bombardment. On 9 July General Banks captured Port Hudson, La. The entire Mississippi was then under Union control and the Confederacy divided. Bond's news about Washington, D.C., was obviously a rumor.

Some have gone nine or ten miles shopping—some visiting the sick—and some *gossiping.* How do the people of this country ever expect to be prosperous when they disregard God's law so! They complain of man's law not being enforced, when they constantly break God's commandments. "Teach us to number our days that we may apply our hearts unto wisdom."

[This entry is not dated]

My husband got back Monday night 21st safe, had not seen a Yankee—although he feared they would catch in whilst in Terrebonne. He visited the plantation, found all the negroes there but a few who had died in camp & at home. All the people seemed glad to see him back in Terrebonne. Laura received a letter from her ma whilst Howard was there, *All were well* at *my home.* Oh, Father this comforted my heart. We also learned that Gov. Bradford of Md had saved cousin Josh's property—Laura has a brother in Va (Oliver) also *Willy Green.*

Vicksburg, Port Hudson have fallen, & Terrebonne taken back by the Yankees—They are at the bay. I know not what this country will do if the Yankees are to have it.

Got a letter from cousin Josh, he writes sadly—has nothing to eat but cornbread & beef and his disease requires something else.

August 9th

I believe the rainy season has set in. It rained every day.

Friday 15th

Howard has been very sick since last Sunday, with chills & fevers. This is the day for him to be worse, but I do hope the quinine will have the desired effect & keep off the chill.

Our material affairs look dark enough—What is to be the issue of all these troubles none can tell! Oh! I wish the war—this miserable war—was at an end.

I walked up to the store the other day, priced some calico, 40 & 50$ a dress pattern—Two dollars for a spool of cotton. What will it be next year if this war continues! How I should love to know what is going on at home today. Two years the 12th of this month since I received a letter from my dear old home! I often ask the question mentally—shall I ever see that dear old spot—sometimes the answer comes no never & then Hopes *bright star* shines out from beneath the dark clouds that surround my horizon, and bids me hope & bide the time for sure 'twill come. Home sweet home, be it ever so humble, there's no place like home.

The house where we are staying belongs to Mrs. Maxwell, a present from her Mother—Mrs. Nixon; her Ma lives here, & her little nephew Clarence. The Ma & daughter live like cats & dogs. Oh! if Mother & children would only consider the brevity of life, & uncertainty of living long with each other—how differently would they live!

Thursday 21st

Yesterday Lieut Patton & Mr. Wiltz paid us a visit. After which, Mr. Wiltz was taken sick. Howard gave him some medicine—which relieved him very much. It has been raining nearly all this week—I suppose we will not be clear of the rainy season till first of Oct. We hear cheering news of our army in Md. I believe Lee has crossed the Potomac in to Va after taking many army stores.[27] Abbeville is as dull as it can be; nothing but the lowest society here—all nearly roman catholic. Mrs. Hall (the queerest looking woman I every saw) Madame Julius de France, her daughter Miss Ursula are about the only visitors of *any* consequence, that we see often. Both of them are illiterate.[28] Poor Mr. Eugene has been in a sad state since Laura left! I pity him![29] This afternoon Mr. & Mrs. Keanan & Mr. Brewster call on us—they live at the Lake. I was much pleased with the ladies. Mr. K- is very deaf, does not hear without the use of a trumpet. Mrs. K- is a Marylander, a graduate of Mr. Archer's (at Patapsco).

Friday 22nd

I was sick all this morning—was fearful I should have another hemorrhage but the worst feelings passed off & I feel better.

Saturday 23rd

Lovely day. Mr. & Mrs. Hatched called on us—they live at the Lake. Rev. Mr. Wren also called few minutes.[30] My cough very troublesome—I walked around to see Dr. Abadie late this evening, he is quite sick—has had cough; we can sympathize with each other. I have been reading in my journal in 58 & 60. Oh, how vividly scenes rise up before my mind's eye. Remarks made then, or rather sentiments expressed, seem but a forerunner of what was to come.———

Sunday 24th

All have gone to church (Baptist) but some of the servants & myself. I have not been to church since last Oct. It seems to me I have not heard a sermon that has

27. Confederate general Richard S. Ewell led the Army of Northern Virginia up the Shenandoah Valley, crossing the Potomac on 17 June 1863.

28. Sarah Hall* was married to Vermilion Parish farmer James. Bond also writes of Madame Juille DeFrance, or Caroline, and her daughter, Uresule, age twenty. Madame DeFrance's husband was a farmer owning, in 1860, real estate worth fifteen hundred dollars and a personal estate worth eight thousand dollars.

29. Eugene Guegnon, the twenty-year-old son of Eugene L. Guegnon,* obviously had affections for Laura. The elder Guegnon was a lawyer and editor of the local French newspaper, *Le Meridional.*

30. Mr. Wren* was the Baptist minister. Vermilion Parish had one Baptist church in 1860.

entered deep in my heart since I came south, like those I've heard at dear old Watters meeting house, and Belair. Oh, I do pray the good Lord will grant me this prayer—that I once more may visit the place of my nativity & be allowed to sit in that dear old church where the warning voice of God spoke to my sin sick heart and be laid under the shadow of its peaceful & hallowed roof. It is my wish to be buried in that loved spot where kind and loved ones can sometimes visit the spot where I am, & plant flowers—sweet jasmine on my grave. Let no marble slab, or monument mark the spot of my resting place. But let the spanish jasmine twine its graceful vines over my body. It is my favorite flower—it is so sweet and pure. My disease seems not to get better—my thoughts are often on death! Am I prepared to go, at any moment. Mine is a disease that may at any time snap the silver thread of life. I feel, at times perfectly resigned to my Heavenly Father's will—to go or stay, again there is a strong desire to live many years. I have a good husband to live for, one who has been kind to me, yes devotedly so—I have my loved ones at home who it grieves to have me separated from them—would they not grieve if they should never see me again. Oh, yes.

But whether living or dying, may I ever have that more important thing before me—to be ready when the messenger comes. God loves me, or he never would *tried*, & afflicted me as he has done. It is a source of great *hope* that those trials & afflictions my Heavenly Father sees fit to punish me with are but true indications of His love & mercy. I have truly suffered with pain & disease for the most of five years, and since last Nov have been more than once near death's door. Physicians have given me out, and I have felt as though my days were fast drawing to a close.

The first of my illness—I felt very unwilling to die. I felt as though I was not fit to meet my pure Saviour. I felt I know my life had been spent unprofitably. O God! grant I may be reminded of the promises I made whilst on the bed of disease—God has answered prayers which were offered up then & there. He has heard and He will still hear. Dr. Abadie, on thanksgiving day—whilst I was so ill—went to church & prayed for the restoration of my health a half hour. He is a catholic. Mr. Wren took dinner here. Howard is complaining very much—I fear he will have another attack. O! when will people learn to keep God's laws, & *His day!*

Monday 25th

Howard *very* sick today. We had three confederate soldiers to breakfast with us. They arrived in Abbeville last night about midnight. One company, 150 men. I do not know their business. Poor soldiers—some are barefootted & ragged—but they are fighting for rights our foes (*the detestable Yankees*) would deprive of us. "Fighting for the property we gained by honest toil." I hear the negroes at Baton Rouge had turned upon the *Feds* & driven them off. Also at Port Hudson the negroes raised a rumpus & the Yanks had to compromise. I believe there the negroes revolted against the five dollars they had to pay for pass to go out of the town. Took a walk this evening up town, saw many soldiers!

Tuesday 26th

My birthday—25—how time flys! Cloudy and cold. Howard better. Two officers saw me as I walked yesterday—took me to be a single lady—asked a servant who I was—surprised to learn I was *married.* I *teased Howard.* Dreamed I went home, last night. Oh! When will my dreams be realized! I feel some little better today. . . .

August 27th

Several soldiers eat here last evening—among them a Western Shore Marylander, a nephew of old Dr. Goldsborough of Balto. I was much pleased with him—he promised us another visit. I was *so glad* to see a *Maryland soldier.* I feel very sick today. Cousin Rebecca got a letter from cousin Josh—he hopes he & I may meet again—Lord grant! O that this separation may be for *our spiritual good.*

August 28th

I went to Mrs. Robertson's this morning. Willy & Emily very sick, from there, I went to Dr. Abadie's—he thinks it is not my lungs that gives me so much pain & uneasiness. Mrs. Maxwell, Howard, & I went to visit some sick soldiers. I sent them some tea.

Friday 29th

Judge Baker of the Teche came this morn.[31] He's a jovial old gentleman, a graduate of "West Point." Has known Genl Lee for a number of years. Genl Lee gained a great victory in Va over General Mead (Federal).[32] Lee took about 100,000 prisoners. General Bragg is dead—Capt. Fuller (of the Cotton) died from wounds received at the Bay.[33] He was a brave & noble man—but a very *ugly one.*

---

31. Bond probably refers to Joshua Baker, a West Point graduate and planter who owned three sugar plantations in Terrebonne, St. Mary, and St. Martin parishes. He served as judge in St. Mary Parish and in 1868, after taking an Oath of Loyalty to the Union, was appointed military governor by Gen. Winfield Scott Hancock.

32. Maj. Gen. George Mead was appointed by Lincoln to command the Army of the Potomac.

33. Gen. Braxton Bragg was not dead, as Bond later notes. He lived until 1876. Bond is correct in stating the E. W. Fuller, captain of the Confederate gunboat the *Cotton*, was mortally injured on 14 January 1863, in a battle with Federal gunboats on the Teche. He died on 15 July. He was captain of the St. Martin Rangers Company Infantry.

Saturday 30th[34]

Judge stayed all night here—left soon after breakfast. He related a very amusing anecdote about a little son of a Mr. Huff (of Huff Island.) It appears when the father saw the Yankees coming in their Gun Boat he told his little boy to run down the other side of the bank, & pretend he was running from Guerilas. He started off full speed, looking back, as tho' he was watching some one to overtake him— when he got opposite to the Gun Boat he stopped short, as if taken by surprise at seeing them, & then started on. The *Yanks* called "hey my little son, what is the matter with you—you seem scared!" "Matter! Why Guerillers! Plenty of Guerillers—them hollers you see thar's full of 'em! I bin running 'fraid thy shoot *me*, but since *you here*, I *spose* they after *you*." The Yankees turned their boat which they had stopped to get wood, being entirely out, & each one grabbed a stick & off they went, full speed. The "little boy" had acted it to perfection. They seem to be dreadfully afraid of Guerillers!

Another anecdote the Judge told was about an old man in Va, who lived in the Yankee lines & who I presume was suspected of not being as loyal as he should be. He was arrested, & brought before the General of the Federal army, who accosted rather roughly & in rather strong language—says he, "well sir I have some questions to ask you & I wish you to tell the truth." The old man replied "I will." "Well sir! do you know of any one who has passed out of the Rebble lines and come into ours, then went back in the rebbles?" "Yes, sir I do"! "Who was it, you d——scoundrel (spoken in a loud & threatening manner) "*Genl Stuart*, sir!" Whereupon the Yankee general grew furious & with many oaths, he replied "You d——rascal—if you don't look sharp, you'll wish you had, and answer my questions *right*." The fellow replied he would. "Did you know of anyone in the Federal lines who furnish the Rebbles with provisions?" "Yes, Sir." "Who is it, you rascal." "*Genl Banks sir!*"[35] Whereupon he exploded & had the old *rebble* sent to the guard house.

Sunday 30th

Lovely day—but cool—Howard quite sick again—chills—chills. It seems he can't get rid of them. I'm not feeling quite so well—we have North wind & I feel always the effect of it.

I heard Brigadier genl Archer is dead—I suppose it is Dr. George's brother Jim. The soldiers (the 1st La Reg) who have been here several days left yesterday morning, excepting six sick ones. Two of them came to see us this eve. Poor fellows! I looked at them & thought ah! me—perhaps you poor fellows may soon be victims

---

34. Bond misdates the following five entries, dating both Saturday and Sunday as 30 August. Because the dates are not clear, I have left them as she wrote them.

35. Nathaniel Prentiss Banks replaced Gen. Benjamin Butler in New Orleans in 1862.

to the Yankees guns. I walked around to Mrs. Patrick's yesterday & got some figs— *They seemed pretty lively at the "Coffee House."* I hear our troops have gone in the direction of the "Bay"—I do hope they may take & keep it for good.

Monday 31st

This morning Howard & I walked over to Mr. Robertson's, stayed till 12 o'c. We started to go to a new store (the goods came yesterday in a boat from New Orleans) but it will not be opened till tomorrow. These men who come with the boat I believe to be *full blooded yankees.*

Tuesday 1st Sept

Went to the store today—did not purchase but two dollars worth—that was for a toothbrush. They ask 40$ for 10 yds of calico, 50 for ladies bootees, 25 for gaiters, 5 for white cotton (muslin) 40 for doz stockens, 50 for doz handkerchiefs, very plain. One of the owners said he would take charge of a letter for me & put it in the office in Havana, to go to Md. His name is Mr. Gury, he seemed very polite. I do hope my letter will safely reach there.

September 2nd

Cousin R- got a letter from Mrs. Barrow & Laura, written in May & June urging us to come back to Terrebonne, offering us a home, also Mrs. Prince wishes us to come—

Cousin Rebecca so often throws up to me, about Mintty, & threatened today to send her to Texas, says there's too much fault found with her by Howard & I. She makes me feel cheap sometimes—but I dare not tell Howard all my troubles, I know what he would do. He would not take it very kindly—for I do not think cousin Josh conferred a greater favor upon me than was his duty, when he let me have Mintty to wait upon me, as ill as I then was. His child's wife, too! It is the first & only favor I ever got of the kind, and then for cousin R to act in this way, it is very unkind.

Sept. 6th

This week has passed away so quickly—nothing of interest has occurred. I have written a long letter to ma; I do hope she will get it. Mr. Gury of New Orleans said he would mail it in Havana.

My cough still distresses me! Can't get any medicine. Paid several visits to Mrs. Robertson's. Heard *such a story* about this family. Mr. & Mrs. Maxwell applied some years since for a divorce. Oh! this world—how much sinning there is in it.

Thursday 10th

Spent the day very pleasantly with the two Mrs. Robertson's & the children. Called to see Mrs. Fontalier. Came back to tea, feel sad—had my feelings very much hurt by cousin R—she said she wished she had gone to Texas with cousin Josh. I think my reply did more good than if I had gotten angry. Oh! Father keep my lips from evil speaking & my thoughts from all guile.

Friday 11th

Howard left this morning, for New Iberia, will be gone several days I expect. I have not felt so well today; did not sleep much last night.

Saturday 12th

Howard returned tonight—brought bad news. The Yankees had taken Monroe between here and Shreveport & they had their fleet opposite "Neblett's Bluff." I suppose there will soon be a fight in Texas.[36]

Sunday 13th

I thought of going to church today—but was not feeling so well this morning, & it is well I didn't as it rained about dinner time, & there was not any preacher come.

Tuesday 15th

Cousin Rebecca has engaged a house on Main Street, we will move tomorrow. The inmates here will be heartily glad to be rid of us all. They are a singular people. They are worse than *heathens*. Mrs. Maxwell is the *greatest abolitionist I ever saw!!* We have been greatly put to it, what we will do when we go to housekeeping, for eatables—for we have nothing to housekeep with & very little on. Cousin R. has had several *cryes*. I tell her I believe Providence will take care of us, and we will be supplied with necessities. God help & keep us faithful.

Wednesday 16th

After tea last night who should walk in, but Dr. Hemlick. We were surprised & delighted to see him. Mrs. H- is in New Iberia. I expect they will live with us. I hope all will be forgiven & forgotten & we still be friends. Dr. brought the sad intelligence of Mrs. McConnell's death. She died of Typhoid fever, & was sick only three weeks. What a bereavement. God comfort the smitten hearts, that thou has seen fit in thy wise dispensation of providence to inflict on them. If the enemy gets here, we think of going to Terrebonne. The Dr. & his family, also. Oh! must I leave my husband, or rather separate—for he will go one way & I another. It nearly

36. Bond was correct in stating that Union forces were focusing on Texas during the fall and winter of 1863. Located in Calcasieu Parish on the Sabine River, Niblett's Bluff was the location of a military hospital and also a place where Confederate troops camped, especially during 1863 and 1864, when Union forces were concentrating on invading Texas.

breaks my heart, to think so. If I get over the Bay "It may be for years and it may be forever," that I can not see my Howard.

I think God is trying my faith by afflicting me this way. Oh! Father I do believe thou art *my* father & my God & Saviour. Let not the rod of chastisement fall so heavily upon me. But what ever may occur, may I be constrained to believe all is for my good! Give us faith! And gracious Redeemer, my dear good husband, shield him from the fierce battles, may he be spared to me, & I to him these many years. Shield *him* from the arrows of that *wicked one who* kills the soul.

I feel very sad—my heart seems like a fountain of tears. I weep—I try to keep them back—but o, how long have I done that! My heart is over flowing—it must find vent, else it will break. But the spirit of Peace seems to breathe gently through it at times, and the star of Hope sends a glimmering beam and the dark clouds for a moment are parted, that envelop my heart. We are going to leave here today and live next door to Mrs. Wise. (She is not *wise* enough to gain wisdom from.) I wonder how we will get along housekeeping—I will give a description—

17th

Came around to the house yester afternoon. Bid the family good bye with as good grace as I could without being deceitful—*Delight* was pictured on their faces, when we left. I enjoyed the setting of the table. Mintty looked surprised at my setting the table—she standing looking on with her arms akimbo—I tell you it was a real amusing scene—the table about a yard long & ¾ wide & when we sat down our heads & necks were visible—I laughed more than I have for a long time. We make boxes answer for chairs, as we have but three & they are rocking ones; we borrowed the table & two pots to cook in. We have a bed a piece, one wash bowl, & everything else scarce. Mrs. Robertson sent me biscuits for tea—also for breakfast. It has rained all afternoon. I just saw a corpse pass. The priest going before chanting & two men carrying the coffin; one gray headed man was all—he laid a cross on the coffin as it passed this house.

18th

Howard away all afternoon.

CHAPTER EIGHT

"Abbeville Independence"

19th

Last night Howard walked 'round to Mr. Robertson's—heard the Yankees were at Franklin & expected at New Town last night. He told me [he] would start from here [at] five this morning. Oh! God, if a dagger had pierced my heart I could not have suffered more. The agony I have suffered ever since. I scarcely slept at all last night. And this morning when he folded me to his noble heart & imprinted on my lips & eyes the last fond kisses—it seemed it was too hard to bear. I said, was I so wicked that God had to chastise me so severly[1]—God forgive me, & grant me grace to bear up under ever affliction—every new trial. I have cried so much that my breast pains me so much I can scarcely sit up. I did not get up till three oc this afternoon. After my dear husband left I took an opium pill & slept till nearly dinner time. . . . .

The sun shines lovely, but my heart is in clouds. My Howard has gone! Gone! Gone! Alas: perhaps for years—perhaps I shall never see him again. Oh! father in Heaven grant we may live to meet again & not be parted as long as we think. Oh! Father comfort our hearts. Keep him from all sin, from *temptation & all* danger.

Sunday 20th

Beautiful Sabbath—all went around to Mrs. R's to eat watermelon. I feel too sad to go. My heart is heavy & sad. Oh! My Howard! My Howard!

Wednesday 23rd

I've been sick in bed all day, till this evening. I had a chill sunday evening & yesterday evening, followed by a fever. The Dr. came to see me this morning—will wait till tomorrow to give me medicine. So many different rumors come to town, in regard to the Yankees' movements. The report that hurried Howard off proved to be faulse. The Yankees are at the Bay yet. Maybe it's all for the best. Lord direct our ways and grant we may follow them.

I went round to Mrs. Maxwell's monday afternoon, to get my account for board, had not made it out.

---

1. Bond begins a sentence with the words "We had taken." She crosses this phrase out.

Oh! my Heavenly Father give me grace to bear under this heavy trial, without thy help I can do nothing. Keep my husband in the hollow of thy hand!

Friday 25th

Yesterday afternoon Mrs. Robertson brought her sewing & came to spend the evening with us. Near sundown a knock was heard at the door, and who should walk in; a man from Houma brought letters from Laura to cousin R. & myself—also New York papers of recent date. He is on his way to Texas to see Pittman, Gaitwood, Miller & Bond.[2] I heard from my dear ma, Coz had seen her at church, never saw her look better. Oh! I am so glad. Thank God for that comfort! All the rest at *home well,* I hope I'll get a letter from there soon. Laura writes they expect the Parish to be garrisoned by negroe soldiers this winter, & if that is the case many families will leave & go to the city. Mrs. Barrow intends moving her establishment there. Mrs. Pierce is anxious for us to go live with her—[3] I believe I prefer *Abbeville independence* rather than *Terrebonne Charity.* Laura also wrote that "Little Mose," Minttie's brother, had been forced into the army, but he succeeded in making his escape & had gone back to the plantation & was there hiding from the Yankees. The Yanks have not got to New Town yet. They came as far as Capt. Fueselleirs, took everything off the place, carried it to the city & went back.[4]

Saturday 26th

I have just returned from [a] catholic funeral across the street (we live opposite the Priest's). It was a Mrs. Brusard who was buried. I never was at a funeral I felt as little solemnity as I did there. It seemed so ridiculous—all that ceremony.

Sunday 27th

At home all the morning, heard of the death of Mr. Barretts son—caught cold in camp, fell on his lungs—came home from Va. last summer, with consumption & died from it. Poor Mr. B- how he will mourn for his (as he told me) "baby boy!" He was the youngest son & was I believe about 20 years old. May he rest in peace![5]

Oh! how uncertain is life. "Lord help us to number our days, that we may apply our hearts unto wisdom."

2. In a later entry, Bond notes that Gatewood is one of Barrow's partners, and thus we can assume the other men mentioned here, in addition to Josh Bond, are his business associates as well.

3. Phoebe Pierce owned a plantation in Terrebonne Parish.

4. Bond probably refers to Gabriel L. Fuselier, a sugar planter on Bayou Teche. Fuselier later became major of the Seventh Cavalry regiment charged with patrolling against Jayhawkers in southwestern Louisiana. Bond, in her entry of 5 July 1863, mentions that after fleeing Terrebonne, she stayed on a lavish plantation owned by one of the several Fuseliers living in St. Mary Parish.

5. John Barrett,* an Abbeville native, was a saddler. His youngest son, Robert, was twenty-two years old.

Monday 28th

Cousin Rebecca quite sick—sick all night. O! I fear she will have another one of her severe attacks. Oh, my Father be with us, we need thy Fatherly protection more than ever! Give us faith—never-doubting faith to believe *all* will work together for our good—*That God is good* to *his children.* The confederate soldiers came this morning & took Martin off, to help fill up the bayou (Bayou Vermillion) to keep the Yankee Gun Boats out. I fear, when they are ready, they will come anyhow—but I suppose it is right to do all we can to prevent it.

The church bells have just tolled, for another burial. There's so much sickness about here. I think it is much more sickly here than in Terrebonne.

Mrs. Nixon here this morning for a little while. She said she'd come twice, but she did not want to meet the Robertsons. I wonder how she will do, if she & Mrs. R- is so fortunate to get to Heaven—will they be happy there? There's naught but *Love* there!

Tuesday 29th

Dr. Helmick came yesterday afternoon, very glad to see him. Is still here. Has been raining all day—quite a storm—must be equinoxal storm. Cousin R- up today—so *thankful* for it—for if she should get ill, I know not what would become of me. In thy hands oh Father do I place myself.

Dr. H- says he believes if I go to Terrebonne, & take cod liver oil & *drinkables,* I would get well. I know not what is best for me—my savior *guide* me as I should go. I have been reading the first of my journal—& there I speak of having too good an opinion of myself, & being self righteous. *Oh my God* keep me from *all such.* I *know* that is *one* of my *besetting sins.*

Wednesday 30th

Dr. H- left early this morning. It has rained off & on all day. Mrs. Robertson came this afternoon, sit an hour or two. No mail today. I hope I'll hear *soon from dear Howard.* I dreamed of him last night. Heard of Mr. Townson's death. Others have deeper sorrow than *I.* Give me a more thankful heart oh, my Father!

Oct. 1st

Cleared off today. Mr. Townson buried before breakfast—he leaves a wife to mourn her loss. Mrs. Robertson spent the afternoon. Mrs. Kerney, her children, & Miss Patton called.

Oct. 2nd

Beautiful day! I feel as though I was getting better; my cough does not plague me so much at night. I have not taken opium for several nights.

Oct. 3rd

I walked down to Mrs. Halls this morning to buy some rag carpeting. She gave me an old piece to lie before my bed. Took dinner at Mrs. Robertson's. Lovely day! I heard the most of Franklin was burned by the Yankees. Don't believe it tho.[6]

Sunday 4th Oct.

Dreamed of home & Yankees all last night. Walked around to Dr. Abadie's— saw a soldier there, who told me he had arrested Mr. Stuart, the man Mr. Barrow sent from Terrebonne to go to Texas. He was arrested at Vermillion Bridge, as a spy. I don't think he can be one. He was going on private business for Mr. B-. I hope he will be cleared & allowed to continue his journey. All the letters on his person will be read at Headquarters. I gave him one to my husband. I hope General Mouton will forward it.[7] Mrs. Spaulding here a little while.

Monday 5th Oct. Afternoon.

All alone—I hear the Yankees are in New Town.[8] *God help us* if they come here!

Thursday 8th Oct.

Last night, about the middle, the Yankees came, & rushed into the coffee house, frightening the gamblers from their favorite game (Poker). There were not many of them, & they soon left. This morning our men came on the other side of the bayou, did not cross over. It created quite a commotion amongst the inhabitants of Abbeville. They commenced gathering up their horses, thinking they were the Yankees. I guess *some* of the Abbevillians stand in greater awe of the Confederates than they do of the Yankees.[9]

Oct. 9th

This morning I took a long walk, called at Madam Patrick's. Soon after I got home I sold my spinning for 8.00$ to Mr. Debroker. He is a rich planter on this bayou (Vermillion).

---

6. Military action around Franklin, located in St. Mary Parish, was at its height in the spring of 1863, so it is likely that Bond heard of damage resulting from this activity.

7. Jean Jacques Alfred Alexander Mouton, a Confederate brigadier general and West Point graduate from Opelousas, La. He was the son of former Louisiana governor Alexander Mouton.

8. The Federal troops did indeed occupy New Town (New Iberia) in October 1863 as part of the Great Texas Overland Expedition. Located approximately thirty miles east of Abbeville, the town remained under Union control throughout the remainder of the war.

9. The Federal visitors could have been part of Gen. William Franklin's troops making their way from Bisland to Opelousas and Washington, La.

Oct. 10

Mr. Wren called this morning, brought me a letter *from my own Howard.* God
bless him! They say we had a fight with the Yankees, at Vermillion bridge.[10] We
have whiped them at the mouth of Red River—taken quantity of negroes, mules
and wagons. We also whiped & captured them at Plaquemine.[11]

Oct. 15th

I was taken sick saturday afternoon, had a hot fever. Sunday, after dinner I had
a slight hemorrhage; put a blister across my breast, have it on there now. I walked
to the bridge & from there to Mrs. Robertsons—I feel so *tired.* They say the Yankees are fighting today at Vermillion bridge. We hear nothing *positively true,* as regards the armies.[12] Oh! *Father,* take care of my dear Howard, grant he may be
safely kept from all harm & temptation. O my Saviour if it is thy will & the will
of my Father & the will of the Holy Spirit that my life shall be spared O! help me
to be ever grateful for it, & if it is not right or best—fill me with perfect *resignation* even as my blessed Saviour was resigned to thy will. O! Father Oh! holy spirit
ever dwell in my heart. Give me faith—O that my faith may never grow less; but
increase more & more. Thou knowest all my weaknesses, & are acquainted with
all my besetting sins. O! Father forgive them & give me grace to take up my cross
& follow the path that leads to thee.

Oct. 16th

I went to see Mrs. Spaulding who is quite sick. I related a dream I once had. I
saw Mrs. Patrick's eyes fill—I believe she is a christian woman. Oh, that I may
have said something that fell upon good ground not for my praise but God's glory!
O that I may let fall words that will enter the heart, & be as dew upon flowers. I
believe I am perfectly resigned to God's will. I feel as though *He will* spare me, that
I am not to go now, but if it is God's wish to take me, he knows best. I place myself in *His righteous hands.* I hear we have whipped the Yankees above & they are

10. In a letter dated 11 October 1863 to Confederate general Kirby Smith, Maj. Gen. Richard Taylor reported "skirmishing on Bayou Vermillion to-day, inflicting some loss to the enemy." See U.S. War
Department, *War of the Rebellion,* ser. 1, vol. 26, pt. 1, 386.

11. As Union forces were looking toward Texas, Confederate troops had success in Louisiana during the fall and winter of 1863. One of the larger battles occurred on 29 September in Pointe Coupee
Parish as the Confederates, led by Brig. Gen. Tom Green, defeated a Union force in the Battle of Stir-
ling Plantation.

12. Union troops camped near Vermilionville in mid-October. On 16 October, Union major general W. B. Franklin noted in a letter to General Banks a Confederate attack "without any result."
Franklin also explained that, because of his troops' location, he expected such attacks to continue, and
thus he soon moved to Carrion Crow Bayou. See U.S. War Department, *War of the Rebellion,* ser. 1, vol.
26, pt. 1, 338–39.

retreating towards New Town. I hope the South will soon be free. I believe it is being punished for its wickedness.

Sunday 18th

Lovely day, tho it rained last night. I heard the Yankees had been reinforced & had whipped our forces at "Carion Cross."[13] Cousin R- got a letter yesterday from Mr. Barrow. He wants us to go home—says he supposes the Federal Army has passed by Abbeville by this time—hopes they will do us no harm. I expect I shall get letters from home soon. We were very much frightened this evening at the appearance of 25 or 40 Yankees in town. They came across the bayou, went to Mr. Frank's house, & arrested him, also Coul O'Brien, Eugene Guigne & others.[14] I believe they did not take Mr. Eugene with them, the others they did. I pity Mrs. Franks. When I saw the Yankees, I felt so glad Howard was not here. They did not stay long. I hope they will not trouble us soon again. Several came in the yard, one asked for something to eat, we gave him all we had cooked—he said he was much obliged—I *am sure we* were *more* obliged he did not come in. Blessed Father may our hearts be lifted up in thanksgiving for thy tender mercies over us! Nothing can befall us while we put our *full trust* in *God!*

Monday 19th

One month since my Howard left us. God keep him from all dangers seen & unseen—Oh! that this horrible war may soon be put to an end, & Peace once more grace our country.

I have been reading this morning a New Orleans "True Delta." It gives an account of our victories in Georgia & Tennessee, Bragg over Roazencrants—We killed according to *their* accounts 1700, wounded 8000, took 50 pieces of artillery, & a large number of prisoners, 5 or 6000.[15] The paper states there is to be a King over Mexico—Patterson Bonapart is one spoken of most likely to get it.[16]

13. Skirmishes did occur in mid-October at Carrion Crow; see also Bond's entry of 22 November 1863.

14. Col. Patrick B. O'Brien was of the Louisiana Irish Regiment. Eugene Guegnon's* oldest son, also Eugene, was mentioned in an earlier entry as Laura's suitor.

15. Bond probably refers to the Battle of Chickamauga, in which Confederate general Bragg forced the retreat of Gen. William Rosecrans from Chickamauga, Ga., to Chattanooga on 19–20 September 1863. The victory helped southern morale but had little strategic consequence, as Rosecrans still held Chattanooga. Moreover, the South lost 18,454 men, with the North losing 16,170. See McPherson, *Ordeal by Fire,* 338.

16. French troops seized Mexico City in 1863, overthrowing the leader, Benito Juárez, and replacing him with Archduke Ferdinand Maximilian of Austria. Southern diplomats hoped to win an agreement with France in which the Confederacy would recognize a French-controlled Mexican regime in return for French recognition of the Confederacy. Their efforts failed, however, as Napoléon III, los-

Wednesday 21st

Mr. Kearney came back from Texas this morning—he brings good news from our army, says 50,000 french troops have landed in Texas for what purpose we cannot exactly tell—there are many conjectures afloat. In the Delta, I read there was seen off the Harbor of New York a Russian fleet. Now if Russia is going to help the U.S., God help us! The *Yankees* are bad enough—but the surfs are *worse*. Mr. Frank came back today—but Col O'Brien they have sent to the city. I attended the funeral of Mrs. Ellis' father this morning.[17] I wrote home to sister Fannie today. I also wrote to Laura—I do hope they may go safely.

Thursday, Oct 22nd

Cloudy & disagreeable weather. I feel the effects of damp air. I heard the Federals were coming back today. I hope they will act rightly. I am afraid of the negroes! Mrs. Maxwell's George has gone to the Yankees & taken her best horse. Went round to see Mrs. Murry—also Mrs. Robertson. When I got home, found Mrs. Sophia Robertson here. After tea Mrs. Robertson came to tell us it was not true the federals were coming to quarter here, as we had heard. We are constantly kept in a state of excitement as regards the enemy.

Friday Oct. 23rd

Very cloudy & rainy—quite a change—yesterday so warm—today so cold. I hope it will not affect me—I feel thankful I am as well as I am. I do hope & pray I'll be kept out of my bed. The servants are all complaining. I wonder how my husband is today, I want to see him so badly. God bless my dear Howard!

Oct. 24th

Lovely cold day, feels like winter has indeed come upon us. This time last year we were at "Crescent Place." I remember it was cold then. Oh! The changes one year has wrought. Mrs. Susan Robertson spent the afternoon here. Her little children are here now playing with sis. No news today. I hope Mr. Fontalier will bring me some letters from N. Town when he comes. I feel sad today—I feel I have not acted altogether right. I hope I may have grace to sustain me through every temptation.

Sunday Oct. 25th

All went to church but the servants & myself—I felt sad—why I cannot tell. I got my hymn book & read several hymns, one in particular gave me much com-

---

ing interest in Mexico and fearing war with the United States, resisted an agreement with the Confederacy. In the following entry, Bond repeats rumors of a French-Confederate alliance.

17. She writes of Victorine Ellis,* a native of St. Mary Parish.

fort—That one was "How firm a foundation ye saints of the Lord." Oh! it seemed to suit me so well—God is consuming the dross within me, & refining the gold, fitting me for his Holy presence. Blessed be His holy name! Mr. Wren took dinner with us (the Baptist minister). He is a favorite with me. I enjoy his society very much. He thinks the Yankees will retreat towards the Bay soon—they find "on to Texas" is like "on to Richmond," easier said than *done*.[18] It seems we have whipped them at *Bellville*, took several hundred prisoners—& 20 officers. I do hope they will soon leave this part of the state. We cry like President Lincoln "*to be let alone*." Mrs. Spaulding here for a short while—she related an anecdote of a woman who lost her husband. When he died she said, "poor fellow, poor fellow! I don't know how he'll fare in the next world—but I hope he'll get where there's aplenty of good *fire*, for he liked *it* so *well here*."

Monday 26th

Lovely day—so unlike one year ago. I walked over to Mrs. R's, then she & I took a walk around by Dr. Young's store.[19]

Tuesday 27th

Cloudy—I feel *achy* & bad. Amanda came home yesterday from Dr. Abadie's & said she was sick. But Mintty seems to think not much the matter—for she is trying to get them off to the Yankees. But M[intty] & Betsy say they don't want to go, they find *home* very good, better than the Yankees can give them. Mandy says she hopes the Yankees will come here; she will tell them to take our clothes & things from us, says she hates the *Bonds*. I hope she will be dispatched from here soon. Mr. Wise returned from New Orleans today—has been two weeks coming, says the Confederacy is stronger now than she has ever been. No business doing in the city. Mrs. Robertson came for a little while.

Oct. 28th

One year since we left Crescent Place. I was then so well & fatter than I had been for a long time. It has been cloudy & raining some. I feel badly. Now it is October. The "deep and crimson streak" which the poet spoke of is disclosed by the dying leaves. Every where is presented flowers of gold and crimson, and scarlet, and russet brown.

---

18. Federal troops in Louisiana under the direction of General Banks were attempting to reach Texas beginning in September 1863. As Bond notes, they did meet with setbacks, such as a defeat at Sabine Pass in early September under Maj. Gen. W. B. Franklin. Banks's troops occupied portions of Texas by November 1863.

19. Dr. Frances Young* was a Louisiana native.

October!
"Solemn, yet beautiful to view,
Month of my heart! Thou dawnest here,
With sad and faded leaves to strew
Pale summer's melancholy hew;
The mourning of the winds I hear,
As the red sunset dies afar,
And mass of purple clouds appear
Obscuring every western star.
I look to nature and behold
My lifes dim nebulous rustling sound,
In hues of amber and of gold—
The years dead horrors on the ground;
And sighing with the winds I feel,
While their low whispers murmur by,
How much their sweeping tones reveal
Of life and human destiny.
Alas for Time and Death and Love!
What gloom about our way they fling!
Like clouds in Autumn's gusty air,
The burial pageant of the spring.
The dream that each successive year
Seemed bathed in hues of brighter pride,
At last like weathered leaves appear,
And sleep in darkness side by side."

Yes, but there comes a spring, when all shall be again renewed: when the flowers shall appear again upon the earth: when the time of the singing of the birds shall come, and the voice of the turtle shall be heard in the land. Precious time of the resurrection of this frail, failing, dying body!—time of the immortal life!

Home[20]
"Take the bright shell
From its home in the sea,
And wherever it goes
It will sing of the sea."

"So take the fond heart
From its home and its hearth,
I will sing of the loved
To the ends of the earth."

20. Bond writes this poem sideways on the page.

Nov 3rd

I wrote a letter to ma yesterday & sent it to New Town this morning by Mr. Wise.[21] I hope it may reach her soon. This is very uncomfortable warm weather for the season. I was around to Mrs. Robertsons yesterday—We heard the Yankees were coming yesterday or today; but the rumor is now they have retreated from Lafayette. I hope they'll retreat across the Bay. I bought a little bottle of claret yesterday 9$ per bottle.

Friday 6th

I have just discovered I had made a mistake & have left unfilled a page & a half of my journal. I will fill it out with poetry or something.[22] I read a New Orleans paper of the 2nd today—Glorious news for us in it. Lee has so out generaled *Meads* that he (Meads) had to *hug* Washington for safety—Lee has burned bridges, torn up railroads & so destroyed the road leading to Washington (the Alexandria & orange railroad) that it will take one or two months to repair it. Bragg has whipped Rosencrans so badly that *Ros* has been called to an account by *Pres Abe,* and his command taken from him. Genl Thomas is now in command of R-'s army.[23] There was a terrible collision on the Opelousas road—The cars bound from Brashear city to Algiers with soldiers, 48 of which were confederate prisoners, 100 soldiers were killed & many wounded, strange to say not one of the prisoners were killed & but *one slightly* wounded. I hear all negroes have been sent off from New Town, negroe soldiers too—to some Island across the ocean—don't know the name. I got some Yankee crackers—paid 40 cts. per lb—good money. If I had paid in confederate it would have been *3.36$.* I got 2 doz. oranges here in town, paid 12$. We have had very gloomy weather this week. I feel badly—my lungs feel sore. Sissy started to school this week—goes to Madam Ameal across the bayou.

Sunday 8th

Had a battle above Lafayette Friday—we whipped killing a great number, taking 500 prisoners & five pieces of artillery. I have not heard our lost.[24] There were two deserters in town this morning, one said he was in the battle but was tired of the war. Lovely day. I went to the catholic church but could not understand french

21. See app. 1 for the letter to her mother dated 2 November 1863.

22. Bond probably refers to the poems she included after the entry of 28 October.

23. Bond again refers to the Battle of Chickamauga. Rosecrans did not rebound from his defeat, and in October Grant replaced Rosecrans with George H. Thomas as commander of the Army of the Cumberland.

24. The Battle of Bayou Bourbeau occurred on 3 November near Lafayette and was a Confederate victory.

so I came out & went round to Mrs. Robertson's. I am invited to Mrs. Fontalier's tomorrow to dinner.

Cousin Rebecca & I had some words at dinner—she accused me of being a yankee because I did not go in for the Confederates stealing everything they get their hands on. It is not the first time she has done so either, and throwing up to me for keeping her in Abbeville. I pray God to forgive me for all I may have said amiss & keep me from provoking anyone in any way. If others have no respect for my feelings—let me be kept from hurting theirs. Lord direct my ways and keep my tongue from evil saying. I can not fathom cousin R—she has a jealous disposition—I believe she is jealous of Howard's affection for me, & is always speaking of his faults to me & saying Howard never should *have married me.* It is hard to bear sometimes. For I am *peculiarly situated.* Lord thou knowest the feelings of my heart— thou seest too my own shortcomings—O help me to forgive as I wish to be forgiven!—Keep under the shadow of thy wing. Oh! how I should love to hear from my Howard. I feel I have few to love me—"Away from home," how sad it is to feel so lonely. *Alone!!*

Nov. 9th

Cold & windy—Mrs. Ellis brought me 20 oranges this morning & the news that our men had whipped the Yankees back to "Camp Pratt," about three miles from Iberia—this side.[25] The Yanks have burnt the bridge at Lafayette. If *I am a Yankee* I hope they may be whipped clear out of La. I hope I'll hear from my dear husband soon—

Tuesday 10th

Spent the day at Mrs. Fountalears with Mrs. Robertson & Mrs. Foot.[26] Had a very nice time.

Wednesday 11th

Mrs. Foote (a refugee from bayou Teche) called this morning—we went walking together, called to see Mrs. Dr. Abadie. I came home to dinner. After which Mrs. R[obertson] & I walked to Madam Gayen—got some roses. Heard the Yankees were retreating & burning as they go. No other news.

Thursday 12th

Took a walk this morning got some oysters—paid the rate of 4$ per hundred. This afternoon went to Mrs. Foot's got some oranges. Mrs. Foot lives in the same

25. On 2 and 3 November, Confederate action under the direction of General Taylor and Brig. Gen. Thomas Green resulted in Union troops, led by Maj. Gen. William Franklin, retreating from Opelousas to New Iberia for the winter.

26. Evelina Foote,* a native of St. Mary Parish, was twenty-eight years old in 1863.

house we did last winter—she's a funny woman—makes me laugh so. Mrs. Foun-talear invited me to ride tomorrow at 10 oc. News now is the Yankees are fortify-ing at New Town.[27]

Friday 13th

I feel badly today—have not been out. Am invited tomorrow to dinner at Mrs. Robertson's. Expect the "big pot to be put in the little one."

Saturday 14th

Spent a delightful day at Mrs. Robertson's, Mrs. Fontalier, Mrs. Foote, Mrs. Louise Abadie,[28] cousin R-, sis & myself—we had a *nice* dinner—lots of good things. The table did not look like "hard times."

Sunday 15th

The Yankees came this morning—about 50 of them. I was so frightened—they did not come in our yard. They stayed about two hours, & then left for Lafayette. I hope our men may catch them.

Monday 16th

Feel badly, throat sore. Went to see the Dr. not at home—took a walk this af-ternoon—saw a man drunk & whipping his wife. Poor thing. Yesterday when the Yankees were here one rode up to where Mandy was standing and said *"We'll hurry."* Oh yes, the negroes are *very very* sweet!!! They seem to gain all their information from the *unbleached gentlemen* & *ladies.* They asked a negroe man if any rebbles in town. "Oh yes, *plenty* in *every house!"*

Tuesday 17th

Quite sick this morning—sent for the Dr [Abadie]—felt so badly, I cryed— The dr. laughed—he told me to get up & take a walk—finds my lungs well. It is my throat that's affected. I hear the yankees have retreated from New Town— Confederates at camp Pratt. I hope it's true.[29]

Thursday 19th

Confederates victorious. Yankees gone to the bay—say we have them in the rear.

Sunday 22nd

Lovely day—I have been feeling worse for several days—such pains in my shoulders & my cough is so bad. I hear there are 1400 confederate soldiers to pass

27. In November Union troops under Major General Franklin established headquarters in New Iberia (New Town). See U.S. War Department, *War of the Rebellion,* ser. 1, vol. 26, pt. 1, 346.

28. Aline Abadie, the wife of Dr. Abadie's* brother, who was a merchant.

29. Bond's information about Union troops' retreat from New Iberia was incorrect.

through this town this evening. We have whipped the Yankees all to pieces—Gens. Green, Sibley, Mouton, Polignac, & Taylor are *our genls.*[30] Genl Kirby Smith commands this division under genl Magruder.[31] Cousin Rebecca went to church this morning—sisy stayed with me. I feel badly—my cough is so distressing. It is said we took a thousand prisoners at the battle of Carion Crow. I think that place had better change its name to *"Yankee Carion,"* since we killed so many Yankees there.[32]

25th

Lovely day—cold, very much a day as three years ago. I then was in Balto, had cold on my breast then. Dr. prescribed a plaster. Yesterday & Monday it rained, cleared off in the afternoon. I was reading over the last days spent with my beloved ones at home to cousin Rebecca. Memory pictured home so vividly I could not help weep, but the sorrow of my heart received no sympathy from hers—she does not know what wealth of affection I left there. She knows not of a mother's love; as her mother died while she was quite young[33]—

My ma, O my ma! how my heart aches some times to see your face. Memory often wanders back to the good old times of youth—Childhood pleasures O, how fleeting.

I believe I am getting to be uncongenial to cousin R- She has a singular disposition, she told me the other day she never but once acknowledges herself in the wrong—that she had a sort of *pride* about her she could not say she was wrong— And if she & I disagree about anything—she never gives up even if she finds she was mistaken. And if she once gets angry with any one—she never forgives them, matters not what they do—she will not see (or let on she sees) their good qualities. I believe she is jealous of Howard's love for me—she so often says I never ought to have gotten married, or should have married a rich man—without my

30. Bond refers to Thomas Green, Henry H. Sibley, Alfred Mouton, Camille Polignac, and Richard Taylor. Taylor was promoted in 1862 to major general in charge of troops south of the Red River and was the son of former U.S. president Zachary Taylor.

31. In February 1863, Lt. Gen. E. Kirby Smith was assigned command over the Trans-Mississippi Department under J. Bankhead Magruder.

32. The region surrounding Bayou Teche was the scene of military operations in Louisiana during the latter months of 1863. In October Maj. Gen. William B. Franklin led Federal forces from Berwick Bay to New Iberia, and from October until December several skirmishes occurred. The most notable ones took place at Grand Coteau, Washington, Vermilionville, Vermilion Bayou, and Carrion Crow Bayou. The Battle of Carrion Crow, mentioned by Bond, took place on 14–15 October.

33. Like many of her contemporaries, Bond saw as vital the role that mothers played in both the domestication and eventual salvation of their children. Domestic novelists celebrated the influence of mothers and mother figures. Bond, for example, writes of reading the novel *The Methodist,* in which the heroine benefits from her mother's influence. See her entry, and the accompanying note, for 12 March 1860.

saying anything to cause her to express herself so. And then again speaking to me of Howard's faults in their most glaring light. I generally reply thus—well I would like to find the man who had not any. These things are hard to bear coming from his family & under existing circumstances.

I wish I could not feel cuts, or anything disagreeable. For that evil member— tongue—will say things that cause many regrets. Good Lord deliver me from the evil promptings of my heart. May I be kept from evil sayings, and doings—

27th

There are so many rumors about our army whipping the Federals, then theirs whipping ours, that we know not what to believe. Several soldiers visited the town today—it seems hard to tell who they are—they were dressed in Yankee uniform but said they were Confederates.[34] At any rate they went across the Bayou which looks very confederate.

I have been feeling very homesick here lately; yesterday I came across a piece of poetry entitled, "Carry me home to die," which were pretty near my sentiments, so I altered them to suit my feelings—and will put them here as *my sentiments*. It is my wish to be carried home & buried there at Watters' meeting house.

> Carry me home to die.
> O, carry me back to my childhood's home,
> Is my earnest earthly prayer
> Where hearts are innocent, pure, and kind
> And wish me ever there.
> I'm pining away in a stranger's land,
> Beneath a stranger's eye.
> O carry me home, O carry me home,
> O carry me home to die.
>
> I sigh in vain for my native hills,
> Their sweet and balmy air
> Would waft away from my youthful brow
> Each trace of gloomy care.
> I sigh to breath the air of home
> To gaze on its stary sky;
> O carry me home, O carry me home
> O carry me home to die.
>
> I long to see my mother again,
> And hear her sweetly say,

34. Because of clothing shortages, Confederate soldiers did wear the uniforms of captured or killed Union soldiers.

"Come weary dove, here's thy home,
Then fold thy wing and stay."
Twould ease my pain to hear her voice,
When death had darkened my eye;
O carry me home, O carry me home
O carry me home to die.

Then let me rest in a peaceful grave
Beside the loved and dead
For the quiet earth is the only place
To rest my weary head.
I would sleep sweetly if you buried me
Beneath my country's sky;
O carry me home, O carry me home
O carry me home to die.
            MITT BOND

Monday 30th

It has been very cold for several days past—ice—warmer today. I took a walk this morning. Saw good many confederate soldiers—suppose they are our pickets. I hear the yankees are not far from here. I hope they will keep away. Cousin R-sold Mandy—she left here yesterday for "Grand Chenier." Mr. Kearney sold her to an old gentleman here; she did not bid any of us good bye. I feel as though an incubus had been removed from my presence. Miss Ann Patten called yesterday. Mrs. Maxwell spent the afternoon.

Dec. 1st

Heard today Genl Taylor had got to Thibodeaux—torn up the rail road. Genl. Price had left Alexandria with 12,000 men[35]—destruction unknown—I do hope we may be able to capture all Bank's army.

We have retaken Port Hudson, burnt it down, spiked all the guns & taken a great many negroes and 500 yankee officers, which were *all dispatched in good order.* I bought 2 hdd of sugar the other day for 300$ a piece,[36] and now they say I can get 400 for them. I hope I may be able to do some thing to help poor Howard out of debt for I have been at great expense since in Abbeville.[37]

I sent Mrs. Nixon two pairs of wooling stockings with a very polite note to ex-

---

35. Bond refers to Confederate major general Sterling Price.

36. The abbreviation *hhd* stands for hogsheads of sugar.

37. See app. 1 for Bond's 4 December letter to her sister Ann Lee, in which she discusses in more detail her speculation in sugar.

cept them, but she returned them, saying she could not except them—but she would buy them. I gave them to her because I thought she needed them, & as I had two other pair, I would do without those for the benefit of Mrs. Nixon. I desired God's blessing on the effort I made. What am I to do? Shall I let her have them? Or give them to some one who perhaps needs them worse than she does. It is her proud & wicked spirit that prevented her from excepting any thing from me. I gave her a grass skirt last summer—I heard her wish for one & gave her mine, one I had not made up. She did take it but in such a manner that I know she meant some thing by it, & then gave it away before *my eyes*.

Dec. 4th

The town has been filled since last sunday with confederate soldiers. Liet. Kelly brought me today a letter from Laura, & one from Peggie.[38] They came by flag of truce. Oh! to hear from home—that all are well—that the household band are still all there, & that I am fondly remembered is enough to fill my heart with joy. I thank my Heavenly Father for his merciful kindness over me, & allowing me to hear from *my dear ones again*. I was delighted to hear brother is not in the army. He is at home & only one of my gentlemen friends is in the Federal *ranks*, that one John Ehlears. My dear old grandma still alive. May I see her again.

Laura going home soon—wrote so affectionately—poor Laura—I miss her much. Liet. Kelly took tea with us—he is from Terrebonne. It was so pleasant to meet with someone from home. I met with Mrs. Patrick O'Connor today—she interested me. I went to see Madam Patrick yesterday, she is better—I sent her a cup of coffee for her breakfast.

Saturday 5th

Settled with Mr. Ellis this morning for the sugar,[39] three hhd, 900$. Also Mr. Foote for hauling[40]—he charged me 45$. I thought it too much, & gave his wife 30 (as I could not have an interview with him—he was too busily gambling). Shortly after my return home, Mr Senette (his overseer) sent me a note saying he would rather make me a present of the money than to take less,[41] & returning the 30 I had sent. I immediately wrote back on the back of his note these words "Mr. Senette, Thank you *Sir* for your *kind* and *generous offer*. When I *desire presents*, I will call upon my *friends*. I enclose you the 45$. M.P. Bond"

I think I let him see *I* could be as independent as *he*. There are the meanest set

---

38. She discusses Peggie's letter in her own of 4 December to Ann Lee. See app. 1.

39. John Ellis* was a sawmill owner in St. Mary Parish.

40. Here she refers to George Foote.*

41. In a later entry, Bond mentions that Mr. Senette is also George Foote's brother-in-law.

of men in this town, I ever saw—they live by gambling and cheating men women & children.

Sunday 6th

Took a walk on the bayou with Mrs. R[obertson]. We had to pull ourselves over on the ferry; went to Mrs. Ameals;[42] saw several soldiers. Had a pleasant walk.

Dec. 7th

Been home all day; had a bedstead put up in my room, Mrs. Fontalier loaned me. This afternoon two soldiers—a Mr. Larette (from Terrebonne) and the other's name I have forgotten;[43] he is from Lafourche came. I went out with the one from Lafourche & practiced pistle shooting—I made three hits out of six. I shot at a tree near Mr. Wise's house—he put his head out, & drew it back as quick—as if he thought I would shoot him. We are not friendly with the family. He has re-sorted to many mean things to *spite us.* I heard the Yankees were 4 miles from here to day. I do hope they will let us alone. I finished writing to Ann Lee.[44] Oh! I do pray Providence will grant it may reach her, & I may hear from them soon. Oh! I want to hear from my husband so badly.

Dec. 8th

I have felt particularly sad all day. I know not why! There are at times mysteri-ous feelings of sadness creeps through out our hearts,[45] the cause we know not.

Thursday 17th

I have had a very severe attack of Neuralgia in my right shoulder; had a blister put on it. But now I'm able to go about—My throat is nearly always sore.[46]

We have had very hard rains several days. Yesterday was the bluest and gloomi-est day I have passed for an age. Today is very bright & lovely—but very cold, plenty of ice this morning. Mr. Aléman took dinner here today.[47] He is a Con-federate soldier. I like him very much.

42. Mrs. Ameal ran a school for girls. (Bond usually refers to her as Madame Ameal.) Cousin Re-becca's daughter, "Sis," was a student there.

43. Mr. Larette is probably one of Alexandre Lirette's sons, Leo or Onver. Lirette was a planter in Terrebonne Parish.

44. This is likely the letter dated 4 December in app. 1.

45. Bond first wrote *feeling* but replaced her original word with *hearts.*

46. In mid-November, Bond begins to note a constant sore throat and increased problems with her cough. She seems to be showing symptoms indicative of the second stage of consumption. Her sore throat was likely caused by throat ulcers, which would have made both talking and eating painful. Her cough would have been marked by increasing mucous. Even at this stage, doctors hesitated to diagnose the disease, assuming that some of the symptoms could have been caused by neuralgia. See Rothman, *Living in the Shadow of Death,* for more details on the stages of consumption.

47. Pierre Alléman* was a private in Company B of the Crescent Regiment, Louisiana Infantry. See Booth, *Records of Louisiana Confederate Soldiers,* 44.

Sometime after dinner—two other soldiers came & got their dinner. They brought bad news—that Bragg had been badly whipped by Genl Thomas, at Chattanooga, and Breckenridge killed in the engagement. But this much is good. *Lee* had again whipped Mead on the Potomac. Gen. Green has gone from Lafayette to Texas to reinforce Magruder. I'm afraid the Yankees will be upon us again *hotter* than ever.[48]

It really makes my heart sick—But I must bear bravely up—The Lord is my helper I need not fear what man can do unto me. Oh! Father grant I may not be entirely cut off from my husband. Oh! that the cruel enemy may be driven from our soil.

Night—I received a letter from Howard & one from cousin Josh this evening. Dear Howard how much I want to see you! Cousin J[osh] wrote me a very affectionate letter; he gives a graphic account of his cutting out pants & patching old ones. Poor Howard has been sick—but now well.

Friday 18th

Mr. Kearny here this afternoon.

Saturday 19th

Mr. Aléman here a little while—also Mrs. Maxwell—she is *wild* again. I think has been to Mrs. Gaigon's.

Sunday 20th

Mrs. Ellis, Mrs. Robertson here this morning—had a big fight amongst the negroes there (at Mrs. R-'s) this morning (Ned & Louisa). Mr. Jackson from Terrebonne called this afternoon, he is a scout, & belongs to the 2nd La Rgt. Liet Kelly called this afternoon—he is a very agreeable gentleman—he gave us an account of one of Mr. Aleman's (or cousin Pete's) feats of agility. Said he with seven others were out scouting one day, & they spied 16 Yankees with a team—they rode up pretty close & an officer rode out to meet them, they halted. Mr. Aleman was anxious to move closer, but the Liet thought best not to do it. Aleman was not to be put off, & he begged permission to advance—he went forward. The Yankee Capt. hollered to know what company he belonged to, *cousin Pete* said it made no difference—that he was his prisoner & surrender this minute, whereupon the Yankee turned to flee & Mr. A- shot him, killing him instantly. He then jumped the

---

48. The Battle of Chattanooga, a Union victory, allowed Federal forces to begin again an offensive to divide the South. The Federal commander was Gen. George Thomas. See Williams, *History of American Wars,* 294. In her reference to Lee and Mead, Bond refers to the Mine Run Campaign in Virginia of November and December 1863 that resulted in skirmishes but no major battle. Mead attempted to attack Lee's forces but thought that the Confederate position was too strong and withdrew.

fence, which was between them—and secured pistol—round—pocket knife & boots, & the other Yankees after him—but he made good his escape.[49]

Monday 21st

A very gloomy morning, looks like snow. I expect they are sleighing in Md. now. Mrs. Robertson here this morning a little while.

Night—Our confederate soldiers are gone. We are now left to the mercy of the Yankees. Mr. Alémán & the Liet called & bid us goodbye. I had to write a note to Liet. Kelly on a little business—& for P.S. I put 'take good care of *cousin Pete.*' The relationship is this way—I had some cottonade woven by a man named Doary, who cheated me, & never brought it to me, I told Mr. Aleman if he would get it I would make him a pair of pants off of it. So he told a Mr. Barrard to go & get it, & if the man would not send it, to tell him Mrs. Bond had a cousin here, a confederate soldier, & *he* would come out there & put him in the army. So that is how he became my cousin. But he has gone & I have not got my cottonade yet.

I have written & sent letters to cousin Josh & Howard by the Liet. Mrs. Sophy Roberston & Mrs. Maxwell met here this evening, were very sociable. I was pleased for I dislike to be in company with persons who are at enmity with each other.

Tuesday 22nd

Our soldiers came back this morning—but left this evening. We had a big scare this evening. Heard the Yankees were in town. I forthwith locked up my trunk, put sister Fannie's ambrotype in the trunk & my watch in my pocket. Mr. Alémán was here this afternoon, had the flag I gave him in his hat. Mrs. Robertson spent the afternoon. Mr. Eugene [Guegnon] called this evening—was quite communicative. Did not ask after "*Miss Laura.*" We are expecting the Yankees here tonight. I hope they won't come & our soldiers will return.

Wednesday 23rd

I was in bed nearly all day today. Got up this afternoon. Mrs. Maxwell brought me some oranges. She came from "Lake Simsonete" this morning where she got the oranges. Mrs. Nixon is very angry at her for going, & also having a dinner on christmas.

---

49. Maj. Gen. C. C. Washburn recounts this incident in a letter to Brig. Gen. Charles Stone on 3 November 1863. The soldier Alléman shot was a captain of the twenty-fourth Iowa Infantry. He was with a foraging party and, seeing a group of soldiers dressed in blue, assumed them to be of the Union. As he approached them, he was shot through the heart and robbed. See U.S. War Department, *War of the Rebellion,* ser. 1, vol. 26, pt. 1, 356.

Tuesday 24th

I hope I was constrained by the divine spirit today to give a poor woman 20$, whose husband is in the Confederate army, and she has to do her own work—cutting & hauling her wood. Mrs. Maxwell sent me Dickens' "Christmas Carol" to read on christmas. It can be better appreciated now than any other time. Oh, if the rich would think of their poor at such a time, it would not require the "spirit of the past" to haunt them to bring forth their *better feelings*. This is a season to bring forth new thoughts—to fill the heart with emotions not felt every day. It is a time to turn out malice, hatred & revenge from our hearts & let sweet peace & forgiveness dwell therein. As the "Star" appeared of old, to direct the "wise men" to their blessed Lord & Saviour, So let the Star of Love arise in our hearts, to our Father in Heaven, & to our fellow creatures here. If we cannot make a merry christmas we can a happy one—remembering the blessings God has given us. The mercies He has shown us since last christmas. We have been spared & those of our loved ones—though war, cruel war—has surrounded some of them. Yet are they left to us.

Christmas eve, I'm all alone, cousin Rebecca & sis have gone to Mrs. R[obertson's]. I am left in the dim twilight to my own sad musing. As I seated myself on my bed, and gazed out upon the full Moon—sending such beautiful streaks of silvery light in my window—the thought of *home & Ma* came, thronging my mind with sweet memories of Christmas past. So vividly was the picture drawn that involuntary escaped from my lips, "Ma O my Ma!" Was she not thinking of *me* then—did her heart cry out "O my child my child!" I feel sure they are thinking of Mitt at home this *eve*. Tears are in their hearts as well as sad memories. Perhaps they are too sad to repeat my name (my heart often is too sad to speak theirs) but it is written on & in their hearts. I know I feel they are *thinking* of *me* at *HOME!*

Christmas Day 25th 1863

20 minutes past two. How shall I give a true definition to my feelings! I have been alone most of the day—that is no one has been around me, in person, but my companions have been sweet & pleasant thoughts. I do not remember of *ever* spending a happier christmas day. I have spent *many merrier ones*, but none *happier*. As I said my thoughts have been pleasant. Dickens has proved an agreeable companion in the reading of "Christmas Carol." I have finished it. It has furnished good & I *hope* profitable food for the future. Have *I* sent a ray of comfort & sunshine into the hearts of any my suffering creatures? Has our hearth been made brighter and a heart lighter by an act of mine? I hope so. I pray so. I ask God to bless the *mite* I bestowed upon the *needy*. May God put it in my heart to do that which is right for nothing can purchase good without the divine blessing. "Con-

tentment is better than riches." Cousin R- has just gotten back—was scared from her dinner (at Mrs. M-'s) by the tap of the courthouse bell: she thought the Yankees were about. Good many of our soldiers are in town today. Mr. Aleman (or "Cousin Pete") was here this morning—brought me a duck. Said he hoped I might live many, many years to come. Mrs. Spaulding called to wish me a merry Christmas & I wished her a happy one. Mr. Robertson came home last night. Cousin R- got a letter from cousin Josh—he has gotten well, *entirely well.* Oh! where is *my Howard* today. What is he thinking of? *His pet no doubt.* Oh, Father grant that I may see him shortly! I am separated from all my most beloved on earth. But the same fatherly eye is on us all!

26th Saturday night

I am like the unfortunate Mrs. Gummidge (in David Copperfield). I am a "poor lone lorn creetur" tonight. Cousin Rebecca & sis have gone to a military & *Creole* Ball at the court house—Sissy went last night. What would Cousin Josh think & what would he say.

Sunday 27th

Rained all day—very lonesome. Saw several soldiers in town today. Mr. Henry Fair advises cousin R- to go home, says he will have us sent by flag of truce in the Yankee lines. He seems to be a man of *fair* speech, at any rate.

Monday 28th

Mr. & Mrs. Robertson & Mrs. Maxwell met here this morning & appeared quite friendly. I was glad to see it—for they have been at daggers point with each other for some time.

About 12 o'c, Mintty rushed in, with her eyes considerably *enlarged* & says, "Oh, Miss Mitt, Yankees in town." She looked so frightened. I did not feel at all afraid, but sit by the window in my room, and watched them passing. They did not make us a call, but I did not feel slighted—though I jesterly remarked to cousin R- I would make up a good fire if they came, would tell them I had a big fire made, I wanted them to get used to fire—for they would see enough of it in the next world. Mrs. Maxwell, who had gone home, returned & dined with us. She talked pretty saucy to the *Feds,* & told them she wished "the Yankees as far in *Hell* as a pigeon could fly." They asked her for some corn bread—she hadn't any bread for them— she had plenty of bread but it was *all* for the *Confederates*—for her *brothers* & *friends.* They were very mad with her. I understand they shot several times at Dr. Abadie. They did not stay more than two hours in town. I hear they met 15 of our men in the bayou, who gave them battle. The Yankees numbered 115 counted. Last Friday, saturday & sunday there was an armistice between our army at Lafayette

& the Federal at New Town. I heard the yanks & rebels met not far from here yesterday, & shook hands, said they were "glad to meet as *friends* if only *for a day*." Mrs. Maxwell told me today, Mr. Eugene said his message to Miss Laura was, "when he first saw she & I, he was prepossessed in *my* favor but when he learned I was married—he of course had nothing to do but be pleased with Miss Laura." Mrs. M- told him a young officer dined here the other day—and in the course of conversation I spoke of my husband. The young soldier started & looked at me, then relapsed into profound quietude. He said he had never shown *his* admiration, but if others did—he didn't see why he should not. I think he is a consummate *goose!*

Tuesday 29th

I walked out this morning the first time for a good while—went to Mrs. Robertson's and who should be seated there but Mrs. Maxwell. I was very much surpprised & very glad to see they had made up. I expect Mrs. Nixon is furious, & will blame it on me.

I went around to Mrs. Patrick's. Old irish John was there drunk—If there is anything, or anybody I am afraid of it is a drunken man. I got away as soon as I could. The confederates carried a young man from the town over the bayou—I suppose will take him to Lafayette. They shot him several weeks since through the face, inflicting a dreadful wound—but not fatal. He deserted our army last fall or spring & went to the Yankees, & several weeks since they caught him as a spy—he would not hault—is the reason they shot him. I suppose he will be delt with according to Law. If the Yankees come now I guess they will nearly take up the town. If our soldiers are about New Year's, Mrs. Maxwell intends giving them a dinner & a ball at night. The old year is fast drawing to a close—Oh! how many sad bleeding hearts this year has made! May God in his infinite mercy put a stop shortly to this miserable war! It does not appear to me like any other period of life I ever spent. The time speeds by rapidly—the same old routine is gone through every day. Some time life is very monotonous—then again, startling change takes place so rappedly that it fills one with intense excitement & expectation as to what shall next appear.

Wednesday 30th

Mrs. Guignon's servant woman, Celestean, was buried this morning.[50] She died of Pneumonia. This has been one of the rainiest days! I think the clouds must have nearly exausted themselves tonight; it has rained so hard. Poor soldiers! How pitiable it is to think so many exposed to all kinds of weather. Doubtless many fire-

---

50. Valerie Guegnon was married to Eugene Guegnon.*

sides are darkened this eve—with the shadow of a vacant chair, besides ours. Ours has not been by death—as many others has this year—but fate has parted us our loved ones; & caused our hearts to bleed. I do not feel well in mind this evening. I have spoken unguarded words—words fraught with anger—where kind ones would have done better. Why is it I can not "bridle my tongue"? It is because I do not ask earnestly enough to be supported by God's Grace, & lack faith. Oh Faith! If I only had the faith of a mustard seed! May the drooping flowers of Faith in my heart, be well watered by the tears of repentance—and the Sun of Righteousness may its beams fall brightly upon them—warming them into new life—bring forth sweet odors, & filling my heart with 'sweet peace.'

Dec. 31st

Very cold & blustery. "Cousin Pete" here for a short while this morning; brought me a duck, wanted to know if I shot my pistol off at the Yankees. I told him no, but I shot it off at the dogs the night after they left. They teased me so, barking I could not get to sleep till very late & not until I made Mintty open my window & I reach over & got my pistol out of the trunk, & fired it at the dogs, who beat a hasty retreat; I do not know if I touched one or not, but it had the desired effect— they did not come back that night, nor since. I have had the *double-breasted blues,* all day. Oh! if Howard was only here. These days surely are dark and dreary. I wish I could get a letter from my dear husband. Cousin R- said today to sis, that "brother Howard" had put her nose out of joint by marrying me. I said *hers* was not the only one—I thought it disjointed *several others.* Why is it she is always saying in around-about way, that "H- oughtn't to have married me," I should have married some one else, &c &c &c & went so far once to tell H she wished he had not married.

New Years Day

Bright, cold & frosty morning. The water in the tumbler in my room froze nearly solid. I had a glass of egg-nogg sent me this morning.

Mrs. Maxwell gives a ball to the soldiers (Liet. Kelly & his men) over the bayou tonight—she has the rooms I understand dressed very prettily for the occasion. She borrowed a dress of me to wear, also colar & headdress. So part of my wardrobe will be there if I am not. Mr. & Mrs. R- called before going to the ball.

Jan. 2nd Saturday

Not quite so cold as it was yesterday. Mr. Aleman called whilst we were at break-fast. As we had loaned the eating table for the ball—we had a little stand drawn up before the fire—with sundry plates, cups, &c & took our breakfast in our laps— so "cousin Pete" found us. We had another breakfast prepared for him—I furnished the biscuits & coffee, cousin R- sausage, corn bread & eggs. He gave a very good account of himself at the ball—as well as others, said he walked home with a young lady across the bayou—does not wish the Madam to find it out—whispered it to me for fear cousin R- might tell Madam Ameal. I was much amused (secretly, for I should dare to let her know I suspected her) at cousin R-'s curiosity—and the way she tried to found it out. She wanted to know what that was Mr. A- said about some one going to Lafourche? I told her nothing—it was something he told me he did not wish me to speak of. I do not believe she half liked my not telling her. Mrs. Maxwell called & sat a good while this morning—I read to her & she to me—She read Gray's Elegy in the churchyard. I think it beautiful. I read some of Mrs. Gordy's pieces[51]—which she admired very much, one piece in particular which I wish to copy here. I have not all of it.

> Lines for Nannie
> There is in every human heart
> Some quiet little nook,
> And hoarded there with tender care
> A cherished word or look.
> Some word perchance that floated
> Across lifes fleeting shore
> Whose music stole, within the soul,
> To echo ever more.
>
> There is some picture of the past,
> Hung up in memory's hall,
> A *name* we trace beneath the face
> And *turn* it to the wall.
> But still we meet its earnest gaze
> Fixed in a mournful stare,
> We turn aside, but can not hide
> From that sweet picture there.
>
> There is some little withered flower
> That's folded down between,
> The pages of the heart to part
> When death shall intervene.
> Carrie E. Plumlee.

In another piece called "Memories of the Past," I have one verse.

---

51. Mrs. Gordy's birth name was Carrie E. Plumlee.* Bond records her death in a letter to her mother dated 2 November 1863.

That life has many a picture bright
Spread out before our view,
But when we touch the *frame* it melts
As sunshine melts the dew.
Yes memories of the ol dear time,
Come thronging round us fast,

There's not a heart, but has its own
Bright visions of the past.
Carrie

Sunday 3rd

Cloudy disagreeable day—got the heartache, and headache. Have had all (except one) of my dear home pictures out looking at them. "Memories of the past rush before me!" Sweet memories! All are there but me around the "old arm chair." I am the first to break one bough from "off our Parent tree." I had such a beautiful piece of poetry, which got burnt I believe May 19th 1862. I will try to call it to mind. It is called The *Family!*

The family is like a book,
The children are the leaves,
The parents are the cover that,
Protective beauty gives.

At first the pages of the book,
Are blank, and purely fair,
But time soon writeth memories,
And painteth pictures there.

Love, is the little golden clasp,
Which bindeth up the trust,
Oh, break it not, lest all the leaves,
Should scatter and be lost!
Mitt P. Bond

I was the first leaf to be scattered from off our parent tree.

Sweet girl-hood hours! Why have ye flown, & left shadows—warning me that life is verging towards the eve. The bright sunshine is leaving my path—& the lengthened shadows of evening are falling around me. The cold blasts of unkindness are chilling me through. Oh! cousin Rebecca—you have a *child* who may one day be separated from you—& a kind word a pleasant smile may be as much needed by her—as it is to me *now*—when I am separated from the sweet and dearest ones

on earth. All, all, not one have I got to rest my weary head on, and tell my joys &
woes. Oh! for my dear Mothers sympathizing heart one word of advice from her
dear lips would—how eagerly be listened to by her poor disconsolate child. I am
blamed for writing even my book—but my thoughts *must* find vent in some way—
though it hurts me very much to write—yet it is one of the few *pleasures* I enjoy.

Monday 4th

I was much surpprised this morning to see Mr. Aleman looking in at the window where I sat. He came with a friend who had just arrived from Thibodeaux, &
who is going back tomorrow, and will carry letters from us to Laura, Mrs. Barrow
& Mrs. Pierce & has also promised to bring letters over for me. Oh, I hope he'll
get there & back safely. It was very kind in "*cousin Pete*" to take so much trouble to
get my letters off—and I thank him much. They came in all the rain and were quite
wet. This man is a paroled prisoner at Vicksburg, & knows Dr. Archer & wife also
Dr. Chamberland, Mr. James Archer, & Mr. Stevy Archer. He also informed me
that *Maryland*—My Maryland—had seceded—that Gov. Bradford has turned
southerner & called all Maryland troops from out the Federal Army. God bless &
preserve the dear old lady—she has been chained, but she now has thrown off her
gaulding chains & is another star in our bonnie blue flag.

Thursday 7th

I have been worse several days. Dr. Abadie came to see me Tuesday. I'm taking
some french pills "Gille's." Tuesday night it snowed. I was much surpprised to see,
when I got up yesterday the ground was sufficiently covered with snow to sleigh
on. It hailed, snowed & rained all day. Mr. Aleman came though, & I wrote another letter to go to Terrebonne by a Mr. Ohan Boussier. I wrote to Laura to send
me medicines & flannel & e. I expect he'll be back about the 20th. I hear the negroes in Fort St. Philip and Jackson turned in & took possession of the forts & one
gun boat & killed all the Yankee officers and fought the Yankees four days before
they gave up. I expect the negroes will turn Confederates yet before the war is over.
I also heard Lincoln had the small pox, & was not expected to live. We have
whipped the Yankees entirely out of Tennessee. *Glorious news!* I hope the time will
soon come when La will be free from the Vandals of the North.[52] I have finished
"David Copperfield," & was charmed with it. Agnes was a lovely character. David
a noble fellow; and Miss Betsy Trotwood a dear old human nature aunt. I like *her*
so much.

---

52. In November Confederate forces won two battles in Tennessee (Collierville and Columbia).
Bond, however, does not mention the Battle of Chattanooga, a major battle and a decisive Union victory.

Saturday 9th

Mrs. Maxwell took dinner here yesterday. I hear today the Yankees left New Town yesterday morning 3 o'c. I hope it's so.[53] I'm writing to my husband to come to see me. Getting warmer. I believe, Cousin R- writing to Mrs. Powell—an old friend of hers from Donaldsonville.

Sunday 10th

Liet. Kelly took breakfast here—Mr. Aleman called—they seemed very lively joking each other. Mr. Aleman is going to call for a letter, to send to Howard, this afternoon. It is raining today. Oh! what disagreeable weather. Old Mrs. Robertson called this evening—Mr. Aleman came back took a list of medicines I wanted.

Monday 11th

Mr. Aleman called again this morning—took a letter from Howard to mail. Damp disagreeable weather—I do hope we will have good weather soon. The soldiers (Liet. Kelly's company) have come back & will occupy the same place across the bayou. The Yankees left New Town & went to Camp Bisland.[54]

Tuesday 12th

Cleared off this afternoon & the clouds resting on my heart seem to have floated off & now sunshine which for several days past been obscured by those leaden clouds, is warming my heart & nature again. We have had such disagreeably cold weather—so hard on a delicate frame like mine. I have suffered from it, but the "Lord has tempered the wind to the shorn lamb." Mrs. Robertson called evening.

Wednesday 13th

Lovely day—I do not feel well—fear I have taken cold—was over the fire yesterday making candy—got heated too much. Cousin Rebecca gone to Mrs. Maxwell's. I have been laughing at something I heard last summer—which borders on the ridiculous so much I can not refrain from dropping it in here—

One evening just at dusk, Rev. Mr. Wren went to Mrs. Maxwell's & as he entered the yard gate, he spied a huge sunflower surrounded by shrubbery so nothing of it was visible but its *face*. Taken it for old Mrs. Nixon or someone else, who I suppose he thought wore *caps*—he made it a profound bow "Good evening Madam," but no reply being made—he thought the lady in question was a very *stiff* one (which no doubt she was) & walked closer up & scrutinized her face; what was his consternation when he beheld the yellow face sun flower! It created quite a laugh when the joke was found out.

---

53. The town remained under Union control until the war's end.

54. Bond could be referring to a detachment of the Twenty-sixth Massachusetts Infantry. Returning from Opelousas, they camped at New Iberia and then, in January 1864, headed to Franklin, La., slightly north of Camp Bisland.

Thursday 14th

Mrs. Robertson here little while this eve. Got a New Orleans paper: old *Lincoln* got the Small Pox. I have written to dear H- to come home. Oh, I hope he'll come. Mr. Aleman took dinner here.

Friday 15th

The third anniversary of my marriage! The years since I looked upon the dear faces of home! How many more, Oh, Father, shall it be till that happy time comes? Mr. Foot came this morning & his little daughter Valerie.[55] I thought perhaps she would not come any more after the note I wrote to Mr. Senette. But were it to do over I should write *just such another*. Oh! what are they doing at home today? Are they thinking of the absent one? Ah yes, many a sigh has been heard—tears too shed & prayers offered up for me & mine.

Saturday 16th

Liet. Kelly arrested Mr. Beldon (mayor of the town) this morning and sent him to camp (Lafayette).[56] The charges brought against him are great enough to hang him. He has been acting as spy for the Federals. There's to be a grand ball given this evening at the court house. Mrs. Robertson & Mrs. Maxwell here this morning. Mr. Aleman came after dinner took a cup of coffee with cousin R- & myself.

Sunday 17th

I have been sitting on my bed watching the congregations coming out of Mr. Poets' church.[57] He had quite a large one today. Sissy went to the ball, with Mrs. Robertson, Mr. Aleman came for her. She is rather young to go to *such places* I think. Old Mrs. R-danced. She is just ma's age.

Night: Liet. Kelly & "cousin Pete" here a short while this afternoon. Liet. Kelly arrested a man, last night in the ball room & whilst he (Liet) was dancing with his half sister. The fellow must have been a bold fellow to venture where soldiers were, after having been arrested once before, & on his promising to join a company (he had deserted) he was released, but failed to keep his promise but went to the enemy. I know *he* brought them in our yard. Mrs. Spalding here spent the afternoon, Mrs. R. also here. Mrs. Maxwell went to the ball. Mr. Beldon's family were there.[58] The arrest of their father does not appear to have had much serious effect on them.

55. George and Evelina Foote's* daughter Valerie would have been about four years old.

56. J. K. Beldon* was mayor of Abbeville from 1863 to 1865.

57. Bond refers to Mr. Poyét's church.

58. Beldon and his wife, Eliza, had two daughters and four sons, their ages ranging from twenty-five to nine years old.

PART TWO

CHAPTER NINE

"Life Almost Seems Like a Burden"

19 JANUARY 1864–31 MAY 1864

January 19th

I have not been feeling so well today—but as the weather is warmer I walked out this morning—called to see Mrs. Dr. Abadie, also Mrs. P. M. Murray. Got a plate of soup at the latter place. I feel thankful I'm permitted to go about—my cough continues troublesome & often painful but I thank my Heavenly Father it is as well with me as it is. I hear the Yankees are leaving Terrebonne but that I do not credit. I hope they will remain away from here long enough for my husband to pay me a *long visit.*

Howard has been gone four months today.

Wednesday 20th

Mrs. Robertson here this morning, also Mr. Peire Aléman who came to invite me to a christening this afternoon; he is to stand God-father, Miss Eursule, God-mother.[1] Mr. A- seems in high spirits. Liet. Kelly call before breakfast to get a list of medicines for me. So he could get them in New Town, for me. I had not finished dressing & had to make my escape into my room.

Night. Went with Mrs. R- over to the Priest's house—saw the wee thing baptized & called "Peter Gilbert" Adderson. The poor little thing cried nearly all the time. I was about to leave the house, without bidding adieu to Mr. Poyét when Mr. Aleman whispered "Mrs. Bond bid the old priest good bye." I was very much obliged for his thoughtfulness & thanked him for it—for I should not like to offend him—he has shown me a kindness & I should treat him with respect. Miss Eusule invited me to dine with them, but that I could not think of doing.[2]

Bond begins her second book with the 19 January 1864 entry. She heads her new diary "Mittie H. Bond's journal. Abbeville."

1. Uresule DeFrance was twenty-one years old and a daughter of local planter Juille DeFrance.

2. Likely, Bond declines the dinner invitation because she sees herself as both morally and culturally superior to the DeFrances, Catholic French Creoles. In her entry of 21 August 1863, she condescendingly remarks that Uresule is illiterate. We can see by this and the following entry, however, that Bond is curious about the culture.

Jan 21st

Lovely day—walked over to the church had no intention of going in, but found so many candles lit—thought I would go in & see what was going on. The priest saying mass. They had a faulse grave made on a table covered with black & about three dozen candles around it: the alter also was covered with black—had great many candles on it. I remained as long as I felt like it, & came out. I heard footsteps following me—but would not turn my head, & a voice called out "Mrs. Bond," & Mr. Aléman came beside me; he commenced taken me to task for not kneeling as others did & going through all of the ceremonies; he said the priest could get after me. I told him I was not afraid of the priest, I was not going to bow when I did not know what I was bowing for. That no one had more respect for religion than *I*, but I could not worship when I did not know what I was doing. He asked me to walk on the bridge. Just then Mrs. Robertson call'd & wanted to know if I go to Mrs. Hall's. I assented, & was glad to get rid of a walk alone with Mr. A— for a married woman can not be too particular in a town—not but what Mr. A- is a gentleman—but my husband is absent. Oh! I wish he would come. I *feel* & *know* if it is God's will he will come for I have entirely left it in His hands. He knows best. I pray my Heavenly Father will give me grace to bear up patiently under *any* circumstance. I hear Mr. Beldon returned from Lafayette where he has been imprisoned since saturday. I hear he got off because he is a mason & Col Vincent is one.[3] I went to Mrs Maxwell's this eve.

Jan 22nd

Mrs. Maxwell came here before I was awake, wants to have a party here tonight; to play some games. Cousin R- has consented—she [Mrs. Maxwell] is to find the refreshments.[4] I took a walk this morning—went to Mrs. Fontaliers, came home very tired.

Jan 23ed (Saturday)

The party of the *season* came duely off; last evening; 13 persons including cousin R- & myself & excluding the children. I believe persons enjoyed their selves very much. Miss Mary Ellen O'Brien, Miss Gus Perry were the *only single* ladies present. We played games & I tryed to make myself as agreeable as possible & I heard of several compliments. The military figured quite extensively—*Liet* Kelly, *Sgt* Lablaus & Corp Sprigue & two privates in the Liet's company. The company left at eleven. Cousin Rebecca received a letter last eve from Mrs. Barrow. I did not venture to read it last night; & it has made me feel sad. I can't at times refrain from

---

3. Col. William G. Vincent was of the Thirty-third Regiment Partisan Rangers.

4. (*Mrs M*) is inserted above *she*.

crying. Laura left for N.O. the 6th of this month, for Maryland. This last link is severed that joined me to my *old dear home*. My heart feels indeed sad sad. Mrs. B requests us to return home. Oh, is it my *fate* to leave my *only love* far behind. To part from all that is *most dear to me! My God! Thou & Thou only* can direct me aright. If it is *thy* will, "thy will be done." Poor blind creature that I am—how can I discern what is right, and best for me. But O Father permit me to see my dear husband again before I leave the country *he loves* so *dearly*. The country he is given strength mind and body to, & perhaps life. Poor dear Mrs. Barrow, how my heart aches for her. She has lost her only dear beloved brother Harris. He was her *all, she writes*. Oh, what a broken-hearted world this war is making!

Night. I walked down to Mrs. Maxwell's this evening. Liet Kelly & Mr. Sprague came before I left. I had to leave before sundown. The young ladies are staying there. We have a good joke on Mr. Aléman. The other evening at Madam de France, they were playing games, & the Priest proposed a *new* play. He took Miss Eusule out & whispered some thing, & then brought her in the room, & seated her on a platform put a veil over her face—and told Mr. A- to go & kneel to the virgin (Miss Eusule) & make a prayer he did so & prayed they might be married in three weeks.[5] She lifted her veil and *spit* on him. The people here are scarcely civilized. Many cannot read one word & *few* very few have even a knowledge of books. Liet Kelly says he heard that Lincoln had announced in congress "he was for peace if they were for peace, if *they* were for war—so was *he*. A vote was there upon taken *19* were for peace.[6] Lee has whipped Mead out of Va & other good news on our side. I expect when we get in Yankee land we will be as good *Yankees* as any.[7]

Sunday 24th

I walked around to Mrs. Robertson's this morning—they insisted on my remaining to dinner, I did so. Liet Kelly took dinner there also. He is a very agreeable gentleman. Mrs. Robertson told me he paid me some very high compliments—said he did not know a more agreeable lady, than I, & he perferred talking to me to any lady he knew. I teased him about Miss Virgina Beldon.[8] Mr. Aleman came soon after dinner. Mrs. Fontalier's servants had a ball, we stood in Mrs. R's pantry & looked at them dancing. After which Mrs. R- & I took a walk.

5. Bond scratched out the word *bow* and inserted *kneel*.

6. The number 29 was written initially; the 2 is crossed over by a 1.

7. Bond refers to Lee's earlier successes before Gettysburg and is aware of the Confederate march to Pennsylvania. Gen. George Meade commanded the Army of the Potomac.

8. Virginia Beldon was twenty-two years old and the daughter of J. K. Beldon,* Abbeville's mayor.

Monday 25th

Mr. Aleman came this morning. I was deep in the mysteries of my trunk—I said not come in yet—but as usual—he disobeyed orders. I hear Mr. Beldon has been arrested again—and ten others; they have them over the bayou. I saw Liet Kelly this morning, as sis & I were taking a walk, he was up all night hunting deserters & caught ten. I have promised him a candy pulling but I'll not be as bad as Miss Virginia Beldon who invited him to come to a candy pulling & never had any. He & five others are dining at Mr. Robertson's today on oysters. I don't feel very well today—I did not get my natural rest last night.

(Night) Old Mrs. Robertson & I took a walk across the bayou last evening. We had a very nice walk. Liet Kelly joined us & walked home with us. Mrs. R. accused him of want of gallantry & I to prove to her she was mistaken (so I told him) took my seat in what I call my seat (the roots of an oak that have grown high & formed themselves into a comfortable seat.) So did Mrs. R- & the Liet had to stand up. Mrs. R- insisted I should let him go into town, with his boots—ones he had to have mended—as the shop might be closed; but I would not consent; she said I had kept him standing so long waiting—I then said, well you accused him of want of gallantry & I wanted to prove to the contrary. He laughed *very much* & said I would have to wait on him to the shoe makers.

Tuesday 26th

Lovely morning—springlike. I was aroused this morning by hearing Mr. Aléman saying to cousin R- "the Yankees are coming & we have orders to leave now, tell Mrs. Howard good bye." If a stone had dropped on my heart, it could not have felt heavier. I raised up & peeped out of the window, had my night cap on, & I presume looked anything but good-looking. Mr. Aléman looked back at the window as he passed & said "good bye." So I suppose he saw *night* cap & all. Liet [Kelly] came & bid us good bye with many regrets on both sides. He sent me some coffee to keep me from telling his sister *all* about him, when I go to Terrebonne. I feel real sorry they have gone—shall miss them so much. I believe they were sorry to leave. The Yankees are reported advancing. The Liet wished me *many sun shiny days* with no shadows, I suppose but the shadows are falling across my path already. I fear my dear husband will not come. Oh, my Father grant I may see *thy hand* in all things! For I have *put my trust* in thee.[9] Mrs. Patrick & Mrs. Susan R[obertson] here this morning. I got some hyacinths & hearts ears——

(Night) Old Mrs. Robertson call'd this afternoon & she & I went walking on the bridge looked over the bayou. It looked so lonesome over there that we both felt *blue*.

9. *Him* is crossed out.

Wednesday 27th

Very far from feeling well today—pain in my right lung—depressed in spirits too. Coughed all day nearly. I try to be trustful & do feel *all* will work together for good in the end. Lord increase my faith! Took quite a long walk this afternoon—called at Mr. Fontaliers, got a nice *cup* of *coffee,* some cake & dryed apples—the latter I have not seen since I left Md. Hear the Yankees are *not* coming, but going towards the bay & crossing over on the other side. Oh! that my dear husband may come yet. I was reminded this evening of a joke I have on Liet Kelly. I heard he had a pet pig on the bayou & *kissed* it the other day. Mr. Kearney here twice to-day—is going to send a letter to cousin Josh. (Night) Mrs. Maxwell here till nine o'c. Very lively, said the day Mrs. Guignon's black woman was buried, Mrs. G-wanted Mr. Eugene to get 12 pall-bearers, but he could not find them in town (since the Yankees been about *unbleached* domestics has been very scarce). The old lady was quite determine upon them. Mr. E- waxed wroth & retorted "that he could not find them & if he had the *material* in *hand* he would make them for her." Mrs. Maxwell thought it very *witty* & said she would *help him.* That beats all I ever heard of. She also told of a custom amongst the creoles. When two old persons meet, say an old lady & gentleman—who have not seen each other since their younger days & were then great friends they will both occupy the same *bed* room at night, & talk all night, if the husband of the lady be living & objects to the arrangement—he is told, *he can occupy another room.* Really this is *funny!* Truly this is something new *to me* under the *sun.* Mrs. Maxwell had been to Lafayette—visited her old home—says she intends buying it back, & go live there—when asked what she would live on—"On past recollections" she replyed. I think she would grow *lean* on such *diet.* I hear some of our soldiers are in the bayou. I hope they will come back.

Thursday night 28th

Have not walked a great deal today—was at Mrs. Robertson's house. Heard our soldiers are in possession of Franklin again. Delightful weather, hazy & like "Indian Summer." I think winter has broken up & we will not be afflicted with very cold weather again.

I have been thinking a good deal today, about Laura going home—It will appear very strange, when I return to Terrebonne, not to see her joyous face there. I shall miss her sadly. I feel more hopeful my dearest husband will shortly visit us. I am weary without him.

Friday 29th

Gloomy, cloudy & rainy today. True—the sun at times played hide and seek with the clouds. I too feel the effect of gloomy weather upon my spirits. I have been troubled in spirit all day. That evil member—tongue—which besets *me* so

much, and which I find hard to control, has given me a cloudy brow & sore conscience. I pray God to forgive me & grant me grace to bear & forbear. Let not my
unruly tongue & temper get the upper hand of my better spirit. I like a high spirit
but mine soars too high. I am now reading Scotts "Anna of Geierstein." It is a delightfully written book. The scenery on the Rhine is described so beautifully—as
being so magnificent. "Margaret of Anjo"—the proud—the selfwill, but heroic
queen of England—figures greatly in it. Margaret the "Daisy flower"—the "Red
Rose" of 'Lancaster.'

Saturday 30eth

Walked out this afternoon—was kept in all yesterday—felt very weak though—
could not go far.

Mrs. Sophia Robertson came after tea—scared me so—hollored "Yankees'
coming," at the door—I was in a "bower study" & it startled me. I chased her
around the table caught her—& gave her a hard smack on the shoulder.

Sunday 31st

Cloudy but warm day—Mrs. Maxwell came from church (catholic) just in time
to get some egg-nogg. She is *quite wild* (*"Martha's wild."*) She has heard from Mr.
M- who has come from Md & gone to Texas. I should much like to see him &
hear some Md. news. Poor "Irish John" was found dead in his bed this morning.
He had been sick for some time. I just saw the procession pass by. Such is life! Oh!
how brittle is the thread that binds the soul to earth. We are here to day—tomorrow we *are not*. The deceased was a drunkard but his religion there is pardon offered to the dead. I told Mrs. M- I heard she was christened a catholic yesterday
& Mrs. Guegnon was god-mother; she denied it though in such away I scarcely
believed her. Mrs. Maxwell, I hear paid the priest 50$ for burying John.——

Monday, Feb 1st

Walked round to Mrs. Patrick's this afternoon—from there to Mrs. Robertson's—sit awhile—Heard confederate money in the city good as green backs, they
only worth 40 cts on the dollar. Very agreeably surprised to see Mr. Aléman here
after tea—came all the way from Generette's (10 miles other side of New Iberia)
to bring me a letter from Howard; He wrote he can not come see me; I feel greatly
disappointed but as my prayer is to my Heavenly Father *"Thy will be done."* I believe it is all for the best, & when it is right for us to meet God will permit it. *He*
has given me strength as my day. I pray I may never be tempted to murmur at any
trials I may have to endure, be they ever so hard. But ever remember they who
"meekly bear the Cross are worthiest of the Crown." Mr. Aléman—cousin Re-

becca says—look at me whilst I was reading my letter with so much sympathy expressed on his countenance & heard a deep sigh.[10]

Tuesday 2nd

I wrote a long, long letter to H- today. Mr. Alémam took it to night—he is going soon in the morning, to Lafayette & will send it by courier. He came this afternoon. I made him an egg-nog; he also took tea with us. I sent several messages to the Lieut by him. I hope he will deliver them in the manner I said them. I hear the confederates got over by Tigerville—tore up the rail road burnt bayou Black bridge—causing the cars to run off into the bayou & capturing 4 Yankees, who they first brought to Lafayette, and then made them walk up to Alexandria, Old Beldon also with them. Howard writes, cousin Dick has been promoted Major, & is at Mobile.[11] Red river was frozen over, & he and Genl Kerby Smith took *a skate on it*.[12] Mrs. Hall spent the evening here—I wrote a letter to *"Hall"* for her, used the most endearing names—told how I sit in the coming of evening smoking my pipe—& thinking of my dear husband.

Night—took a walk this afternoon with Mrs. Robertson Jr. who expressed herself very sorry at my leaving Abbeville. I came home soon for was quite tired, & cousin R- then walked with Mrs. R. Mrs. Patrick came in soon after, told me the Yankees were reported to be in New Town. I hope it is faulse. *It is all right my husband* can't come, he might get caught by them. Mrs. Patrick Murry is a dear old lady. I love her much. I believe she is a good christian, a strict catholic though. Mr. Alémam's sentiments of this war are mine exactly—He said last night, that God had brought this war upon the south for her wickedness—for her utter disregard to the sabbath, & to the souls placed in her charge. Of course he meant individuals. If peace should soon be ours—God grant it may—& we forget this chastisement, God will send worse plagues upon us [than] this war.[13]

10. Here Bond crosses out what at best estimate is the following sentence: "I did indeed feel wretshed that night but I feel more resigned now."

11. Richard C. Bond was a major in Company H of the First Heavy Artillery, which was organized in 1861 as part of the Louisiana State Army and soon transferred to Confederate service. His company did go to Mobile, as Bond reports, arriving in January 1864.

12. She writes of Calvary general Edmund Kirby Smith.

13. While Bond expresses elsewhere in her diary the prominent view that war was punishment for the South's sins, this is the first time she has alluded to slavery as a cause of war. Before the war, prominent southern clergy, while not sanctioning abolition, had preached reform of slavery as it was then practiced. Most notably, they argued against the separation of slave families and against the literacy law that made it illegal to teach slaves to read. As the South's early victories in the war became fewer, many

Thursday 4th

Lovely afternoon. Been writing to ma. This morning, a funeral at the church—two little children died with diptheria & were buried I presume in the same grave. So many warnings the living have & yet we are so careless, about death No news of any account.

Friday 5th

Lovely day. The weather cool—but feels reasonable. I spent several hours at Mrs. Hall's. Our conversation mostly on religion.

Saturday 6th

A real march day, wind blowing very hard. Mrs. Maxwell here this morning—Came from Lafayete yesterday, talks kinda crazy. The soldiers in town looking for deserters. They are passing now—hunting for Mr. Fontalier, who joined a company & did not report. I walked round to Mrs. R-'s this afternoon, although the wind was blowing quite hard.

Sunday 7th

Lovely day, took a walk this morning, also this evening, went to Mrs. Nixon's—poor old wretch—she is in deep trouble about Mrs. M- but she hunts up trouble herself. I pity & blame her at the same time.

Monday 8th

Mrs. Sophy R- & I went over to Madam Ameal's this afternoon—We had to cross the bayou on ferry but neither of us said a word about paying—but thanked Mr. *Ferryman* very politely. I guess he thinks he does *not live on thanks.* It is lovely on the bayou—looks some thing like Md scenery.

Tuesday 9th

Pa's birthday—64. Oh how I wish I was there to day! I feel sad—sad. Nothing but sickness sorrow & pain in this world! I dreamed about dear Howard last night—I dreamed I saw tears in his eyes. Oh that I may ever remember his request in the last letter I received.

Thursday 11th

I was in bed all yesterday—up today though, took a short walk. I cough a good deal. The weather warm & looks like *"Indian Summer."* Have finished reading lately, "The Fair Maid of Pearth" & "Castle Dangerous," both of which are very interesting & highly historical, but "Anne of Geierstein" bears off the palm. *This*

Christians again turned their attention to slavery, wondering if their defeats were the results of God's displeasure of abuses within the institution. (For further detail, see Genovese, *Consuming Fire,* 51–61.)

is the time to read and appreciate Scott's novels, whilst *war,* is in the land; we can better understand them.[14]

Saturday 13th

Mrs. Maxwell & I went to Mrs. Col O'Briens & Mrs. Perry's yesterday[15]—I enjoyed the ride & visit very much—but disgraced myself at both places for I drank too much wine & became *tight,* we came home to dinner. I sent my letter to ma, by Dr. Poyét this morning who started for the city. I do earnestly pray God, it may reach her, & *I feel it will.*[16] I found Dr. Poyet very agreeable. He use to be a priest— but has been excommunicated from the church. I saw a few minutes ago, a funeral go to the church, and a man was sitting across the coffin driving. The people *here* are worse than *heathens!* I feel very badly today—I cough a good deal, & feel so weak. My heart feels so *sad.* Life *almost* seems like a burden. Lovely day.

Sunday 14th

I was in hopes I should have been able to attend church this morning, as Mr. Wren preached—but I rested so badly & coughed so much last night I was not able. I feel I have taken cold—but how or when can not divine. I feel low in spirits! sad, sad. "Oh! why o why my heart is sadness." I have just read a lovely piece of poetry to cousin Rebecca, which affected her to tears. It is this

> Nearer Home
> "One sweetly solemn thought
> Comes to me o'er and o'er;
> I'm nearer my home to day
> Than I've ever been before—
>
> Nearer my Father's house,
> Where the many mansions be—
> Nearer the great white throne—
> Nearer the jasper sea—

---

14. Several times, Bond mentions reading Sir Walter Scott's novels. His works, especially the Waverly novels, were hugely popular in the South even before the Civil War. Literary critics have linked Scott's novels to the creation of southern nationalism. Mark Twain went so far as to claim that "Sir Walter had so large a hand in making Southern character, as it existed before the war, that he is in great measure responsible for the war. . . . The Southerner of the American revolution owned slaves; so did the Southerner of the Civil War; but the former resembles the latter as an Englishman resembles a Frenchman. The change of character can be traced rather more easily to Sir Walter's influence than to that of any other thing or person." *Life on the Mississippi,* 376.

15. Mrs. O'Brien's husband was Col. Patrick B. O'Brien, of the Louisiana Irish Regiment.

16. Bond underlines *will* twice.

Nearer the bound of life—
Where we lay our burdens down—
Nearer leaving my cross—
Nearer taking my crown.

But, darkly lying between,
Winding down through the night,
Is the dim and unknown stream
Which leads at last to the light.

Father, perfect my trust!
Strengthen my feeble faith!
Let me feel as I would when I stand
On the shore of the river of death!"

How lovely those lines are! They are my own sentiments. "Let me feel as I would when I stand on the shore of the river of death!" And how soon that may be God only knows! My heart tells me I am not as I should be, though sickness & pain are my constant companions, yet am I heedless of these warnings. Oh! "Father help me to number my days that I may apply my heart unto wisdom."

Monday 15th

Rained last night & cloudy today, partly cleared off this afternoon. Mrs. Robertson came & set till dusk—I saw sympathetic tears in her eyes, as I gave her *some* scenes I had passed through since I was married—the burning of the house ("Crescent Place") & the horrible feelings of anxiety I endured. My separation from my beloved home & my husband. She thinks of changing her present abode, & moving into the hotel—if she does—I think it probable we will take part of the house; as it is a very large one.

Tuesday 16th

Beautiful bright day. I have not been feeling near as well since saturday—I cough a great deal, especially at night and my lungs are sore & sometimes painful. Mrs. Maxwell & Miss Virginia Beldon, spent the afternoon here. I hear the Yankees have again returned to New Town. I hope they will not pay Abbeville a visit again.

Wednesday 17th

I feel very badly today—pain in my head, & cough a good deal. Mrs. Robertson sent my breakfast to me, yesterday & this morning. She is a *true & tryed friend.* May the good Lord bless and reward her for all the many kindnesses she has shown us. I have been suffering from neuralgia & my other disease very much today; also much depressed in spirits; Oh what would I not give to feel the loving arms of my dear husband thrown around me, To feel I am dear to him yet I *know* I am—but I long for a word of love—of sympathy-of *pity!* My heart grows so sick for the *loved* ones.

I know it is all right I am separated from them. I have much to be thankful for. God has *been very merciful.*

Since I left my home, in Maryland, the circle has remained unbroken, & while the death-pall has draped other homes, *mine* has been spared, and the dear frail Mother, whose life has been watched so anxiously by all of us for many years—has been spared & *hope* still holds out some encouragement I may see her again.

Tuesday 23ed

I was taken to my bed last Wednesday & yesterday was the first day I've been up since. My suffering has been very great—neuralgia in my head & shoulder. I have six blisters from mustard on me now. I feel very much better today. I received a letter saturday from dear Howard, brought by Dr. Hardie of Shreveport who came down for the purpose of examining those persons who have had discharges from military services, on account of diseases, & see who was able & who not. Mrs. Robertson was very much distressed, on sunday, fearing her husband would not get a discharge—I believe he will, on certain conditions—that he in some way assists the Government. Mrs. Robertson brought Dr. Hardie to see me yesterday afternoon. I found him a pleasant & agreeable gentleman. He said he hoped I would come to Shreveport; and promised to go see Howard & also took some articals of clothen for him & letters from his ma & I.

The Dr. left this morning. This is a pleasant day, a little cloudy. I am about to have the bedstead taken down I've been using some time & have one put up in its place, Mrs. Ellis loaned me a very handsome mahogany one. Mrs. R- called this afternoon, & told me what Dr. Hardie said about me. He said "if he had such a pretty wife as I,[17] he would be sure and come see her if he had to desert." Cousin Rebecca insisted I should not be told what he said, for I was too vain now. I hope if I entertain vain & foolish feelings God will forgive me & give me grace to over come them. Oh! My Father teach me to be an humble and consistent Christian.

Wednesday 24th

Brother's birthday. I hope he may spend a happy one, & live to spend many more. Dreadful pain in my shoulder—so sore inside—down my breast, & where my food goes down—can't swallow any thing but liquids; felt hungry too for breakfast, but must endure it. Could not help crying when I tryed to eat some dinner—

17. Bond crosses out the phrase *I was him* following *if.*

swallowed a little piece of sweet potato, but hurt so badly the tears would come; just eat a little clabber. Cousin R- gone to see Mrs. Nixon who is very sick, left me this morning without any breakfast again at dinner time. I can not comprehend cousin R—at times, she seems to enjoy my society—then again is so cold & taciturn in her manners, Calls me by names, she dislikes herself—such as *"New Josh Bond."* If I found fault about things not being kept nicely by the servants, or about the house being dirty she will say "Well you are old Mrs. Robertson over again," and she don't like her much. I try not find fault—but when I see Mintty allowed to be so filthy about the house I can not help speaking. She has an idea I am vain— and acts like she was jealous. Mrs. Susan R[obertson]- seems to take a great interest in me & is very fond of my society—She & her husband have told me I was agreeable to them & of course I feel glad I am; but that isn't vanity!

Now Mrs. R[obertson] said to me this morning—Mr. R. was anxious to get another house—so he could give me a room in it; for they would like to have me there all the time. I of course could not think of leaving cousin R- nor would I do it but it shows how much they like me—one too who is always sick, I thank her for her goodness. It warms my heart to know *all* are not indifferent to me; some hearts draw near me in these dark days of sorrow.

I pray God to give me grace to bear up—to see & not see—to be blind to all faults in those around me, & to act & think charitably to *all*.

Saturday 27th

Been suffering dreadfully this week. Dr. sounded my lungs, says the right one is also affected, I can't breath through it well.

Liet Kelly has been to see us again—came yesterday; I was in bed—had the curtain drawn & talked to him through it. He accused me of sending him a valentine. I read it & told him if I had sent him one, it would have been worse than that. He called this morning to bid us good bye, & seemed glad to see me out of my room.

Mrs Valco Verzie died yesterday. I suppose she will be buried this evening or in the morning. Mr. Beldon has gotten back; *honorably acquited.* Mr Suane & family run off this week—gone to the Yankees and a number of men with them.

March 2nd

Sitting up today—feel little better—suffer very much—Been very sick since I wrote in here. Dr. sounded my lungs—my right lung affected. I can not breath good through it. *Thou* has afflicted me in thy righteousness Oh Father. I am thy child through grace, but a wayward & disobedient one, and only through tribulation & suffering will I be as a little child. Rev. Mr. Wren prayed with me the other evening. He prayed so beautifully for me that if it was the divine will I might be

restored to health, and for our absent ones. Oh! the tears fell fast from my eyes—
It was the first prayer I had heard for so long. I feel nearly always that I shall not
live long. Some times hope springs up in my heart & then I think all things are
possible to God, & if it is his will, I *know* I shall be cured even if I can not get medicines. Oh! my savior if I—like the woman who had the issue of blood could but
touch the hem of your garment, I should be healed, "*Only Believe.*" Those words
strike deep in my heart! I do believe Oh! my saviour—"help thou my unbelief." If
I felt perfectly *sure* I should reach the Heavenly Shore where the "jasper sea" continuously roles—I do not believe there is any thing in this world could make me
desire to remain in it. I feel I'm so unworthy to enter those pearly gates—that I
fear—"*Fear not I am with thee*" is another encouraging promise.[18]

Mr. Aleman came on us this morning—left this evening—right sick—poor
fellow. I pity him—away from home—How sick the heart grows, away from
home—when the body's sick.

4th Friday—

Yesterday afternoon, Miss Virginia Beldon & Mrs. Maxwell came see me.
Cousin Rebecca received a letter from her husband. The sun played hide and seek
with the clouds to day. I fear bad weather will be the issue. Have the small pox in
the village—several cases—I do pray it may not spread. I still have such a dreadful sore throat.

Saturday afternoon 5th

Looks pleasant out of doors. I feel little stronger today—did not sleep well last
night. Mrs. R- here this morning; says the Confederacy looks more cheering. Yankees been whipped badly at Mobile, also in Tenn, & Miss.[19] Confederate money
worth 25 cts in the dollar in N.O. 18 cts in New Town. I hope France will recognize us as a nation soon—and this wicked war put to an end.

6th

Lovely sabbath eve. I can only look out & enjoy lovely nature. We have been &
still are much alarmed about the *Jay hawkers,* who are very bad. They commit *all*
kinds of outrages upon men, *women* & children, rob murder & rape—Oh it is
dreadful! What is our once happy country coming to! As Dr. Hardie remarked, "he
believed God sent this war as a punishment upon the south—for her manifold
sins—yet it seemed she was more wicked than ever. They tell me there is prospects

---

18. Bond underlines the biblical phrase quoted here with wavy lines.

19. Around the time Bond writes, there were no major battles in Mobile. On 17 January 1864, the
Confederates had a victory at Dandridge, Tenn. In Mississippi there was a Confederate victory on 22
February with the battle of Okolona, near Meridian.

of peace *soon;* I have heard it so often that I shall not believe it, till I feel the effects of it. Twelve Jayhawkers were shot at Lafayette, last week.

Night. Mrs. Broussard & Miss Guss Perry called this eve. After they left, Mrs. Foot & child, Mrs. Spaulding, Mrs. Maxwell, & Mrs. Robertson came.

Monday 7th

A real March day. I feel achey—did not rest well last night. Cough so much today. Dr. Abadie quite sick—coughs a great deal. I have no appetite—all I eat I force. All friends are so kind. Mrs. Ellis let me have milk for nothing; gave me two chickens since I've been sick. Some one always giving me something. Perhaps it is childish to write such things in my journal, but it may be my loved ones at home will not know of the kindnesses their loved one met with in a strange land, amid strangers, & foreigners unless they see it here. Where ever I've been the Lord has raised up friends for me. And I believed the good Lord, raised up Mrs. Robertson for my friend; she has indeed proved herself a *true one.*

8th

The sweet birds are singing so delightfully at my window. I believe they are building their nests near by. I shall enjoy their sweet notes very much, when I can't go out of doors. Old Mrs. Robertson spent yesterday afternoon with us. She is a singular old lady—but has many good traits of character.

9th

A very disagreeable day—cloudy & rainy all day, till near sun set then the dark clouds rolled back, & the orb of day through back upon us, its last lingering rays, as a parting blessing & filling our hearts with a hope of a *brighter to-morrow.* But I believe as it descended beyond the horizon a cloud covered its face; as it was about to give the last glance. Old Mrs. R- spent the afternoon here.

10th

Another disagreeably cloudy day.

Friday 11th

Lovely day—cold wind blowing. Quite a little scene occurred next door, this afternoon. Our neighbor Mr. Wise & us have not been on friendly terms for several months,[20] and also the owner of his & our house have had some words with him several times. Mr. Broussard (the owner) had threatened several times he would break Wise's head if he did not behave himself. One day he said to me he was going to whip him, and after he left, I remarked to Mrs. R[obertson] I hope

20. Soloman Wise.*

he would—& if I saw him at it, I would say "give it to him—you won't give him a lick a miss unless you miss him." I did not think he really was going to give him a lamming, but sure enough this afternoon, I heard such an out break in the street, in the direction of Wise's store. At first I took it to be children & thought one of them were hurt; as shriek after shriek met my ear, I concluded it was some thing of a very serious character. It frightened me so I did not know what to do; my heart beat so rapidly. I looked out of my window & there was Wise & his wife throwing bricks & cursing Mr. Broussard, both of them cursing. It appears Mr. B- was in to have a settlement, some dispute as regards the paying of certain money arose, & B- had a pretty big stick in his hand, which he used too freely over the said Wise's head & hand, causing the better half to cry out, & that's what created such an uproar.

Cousin R has just gone to see Mrs. Hall who is quite sick.

Monday 14th

Very disagreeable weather, cloudy rainy and windy. Yesterday afternoon, Mrs. & Mr. Robertson came, also, Miss Virginia Beldon & Mrs. Spaulding. They say the Yankees are coming sure enough.

A man across the bayou buried this morning, another corpse to be buried this evening. The small pox has spread to several houses, one or two cases very bad.

Thursday 17th

The Yankee's have truly & really come up to New Town, are passing up towards Alexandria where I hope they will be well whipped. Their number is supposed to be from 15 to 18000 men.[21] I fear I shall now be cut off entirely from my dear husband for a long time. God give me strength to meet every disappointment with a strong & trusting heart! Believing all things will be well in the end. Oh! Father strengthen my feeble faith.

Night—I was made so indignant and angry at the dinner table, by the idea I was thought *clannish*. And I gave way to my passion in an unguarded moment. I felt exceedingly sorry & after all things was explained I begged God's forgiveness as well as the one I had done injustice too. Although I feel I was not entirely to blame—but I acknowledge my fault & begged pardon—if pride prevented *her* from doing the same, *I* have the satisfaction of feeling I have over come my pride & the temptation of not doing what is far nobler, confessing faults, rather than concealing them—Thank God for *Grace!*

21. In early March 1864 Banks's troops began increasing their numbers at Berwick Bay. By 15 March, however, most had left the area and were moving up Bayou Teche.

Friday 18th

I feel very sad to day. My disease I think is getting worse. The most favorable sign I had, has vanished. Oh! how truly thankful I have been taught to love my God—my Saviour, and have by the divine spirit, been led to the foot of *cross*. That I commenced serving God (though falling far short of my duty) in the flower of my youth—ere disease had shattered this now weakly frame—when life was most joyous & I was most intoxicated with the gayeties of youth. Oh how gay was I *that* summer! If I had continued as I then was, where would *now* be my *hope* of a better country? But that good Shepherd who is ever watchful for the foal—snatched me from the devouring wolf—& took me under His most gracious care. And blessed be God, I am still with a bright hope of ever being a lamb of His, and the time appears not long, when I shall be released from the snares of the tempter,[22] having had my robes wash[ed] white in the blood of the lamb. Oh! blessed trinity! Oh blessed Heaven where the many mansions be! Shall I not have one prepared for me—unworthy as I am. But my dependence is on the atoning blood of my saviour & the endless mercy & love of the Father, who has said I will not leave or forsake thee.

Tuesday 22ond

I have for the last few days been feeling badly—low spirited about my disease and dear husband. Yesterday I was sick in bed all day. Mrs. Robertson spent the evening with me. I feel better in spirits to day; though I hear bad news. Our troops at Lafayette, Alexandria, and "Fort Derussy" have evacuated & gone to Shreveport.[23] I expect soon to hear of evacuation at that place to the Yankees. They have all the above named places.[24]

This has been a real March day; yesterday it rained all day, today is bright & windy. There are only a few federals in New Town at present. I hope I may get a letter from home soon. I suppose I am entirely cut off from Howard now. Oh, I do hope I shall in some way hear from him soon. It was *all* right he did not come down to see me. The Lord's ways are the best!

Friday 25th

Lovely day—very windy—yesterday until 2 it rained in torrents, but cleared off about three. We hear no news, they seemed to have stagnated. I have not rested well the two last nights—coughed nearly all the time. I can not tell whether I am

22. The words *and shall have* are crossed out.
23. The word *forces* is crossed out and replaced by *troops*.
24. The Union flag was raised over Opelousas in mid-March; Fort DeRussy, on the Red River, was captured on 14 March, opening the way to Alexandria, which was occupied the next day.

getting better or worse. I got the other day a bottle of claret—paid the enormous price of 2.50 in silver. It strengthens me some. I wish I could get Port wine.

Monday 28th

I took a walk saturday, & my limbs were so weak that several times I came near falling in the street—once my limbs got so weak that I tumbled over—but fortunately steps were there & I sit upon them. I hear much news—some confirmed— Coul Vincent's reg. was captured by the Yankees—excepting the Coul & a few men.[25] They are now reported to be retreating from Alexandria, this way. I do hope they will get a good sound whipping. The N.O. Picayune states we have whipped the Federals at Richmond—capturing a great many arms, they had taken with them for the purpose of arming the Yankee prisoners there—*they felt so sure of capturing Richmond that time.* Also our victories in Florida & Alabama.[26] I am daily expecting to hear of an attack on Shreveport. Oh! Father spare my husband. I felt very sad last night about him & I dreamed he was trying to escape from them & I was hiding guns & ammunition. All I can do is to pray for him, & that God will give me grace & strengthen sufficient as my day. He has hitherto done so & I have every cause to believe he will. Oh how many mercies I enjoy—all from my Father's hand & that blessed Jesus who has bled & died for such as I! Oh amazing love! I receive so many little kindnesses from the people here—though poor, they have some little nice thing to send me most every day. One lady supplies me with milk, & has given me several chickens, others send me lettuce—preserves, and other delicacies. Some send or bring me flowers; & what could be pleasing to the eyes of an invalid than the sweet & fragrant blossoms of spring!

I wish my meditations were oftener on the goodness & mercies, longsuffering & patience of God. Of the deep humility, gentleness, & love of the Savior. Though my afflictions are at times very *great,* yet it does not make me think of the shortness of life as it should. I do indeed at *times* feel *little* desire to remain in this world but still there is yet a little left to live for. I often ask myself of what use I am? I have never got an answer. Do I ever do any good? Is there ever a word from my lips dropped in the heart of any one that will germinate & bring forth *precious* seed! Lord grant! Oh! that I may be an instrument in *thy* hands to do good. I feel perfectly willing to suffer all the afflictions & trials I may be called upon to meet, if

25. Col. William G. Vincent's regiment was overrun by opposing troops at Henderson's Hill on 21 March 1864.

26. In her reference to Richmond, Bond must be referring to the Battle of Walkerton on 2 March 1864, a Confederate victory north of Richmond. In Florida on 20 February, a battle at Olustee, part of the Florida expedition, also resulted in a Confederate victory; however, there were no significant Confederate victories in Alabama around this period.

they will be sanctified to the good of the souls of my dear & beloved ones, here & every where.

Tuesday 29th

This has been one of the windiest days I have seen in La. The chimney caught fire this morning—the blaze was very high—but nothing caught from it—if it had, I suppose the whole block of houses would have gone ere it could have been stopped. Surely Providence is very good. Cousin R- was summoned at court this morning as witness against Mr. Wise in the case of Broussard. Mrs. R- here this evening.

Wednesday 30th

I dined at Mrs. R-'s, had the head ache all day—beautiful day! I finished the life of Wm Tell yesterday.

Thursday 31st

I am teaching sis, now, I find I have to be very firm, she is so in the habit of doing what she pleases & not being controlled. I am going to teach Alice Ellis next week.[27] I do not think so much of my troubles when I'm teaching.

Friday 1st

April has come in blustering & cold. I am feeling the affects of the bad weather; last night some time in the night, I suppose I had a small hemorrhage, for this morning when I commenced to cough—I coughed up a good deal of old blood, & have off & on all day. I slept very well last night though, and feel very thankful to my heavenly Father for his watchful care over me. If I were to have a large hemorrhage in my sleep—it might prove fatal. I sent an April-fool to old Mrs. Robertson, this morning—some moss nicely done up in paper. I don't believe the old lady half liked the joke, at any rate I didn't *fool her.*

Evening. Mrs. Foot fooled so many persons to day, about the soldiers—had people running to see them, & to hear the news.

Sunday 3rd

I walked out yesterday—called at Mrs. Patrick & Mrs. Robertson's. Mr. & Mrs. Robertson called after tea. This is a gloomy & windy day, I have been housed all day. Old Mrs. Robertson came this afternoon—brought me some flowers. When she heard I had made a very light dinner, on account of not being able to eat the beef—she insisted upon going home & getting me a piece of chicken which was left from dinner—She brought it, a biscuit, & some preserves; I eat them with a good appetite. "Surely goodness & mercy has followed me all the days of my life."

27. Alice Ellis was the young daughter of Victorine and John Ellis.*

We hear we have whipped the Yankees dreadfully, above Alexandria I hope its so!![28]

Tuesday 5th

Lovely day—been walking a good deal, feel good deal better. I've such a lovely boquet of flowers on my table, fixed Maryland fashion.

Friday 8th

Mr. Murry Robertson is very ill—did not expect him to live yesterday—better today. Old Mrs. Beldon very ill. Mrs. Hall called this afternoon. Had very disagreeable weather last few days—cleared off now.

I was fortunate enough this morning to sell a white swiss dress 30$ in green backs (Yankee money)

I have been sympathizing with Mrs. R- so much & prayed earnestly God would spare her husband, & I *believe He will*. I feel I have very much to thank God for. Many are far worse off than I. Last sunday, I noticed a lady & two gentlemen pass my window, who appeared to be travelers, and they proved to be strangers from Texas. The lady not feeling very well concluded not to follow her companions to New Town then, but remain a day or two to rest. The second night after her arrival she gave birth to a babe. It appears from what I hear—she & her husband left New Orleans & went to Texas; there he was obliged to go in the army, and she started back homeward, with two friends. Thus she was left amongst strangers in a strange place & unfortunately got in a french family who do not understand english, nor she french. How lonely she must feel—& how much she must miss her husband—especially if he is a good one. Mrs. Robertson's little children are staying through the day, so Mr. R- may be kept quiet.

Saturday 9th

We had just now such a scare—the cry of fire—but I believe nothing serious the matter—only Dr. Young's chimney on fire.[29] The sick folk better today.

Sunday 10th

Went to see Mr. Robertson this morning—very sick—not so well this evening. Went this afternoon to see Mrs. Wright (the sick lady at the hotel);[30] found her

28. Bond must be referring to one of the several skirmishes that preceded the Red River Campaign, the goal of which was for the Union general Banks to seize the strategically important city of Shreveport. After several Confederate successes, the campaign failed, and Banks withdrew from western Louisiana.

29. Bond refers to Frances Young.*

30. Mrs. Wright* was from New Orleans. Bond explains how she came to Abbeville in her entry of 8 April.

very pleasant; she has been married just the same length of time as I have, with the exception of two weeks. She sayed I cheered her up a good deal. Mrs. Spaulding here a little while.

Monday 11th

Mr. R- so ill—cousin R- there all day—going to set up tonight with him. Had a lovely bouquet sent me. Hear promising news of *our* confederacy: great victory over the Yankees, in Tenn.[31]

Tuesday 12th

Children here all day—tired of so much noise. I felt glad I hadn't any. Cousin R- going to see Mrs. Ellis, who is sick.

Friday 15th

I have not been feeling so well for several days past. I cough a good deal & feel nervous, and low spirited; one thing cousin R- has been away much of the time, & all Mrs. Robertson's children have been here everyday; & with their noise I felt like going crazy. The sick are all getting better! I have felt so uneasy about Mr. R-'s recovery—but I believe he is out of danger now.

This has been a real April day. Sister Fannie's birthday! May she be happy & have many returns! I have been reading "Domby & Son" and "The Cricket on the Hearth."[32] I like the latter very much indeed—the other not much though I could not help seeing some resemblance to some of my relations in some of the characters—especially Mr. *Domby*.

Saturday 16th

Had a visit from Mrs. Maxwell this morning; came to see me about my board. And got very angry with me, because I would not give her all my sugar for it. Said I was dishonest, & she hoped she would never act that way—that my acting as I had did not increase her good opinion of me. I told [her] if walking across the room would make her think more of me, I would not do it—for if her previous knowledge of me had not gained her esteem & friendship I can not that she should have it. Oh! what a cruel school this world is—especially to one who has hitherto lived in a little world of loving hearts and *true*. I have met with an opportunity of sending a letter to Howard, I wrote one to him & Mr. Hall—for his wife.

Night. Went around to see Mr. Robertson this afternoon—found him better. Mrs. M- came soon after I got there, did not speak to me. I also went to see Mrs. Beldon—found her better.

31. There were no key battles in Tennessee at this time other than the Battle of Dandridge on 17 January.

32. Both books are by Charles Dickens.

Sunday 17th

Miss Gus Perry here this morning; brought me a lovely boquet. I went to see Mrs. Wright this afternoon—also Mrs. Abadie. Have a case of the small pox at Mrs. Robertsons, also Mrs. Patricks & Dr. Abadie's.

Monday 18th

Heard the Yankees have possession of Shreveport. Oh! Howard where are you this morning—are you dead or alive? Oh God strengthen our feeble faith![33] Walked over to Mrs. Ellis's this afternoon—went to Dr. Young's also. Hear Genl. Mouton is killed & his battalion cut up; but we gained the victory.[34]

Tuesday 19th

Seven months today since dear Howard left me; my heart's nearly, if not quite as sad this morning as it was then. Oh! my poor heart. I had such a dream last night. I fear it is a warning. I do not as a general thing believe in dreams—but this is so singular I cant help but think some *great trouble* is in store for me. I dread to think what it might be. I dreamed I was in great distress about brother's going away some where—& my heart ached so badly. Then I dreamed I thought he was going to Shreveport, & I commenced to tell him what I wanted him to say to Howard; he looked so strangely at me—he bade all good bye but me, & left me for the last—all looked sorrowfully at me. At last the thought struck me he had been at shreveport, & I asked him—he said yes—I then begged him to [tell] me of Howard—he said I could not stand it. I told him yes I would, to tell me if he was sick, & he said yes—he saw him & he was sick—that the *prayers of the people were requested for him.* I thought I lifted up my eyes & hands towards Heaven & said "Oh God give me strength," brother then said, "now I shouldn't of told you, but I told him, I would fast & pray all that day for H-. I then dreamed I was dressed in my wedding dress, bonnet & all, & weeping as though my heart would break— & was walking along a road, when I met a funeral, when they got to me, they halted & stopped & came so close to press against me. I then awoke, my heart sobbing— though no tears had I shed in my sleep. I burst into tears, & cryed bitterly for some time, for it seemed as though dear Howard was dead. Oh! my heart is sad sad. My Heavenly Father, thou knowest every pang my soul hast—thou knowest all my mental & bodily sufferings, O give me grace & strength to bear up under every dispensation of thy divine will. Prepare me for every *coming event.* Keep me from

33. Bond is mistaken about the fall of Shreveport. The Union forces were unable to seize the city in April 1864.

34. General Mouton was killed in battle on 8 April 1864 at Mansfield, La. The battle was a Confederate victory, but both sides sustained heavy losses.

asking for things I should not have. Oh! *my father* give me faith—that I may see thy hand in every event, & believe all things that happen to me is directed by thy unerring wisdom & love.

Wednesday 20th

Feel better to day in spirits, visited Mrs. Beldon this morning, Mrs. Wright this evening. She seemed cheered up some by my visit. I hope I may be able by God's help to bring sunlight to some benighted heart like my own.

Thursday 21st

I went again to see Mrs. W[right] this morning. I entertained her about the burning of the place. I was much amused at her waiting maid, who it seems is from Illinois; after I had finished speaking of the outrage they had done us, she looked up, & said she had no idea the Yankees were so bad—she had been telling every one, she had relations in their army, but she was not going to say so any more; & she was ready to go back to Texas. I laughed very much at the astonishment she evinced, on hearing they were such wicked wretches.

This afternoon I'm alone. *Rina* our little pet is here, a very lovely child.[35] Cousin R- & sis have gone to Mrs. Ameal's. The weather is cloudy & damp—I think we shall have rain soon. My spirits cloud with the sky!

We have had a great victory at Mansfield, between Nakatoche & Shreveport. Genl Mouton killed;[36] do not know who else. Yankees surrendered at Nackatoche on their gun boats—can't get away because the water is so low.[37] God grant this war may soon be put to an end! I have just received some dryed apples from New Town, they are so good & remind me of *home*.

Saturday afternoon, 23rd

Mrs. Murry Robertson just left. We've have had a decisive victory over the Yankees at Mansfield, I believe on the 7–8 & probably other days—at any rate the enemy's army has been completely routed, what is left & put to flight towards Natches. Their gun boats have gotten aground & we have captured several. As soon as they saw we were capturing their wagons, they set fire to & burned up all of 300, but the rest we got, which must have been quite a number—for their train up had about 800 wagons. We have lost a great number of our men, Gen. Mouton & Gen. Green both dead, but genl M. was shot through by 7 balls, by men after they had

35. Bond likely refers to Martha Maxwell's* eight-year-old daughter, Clarena.

36. Bond also mentions Mouton's death in her entry of 18 April.

37. Retreating from the failed Red River Campaign, Union general Banks's forces were stranded in low waters on the Red River. They were fired on by Confederates and escaped eventually only after building dams to raise the water level, thus allowing the fleet to move downriver.

been taken prisoners; I hear the company that did it, were killed, all except two, who escaped.[38] I hear Gen. Banks had one arm shot off or broken. I do hope the Yankees will let this part of La alone & the time may not be long before I shall see the smiling face of my beloved husband. I have felt sadly, thinking perhaps Howard may have volunteered, & been in that battle, Oh! what if he has, & been killed or wounded. But I will not—must not think so. Have I not placed him in the hands of my dear Father who *will* shield him from all danger, and I shall behold him again, if it is right. I succeeded in getting a fine pair of bootes yesterday,[39] paid 10 in green backs.

Sunday 24th

Lovely cool day; hear Yankees are whipped out of La & we have them surrounded in Miss.

Monday 25th

Been trading off sugar for calico & flannel shirts for Howard. Got cousin R- calico dress for 150$. Went up to see Mrs. Wright this morning—she always seems glad to see me. Read a New Orleans paper of the 20th. There was a strong debate in the House in Washington; great excitement! They are actually bold enough to cry for peace & a *recognition of the Southern Confederacy."*

They are very much opposed to Maximillion taken the throne in Mexico.[40] I suppose there'll be a little work then.

Tuesday 26th

Our town has been in the greatest excitement today. Last evening an hour before sun-down a body of detailed soldiers, to hunt & kill jay-hawkers, entered the town; arrested Mr. George Foot & Mr. Beldon & carried them out of town. Mr. Kearney *the pilot.* They kept their prisoners till ten this morning, when a party of friends went over the bayou & interceded in their behalf. Mr. Foot was released, but Beldon still a prisoner—but they accompanied him to his house—guarded him to the bed of his sick wife, & then they all walked down town. As Mr. Beldon had been honorably acquited from all charges brought against him by Gen. Tay-

---

38. The military action Bond mentions is that which occurred as Banks's forces were retreating after the battles of Mansfield and Pleasant Hill. At Blair's Landing Confederate general Tom Green was killed as he led troops on an ambush of the Union vessels. Bond also reports Mouton's death in her entries of 18 and 21 April. In this entry, she is incorrect about the way he died. He was killed by a Union marksman. The Confederate field officers had agreed to remain mounted during the Battle of Mansfield, but this decision made them easy targets. See Brooksher, *War along the Bayous,* 97.

39. Bond initially wrote *shoes* but crossed out the word and specified her purchase as boots.

40. See her entry of 19 October 1863 and accompanying note for information on Mexico.

lor, he thought he could get off. But it seems this party of men (or brutes) are perfect desperadoes, and are *from Texas*. Well, it seems they treated Mr. Beldon very unkindly, took his watch, & because he wouldn't own he was no better than a dog, some one held him whilst several stepped close up & shot at him, some of their balls taken effect, he fell, & whilst down one of the Liet's shot at his head, but missed fire, when upon he jumped up & fled; soon after—Beldon's son came in the room where they were eating dinner,[41] & deliberately shot this Liet down, & made his escape—so far, neither have been heard from. I heard the dieing groans of the soldier—he did not linger long. The whole town is arroused. The citizens are obliged to search for them & if found to bring them in—under the penalty of their own lives. I visited the family this evening; found them much more composed than I expected not a tear did I see; they may feel very deeply though. I tryed to say some cheering & comforting words. Poor old Mrs. Beldon, how I do pity her. She is still very sick, unable to be up, only for a little while at a time. The soldiers went into the house to search for "Jim Beldon," & went into her room, threatened to shoot the negro woman who was at her Mistress' bed, if she did not tell where he was. She protested she knew nothing about him.

I can sympathize with them, for I know the feeling of anxiety for my dear husband, when the Yankees were after him. I suppose this town will be strictly guarded to night. They even say if they are not found, the town will be burned, but I guess that is all wind that will blow over. I hear cheering news of our army above. We have fresh supply of troops from Texas. Taylor crossed red river—cut off Gen Steel's from reinforcing Banks, & has the enemy entirely surrounded, so they can't get provisions. I hope we may soon hear of another victory on our side.[42]

Friday 29th

Since wednesday morning our town has been pretty quiet; the soldiers left that morning. Old Mr. Beldon came back yesterday. I do not know whether he is going to remain or not. There seems to be a great deal of sympathy for him in the town. A schooner arrived last night. I hope we will be able to get some goods. This is a lovely day. I walked down to see Mrs. Hall—she is more cheerful about her husband. Met Mrs. Maxwell there. I spoke in as lady like manner as I could & said "good morning Mrs. Maxwell," she only inclined her head *stiffly* & that was the only recognition I received.

I gathered a lovely bouquet & as I was on my way home—I stopped at Mrs. Beas, to purchase some strawberries; she gave me a large cup full, which made me

41. James Beldon was nineteen years old.

42. Bond has received accurate news about General Taylor. Her hopes for victory were realized on 25 April 1864 with the Confederate win at Mark's Mills in Arkansas.

feel very kindly toward her for. When I reached home, I told all I was going to be stingy for I felt very *strawberry hungry*. Whilst I was stemming I thought of my invalid friend at the hotel,[43] whom I suspect loved them quite as well as I, and I thought it will be a struggle to part with any—for I could easily eat *all* myself, & then have a spare corner. But the good intentions triumphed. I divided & sent them. I shared the rest with sis. Cousin R- cares little for them. When I went into Mrs. Beas' Mrs Nixon was coming out. I met her with the same cheerful good morning Mrs. Nixon—but she drew herself up—drew her lips in & looked altogether so savage—that one might have supposed she could have used her teeth quicker (that is if she had possessed any) on me, than her tongue. Well at any rate I feel comfortably towards them; & sorry & sad any one at her turn of life should bear such malace & revenge. I leave it in God's hands to work out right.[44]

I have just finished "The two Guardians" by *Marian Harland*.[45] It is beautiful. Right & Wrong are set in contrast—showing what peaceable fruits right will bring forth in the end. It easily is my principle but O, not always my practice. I wish I could always be firm when I'm sure I'm in the right & not care at all what others may think of me. Oh! Father show me my duty—& give me *strength* & wisdom to do it. What a lovely character Marian was! I have finished the "Lamplighter," & have recommended to sis; she seems well pleased with Gerty, & admires her pretty thoughts about the stars being lit by [a] *good one*.[46] She is a child, that takes in beautiful ideas very soon and I like her to read Mrs. Herman's poetry.[47] She says her lessons very well, & is improving quite fast. I hope I may be enabled to do some good, & be of a little use. I have just given her her first lesson in long division, & more than once came near loosing patience.

This afternoon I walked over the bayou with Mrs. Murry R- & then to Mr. Beldon's, found he had come back. His son also.

Saturday 30th

Mr. & Mrs. R[obertson] came this afternoon, whilst here Mrs. Hall bounced in & sayed there was 1000 Texans on the bayou; when we come to find out it was

---

43. Mrs. Wright,* see Bond's entry of 10 April.

44. Mrs. Nixon, Mrs. Maxwell's mother, was likely angry because of Bond's refusal to pay Mrs. Maxwell what she requested for rent. See Bond's entry of 16 April 1864.

45. Mary Virginia Hawes Terhune was a popular author whose pen name was Marion Harland.

46. Maria Susanna Cummins's best-selling domestic novel *The Lamplighter* (1854) tells the story of an orphan girl named Gerty and her journey to "true womanhood." After the kind-hearted lamplighter who adopted her dies, Gerty imagines him in heaven lighting the stars.

47. The first spelling of the name is crossed through and corrected above the line. It is not clear to whom she refers.

7 men after beef. I went up to Mr. B[eldon]'s & there was the greatest excitement. Mr. B & his son were hiding—& his wife so sick & of course greatly excited.

Sunday May 1st

Cloudy disagreeable day—home all day, old Mrs. R- here in the afternoon.

Monday 2nd

Went to see Mrs. Foot this morning who has been sick since her husband was treated so badly by the Texans. Spent the afternoon with Mrs. Wright. She seems to regret our separation; expects to leave this week on her way home. I shall miss her sadly. She is so pleasant and agreeable. Says I seem like an old friend; she will take letters to send to Md for me.

Tuesday 3rd

Last night the whole town was up in arms. News came that the jay hawkers were 6 miles from here. The town was strongly guarded all night & a large force went to meet them. But I do believe they were our soldiers—for nothing was seen of the jayhawkers and this morning a lot of them came in town & are picking up deserters and all the men. They have Wise under arrest & I suppose will carry him off because he is a deserter.

Wednesday 4th

Made several calls to day—do not feel very well. I hear the Yankees are in Alexandria, & we have them surrounded & are shelling out the town.[48] The soldiers took Mr. Wise & John Ellis. Mr. & Mrs. Robertson here this afternoon, but I was up at Mrs. Wrights.

May 5th

Cool & bright this morning, saw some soldiers pass by—I hear there is a regiment to be sent here.

Friday, 6th

Went up to Dr Abadie's, going lost one 50$ out of my porte-monnaie,[49] but was fortunate enough to find it again. From there went to Mr. Beldon's—found the old gentleman quite "jolly under creditable circumstances." I believe he had a glass too many.

The 4th and 2nd La Regs have gone down to the Bay.[50] I hear others have gone

48. The activity Bond mentions in Alexandria was part of the Red River Campaign that took place from March to May 1864. Union forces occupied the town on 19 March 1864. Shortly after Bond's entry, on 13 May, Alexandria was burned to the ground by Gen. A. J. Smith's troops.

49. The French word for *purse*.

50. In April Col. Louis Bush's Seventh Regiment, sometimes erroneously called the Fourth, and

on Lafourche to cooperate with them in endeavoring to capture the Yankee forces down in that county. I hear we have the Yankees penned up in Alexandria & will capture them. I hope so. Four *long* dreary months have passed since I heard from Howard. I am expecting daily news from him. Oh I hope they will be cheering accounts, I most fear to hear.

Saturday 7th

Cloudy disagreeable day. Mrs. Wright spent the afternoon with us. I really feel drawn towards her. I walked as far as Mrs. Patrick's with her, and as I was returning home—heard there was some good news in town—so I went over to the Priests (Mr. Poyét). He told me Genls Polk and Forrest are at camp Moor (15 miles from New Orleans). Our troops are in possession of Placemine,[51] and Baton Rouge; others have gone to the bay. Beauregard & Lee had a fight with Grant in Va, whipped Grant all to pieces. Gen. Banks has not yet been taken but there's no possible way for them to get off—though they are trying hard.[52]

Sunday 8th

Not feeling well this morning—have the headache. Cousin Rebecca gone to see Mrs. Wright——This afternoon I felt better—after enjoying good cup of coffee went to see Mr. Robertson who is not well—then up to see Mrs. W- she said the sun always seemed to go down sooner when I was there. I am obliged to be in before sundown.

Monday 9th

Went up again this afternoon to see my friend Mrs. Wright, who leaves to morrow *en rout* for New Orleans. I was taken soon after eating dinner with a violent pain in the left shoulder—I made Mintty rub it well with salt, which partly relieved me; but soon after it extended in my lung—I was feeling too unwell to venture out—but it was my only chance of seeing Mrs. W- so off I went—suffered terribly all the time I was there, & had at last to leave before cousin R-. Whilst there, a bridal party arrived. The "loving couple" were covered nearly with dust;

Col. William G. Vincent's Second Regiment were ordered to southern Louisiana to patrol the area for jayhawkers and small enemy garrisons. See Bergeron, *Guide to Louisiana Confederate Military Units,* 43, 51.

51. The proper place name is Plaquemine, La.

52. Baton Rouge was captured by Union forces in May 1862. The Confederates attempted to retake it and failed in August 1862. Plaquemine, near New Orleans, also remained under Union control. In Virginia there were some notable Confederate victories in the summer of 1864, but Union forces under General Grant continued their offensive. With her reference to Banks, Bond refers to his withdrawal from western Louisiana because of heavy Union losses at Mansfield (8 April) and Pleasant Hill (9 April).

they sit on the gallery where every one had a view of them & *he with* his *legs thrown across her lap—Loving possession* truly! I felt very sad bidding good bye to Mrs. Wright—she has won my affections so completely. She gave me a very pretty crochet hood for winter. I shall always keep it. She leaves to morrow morning for New Iberia where she expects to take a boat at Plaquemine for N. Orleans.

Tuesday 10th

I had to go to bed early last evening on account of the pain in my left lung. I am suffering some with a blister there—I put a mustard plaster on & went to sleep, & when I awoke it was like my breast was on fire—it has scared away the pain though. I feel that another friend has left me, in the departure of Mrs. Wright. I'm led to believe Mrs. Beldon's philosophy is true—when she said the reason she had never visited us—she thought she might become fond of our society and we were only temporary dwellers here—when we had to leave she would regret it so much, that she'd wish she had never become acquainted with us. And now I *feel* what she must, I *do almost* regret I made a friend who has taken such a large share of my affections—and had to loose her so soon.

It is very probable we may never meet again in this world. It will afford me great pleasure to do so; but if we never shall—Oh, may [we] meet on that other shore where parting never comes!

Had some black berries sent me this morning: the first of the season. Sissie & Mintty have gone to gather some this afternoon. It has tried to rain today, but not succeeded very well. Every thing greatly in need of it, I believe more than a month has passed since rain fell.

Friday 13th

Had a visit from Mr. Larett;[53] has been in Lafourche—got dry goods &e, says they are fighting the Yankees at Alexandria.[54] The Texans took two gun boats, not far from here, the other day & about three hundred yankees. He also states Howard is in Texas: but that's all I can learn. Why is he there? Has he joined the army under Col Lanlicoskia, or is his father sick & sent for him. I feel so anxious I can scarcely content myself—so restless, I walked down to the bridge this morning; I felt so unhappy—I think perhaps—if it had been no sin I should have been tempted to jumped over. God keep me from all such temptations, even in thought.

I did not sleep well last night—we had another alarm of jayhawkers. I am not afraid—but nervous.

---

53. Alexandre Lirette was a Terrebonne planter.
54. In late April, the Confederates frequently attacked Union forces in the vicinity of Alexandria.

I hear Laura did not leave for Md till three or four weeks ago, and is engaged to Rodney Woods.[55]

Saturday 14th

Had a visit from Mr. Gatewood, who is just from Texas. He is one of Mr. Barrow's partners. Leaves to morrow—will take letters for us. I wrote to Dr. A[rcher] & cousin Josh. Hear Wellie is about joining the army. Poor fellow not quite 18, with little education! I suppose he'll never go to school any more; his father's to be blamed for his not having a better one.

Sunday 15th

Not feeling so well to day.

Monday 16th

Lieut Kelly here a little while this morning. Just over from Lafourche, where he has been making a raid. Looked thin but well. I received a letter from Mrs. Wright yesterday; she had made an attempt to go but was turned back on account of Charlie's illness[56]—but a day or two made him so much better—she startes again—gets some distance on the journey & is turned back by our picket—her pass wouldn't do—"must obey orders." She writes—she cried at him—laughed at him, & talked at him all to no purpose, and she was obliged once more to wind her way back to New Iberia, where she wrote me from. But expected to start next morning for Franklin. Poor woman how I pity her in her utter loneliness!

Wednesday 18th

I in bed nearly all yesterday with my old enemy—neuralgia—I was taken in the night with it in my shoulder & left lung. I sent for the Doctor [Abadie]. He came—examined my lungs & pronounced them better than they have ever been yet. I told him he was a humbug—& was trying to hum bug me, but he said the *french* had no humbug about them.[57] Mrs. Robertson—the dear soul—sent my dinner to me yesterday. Mrs. Ganble here this morning.

55. In the 1860 census, Woods was a student living with Mrs. Phoebe Pierce, a Terrebonne plantation owner. His sister was Susanna Woods, whom Bond mentions when writing from Crescent Place. The 1880 census shows Woods still living in Terrebonne. He was a planter and was married, but not to Laura.

56. Charlie is her newborn child.

57. Consumption caused pains and aches similar to those caused by neuralgia, and thus, until the last stage, doctors frequently misdiagnosed the disease.

Saturday 21st

Spent the day at Mrs. Ellis'—I think I paid a very good penance—for I felt entirely out of *my* element. She is a good hearted creole—but no education or refinement. Good many soldiers in town, no news of any consequence.

Sunday 22ond

Howard's birthday, 25. Poor fellow I hope he is well, & may enjoy a good sermon. May God bless him, & if he is in danger—may He bring him safely out & if he is sick, may that good Physician make him well! Oh, protect him my Father, & restore him to me again. I do not wish he were here now unless it would be right for him. I leave it to my Father to direct. He knows what is best. Give me grace, Heavenly Parent to bear up, and faith to believe *all* is for the best.

It is very warm to day. I took a walk early this morn, through that beautiful wood over the bayou; had to cross in a flat & not a very safe one. Louisa, Nannie R. & Temperance Ellis went with me.[58] I enjoyed the walk very much. The wood reminded me of my own dear home wood.

Thursday 26th

Nothing of note has occurred this week. Of war news, there is some thing against us. Our forces have let the Yankees get away, not without having a dreadful battle—large numbers killed on both sides. They, I believe have retreated to Simsport.[59] The town has been kept in great commotion this week, Capt Perry picking up deserters & conscripts. It has been quite amusing hearing of their hiding. One man could not be found till the capt seized his horse, then he came forth.

We had quite a laugh at our dinner yesterday, it was made up of donations. Lets see, we had soup from the beef given by Capt Perry (as I'm a soldiers wife) broil'd beef, beans—a present from Miss Virginia [Beldon] and some butter Mrs. Young sent me.[60] Whilst we were eating, old Mrs. R- came in & brought us a plate of delicious blackberry pudding. Today was pretty much the same thing. Sis went walking last evening, & whilst out in a field, a negro man killed a rabbit & gave it to her. She told him if he killed any more & did not want them please bring them to her *sick sister,* she had a *sick sister* at home; didn't he know her, Mrs. Howard Bond? "Oh yes! He knew her."

58. Temperance is John and Victorine Ellis's* twelve-year-old daughter.

59. In May Banks's troops retreated from Alexandria with Confederate forces following. An engagement at Mansura did little to stop the Union's move to Simmesport. The battle that Bond discusses is the Battle of Yellow Bayou that took place on 18 May in which 608 Confederates and 350 Union soldiers were killed.

60. Jemimah Young was an Abbeville resident and wife of Dr. Frances Young.*

Home most of the day; wrote a letter for cousin R- to Mr. Kearney. Went to
Mrs. R-'s this evening, had such nice blackberries.

Friday 27th

Mrs. Murry R- dined here to day; she & I walked down to the bridge this morning to see if we could buy some coffee from the boat. We asked for the captain,
who came & seemed as if he knew me, Called me Mrs. Bond, asked after my
health. I enquired if I could get a few lbs of coffee, he said "Oh yes. He would not
sell me any but gave me about *four lbs,* which would amount to 100$ in confeder-
ate. I was *very grateful.* Another proof God is watching over me. All blessings come
from God! I also received a letter from my own dear Howard—written 1st and 10th
of March. Long time ago! He write so lovingly & sadly; had been very sick—had
not recovered then. Says he loves me more & more each day, that he is perfectly
willing to bear any punishment God may see fit to put upon him if He'll only let
us meet again and never part in this world. Oh! my dearest beloved husband, we
are tryed for a *good purpose.* May it be the sanctifying of not only of our own souls,
but many others! God bless, keep & be our everlasting Father, for Christ's sake.

Went up to Dr. Abadie's this evening, Lieut Reading, has been sent down by
Government, for the goods on the schooner, and I believe will let me have some
shoes.

Monday 30th

Had such agreeable & great surprise yesterday; just as we were about finishing
dinner, Wellie came. I didn't know when cousin R was going to give me a chance
to get a *hug* & a *kiss.* Has grown so much taller than Howard. I tell him I'm going
to put a *brick* on *his head.* He has been in two battles, had others killed right beside him. He fought the Yankees from Alexandria down to near Simsport. Was at
the battle of "*Yellow Bayou.*"[61] I talked so much to Wellie—that I have exhausted
my strength to day, I feel so badly. Wellie seems changed for the better. He says he
does not wish to swear, & only does it when he forgets himself, has told several of
his companions in his company, when they heard him swear, to give him a good
thump. I told him that was a *step in* the *right direction;* God help him to persevere
to the end. Oh! that the divine spirit may lead me to say some thing to sink deep
in to his heart. Lord baptize him with thy holy spirit! Spare him for the namesake!
He told me last night, when I bid him goodnight with a kiss—he would try to be
a good boy always. Oh, I do pray he may be an humble christian, & that the *sins* of
the *father* may never fall upon the children!

61. For information on the battle, see Bond's previous entry of 26 May 1864 and the accompanying
note.

Night} Had such a delightful trip on the bayou with old Mrs. S. Robertson, Wellie & sis, went up & down about four miles. It looked so lovely, as smooth as a glass, and the wood along its each side was so sweet, with magnolias & grape blossoms. This is the first time I ever took a row on the waters.

Tuesday 31st

Wellie & I took dinner at Mrs. R-'s, had a nice dinner—we walked down on the bridge & got weighed. He weighed *138¼, I 105.*

I hear Grant, has been whipped again "on to Richmond," & calls for 400,000 men by the first of June.[62]

62. Bond refers to two battles in Virginia: in the Battle of the Wilderness (5–6 May) General Lee attacked Grant's army in a three-day battle, inflicting eighteen thousand Union casualties to approximately ten thousand of his own. At Spotsylvania (8–12 May), Grant counterattacked Lee, and Union forces suffered another twelve thousand casualties.

CHAPTER TEN

"This Suspense Is Dreadful!"

1 JUNE 1864–8 JULY 1865

June 1st

Poor dear Wellie left us this afternoon, about half past one, dear fellow I pitty him so much, so young to go to war. It's hard to part at all times from *those we love*—but when we know they are leaving us for the bloody field of battle, it is *agonizing*. Oh! may "Our Father" protect him from *all danger*—seen & unseen, & restore him to us again.

Have been so busy all day—wrote a letter to my dear Howard. Gave Wellie a little Testament, he promised to read it whenever he could. I marked several places in it, hope he may be lead by the divine spirit to understand it.

Oh, my *Father*, I feel *thou wilt* speak to his heart—I know thou wilt keep him for Christ's sake, who died for *him*

{Night} Went on to Mr. Poyét's to hear the news. Heard Genl Lee had whipped Genl Grant out of the most of his army; Captured 50000 men. I don't know how much to believe.[1] Old Mrs. Robertson spent the evening. Very warm.

Saturday 4th

Has been raining all yesterday, & today with the exception of short while. We needed it so much—every thing parched up. I have not felt lonesome as I usually do [on] rainy days for I've been reading such an entertaining book by Mrs. Southworth,[2] the "Initials" it is called. I have felt very heart sick about my dear husband, & if I did not occupy my thoughts by such reading, I believe it would make me *truly sick*. What has become of him—why don't he write? Are questions I often ask myself. Oh! this suspense is dreadful! My heart aches for him. I often catch myself turning towards the window, half with the expectation of seeing him ride up. I dare not wish him here, for I pray he may only come when it is the Lord's will for him to do so. My prayer is to be patient & have perfect faith. The last few days past, I have felt *he* would *come soon*—perhaps it is because I wish to see him so much—or may be I will get a letter—at any rate I must patiently await future events.

1. Bond refers to the Virginia battles she mentioned in her previous entry.
2. She is reading the popular novelist E.D.E.N. Southworth.

I have not felt near so well since the damp weather commenced—too much electricity for me, my cough troubles me more, & a soreness in my breast & sides. I have so many pains & aches, I fear *all* get tired of my complaining. Oh, how often—when my head aches—my temples throb, do I wish for some loving hand to smooth back my hair and '*just* pet *me* a little," to feel I am an object of love & *pity*— yes *pity*—who does not when in pain love to hear the voice of a *loved one,* say "poor child! Or "my pet! can I do any thing for you." Oh! Howard, how I miss you at all times especially when I'm alone & sick—no one to say "dear pet can I do any thing for you"—to whisper dear words of love & sympathy, which helps me bear the pain. No dear ma to look at me with her sweet eyes full of love & sympathy—& say "dear baby I feel all your pains." Oh, my ma I never knew your priceless value before I left home——How my heart yearns for you, Ma Oh Ma, shall I ever in this world meet you again! God grant me that prayer!

Sunday 5th

Rained all the morning—sun shining now, but the sky is very leaden. I feel something better to day. Have been reading a book called "A Serious call, to a devout and Holy Life."[3] The exhortation to *Humility* & prayer particularly struck me. I earnestly pray I may profit greatly by its perusal. Father I pray *thy* devine blessing upon it! Old Mrs. Roberts went & picked me some blackberries this evening—sit with me till dark.

Monday 6th

Another rainy day. Wrote to H- will send it by courier. Mrs. M[urry] R[obertson] spent the evening. Also Mr. Gatewood—who came from Texas. He was very kind—offered to loan me any money I wanted. I hear the Yankees are coming up this way from the Bay, about 7,000.

Tuesday 7th

Pretty clear to day—but I fear will have a gust this afternoon. Mrs. Spaulding came this afternoon & cut out Mary Huff's dress (a poor girl in town, who I gave a calico dress to). Mr. Gatewood took dinner with us.

Thursday 9th

It is very warm weather. Sent H- a letter. Sent 2.25$, this morning by Mr. Calrole to Opelousis to be scaled, will get 175$. Mrs. Belden called this afternoon— the old wretch!

---

3. The book, written in 1728 by William Law, influenced leading evangelicals, including John Wesley.

Sunday 12th

Received a dear letter from my dearest husband, dated 20th May. He is in very poor health. Expects to be transferred from the Ordnance Department to the chemical, as druggist. Sent me a dispatch from army in Va. We have gained a glorious victory over the *Feds.*

Walked round to Mrs. R-'s little while this afternoon. Mrs. Ellis here. Oh! I feel so thankful I have heard from my Howard. I feared he was sick, or dead. I hope I shall see him soon.

The Yankees 300 strong have come up to fort Bisland. Had the present of some writing paper & envelopes from Mrs. Robertson.

Tuesday 14th

Wrote to my dear husband today—sent the list of my medicines. Mr. Debroker will take it.[4] I sent old Mrs. Nixon some coffee at dinner time. I thought there was a probability she'd send it back; but sis says she received it very kindly. I heard she was sick & thought a cup would do her good.

Wednesday 15th

Got a letter from Howard, dated May 25th. Still sick—poor fellow, without one loving hand to smooth his fevered brow. Sends me good news. Kentucky has seceded & withdrawn her troops from out the Federal army, & *offers 50,000 to the Confederacy.* We have had 12 victories with no reverses, within four months.

Heavy battles in Va 10 days fighting; stopped to rest & have resumed the fight. I feel anxious to hear more. Oh, I hope we will whip them *this* time there; then there would be greater prospects of peace.[5] Mr. Wilcoxen called to know what news my letter contained. He is a perfect gentleman.[6]

Sunday 19th

Have been in bed most of to day; spit up some blood this morning—my left lung pained me yesterday & today. Have such intensely hot weather & gets cooler by low gusts in the evening. I have been dreadfully low spirited for a week—My heart seems like it would break, some times. O! Howard, why do you not come see me? Are you too sick to stand the ride here? I feel you are sicker than you tell me.

4. Debroker is the planter to whom Bond had sold her spinning. See the entry of 9 October 1863.

5. Bond's news about Kentucky seceding was a rumor. When she writes of battles in Virginia, she refers to Grant's Union forces pursuing Lee's army during May and June 1864. The specific battle she mentions was likely Cold Harbor; although Union losses were more than double that of the Confederacy (sixty thousand to thirty thousand), Lee's army never fully recovered from the losses.

6. T. Wilcoxen, a St. Mary Parish planter who, in the 1860 census, owned real estate worth fifty thousand dollars and had a personal estate worth sixty thousand dollars. He was sixty-four years old.

Oh! my Heavenly Parent make my dear husband well, & restore him to me. 9 months this very day since I bid him farewell!

Thursday 30th

I have been very ill since I last recorded in here, with Bilious fever; but the good Lord has raised me up again; & cheered my drooping spirit (for I had been sadder than usual the two weeks past) by letters from Md. One from sister Fannie, March 11 & 12th. One from Peggie [Bond] & aunt R[ebecca Bond] bearing date April 21st & 17th. Oh! I feel so thankful to my Heavenly Father—He has permitted me again to get news from home. All are well there—brother has paid his bounty for the drafts & stayed out of the war. Sister Fannie says they would not have him go for any thing in the world. *They are truly southern!* Ann Giles has passed away, another redeemed one entered the portals of glory. Who will be next? Our dear aged grandma still spared us to cherish & love. Ann Lee was on a visit in Balto, aunt Rebecca writes, she believes Ann Lees tryed to be a christian. Bless the Lord Oh my soul! My heart is filled with joy & thanksgiving to that blessed Being, one prayer has been answered—Oh Jesus when will the rest of *my family band,* yield their hearts to thee. Blessed Lamb draw not thy holy spirit from them—still continue to knock at the portal of their hearts. If I could hear sister Fannie & brother were trying to be christians O, how my heart would bound with *Heavenly Joy.* Shall I not, before I close these mortal eyes! Then I should exclaim like good old Simeon, "Now Lord lettest thy servant depart in peace"; For my eyes have beheld what my prayers have been for years.

So many deaths amongst my friends, & many marriages. Old Mr. Judge Archer gone after a few minutes illness of heart disease. They write for me to come home this summer. They urge me—tell me I shall be petted, amused & waited on, & by those who love me devotedly. Oh! such sweet dear comforting letters. They have done me more good than medicine! Dear aunt, writes—she thinks & prays for me every hour—that I'm never forgotten by any [of] my friends. And she prays for all those who are kind to her dear niece. God bless her for those prayers. I knew I felt *all* were praying for Mitt & Howard, & dear pa invokes God's blessing upon his absent children. Oh! how oft when pain hast fill my body with agony & sorrow bows my heart down 'till it seemed 'twould break—has the sweet thought—there are prayers ascending the throne of grace for me that will be heard & answered. O, I have great faith in Christian prayers. Perhaps the very angels tune their harps anew to chant the prayers that come from the hearts of earthly saints.[7] Peggie's letter was indeed hopeful & cheering. Oh, I hope I may soon get a chance to send

---

7. Bond initially wrote *swell* but changed the word to *tune* above the line.

back returns. We also got letters from Terrebonne, urging us to come home, Mrs. B[arrow] offering us a home & share every thing she has, as though we were her sisters.

I expect they see right hard times there; the Yankees are pretty strict.

July 18th

I have been very ill since I penned in here. Have suffered a great deal; but God has been my helper. I believe cousin R- thought I was going to die. The joy of hearing from home was too much for me. Several nights I scarcely slept for thinking of home & when I did all the contents were mixed up in my dreams. Every one *so* very kind to me. Cousin R- a second mother—setting up so many nights till twelve & two o'clock.

I have drawn those who were angry with me around me—Mrs. Nixon sends nearly every day to see how I am, she is very sick. Mrs. Maxwell came *to see me.* Mrs. Robertson & family are just as kind to us as if we were their blood kin. Mrs. R- seems more like a *sister* to *me,* any thing she has she tells me I'm welcome too. Mrs. Foote too is just as kind as she can be—she made me a home dress, & sent me word to day she would do another for me.

July 23rd[8]

Thought a great deal of my dear ma to day, its her birthday. May God spare her to her family many years to come. My health is very feeble—

July 26th

Ann Lee's birthday. May the good Lord baptize her heart anew with his Holy Spirit. Oh my gracious Father *protect* & *direct* the young Christian. Thou knowest the temptations that beset them every way they turn.

August 2nd

All I have written here with pencil I wrote today for those dates I've used found me to ill to sit up even in bed. I have been threatened with dysentery—my bowels very bad for six weeks, caused by a dose of calomel Dr. Abadie gave me, 12 grains of calomel & 25 of rhubaurb.[9] Last tuesday 26th I called in Doctor Young his medicines have relieved me very much, I'm still very weak—every night I have to change my clothes every stitch—some times twice in the night. I perspire so much. This afternoon old Mrs. Robertson called. This is her birthday & she dress up &

8. The entries for 23 July to 2 August are written in pencil, and the print is larger than what Bond usually writes. In the 2 August entry she explains that she wrote these entries in one sitting.

9. Both rhubarb and calomel, a mercurial compound, were commonly given to purge the patient's system, causing vomiting and diarrhea. Also, the last stage of consumption was marked by diarrhea.

said she was going to walk around town; I told her she looked like [a] Marylander. The report now is the confederates are in possession of Balto. We are whipping the Yankees every where. Had favorable fights in Va around Richmond during the month of August.[10]

Cousin R- has waited on me truly like a mother since I've been sick. And I bless her for it. But she thinks I am ungrateful because I'm petish & cross some times, I do try and pray not to be, but I can't help it. If she would not notice my petish-ness, but she will contend about the least thing, till some times I feel so miserable I do not know what to do with myself. I told her (as I would my own Ma) of some thing she said to Mrs. R- which mortified me so much and begged her not to do it again, and she has been mad with me ever since, she can not bear the *least* fault found with her by any body.

I do pray the good Lord will direct me in thought word & deed, she tells me she wants me to look upon her as my own Mother, but if I go to advise her about any thing she does not like it, & of course I can't be free with her as I could Ma. All day to day she has sit with her back towards me & never spoken half a dozen words to me, only about my medicines. I believe some times she hates the *very sight* of *me.* Then when I get ill & thinks I'm going to die—she cries around me and does every thing she can—but just as soon as I'm better she spites me in every thing.

August 4th

Oh! so warm to day & in fact I never spent such a warm summer. I scarcely slept at night for the heat—change my clothes some times twice in the night. I talked to sissy yesterday evening about the love of the Saviour—faith in Gods protec-tion—& the effect of prayer—she seemed deeply interested in all I said & read several hymns & texts to me. Cousin R- was listening & I think it made by the di-vine spirit some good impression on her[11]—This morning we commenced talk-ing about christians. I hope *I,* by the Divine Spirit was led to say things which sank deeply in her heart. "One thing—she said—she never could bring her mind down to believe—" I asked what that was; she burst into tears—I felt mystified & said if there was any thing which troubled her about the plan of Salvation—she must go to her Father & beseech Him to make it clear before her. She told me she could not believe *Christ* was equal with *God.* I reminded her of Christ's saying when

10. On 19 April 1861, Union troops occupied Baltimore, and the city remained in Union hands throughout the war. Confederate armies did enter Maryland and threatened Baltimore and Washing-ton, D.C., but Union troops successfully resisted those attacks. Bond is correct about Confederate suc-cesses in Virginia, although she mistakes the month; the Confederate victories occurred in July and in-clude battles at Cool Spring (17–18 July), Kernstown (24 July), and Darby Town (27–29 July).

11. Bond first wrote *had* but replaced it with *made.*

asked by some of his hearers if they had seen the Father, & He said they that have seen me, have seen the Father, I & my Father are one, I in him & He in me. I pray earnestly God will baptize her *heart* & the *Love* of *the Saviour may abound in* it—

25th

My dear Howard came last sunday 21st—O! *how rejoiced* I was to see him. I wept then laughed. He has been appointed State chemist & lives at Mount Lebanon above Shreveport, about 50 miles.[12] He wishes me to go there—and now expects to come for us in a month or two. He will leave me next week—May the good Lord direct us—if it is right for us to go I hope we shall, & if not O, give me grace to bear the separation. I have written a long letter home to sister Fannie bearing dates June 19th August 17th & 24th. I sent it this morning by Miss Virginia Belden who started for N.O. I pray they may get it.

We were visited, last week by Arthur Cowley—who had just made his escape from out the federal lines. They are making all ladies from 16 to 100, if such there be, take the oath.

Sept 17th

Dear Howard left yesterday for Mount Lebanon. I felt comforted more this time parting with him than I ever did because he thinks he will be here in five or six weeks to move us where he is. I have been again very *ill.* One day whilst I was sick I was taken with cramp colic—sent for Dr. Young (my Dr.) & he sent me word, "he was drunk to send for Dr. *Abadie.*" So we sent for him—but unfortunately had gone out of town. I felt more like dieing then than I've ever done. They say I was just as white as could be. Dear Howard held me up whilst cousin R-rubbed my hands & face, they both cried so, I felt my time had come, they did not seem to know what to do for me. I directed that hot water should be brought & my feet put in—then mustard on the inside of my legs & hot hops on my stomach—Howard gave me [illegible] & I threw it up with quantities of green bile. I soon got some relief. I suffered terribly—from inflamation to the bowels and stomach, am better now—very weak & thin.

Thursday 22nd

I wrote to Ann Lee & grandma,[13] yesterday & sent it by Mr. Larette, who will take it to Terrebonne soon. I do hope & pray they may reach home safely. I'm read-

---

12. Under Governor Henry W. Allen, a state laboratory that made and distributed medicines was organized in January 1864 at the Mt. Lebanon Women's Academy in Minden. Allen was attempting to meet the needs of Louisiana citizens who were suffering from severe shortages of medicines. A medical dispensary was also established in Shreveport.

13. Ann Lee's letter is included in app. 1.

ing now such a beautiful book called "Serious call to a Holy Life." Oh! that I might be as perfect as Marinda, Lord fill my heart with thy spirit, & give me grace to over come *every* temptation; to take up my Cross heroically & follow my Divine Saviour![14] The more I look into my heart—the more I see my short-comings—my utter inability to do any good thing on my own strength.

Sunday 25th

My heart has been made so joyful to day at the reception of a dear letter from my sister Ann Lee & one also from my dear friend Mrs. Wright of N.O. Ann Lee accompanied her dear letter with a photograph of her own dear self. Oh! how my heart does rejoice once more [to] hear from that dear home I left so long ago. *All* are well—she writes—Ma looking better than she ever saw her. Oh how much have I to be thankful for. God is so good to me. I have been looking into my heart more within the past week. O, I see so much to disgust me with myself. So corrupt—so vile—so full of envies—pride & vanity. I have & am reading "A Serious Call to a devout & Holy Life" which has opened my eyes to many faults in myself. I pray God most earnestly *he* will sanctify it to my soul.

Ann Lee writes in good spirits—wants me [to] come home—pa will send me money. Oh! poor pa—it is out of my power to go to you—even if I had money. God grant I may be able to go next summer.

Tuesday 27th

Spent the day at Mrs. Foote's—had a fine dinner & a nice cup of coffee, afterwards. Feel good deal better—Dr. says I have not the consumption—

Wednesday 28th[15]

Spent the day at Mrs. Robertson's got caught in the rain—Ned had to bring me home in the cart, he acting horse—my appearance created quite a laugh—perched up in a high chair in the cart—feeling very much like I should turn over.

Sept 29th[16]

Had hard rain today—Capt Marelle brought me a letter from Howard written last July—before he came to see me.[17] I sold a hhd of sugar to day for 60$ in gold. Betsy quite sick—Dr. Young to see her twice.[18]

14. Bond also mentions this book, by William Law, in her entry of 4 June 1864. Miranda, a character in the book, rejects earthly concerns and serves as a model for devout Christianity.

15. The date was originally written as 1 October, but Bond corrects herself.

16. *Oct 2nd* is crossed out and replaced by *Sept 29th*.

17. Morelle, a former Confederate captain from Terrebonne Parish, was implicated with Howard Bond in leading the 1862 ambush on Union soldiers outside of Houma.

18. Betsy is one of the Bonds' slaves.

Oct 26th

Some time has elapsed since I penned in here. Nothing of much interest has occurred in that time. Mr. Robertson started for Texas last Monday (17). I hear the Yellow Fever is raging in Houston & Galveston brought there by vessels running the blockade from Havana.

I'm not feeling so well, as I have for the past three weeks—Since Betsy's sickness I have been exercising more & sewing a good deal. Day before yesterday, I had a hemorrhage from my lung. I immediately sent for Dr. Young who came—It did not prove very severe—but I feel fearful I may have more of them. I know God my good Shepard is watching over me; and nothing can befall me, without His knowledge. My health seems much improved here lately. I have gained good deal of flesh—my face looks quite full. The Dr. thinks perhaps I'm pregnant, but I guess not. I heard of the death of Mrs. Albert Woods, died with consumption.[19] Her husband cared nothing for her—I believe it was brought on more from a breaking heart.

Friday 28th

Lovely autumnal day. Mrs. Murry Robertson spent the morning with us—I believe she offended cousin R- finding fault with sis—who is dreadfully spoiled by her ma; but no one must say a word to any of her babyness, or obstinacy. I feel far from well—I slept very little last night. Was so disappointed I did not get a letter from Howard this week. Last night I set up till after 10 o'c talking about home and *loved ones*. I expect I'm the only interested person but I *do* love to talk about home & when H- is here we often enjoy those kind of chats—he is *almost* as fond of the subject as I. I have been very fortunate here lately getting presents. Mrs. Foote (a french lady—a great friend of mine) has given me articals of clothing which I could not well do without, and that which is impossible for me to purchase here. Four flannel drawers, three pairs of woolen stocken & a pair of worsted gloves. Providence surely is watching oer me. God *will* provide for *all things needful I will* trust Him *for all*. I am nearly bear for flannel shirts—but I'll trust it will come when I absolutely need it. I can still patch what I have & wear them. We have no news, every body is awaiting the result of the election in the North, for President which will take place next Tuesday week.

Then I suppose we can form a better idea when we shall have *Peace*.[20] Oh! Peace

---

19. Albert Woods was the brother of Rodney Woods, the Terrebonne planter with whom Laura Bond was rumored to be engaged. He was also editor of a Houma newspaper, *Ceres,* and was implicated along with Howard Bond in the 1862 ambush of Union soldiers. His newspaper office was burned in retaliation.

20. Bond could have in mind the Democrats' platform that called for immediate restoration of peace.

glorious Peace how I long for it—Yes on any terms—what is all this blood shed for—for the negroes. They say I'm a Yankee—but if wanting peace is Yankee—then *I am one.* I am tired of *Disunion* of husband & wife.

Oct sunday 30th

Been raining the most of this morning. No letter yet. I've felt so sadly ever since friday. Cousin R- has not spoken half dozen words—I believe—to me since then (only words of necessity) she got angry with Mrs. Robertson & I because we laughed at sis about being such a baby & not studying her lessons better. Then too I spoke of her calling me "old Mrs. Robertson" when she was not very well pleased with me, which I should not have done—I suppose. But it is so provoking to be called names. I hope she will be more careful in [the] future calling me *names.* And for *trifels too.* I tried to carry on conversation at first but I soon found I was making myself more disagreeable & therefore hold my tongue—I find it the best. She is so jealous of me—about Howard—says its no use for her to ask him to do so & so for her—if I'll ask it will be done. The other day several articals for the table that Howard had purchased for us to go housekeeping was missed—some had been stolen & others broken—I enquired into the matter of the servants, as I believe it my duty to take care Howards property—who has often told me to do so, but what was my astonishment, when cousin R- informed me she thought I was talking of things that did not concern me, she considered belonging to her—I told her they did belong to her to use—but still I considered them my property & thought my duty to enquire about them. I also told her when a man marries, his property of every description belonged to his wife & it was her place to take charge of all that came under her care. She said if she had known that she would not have had any thing to to of done with them. And as to living on Howard if she went up to Lebanon—she could not think of such a thing—I said—cousin Rebecca, you know you will be perfectly welcome to all Howard can provide for us & not be considered spunging—that is his duty to take care of his mother when he can—no! she replied if he was single I might think so—but now he has a *wife*—makes a great difference—I said—you know you are welcome to all H. & I have, & as to his being married will make no difference—He will think it *his* duty to take care of you & sis. No! she replied (& the words sank deep into my heart) I could not live upon H- with the *wife he has got.* What have I done to enrage her so against me. I can not tell unless it is because I have talked plainly to her—& given her advice which if she had taken she would have been better off—& made friends—where as it is she has carried out her own plans—lost the regard & respect of her best friends here—& found out she was mistaken—when too late to remedy it, no not too late—but her *pride* would not let her give up & acknowledge her error. The least fault any one finds with any thing she does & tryes to show her wherein she could better herself—she thinks they do it with a purpose of letting her see how much better they could do—never once thinks they have her interest at heart. It is not only with me—but every one else who would befriend her. She told me one day—after I had advised her about some thing & told her I gave the same advise to her as if she were my own dear ma, whom she knew I loved dearly, she did not think it a childs place to find fault with a parent even if they were not right—nor would she thank one of her children for doing so. I resolved then I never would try it again. But have broken through my resolution several times since because I saw she was going to do some thing so disadvantageous to her.

I do pray for *grace* to bear up under those family disagreements—& see & not see—hear & not hear. But the flesh wareth against the spirit when I would do good evil is present with me. I feel God is with me—who then can be against me. I know I fall short of the Knowledge Grace Wisdom & Charity I should have—my desire is to have more & my love for all to increase daily—to be more *Christ like* in my daily walk.

Oh! how oft do I yearn for a sister or dear precious ma, to unburden my heart to. Surely wishing human sympathy can't be sin. Did not even Christ have a dearly loved disciple who he unburdened his trouble too! When I think of my situation—with husband hundreds of miles from me—my fathers house thousands of miles off & my utter inability to go to either—then of my dwelling amongst those whom I am so disagreeable & being compelled to live upon. Where they tell me I should consider my self at home & not feel my self dependant but as one of their own family—how can I, after having been told by cousin J- he was sorry I ever came to La, *he* never wanted me to come—and Oh, so many *bitter* things which has caused my *heart* to *bleed ever since.* Then cousin R- who has acted more my friend then *he*, to say she could not think of living on Howard,[21] with the *wife he has got.* I pray God will direct *all* things—if it is right I hope my husband will come for us if not, O! God give me strength to bear it, & grace to overcome every evil feeling that may arise of disappointment & circumstances.

Monday 31st

Rained all day. Mrs. Foote spent sunday afternoon with me, otherwise I should have been alone. She has written in my Album. Conl. O'Brian arrived home last night after an absence of 10 or 12 months.[22] He was taken prisoner by the Federals last fall when they made a raid, & taken to the city where he had been held in

---

21. The word *not* is inserted above the line.

22. Bond refers to Col. Patrick O'Brien of the Louisiana Irish Regiment.

confinement ever since. I presume his family were rejoiced to see him "home again."

Tuesday Nov 1st

Another rainy day—Oh! so cheerless & dreary—my heart too seems like the weather—clouded over—filled with storm. I am made to feel my self a stranger, an encumbrance—If I try to look pleasant & not notice that brows are clouded—& try a few pleasant words at conversation—I meet with such cold returns that I sink back into my own coldness & silence. Oh! I wish I could always feel careless & indifferent; & overcome such feelings—know all will work right in the end. I find it is generally *little things* which sum up the *miseries of life.* I have endeavored to keep quiet, for one week. I have said little, but what is in answer to some question—nor have I had much said to me. Cousin R- treats *me* just as she did cousin Josh when ever any little difference would occur between them & therefore I know she *despises the very sight of me.* When she would get angry with him—she would for *spite* (for she told me she did it for that purpose—she said she didn't say much but she knew they hated that more than if she said any thing) wait on him—take extra pain to show she was doing him a *favor.* Cousin Josh is very *queer,* but I believe with a *different* wife he would have been a *better man,* one who was willing to look over his failings some times—was kind & affectionate towards him & willing to acknowledge her self in fault when she was in fault.

Nov 11th

Some time has passed without my writing in here. Last Tuesday 8th The Election for President in the United States, came off. I should like to know who has been elected. I hope any how we'll have *Peace.* Wednesday, I got a letter from dear Howard dated Oct 4th, I fear he'll not be able to come for us this winter; I hope the Lord will direct us *in all things* & if we should not be able to go there that *I* may be enabled to see *His* hand in it.

I spent the day yesterday at Mrs. Robertson's, had a fine dinner—as they generally have. This morning Old Mrs. R- spent with us—she sewing on my yellow dress, & I knitting on Henrys sock. I also answered Henry's letter[23]—will send by Capt. Favrot,[24] as far as Alexandria, where he has promised to *mail* for me. Cousin R- still keeps silent towards me—treats me as a piece of furniture in her house.

23. In her Louisiana entries up to this point Bond has mentioned two Henrys. One is Henry Calhoun from Terrebonne, who flees the Union soldiers with Howard and Wellie Bond. The other is a Mr. Henry Fair in Abbeville. Bond could be speaking of one of these men.

24. Henry M. Favrot was lieutenant colonel of the Second State Guards Battalion. This battalion eventually combined with other regiments to form the Eighth Regiment and, as a member of the Eighth, Favrot was likely going toward Alexandria to perform picket and outpost duty. See Bergeron, *Guide to Louisiana Confederate Military Units,* 52.

Thursday 17th

Has been raining several days—& I feel the effects of the damp weather—my cough is very troublesome. I sent a letter to Mrs. Wright, one enclosed for Ann Lee on tuesday. I do hope they may reach home safely. I wrote to H[oward] this week also. Mrs. Hall came this morning for me to write a letter for her, to her husband in Arkansas. I wrote a very affectionate one; she said it just as she should have written herself. She reminds me more of *"Widow Meclot"* than any one else. I feel glad to do any thing to comfort a soldiers wife—I'm glad to be favored myself some times. Old Mrs. Robertson spent the afternoon yesterday with us.

Friday 18th

Raining—still raining. Dr Poyet called to see us this afternoon. He is a tremendous man—and a brother to the Priest who is a very good neighbor—he sent me a glass of milk to day saying he had but little, but as I was sick & he well—he'd much rather I'd have it than he. I have been quite industrious this week—am trimming my winter hats.

Sunday 20th

Gloomy weather! Commenced a letter to aunt R[ebecca Bond]. Have written sadly—but my feelings must have vent in some way.

Oh, for a sympathizing christian to commune with!

Monday 21st

Cleared off this morning—cold north wind. Had a fracas with cousin R—she says I think my self so *smart* & she a fool, crying at the same time, I told her (I could help laughing) she need not cry about it if I was smart—of course I thought myself smart. I see through the whole *matter*—she is *jealous* of me with her son, & in every way. Every body seems to prefer my company—I can't help it, it is not a fault of mine. I told her I had plenty of friends. I had never gone any where without making friends & just as soon as I could find a place to go I would *release her* of my presence—which had become so obnoxious to her.

Old Mrs. Robertson spent the evening here. Several sunday's since—Mrs. Maxwell sent to me for my chess men, as she had company & I suppose wished them to be *badly* entertained—I was absent when the servant came & she not being learned in the mysteries of *games*—nor intimate with said *gentlemen*—by the time she reached here could not come nearer the name, than *"Testament"* (quite a different thing) cousin R- could not imagine what Mrs. M- wanted with my testament but however sent hers. Of course Charlotte soon returned & her memory becoming better, she asked for Chess-men. As cousin R did not know where they were—she went back without them. If I had been here she would not have got them on *Sunday*.

Tuesday 22nd

Mr. Ellis called this morning—he has been home several days on furlough—to see the stranger at home—a little baby girl of two months. The Northern papers, say Lincoln is elected for four more years—no prospects of peace! Old Mr. Foote here this evening.[25] Annie R- & sis picking cotton for me; they are running a race.

I, at last have received my poems Howard sent me. I prize them very highly. Last night I suffered with the cold most dreadfully. I had to make Mintty get up & make a fire & pile the clothes on me. This morning the ground was frozen till dinner time—I suffer more with the cold here than when in Md.

Great many of our soldiers are deserting & going to the Yankees. I have been reading to day pieces in Montgomery. One piece particularly struck a cord in my breast. Speaking of his native land (Briton) he says[26]

> "I love thee:—next to heaven above,
> Land of my fathers! thee I love;
> And rail thy slanderers as they will,
> With all *thy faults I love thee* still."

So it is with my native shore, I love her with *all her faults.*

Wednesday 23rd

Last night after tea, I was made happy by the reception of a letter from home—from sister Fannie. But it was written Oct. 63—which of course made it rather stail—but it was overflowing with such warm affection & sympathy for me & mine. They want me home so much; their cry is "come home! come home!" Oh, what a comfort it is to read *such* letters—breathing *love* from *warm & sincere hearts.* My dear ma says, "if she could, she would most willingly bear my pains & sorrows for me." Oh! *Love* divine. Who but a mothers heart could feel so. My precious ma! My precious ma! God in His wisdom has seen fit to afflict your *poor child*—it surely is *mercy* in a *cloud*—I will write her soon; while they are fresh in my mind. It is so cold & bright to day. I believe I will take a walk after dinner; my breast is painful today.

24th

I took dinner at Mrs. R[obertson]'s with Mrs. Hall—who had called here—cousin R had gone there early—she returned home to dinner; whilst there con-

25. Henry Foote, George Foote's* father, was also a planter in St. Mary Parish. He would have been eighty years old in 1864.

26. Bond begins the poem on the same line but crosses it out and writes, instead, in verse form.

versation turned on doing good to those who did us evil, and our dislike to persons. Cousin R said, when she did not like any one—she would do all she could to favor them—but she would not receive any from *them;* I was reading an old news paper; & as she spoke, I raised my head & fixed my eyes on her face, with the most penetrating gaze I could—my whole soul was in it. She would not return the look but I felt she saw me, & was not mistaken for to night some thing was said to bring the subject up—Oh yes! she said last summer when H- was here she had no sugar of her own, & she did not feel at *liberty* to take *my sugar* to make surup for Howard. I then asked her if she saw me looking at her: her face turned red & she said yes— but she did not feel that way towards *me*. Why does she *act* that way surely if *love* prompts her to do the *same things* that hatred does how can I distinguish between the two? Another schooner in the bayou—for the Government—come from Havana.

Friday 25th
    Bright day.

Saturday 26th
    Sent a letter to aunt Rebecca—hope she will get it. Cousin R- busy about making sausage & drying up lard. I was at Mrs. Patricks till dinner time—went up to the drug store with Mrs. R-, the druggist not there—store full of men—one old gentleman seeing my searching eye enquired, "what do you wish *Miss?*" After I left the store a gentleman from the "Lake" enquired of old Mrs. R- who that *pretty young lady* was with her. I must write Howard and tell him the folks about here think I am a *"pretty young lady."* I *had* an agreeable chat with Dr Poyet this afternoon, he gave me four U. S. stamps to send letters homeward. I saw Dr. Young this evening—he says if I'm not better my *looks* are very *deceiving,* for I'm so fat. He thinks there is some thing *the matter—*

Sunday 27th
    Lovely day—southern breeze blowing not good for me—my breast is so sore inside, coughed up blood some this morning—went around [to] Mrs. Robertsons, Mrs. Foote there with her pet 'flying squirrel,' carrying on her mischief, came home to dinner—after which took a walk with old Mrs. R- down to the bayou to see *another* schooner that came up last night—quite a long one too. Mr. Poyét gave me Northern & London papers, took them to Mr. R- to read aloud so all could enjoy them. They gave him the blues so dreadfully—thinks the Confederacy is at a low ebb—when our head men are recommending the negroes to be armed and put in the army—that is each planter shall free so many slaves, according to the number he has—& put them in the army as free men fighting for their liberty. I was in

hopes this cruel war would soon be over—but from present appearance, it is as far off, as when it commenced. Lincoln says he *can* subjugate the south *in 4 more years.* Yes four more years of *heinous crimes*—of *diabolical outrages,* and bloodshed! and then, what then! The south *will not be conquered.* After tea Mr. & Mrs. M Robertson called.

Monday 28th

I feel sick to day, coughed good deal last night & this morning & blood—Had the tooth ache & neuralgia in my face & head—did not eat breakfast till about 10, have a large blister on my breast now. I am sitting up with my hand pressed on my breast to keep the poultice in its place. Mintty is combing my hair. Mrs. R- just sent for cousin R- to come *Risie* is very sick.

Tuesday 29th

This morning cousin R- & I had quite a exciting talk[27]—I told her I was going crazy—I could not stand it any longer it was killing me by half inches—After awhile I burst into a flood of tears—she could not stand it any longer—but came and put her arms around me & told me not to cry,[28] that she knew she had acted wrong. So *we* mutually agreed to be as we once was loving & true to each other & let no more such misunderstandings occur. I feel happier by this explanation—for I was miserable before. I feel the effect of the intense excitement I was in. I have a very large and sore blister on my breast & neuralgia in my face & head, owing to a decade tooth I think.[29] Dr. Young was to see me this morning—he was drunk last evening when I sent for him.

Wednesday 30th

Warm summer like weather. I took Mrs. Patrick several biscuits this morning—she has not been well for a long time. Got a letter from Howard to day—just a few lines—he had not heard from me since he left here & seemed very uneasy about it—prays God to spare me to him—he does not care what trials he undergoes if I am left him. Poor fellow! how sadly was beat his noble heart for his pet.

Walked round Mrs. R-'s this evening; do not feel well. Old Mrs. R- called this evening late. She & Mrs. Maxwell are about to have another fuss about Mrs. M-'s mother's Bible, she accuses Mrs. R- of stealing it. I never saw such folkes as Mrs. M & Mrs. R- are; there is not a neighbor goes to see them, Mrs. Maxwell

---

27. Bond initially wrote "an exciting time" but changed her phrasing to that shown here.

28. The word *your* was written first but was crossed out and changed to *her.*

29. Bond's toothache could have been a result of the purging medicines, such as calomel, that she frequently took. These toxic remedies could cause patients' gums to turn black and their teeth to fall out. See Sewell, *Medicine in Maryland,* 4.

has left her house—where her mother is—& gone to one of the negro cabins to live. There is some strange talk about her. I think she acts very strangely.

Thursday 1st

First day of winter, cloudy & warm. Mr. Dupry called this morning to show me some flannel he had purchased for himself at 2$ a yd in silver—that is most too high for my purse. Mrs. Patrick spent the evening here—she is a dear good old lady.

Friday 2nd

I'm not feeling well at all—my bowels are very weak, commenced a letter to Howard—but feel very little like doing anything. I feel so sad all the time, so lonely—so heart-sick.

Saturday 3rd

Rained hard last night, cloudy & disagreeable to day. Mrs. Maxwell gives a spinning party to day, quite a select affair judging *by some* she sent for—a negro woman who has a white husband, & lives here in town.

Sunday 4th

Lovely day—I was walking about nearly all day. Mr. Foote sent me several ducks.

Monday 5th

I sent Howard a letter by *courier* directed to Governor Allen—rainy cloudy disagreeable day—feel badly. Old Mrs. R- here this evening—giving Mrs. Maxwell *fits*, didn't want me to loan Mrs. M- my "*Chess men*," but I did. She gives a ball to night—old Mrs. Nixon in *furies*.

Tuesday 6th

Mrs. M's ball I think must have been a failure; had nothing to eat, though things were prepared—no one to cook them; she having falling out with the servants, & got so angry with Harriet (her negro woman) she threw her clothes in the fire. I never saw such conduct from *virtuous* people. She had but few *females* there, much of the guests were males, & they played games where *kissing* is a part & permitted them to kiss her, & *all* the rest. Had the captain of a schooner being there, who she does not know—& from his appearance would take him to be a vulgar person, a great big *bully* of a *man*. I do not blame Mrs. R- for feeling ashamed she is in any way connected with the family. Old Mrs. R- here this afternoon.

Wednesday 7th

Mr. Robertson left to day for Texas; he looked so sad when I bid him good bye that he has made me feel sad the rest of the day. Sadness, like merriment must be infectious. The town was in a blaze of excitement this afternoon. Mr. Lazene Landry shot at the priest.[30] He has had a grudge against Mr. Poyét for some time—because he plays cards, & this is the third time he has shot at him. It appears Lazene, went to the church where the priest was confessing a young man (about 60 males & females are preparing this week to take their first communion next sunday, & are in church neary all day.) Landry said the priest was confessing black & white altogether, & he had his cousins there & they should not go with negroes. So he prepared two revolvers & one bowie knife & would have shot him in the confession box; but some saw him & told Mr. Poyét, who immediately passed to his house & got his gun—& told him he was ready—they both shot at the same time—neither receiving a scratch. Landry was very drunk, or he would not been such a dare devil—but he has it in his heart to kill the priest for he has expressed himself whilst sober, to several persons and said he will kill him. But Mr. Poyét made an affidavit against him & had him arrested & he is now guarded in the court house. I hear they will lodge him in jail at Lafayette. Every body is afraid of him—he is such a dangerous man when drunk for then he is perfectly crazy. The sheriff is afraid to arrest him & got some soldiers to do it. To day has been almost like a summer day—south wind blowing—I have felt truly sad all day. I walked about good deal to day.

Thursday 8th

Just as cold rainy and disagreeable to day, as yesterday was pretty & agreeable. Early this morning just as I finished breakfast Mintty came in, said "Oh! Miss Mitt just look out & see what all that is about." I looked & there was a crowd of people coming out of the priest's house—one carrying a white flag & one ringing several bells. We could not make out what it could be for. I noticed a very tall lady leaning on the arm of an oldish looking man; it seems they were an old couple and they (the crowd) were serenading them. Miss Gus Perry took dinner with us. I have just heard Mr. Robertson has come back, I don't know why. Rain & cold.

Dec. 10th

Sick in bed nearly all yesterday with cold in my face, it is dreadfully swelled. I wish I had courage to have them drawn. I hear they tried Landry yesterday & let him off—I suppose he is bound over, to keep the peace.

Sunday 11th

Cleared off bright & cold—north west wind blowing all day. Mr. Robertson here yesterday for a little while. Left to see if he could obtain some flannel for me,

---

30. Lazene Landry, of Vermilion Parish, was a farmer owning property valued in 1860 at almost nine hundred dollars. He was fifty-four years old in 1864. His wife was named Carmalete, and the couple had two teenage sons in 1864.

from the officer who has come down from headquarters, about the goods on the schooner in the bayou. Mrs. Maxwell & Mrs. Foote called this morning. Grand ceremony at the catholic church, about 80 took their first communion—The ladies all dressed in white with white vails on their heads. I guess some will suffer from the exposure dressing so thinly [on] such a cold day. I hear Mr. Maxwell is in N.O. I hope he has letters & money for me, & I will get them soon. Old Mr. Foote was also here, says he don't come to see me—as I told him I was a *yankee* yesterday. My tooth is still painful & face swelled very much.

Tuesday 13th

Lazene Landry's trial has been going on since thursday—has not been decided yet. He has three lawyers.

Wednesday 14th

I spent the day at Mrs. Robertson's made the acquaintance of Liet Collins;[31] he's a great friend of the Eastens. Did not get a letter from Howard—feel sad and disappointed.

Thursday 15th

Lovely day—like spring—walked round Mrs. Patricks—sit a while then went down to the bayou—had not returned home long before I heart the report of a gun—rushed to my window, & there was Dr. and Mr. Poyet both with guns—& Mr. Landry out in the road. It appears after the priest found the case had gone against him—he determined to kill Landry any how. (Landry had gotten off by several gentlemen going his security to keep the peace, till court in the spring) so Mr. Poyét sent word this morning, he & his brother were walking the yard waiting for him, & they intended to kill him. Mr. Landry came riding by with the Sheriff & some one else (Landry going to the bayou—where his wagons were, already loaded with sugar for Texas—& expect to start right off with Mr. R- for that place,) when Mr. Poyét called out to the others to get out of the way, he was going to shoot, & he Mr. P. fired first, Landry returned the compliment & wounded Dr. Poyét in the hand—no other damage done. Liet Collins immediately summoned a guard & arrested the priest and his brother—they are now in the jail. The whole town is down upon them. Several persons swore in court, they had heard Mr. Poyet say, "there was not a virtuous woman in town" & named over the women he had spoken particularly against, & who their *admirers* were. I sent Laura a letter to day by the underground rail road. Four soldiers have been having their meals prepared here, the names of them are Mr. Dirgen—Mr. Anderson, Mr. More & Mr. Hymes. Mr. Dirgen took my letters & will send it to Captain B. P. L. Vinsan.[32] [T]hose

31. Probably Lt. Col. Joseph Collins.

32. Capt. Bailie P. L. Vinson was a member of the independent Teche Guerrillas Company Cavalry. The company was on scout and outpost duty on the lower Bayou Teche.

gentlemen belong to his company, and are up here for the purpose of guarding the Yankee boat lieing in the bay—the crew are *real* Vermonters & they are not allow to come ashore. We are expecting other schooners in.

Friday 16th

Mr. R- got off this evening, & at last went without Mr. Landry who was arrested just as he was about to start—Mr. Eugéne Guegnon had him arrested because he wounded Dr. Poyét in the hand & shoulder. Mr. Poyét was let off by some one giving a security—1000$. Mr. Lirette here this morning just from Terrebonne—he thinks war is going to last 4 more years; he seemed low spirited. I wrote a short letter to ma & he will give it to his father to mail—I hope it may reach there in safety. Several mornings we have had dense fogs—real *London fogs:* very unhealthy weather—very warm & unseasonable. Mr. Lirette tells us Jonny Pierce is dead—died at Mr. [Mathern] McConnel's. Poor Mrs. P. how I pity her![33]

Saturday 17th

Cloudy most of the day, very warm—so bad for my lungs. I cough a great deal & the phlegm is mixed with blood. I often think my life is drawing early to a close, & ask myself "am I ready & willing to die." Those are serious and solemn questions I scarcely know how to answer them—"*am I ready*." I feel I am *very sinful*— that there is not one thought pure & free from sin. My very best endeavors are filled with impurity. If my *trust* was in *myself* I should be lost but I trust in the *mercy* & *loving kindness* of my Father—He knows the frailty of *his* human creatures. He remembers they are but dust, & His hand is stretched out yet he will save *all* who rely upon his word. "Am I willing?" If I believe God is *my Father* who *directs* & *wills* every thing pertaining to me—every event of my life—& *who* holds the life of my body in His hand—should I not be resigned to His will—tho I might wish life prolonged—as there are ties still dear to me—ties which bind me to earth, yet if God saw best to call me—should I not be willing to go. And thus are the questions answered [illegible word], I believe I shall not be taken till I be prepared, I must be refined by affliction & sorrows.

Sunday 18th

Rained this morning. Mrs. Robertson here little while—I see Dr. Poyet walking the yard. I do not know whether he is released or not. He has been held in close confinement at this brother's since friday—The trial comes on to morrow. I hear I'm to be summoned as a witness against the Priest. Capt Brouster here yesterday—going to kill me some ducks. Had a good deal of excitement next door—

33. She likely refers to Mrs. Phoebe Pierce's son. Bond mentions her when she is writing from Crescent Place; see, for example, the entry of 20 July 1862.

yesterday evening—with drunken folks. I gave Mrs. Wise a peace of my mind—
I told her I believe she would sell her *soul* for a *dime* and her character was at *stake*.
If she didn't feel *that*, she can't feel *any* thing. A woman to sell liquor to drunken
men!

Wednesday 21st

Rained good deal yesterday—cleared off last night. To day is clear & cold. I
received a nice letter from Laura written last June—quite stail—but nevertheless very interesting. Very disappointed did not get a letter from Howard. I do
not see why he doesn't write oftener. Went 'round Mrs. Robertson's read part of
Laura's letter; they are delighted to hear. Mr. Maxwell should say what he did
about Mr. R-. No news of importance, some say the yanks are going to make another raid on the Teche. I don't much believe it though. I have commenced reading Goldsmith's works. Am very much interested in the "Vicar of Wakefield," &
the life of the author.

Friday 23rd

Gathered a dress for old Mrs. R- yesterday and carried it to her after dinner—
made them all laugh so heartily at some of my ups & downs in Abbeville. I hear
Mr. Robertson came home last night with the small pox, driven back third time
from making his trip to Texas. Surely Providence has detained him for some good
cause—Oh, may it be the means of trusting in Providence & asking God's direction in all things. Went round to Mrs. Foote's this afternoon—had the Dr. called
whilst there to consult with him.

Saturday 24th

Cloudy day—walked up & down the street for exercise. Had a little kitten
brought me for a christmas gift.

Sunday 25th

Still cloudy & damp—rained last night. Mrs. Guidry sent me a feather fan for
a christmas gift, the two gifts are the only ones I expect I'll get. Mr. Ellis here this
morning. I wonder what they are doing at home to day? I fancy Ma is thinking
much of her dear one far away—four years ago I was in their midst—but spent a
unhappy day—thought made sad by the idea of leaving my dear old home—O!
how vividly comes back the scenes I passed through that *memorable time*. Were they
forbodings of sorrows & trials to come? Mrs. Spaulding took dinner with us:
notwithstanding *bad times* we had a very large turkey for dinner—nice pieces of
roast beef—sweet potatoes—rice pickles—& sponge cake & pie—melon to eat
with the cake.

Mrs. Patrick called after dinner. What has Howard been doing to day I wonder!

Monday 26th

Was walking nearly all day—with old Mrs. Robertson, went to see Dr. Abadie found him looking very thin. I was very tired when I reached home, & soon after dinner I laid down & finished reading "She stoops to conquer." Saw Mr. R- this evening, he has recovered from the varioloid—which he had instead of the small pox.

Tuesday 27th

At Mrs. Robertson's this morning—After dinner Mrs. Sophia Robertson & I went to Mrs. Hall's; her niece—Mrs. Whittington is staying with her. I received an invitation to a ball of Mrs. Foote's this evening. I forgot to say, Betsy was delivered of a fine daughter this morning, had a great time getting a *granny* for her—had to send three miles for her. *I told her to be ready for me when I called for her.*

Wednesday 28th

New moon to day. Lovely day. Disappointed again not getting a letter—Mrs. Foote & I went to the office—very windy—I made the acquaintance of Dr. Reid & Mr. Bradly. [W]ent to Mrs. R-'s this afternoon—got some salad.

Thursday 29th

[W]alking nearly all day; feel *so* sadly. Thinking of home & ma so much especially twilight, I felt as though she was beside me smiling one of her sweetest smiles upon her poor child. O how oft I know she is with me in spirit. I dreamed the other night, I went home & O, I felt so happy to see them all again—thought we *all* cryed of joy & after a while I said, "well ma I'm here, but *half my heart's* in La, I want to see *Howard so badly.*"

Friday 30th

Cloudy but warm south wind blowing. Can not hear any tidings of Howard—my heart grows sad, with *hope* deferred.

Cloudy, windy day—at Mrs. R-'s this evening—Mr. R- had the blues so badly about going to Texas. Mrs. Susan Robertson & Mrs. Maxwell had another *blow up*—

Saturday 31st

Last night had a storm of wind—I thought some of those surrounding buildings were sure to be blown down—but I believe there was no damage done by it. Has cleared off as bright as can be but cold & windy. The old year seems to be determined to bluster out. This past year has been a very short one to me notwithstanding I have been separated from my husband & other dear ones. How many broken & bleeding sad hearts have been made by this year's war! How much we have to be thankful for, we are still spared & the dearest ones of our hearts are too. Dear old home—how fancy pictures the dear domestic hearth—brighten by so many smiling faces—one only absent there—only one vacant chair. Does the *name* of that absent *one* flit through their minds when the jest goes 'round causing a momentary check to the merry voice? Laugh on dear ones—let not one absent grieve or mar your happiness. But remember me in your chambers—when all is hushed and the deepening twilight warns you 'tis the vesper hour—the hour for prayer— remember me then—let your voices ascend to the thrones of Heaven[34]—pray for the ones far away—& may thy prayers be heard.

New Years eve—Have been busy making *Confederate cake* this afternoon— made with *corn meal* instead of flour. Old Mr. Foote here little while this morning—but he's so deaf I find it makes me cough to talk to him. The year of '64, is fast ebbing away, it will soon be gone.

Sunday Jan 1st

I dined at Mrs. Robertson's—came home after dinner—found Mrs. Hall & Mrs. Whitington here. [B]eautiful day.

Monday 2nd

Mr. R- started again for Texas—

Tuesday 3rd

Took dinner at Mrs. Robertson's—took a walk with Mrs. R- & Mrs. Foote after dinner.

Thursday 5th

Finished a letter to Howard going to send it to morrow up to Shreveport by the Sherif. Betsy's baby died tuesday from lock-jaw—Raining to day.

Friday 6th

Rained.

Saturday

[B]right cold day.

Sunday 8th

I was taken yesterday about half past 12 with cramp colic—had to send for Dr. Young—suffered good deal—up to day—feel little better—pains all over me. Mrs. Sophy R- here with the children this morning, Mrs. Susan R- here this evening. It has commenced to rain again.

---

34. The word *upward* originally followed *voices* but is crossed through.

Friday eve Jan 12th

I have just handed Mr. Durgen a letter to ma;[35] he will leave here in an hour or so for "Cuba," & has promised to mail my letter there, or if the schooner's captured by the Federals will endeavor to have it mailed by them. I told him if he was captured the yankees might read the letter—but he mustn't. He laughed heartily. I have been walking a bout most all the evening. Got some soap—two bits a pound—home made.

Sunday 15th

Cloudy & rainy—pretty much such a day as four years ago—the day I was married. Four years since I saw dear ma's sweet face! I wrote a letter to H- will send it by Henry Foote to morrow,[36] he goes to Shreveport. I hear there are 18 gun boats in Red river, & an attack is expected soon either in Alexandria or Shreveport. I hear the Yankees have Savannah Ga.[37] Every thing looks gloomy enough for the confederacy. Mrs. Ellis had a spinning party yesterday—cousin R- & Mrs. R- went in the evening—Mrs. Ellis sent us pie & cake. Mrs. Maxwell moved home yesterday—had a making up with her ma, I wonder how long its going to last.

Tuesday 17th

Mr. Robertson returned home to day frightened us all very much—thought he was sick again but not much the matter—will go back next week.

Wednesday 18th

Mr. Wise came up from New Town—made us feel happy by the news, France & England had recognized us—they say they only recognize Abe Lincoln President of the "Northern states" & not the "United States." I hope its so. Mrs. Foote (old lady),[38] old Mrs. Robertson, & Miss Mary Wilcoxen spend the evening here.[39] Miss Wilcoxen is a very agreeable & intelligent lady—but very much afflicted in her hand; caused by a spell of sickness. Old Mr. Foote is quite a jolly old fogy, he & I joke each other very often; he comes most every day.

Have not received a letter from Howard yet. Can not imagine what is the matter. Thank God I have grace & strength to bear it. I feel very low spirited this eve.

---

35. Bond corrects the spelling of Dr. Durgen's name above the line.

36. Henry Foote was a St. Mary Parish merchant and landowner who in 1860 owned property worth thirty thousand dollars. Bond more frequently mentions George Foote,* Henry's brother.

37. Savannah fell to Sherman's forces on 22 December 1864.

38. Bond refers to George and Henry Foote's mother.

39. Mary Wilcoxen was the daughter of St. Mary Parish planter T. Wilcoxen (see the entry of 15 June 1864 and accompanying note). She was thirty-four years old.

Thursday 19th

Am feeling quite achey to day—cloudy weather. I feel truly thankful the Lord has answered my prayer—& am perfectly willing to suffer the pain. I heard of the death of dear Mr. Rand, this morning, dear man! [W]e should not grieve for the righteous. I feel he is better off. Has only exchanged a sorrowful world for one of perpetual happiness. May the Great and wise God be with his sorrowing family—give them grace & strength to bear up under the burden of this affliction, and provide for them as He sees they need. Mrs. Hall & her niece here this evening.

Saturday 21st

I was in bed yesterday—not much the matter—amused myself reading "*Adéle*" by Julia Kavanagh.[40] I was extremely interested—it shows if we only trust in *Providence* all things will work out right—every cloud will be dispelled and those crosses will only purify our hearts—the clouds when gone will leave a serene & clear sky, which will be enjoyed the more for having been over shadowed by them. I hear it is faulse, Mr. *Rand is not dead*. Rained all yesterday, & last night—has cleared off now, & the sun's shining beautifully. I hope it will keep good weather for some time & let me enjoy a walk.

Night. Old Mr. Foote came this evening—seemed in great distress about his grandson who is in the army, & sick—they have sent for him. He like myself is threatened with consumption. Mr. Robertson called to ask permission to bring Dr. *Shipy* to see us (a physician from Shreveport who has been sent down to examine those who excuse themselves from military duties, through the plea of sickness.)

Mr. R- made me feel as *blue* as *indigo*, about our *national troubles*. He seems to think it is so, Richmond, Charleston, & Wilmington are given up & the Confederacy played out. *I* believe "*Rebels*" are "*truimps*" yet.[41] This seems to be generally believed, that Lord John Russel, has said England, *does not* recognize "Abe Lincoln" President of the United States, but the Northern States; and I believe his election will be protested in March, as England only recognizes him president of the Northern States[;] 'till *then*, I'll hope for the best. Some thing I *feel* will be done to bring *Peace*.

Sunday 22nd

Rainy day! Some days must be dark and dreary! surely *these* are *dark days*. Mrs. Spaulding called this evening.

40. A popular Irish novelist whose work was often reprinted in America, Kavanagh set much of her fiction, including *Adele* (1858), in France.

41. Mr. Robertson's news was incorrect at the time. These cities would fall to Grant and Sherman several months later.

Monday 23rd

Old Mr. Foote & Mrs. Whittington here after dinner—I spit blood all to day. Young Mrs. Foote came to see me little while this evening.[42] Dr. Shippy left without coming to see us. Mr. R. will send him my letter to Iberia—I hope Howard may get it.

Wednesday 25th

I feel badly—have a cold in my head & fresh cold on my breast; have been spitting more or less blood since Monday. Mr. Robertson left again this afternoon for Texas. Mrs. & Mr. Robertson here this afternoon. I received a long letter from my precious darling husband. The first few pages were *very laughable*—but the latter part made my heart ache. Oh! *to act* right. My precious Saviour direct me and give me more of the spirit of thy own self! I feel truly sad tonight—*Home* and *Heaven seem far away*. Ma, was *your spirit* around your *lone* child to night; when she gaized so sadly upon the beautiful star lit sky? There was a some thing whispered it in my heart. Were you beseeching Heavens blessings upon one thine. May that "all wise Being" hear and answer your prayers.

Saturday 28th

We have such cold weather—looks like it might snow. The sun hasn't shown for several days. I still feel badly—Have been busily engaged this week making *baby clothes* for Mrs. R-.[43] Had a negro wedding at the church this morning. They had a white & red flag & blue flag. I presume one had been married before. That is the way the *french do*.

Sunday 29th

Lovely day. I walked out with Mrs. M. R- saw Dr. Young who told us George D. Prentice had been sent from Washington to Richmond to negotiate for Peace. Saw the new enrolling officer who has been sent to take Captains Favrot's place—he goes above.[44] I commenced a letter to dear huss this afternoon. I fear we shall have bad weather soon.

Monday 30th

Sure enough—been cloudy all day with little showers—not very cold. I received a dear little letter from Howard this morning—brought from Shreveport by Cou[l] Wilson & to Abbeville by Mr. Ewing. It contained 250$ new issue, said he would write again in a few days, so I anticipate getting another missive in a short

---

42. Young Mrs. Foote is either Evelina* or Amelina, Henry's wife.
43. Bond underlines the words with wavy lines.
44. Lt. Col. Henry M. Favrot was of the Second State Guards Battalion.

time. I finished my letter & sent it to the office—will go tomorrow. Mrs. R- here this afternoon.

Tuesday 31st

Cloudy disagreeable day—east wind—so bad for me. Howard wrote me of the death of Mr. James Wilson. He was a Marylander—but has for a number of years resided on Lafouche bayou La where he had a plantation. He it was, who was so kind to come for me, to go see my husband at his house, when the Yankees [had] driven him from his home, an exile on Berwicks bay; And after many weeks had elapsed, he succeeded in reaching Mr. Wilson's—by crossing *the lakes* in a skiff at night, being secretly piloted by friends. We traveled all night through a fog & reach there after sun up. I remained with my husband two days—when he was obliged to leave as secretly as he came. The family were very kind to us. I became very much attached to Mrs. Wilson, who is a very agreeable & kind french lady. I do not know why he went to Md. or what disease he died with. Old Mr. Foote here to day. I could not talk to him—I felt too unwell. Young Mrs. R- spent nearly all the afternoon here, she looks quite *respectable now.* We have a new drug store—very near—from New Iberia, Dr. Blanchard, & Dr. Lablou.

Wednesday 1st

Rainy disagreeable day—did not get any letter. Mrs. Ellis's woman died last night—buried this evening.

Thursday 2nd

Still bad weather. I expect we will have rain all this morn.

Saturday 4th

Cleared off this afternoon. Mrs. M.R- here till near dark.

Sunday 5th

Rained all day—Cousin Rebecca got a letter from Wellie yesterday. Poor fellow—he had been suffering with his foot—had gotten a thorn in it. He said, "tell sister Mitt I & two others take turn about in reading a chapter in the testament she gave me, every night before going to bed, & one of the men is very religious, & explains the parts we don't understand." Dear fellow. Oh, I pray the dear Lord to be ever with him—blessing the words he hears—may each word be a seed of righteousness falling deep in his heart, & there germinate & bring forth good fruit—

I have been writing to Peggie & Laura to day—expect to send them by Dr. Abadie.

Tuesday 7th

A large funeral at the church this afternoon. The lady who purchased a white dress from me to be married in about 10 months ago; she died in child-birth—her babe was born dead—she had three physicians with her. Her husband was Mrs. Dr. Abadie's brother. Poor man! they say he is dreadfully distressed. Her father is very wealthy & the priest had all the ceremony of the church. Mrs. Young said 'he got paid for very knock of the *bell*."

Wednesday 8th

I fully expected a letter from H- to day, but am disappointed. Mrs. Hall, & Mrs. Whittington here after dinner. Mrs. Ellis came & offered her hand to me—but I refused it, because she had told a story on me to Mrs. Hall—& prevented her from using my candle mould when she sent for them. I told her why I did not give her my hand & she said I was mad with her—I said no but I am hurt, "yes," she says "you are mad & I am too" & out the door she went; so let her go. She is a very foolish woman.

Thursday 9th

Pa's birth-day. I hope he is enjoying all the comforts of mind & body he can. I felt sad to day. Went to see Mrs. Foote who is quite sick—After dinner went to Mrs. R-'s, found Miss Mary Wilcoxen there. Old Mrs. R. & Mrs. Murry R- gave the Methodist particular gause. They were not very respectful to my feelings. Old R- said "*All* the *Methodist were grand rascals*—they were a *set* of *rascals*." She knew my parents were Methodist & I had belonged to that church. What makes the Episcopalians so uncharitable to other denominations? surely it is not the spirit of Christ. My feelings were truly hurt. From what Miss Mary said I should think she is a methodist, or her family are. I called to see Mrs. Patrick.

Friday 10th

Lovely morning—cold—very heavy frost. The negro man who has been staying in the yard a good deal & who I suspect was *Minttie's beau*, was taken out of the kitchen last night before cousin R- had gone to bed—by Dr. Reed & others—& shot so dreadfully in the face that they say he must die. I suppose the men were drunk—We had never seen any thing amiss with "Dave" & allowed him to stay here at nights.

I went up to Dr. Abadie's this morning, but both he & his lady were absent from home. The day has been so charming I have passed it mostly in walking. After several days of inclement weather, I can fully appreciate the sun-shine.

Saturday 11th

Called to see Mrs. Foote a little while—found Mr. F- busy packing up & sending his things down to the place; his wife is to sick to be moved—but he (*man like*) has set his mind on moving now & regardless of sick women does so. I believe his wife will not go now—the Dr. has forbidden her removal.

This morning old Mrs. Foote & Miss Mary spent with us. I made them laugh very much at the "old woman's Raid" in Maryland. It is jolly! I walked home with them. I met Dr. Abadie as I was returning home; he said if I would go to France, he was sure I would be cured. I could scarcely hear him speak.[45]

Sunday 12th

Went to see Mrs. Foote. Old Mr. Foote & Miss Mary [Wilcoxen] called before we had eaten breakfast—on their way to the bayou to take the boat for the plantation. I felt very sorry to say "good bye." I eat my breakfast as fast as I could & run down to the bayou to see them off but too late—the boat was gliding down, & I only had the sadisfaction of seeing at a distance my friends again. It was such a lovely morn—but clouds soon gathered thick over the blue sky, & by 12 o'c they had every appearance of rain—but the sun occasionally peeped out at us: & I went to see Mrs. Hall—who I found quite unwell. Mrs. Sophie R- walked that far with me—then went to see Mrs. Ellis. I found Mrs. Spaulding there, who walked home with us—we visited the grave yard—found some of the tombs blown over & completely ruined.

Monday 13th

Rainy all day—wind blew good deal—some thing like March.

Tuesday 14th

The sun has just paid us a visit which I hailed most joyfully. I shall have to be housed as the roads are too muddy for *me* to walk.

Wednesday 15th

Gastal & *his wife* were married last night by Mr. Eugéne, after living together 10 or 12 years & having several children.[46] I hear he embraced his wife & kissed her several times. Mr. Poyet will marry them over. That must be Abbeville fashion.

Disappointed again today not getting a letter. I hear there is an armistice of 90 days between the United States & Confederacy—if such is the case, the war is over. God grant it be so. Davis I hear has sent commissioners to Washington.[47] I visited Mrs. Foote this afternoon. Mrs. M. Robertson & Mrs. Spaulding there.

45. French medical schools were thought to be cutting-edge. This view was especially strong in the Creole culture of south Louisiana. See Crete, *Daily Life in Louisiana*, 181. Dr. Abadie was also suffering from consumption, and his difficulty speaking was likely caused by throat ulcers.

46. Bond refers to Francois Gastall, a carpenter, and his wife, Lody. The couple had three children.

47. In early February, Jefferson Davis had agreed to send Vice President Stephens along with other delegates to meet with Lincoln and Seward. The conference broke up, however, after Davis insisted upon the recognition of southern independence.

Thursday 16th

Lovely bright morning. I had just a cup of milk & a slice of light bread sent me—quite a treat! Dined at Mrs. R's to day—took a walk with old Mrs. R- went to see Dr. Abadie this afternoon met there Dr. Lablas & Capt. Mouton our en-rolling officer—was very much pleased with his manner; he had visited Maryland several times—knows my husband very well.[48] As we were returning from Dr. Abadie's [we] saw the "bride"—she was walking on her gallery—had on a green dirty cottonade blouse, which did not reach her feet by a foot, exposing to view her bare & red legs—her feet had shoes—but not tied, & her face did not look like it had been washed since she was married. Great bride!!!

Friday 17th

Lovely day—I called on Mrs. Henry Foote and Mrs. Senette (Mrs. George Foote's sister) who reached here last night.[49] I also took a walk with them & Mrs. Robertson to show them the beauties of Abbeville. Dr. Lablas loaned me Frank Leslie's ilustrated news, a New York paper. There seems to be grounds for hope for speedy peace—I pray God it may shortly come.

Saturday 18th

Another lovely day—I'm not feeling well to day—feel rather achy. I walked around to Mrs. Patrick's this morning—whilst there Mrs. Robertson sent for me to come dine with her. I did so—after which she & I took a long walk. [S]he came home with me. I was very tired—had not been home long before old Mrs. R-, Mrs. Henry Foote & Miss Sennette came—they remained 'till dark—Giving us an ac-count of the Yankees down on the Teche. Madam Henry would go into Franklin nary every day & gather up all the news regarding the yankees,[50] then at night some where between 12 & three o clock our scouts would come to her house—she would get up & cook supper for the poor fellows & tell them all she could learn about the enemy. One Yankee dressed in confederate clothes (for the purpose of spying I suppose) asked Mrs. Fuséliar for ducks,[51] she did not know what to say to him, & appealed to Mrs. Foote in french—which language the Yankee did not understand. Mrs. Foote told the yankee, "did he expect to take all the fowls from them? [A]nd what were they to live on? his reply, "live on feathers." [S]he told him—"if he was used to live on feathers, 'twas more than she was, & she never ex-pected the Yankees to bring her to that. The fellow went off biting his lip.

48. Eraste Mouton was captain of Company A, Twenty-sixth Louisiana Infantry.

49. Mrs. Henry Foote was Amelina Foote was George Foote's* sister-in-law. Her husband, Henry Foote, was a merchant and landowner in St. Mary Parish. Mrs. Foote would have been thirty-one years old in 1865.

50. Bond refers to Mrs. Henry Foote (Amelina) as Madam Henry.

51. See entries of 5 July and 25 September 1863 for more information on the Fuseliers.

Sunday 19th

Cloudy & windy—after yesterday's lovely sunshine, this gloomy weather makes me feel gloomy. The sun set, last evening, perfectly cloudless, giving us every reason to expect a bright one to day, but alas! like many of our brightest visions brings but gloom & sorrow. Mrs. M. R-, Mrs. Spaulding & Mrs. Patrick called this afternoon—they, cousin R-, & myself took a long walk—I laughed so much my sides ached—

Monday 20th

Went to Mrs. Foote's this morning[52]—They were busy packing up to move to the plantation. Mrs. M. Robertson, Miss Senette & myself took a long walk—I remained at Mrs. Foote's till after 12 o'c, laughing & making them laugh. They said they wished I lived close by them; but I told them they would get tired of me. They told me all about Mrs. Gordy's death.[53] Poor creature, I cannot believe all that was said of her is true! I came home to dinner, after which I finished a letter to Howard & enclosed Wellie's in it to send by courier to morrow morning—Captain Mouton will send it for me; I went back about 2 o'c to bid adieu to the ladies—stayed 'till their carriage rolled off. I read several verses of Mrs. Gordie's poetry to Mrs. Henry & Miss Lelia Senette—they were very much pleased with it. Mrs. Henry Foote gave me a cordial invitation to pay her a visit, which I hope some day to do. I liked her manners very much. They left about 4 oc. I called upon Mrs. Dr. Young—gave Mr. Eugéne the "Rebel Sock," to republish for my benefit.[54] Came over to Mrs. R-'s. We took a walk down the bayou. I purchased some oysters for sugar—8 lbs for 100 oysters. Captain Mouton called to get my letter, such a time as he had making me understand about the direction of my letter. I laughed till I really scarcely had *an idea*. I expect he thought I never had a very *bright one*. He insisted upon [me] giving him another envelope to put my letter in—but at last he directed one to Dr. Master's Surgeon General of Shreveport. I took it, quietly put it back in my book when he was going he again insisted I should give him an envelope—I laughingly called on cousin Rebecca to see how *stingy* he was—he was determined I should give him that envelope. At last I give him one not directed. I have been laughing since every time it has passed my mind. And I expect he has indulged in the same. I really would like to know his opinion of me after this evening's chapter of mistakes.

---

52. Evelina Foote.

53. Bond refers to her friend Carrie E. Plumlee.*

54. Bond refers to a poem by the popular North Carolina writer Mary Bayard Clarke, whose work was often published in periodicals under the pen name "Tenella." Bond asks that the poem be reprinted in the local newspaper, *Le Meridional*.

Tuesday 21st

Mrs. Robertson came, set till dinner time—Captain Mouton sent me paper to make him some envelopes this morning, I did so; they were for official documents— He said last evening he wishes I would lend him my *journal* as he had nothing these long evenings to amuse him. I told him I would exchange mine for *his*, as I want to be *amused* too. He did not have one—but after studying a moment he seemed to have received a "bright idea"—for he proposed his wife's should be *his substitute.* I recon his wife would have the same objection as I have to the exchange.

He also expressed a desire to see one of my "blow up" letters to my husband (as I expressed my intentions of treating said individual to "one," if I shouldn't get a letter from him wednesday) as he had never seen one—never got one himself—I told him never mind Madam Mouton would favor him with one doubtless in the course of time—he hadn't been married long enough yet (only six months.) "Ah, but she don't know how—besides I never give her cause—for *I* write *every day.*" Well I said—perhaps you haven't given her cause *yet*, but as to her *knowing how*, I'll bet she'll find out—if she comes down here—I'll give her *some lessons.*" "No! no! he cryed—you shall not go see her," but I persisted I most *assuredly* would call upon said lady. I had a buggy & horse promised me, when ever I wished to ride. But he contended, "I will proclaim "*Marshal Law*," and you can't get out of town without a pass from me, and I won't *give* you one." He had me there. But, woman like, I said I would be *sure* to get out.

Wednesday 22nd

Washington's birthday! I really had forgotten it was till I wrote 22nd then as by instinct it came to me. We have so much else, these troublesome days, to fill our minds; we nearly forget the Father of our country, Ah, too few follow His example *now!*

Again am I doomed to disappointment! no letter! I really felt so provoked when I heard "no letter for *you*," that I resolved I would not send another line to Howard till I received a letter from him. I can not conseave why he *don't write.* Well the best for myself is, to *bear* it just as well as I *possibly* can. Rain all day! Will it ever be good weather for a walk! Cousin R- got a letter from Mrs. Powell—who wrote in good spirits—just heard of her son's escape from prison in Bolto—I should like to hear the particulars. Cousin R- too disappointed did not hear from her folks.

Thursday 23rd

Has been raining all day. Such gloomy weather! nevertheless I have kept myself from feeling it so much—by sewing reading, & writing—My books are my chosen, choices friends! How I *do* love them! They & I seldom quarrel—sometimes I find a little fault with part of their expression.

Nothing is heard but Peace! peace! peace! in March. Some of the soldiers wives are nearly crazy about it. Mrs. Wise—our next door neighbor—makes me laugh out right. "*Vell*—she says—*vot* for they want to fight any more? I *tinks* they be at it long enough—for my part, my heart hurt me so bad all day—and every thing make me so skeered I hear. I wish Mr. Solomon would come home—I tink & tink all the *vile* about him."

Friday 24th

Another gloomy day—rained hard all night—we kept "high & dry"—but some of our neighbors suffered a small deluge—Mrs. Robertson for instance—one of her servants—Jack—was sleeping in the hall—when he awoke he said he thought he was in a *skiff*. Cousin R- heard there was a letter in the "office" for Mrs. Bond. She posted Mintty off quickly—both of us expected one—she wished it might be for her—I did [not] say any thing—I thought if it was for me—"all right"—if not couldn't be helped. When it came we could not tell for a long time which it was intended for. I believe it was for cousin R-. It was from Rev W. McConnel—our former pastor. He wrote as though *I was dead;* and I expect he had heard I *was,* as *such* was the report some time ago. Mrs. Murray R- here this morning—seems in rather low spirits; I feel gloomy too. Dr. Abadie left, this morning in a schooner for Cuba, where he intends to go to France if his health will permit. I did not know I thought so much of my *old* Dr. till I saw him leave—perhaps, & its more than probable, we will never meet again. Tears fell thick and fast—I pity his poor wife— she is left alone with two little girls one sadly afflicted with spinal affliction—it can not walk & often screams on being touched. I sent a letter to Peggie & Laura Bond, their dates were the 8th Feb.

Saturday 25th

I went to bed last night very sick—had quite fever, feel something better to day—suffered dreadfully with headache this evening—went round to Mrs. Patrick's this eve—met Mrs. M. R-, took a walk—she came home with me, had a romp together.

Sunday 26th

Very pretty day—dined at Mrs. Robertson's came home—found Mrs. Hall & Mrs. Whittington here—after they left, old Mrs. R & I took a walk—could not go very far—felt too unwell—Mrs. Patrick came & sit awhile—also Mrs. M. R.

Monday 27th

Raining, gloomy enough. I feel very badly, coughed nearly all night. Young Mrs. R- here early—in rain & mud.

April 5th

I have been very sick ever since I penned in this book—have suffered a great deal—but have been well *nursed* by *Mintty*—she doing every thing she could for me. And from *her alone* did I get attention or *sympathy*. I received a part of a letter from Ann Lee, yesterday morning—I suppose the other portion got lost out. They were all well at home, though Ann Lee was in Balto. She told me she had seen brother once since she had been there. Oh, I fear he is in the army! It would grieve me so if he was. I have made up my mind to prepare to reach Md this summer, I have sent for a pass so I can go to Terrebonne—from there I will go when pa sends for me. Mr. Robertson returned from Texas the 3rd bring lots of medicines & goods. He brought me 20$ worth of medicines. Mrs. R- gave birth to a daughter yesterday Lela, I believe is its name. Mrs. Hall & Miss Caroline Ewing have just left. I got a present of two bottles of wine to day.

Thursday 13th

Have been kept by illness from writing—Been very sick—still unable to leave my bed. Had a visit from Mr. Barrett this week—he, I think is a truly *good man*. And oh, we had such a nice long talk on *religion*.[55] God surely *answered* my prayer to see *one* who could speak words of comfort to my heart. O! I do love to talk my *blest Jesus,* and what My Heavenly Father does for me. He said my conversation had done him good—had given him a ray of joy in his heart. Thank God for *that*. I have felt happier ever since.

Yesterday morning Mrs. Maxwell came see me. We also had such a sweet talk about God. I really believe she desires to do right, but as St Paul says "What I do that would I *not* do, But what I would do, that do I *not*." I received a note from H- last friday—in it 75$ also sent lots of medicines—dear dear *huss*. He [wants] me to come [to] Mount Lebanon to live but left me entirely to my own feelings about going home. I have not gotten my pass yet. I hope I shall for I want to go home. They say Richmond has fallen, & I think *all* will go soon.[56]

May 10th

Many startling things have occurred, since I penned in this book. Va has been taken back in the Union. Gen Lee & his army surrendered to Gen Grant. Gens Johnson & Taylor have also surrendered. And Lincoln & Seward have been killed, Lincoln was killed by Wilks Booth, the actor, shot through the head. Seward shot & stabbed by Booth's friend. I think the Confederacy must be pretty nearly played out.

55. John Barrett.*
56. Richmond was occupied by Union forces on 3 April 1865.

I received a letter from Ann Lee, on sunday, also one from brother. Oh, how glad I was to hear from them all—dear ma is fat and rosy. How I should love to see their dear faces! Lord direct my ways. Laura Bond has lost her brother Oliver.

Thursday 11th

A council of war is being held in Alexandria Va. between our officers & the Yankees, to come to some terms of peace. Seward is not dead as reported—but recovering from his wounds. Booth has *not* been captured. We have had such unseasonable weather this month; so cold rainy & windy.

Tuesday May 17th[57]

I have gathered all the articals of clothen &e which I think I can do without, & selling them. I laugh at my self; when I take a walk, I generally fill my *pocket*, or a little basket with needles, pins, tape, cotton, & buttons, & if I see any one who looks like they needed such articles I offer for sale my *stock on hand.*

We have had so many rumors of late which conflict with one another. Some say they are going to fight at shreveport, Gen. Smith won't give up. He might as well—for every one knows we are whipped.[58] I received a letter from Howard last saturday—he sent me two nice congress booties—stockings, & lots of little things. He wrote gloomy of our country. If they have a fight there, I would not be supprised if he joined in, or perhaps be drafted in. My Heavenly Father watch over my precious husband, & keep him from all danger. I met with some soldiers from Lee's army—returning home, one had Booth's likeness, the image of him.

Sunday 21st

One week yesterday I commenced selling articals I could do without—so as to get money to take me home. I have done very well so far, I believe I have sold 25$ worth in silver. Most of folks seem to sympathize with me very much & do all they can to help me on. The war must be over! [S]oldiers are leaving their commands by companies—even regiments leave. I hope soon to see dear Howard here. Perhaps *he* can get me off for home sooner. I had such a lovely letter from Mrs. Barrett friday—so full of sweet council & sympathy.[59]

---

57. In this entry, the writing changes, becoming larger and slanted heavily to the right. It looks as if Bond is writing quickly. This pattern continues in the next entry as well.

58. Bond heard correctly that Kirby Smith resisted surrender after Lee's defeat in April. The Trans-Mississippi Department did not surrender until 26 May. Many of the troops and Shreveport citizens, however, disagreed with what they deemed futile resistance and became demoralized. Soldiers began deserting and pillaging government warehouses and stores. See Winters, *Civil War in Louisiana*, 418–26.

59. Charlotte Barrett,* fifty-three years old and the wife of John Barrett, an Abbeville saddler.

June 16th

Month or more has elapsed since I penned in here—Many changes in our National affairs has occurred. Peace is being established over the land. The Federals are at New Iberia where they have been for several weeks. They have black soldiers & white commanders. The country is still infested with Jayhawkers. This town is threatened now. I do not feel afraid of them.

My heart is filled with so much troubles, about Howard. I have not heard from him since Peace. The last letter he wrote me he said if we were conquered—he would leave the country & go to Mexico, he had made arrangements with an officer who would furnish him with transportation.[60] Every thing goes to prove he has deserted me, Oh my heart feels at times as though it would break. I wrote to ma last week, & brother this week to come for me immediately.

I have just finished a letter to Mrs. Wright[61]—going to send it by Mr. Wise to the city—hope she'll send me "something good."

26th

Had a house full of company nearly all day. Mrs. Barrett & her two daughters, & Mrs. Foote took dinner. Mrs. B- is a lovely christian—she comforts me so much by her kind council & advice.

Wellie came home the first of last week, brought no tidings of Howard. I feel *sure* he has gone to Mexico. I have suffered a great deal in mind & have nearly been made crazy by *unkind remarks.* But since sister Barrett's visit I feel more cheerful. I took off my wedding ring to day—It almost felt like a snake around my finger. If *he* has gone to protect [h]is own life at the expense of *mine* I say I have no farther use for *such a man.*

27th

Abbeville begins to show some life. Merchants from N. O. & Houma have arrived within the past week & have filled up several stores with their goods. Wellie left here last saturday evening for Terrebonne. A lady called the other sunday, who I never remember of seeing before & after sitting a while she took from a little basket a sweet bouquet of flowers & presented me. I found out afterwards she was the Sheriff's wife—all are so kind. Yesterday a creole woman brought some not half grown chickens & asked 15 cents apiece in silver—I told her I would give her 75 cts for the 7 she had (they were very little) at last knowing we were going to have visitors to dinner, I told her I'd give 15 cents—no, she says they are already sold. I

60. Gen. Kirby Smith, along with other military and civic leaders, went to Mexico to begin a new life there after the Confederacy surrendered.

61. Mrs. Wright* was in New Orleans.

told her to begone with her lies—After awhile she comes back saying I might have them for 10 cents. I told her I would give her one cent. I would not encourage any one in such sins if I had to go without for a week. I didn't then know where the meal was to come from. Not more than a half hour a man came with 20 fine half grown ones, 10 cts apiece—& it really seemed as though God had sent him to me. I got 12. After awhile Mrs. Barrett came & brought me 5 as a present. Mrs. Foote spent the day, also Mrs. Barrett & two daughters, Laura and Kate.

July 7

Wellie returned today from Terrebonne bringing the blest news. Mr. Bond—dear old huss, was in Terrebonne—he had been terribly burned by sulfuric acid in opening the bottle it exploded burning him dreadfully—he just arrived in the Parish tuesday—will be here in a week to move us down. I feel as though about 500,000 lbs were lifted from my heart. No letters from home.

Thursday

Howard reached here last night.[62] I shed tears of joy just to think he is with me & will go to Md. with me. Mrs. Foote here this evening. The weather extremely hot.

---

62. According to military records, Howard was captured at Monroe, La., on 24 June 1865 and took the oath of loyalty to the Union on 1 July 1865. Upon his release, he stated his destination as Harford County, Md. The burn that Bond mentions likely resulted from his work as a chemist. See Booth, *Records of Louisiana Confederate Soldiers*, 30.

Postscript

AS SHE WROTE her last diary entry, Priscilla Bond's desire was to return to her family in Maryland. She did achieve her goal of returning home, but she died shortly afterward, on 2 January 1866, at age twenty-seven. She was buried in the graveyard at the Watters Methodist Meeting House in Bel Air, Maryland, the church she frequently longed for when she was in Louisiana. In her diary entries of 24 August 1863 and 27 November 1863, she stated her desire to be buried there, calling it her favorite spot and one that her family could easily visit.

During the war, Harford County was spared significant military action, with only one minor skirmish occurring there.[1] The national conflict, however, did little to improve the Munnikhuysens' finances. While Bond had indicated before the war that her family had some financial worries, by 1864 she was concerned that her father did not have the means to pay for her return home or to support her once she got there. According to the 1870 census, the family owned assets worth nine thousand dollars, the same amount listed in the 1860 census.[2]

In spite of difficulties, the family seemed to remain close. After the war, Bond's maternal grandmother, Mary Bond, left Baltimore and moved into Maiden Lane. Bond's brother, William, also remained in his family home and helped his father with the farm. He eventually married Louise (Lou) Wyatt, whom Bond often mentions in her diary, and they had four children. In 1868 Bond's sister Fannie married James (Jimmy) Watters, who had served in the Confederate military with the First Virginia Regiment and then the Maryland Cavalry. After the war, he practiced law and later became judge of the Circuit Court of Harford County. The couple had one daughter and named her Anna. Ann Lee, Bond's youngest sister, remained at home and did not marry. While Bond frequently worried about her

1. Wright, *Our Harford Heritage,* 378.

2. For Bond's references to family finances, see her letter of 21 September 1864. The relevant census records are the 1870 U.S. census, population schedule, Harford County, Md., John Munnikhuysen household; National Archives microfilm publication M593, roll 588.

parents' health, they both lived well past Bond's own death. Her mother died in 1875 at age sixty-five, and her father died in 1877 at age seventy-eight. They were buried near Bond in the graveyard at Watters Meeting House.

Charlotte and Betsy, the household servants Bond inquires about while in Louisiana, were no longer part of the Munnikhuysen household after the war, possibly because the family could no longer afford to pay their wages or support. Because they resided in a border state, they likely had an easier time forging independent lives in postwar Maryland than they would have in other southern states; nevertheless, former slaves and former free blacks in Maryland did not find emancipation to be as liberating as they had expected.[3] They faced resistance and violence as they struggled for the rights of full citizenship. The state did not support the Fifteenth Amendment, and black men received the vote only after the amendment was ratified in 1870.[4]

Howard Bond had accompanied his wife to Harford during her last illness, but he returned to Terrebonne after her death, likely feeling responsible for his family there. In the wake of the war, south Louisiana was in turmoil. Many of the parishes were marked by poverty and violence, oftentimes racially or politically motivated.[5] The Bonds assuredly faced hardships as they attempted to rebuild their lives and to adjust to a postwar reality that was far different from their former lives. In sharp contrast to the 1850 *Debow's Review* article cited in my introduction to the diaries that describes a thriving and prosperous region, a northern journalist's account written shortly after the war describes the area as dilapidated and neglected.[6] Likewise, an 1866 article in the local Houma newspaper contrasted the postwar plantations on Bayou Black to their prewar opulence, concluding: "Those fine plantations present a very different appearance now. . . . The buildings and fences are going to decay and have a very dilapidated appearance. The ditches are fast filling up, and their sides growing up with briars and bushes."[7]

The Bonds' plantation was among those on the bayou that stood in disrepair. By 1872, their property was in foreclosure, and their land was seized and then sold in January 1874.[8] While the Munnikhuysens continued farming after the war, the Bonds did not. Along with many planters in the state's sugar region, they were unable to recover financially from the war. The nature of sugarcane planting contributed to planters' difficulties, as supplies were numerous and expensive. Many

3. Brugger, *Maryland*, 308; Fields, *Slavery and Freedom*, 131.

4. Fields, *Slavery and Freedom*, 134.

5. Taylor, *Louisiana Reconstructed*, chap. 3.

6. Reid, *After the War*, 457–72.

7. "Bayou Black," *Civic Guard*, 9 June 1866.

8. "Abstract of Title Number Seventeen Hundred and Ninety 'C,'" 68–69.

planters had lost their equipment and sugar mills, and replacing them was an ex-orbitant expense, significantly greater than replacing equipment needed for plant-ing cotton and other Louisiana crops. Additionally, planters faced difficulties as they attempted to rebuild because their credit had been based on slave property, and at the same time, New Orleans, the area's financial center, suffered with bank and commercial failures.[9] Expectedly, then, sugar production dropped drastically: in 1860 and 1861, respectively, 229,000 and 459,000 hogsheads of sugar were pro-duced. In contrast, 1864 saw the production of only 7,000 hogsheads. In 1865 the number had improved to 15,000 but still was far short of earlier production.[10] While there had been 1,291 operating cane plantations in south Louisiana in 1861, by 1865 only 200 were still operating.[11]

The Bonds' financial problems could also have been a partial result of Howard's participation in the ambush of Union soldiers in 1862. While most Confederates were granted amnesty and allowed to reclaim their property after defeat, those who were worth more than twenty thousand dollars or who had held a high military office had to appeal for a personal pardon. Howard's implication in the murder of two Union soldiers could have prevented his family's pardon. In either case, the family could not recapture its prewar position.

Josh Bond did not live long after the war. Property records indicate that by 1868 Rebecca Bond was widowed.[12] The 1870 census shows Rebecca Bond as head of a household that consisted of Howard; Wellie; their youngest brother, Barrow; and their sister, Louisa (Sis), who was then sixteen. They claimed no personal wealth. Also, with the loss of his store, Howard apparently could no longer work as a phar-macist; he lists his occupation as machinist. Wellie and Barrow list no occupation. Howard did, however, continue his interest in science, serving as librarian of Houma's Scientific Association. It is unclear if Howard remarried, but he did live into old age. According to the 1920 census, he was eighty-one years old and still living in Houma, Louisiana. He was living alone.[13]

9. See Rodrigue, *Reconstruction in the Cane Fields*, 59.

10. Taylor, *Louisiana Reconstructed*, 316.

11. Roland, *Louisiana Sugar Plantations*, xiii.

12. "Abstract of Title Number Seventeen Hundred and Ninety 'C,'" 68.

13. As the Scientific Association's librarian, Howard posted notices in the local newspaper re-minding patrons to return to their books. See, for example, the 23 May 1868 issue of the *Civic Guard*. Other details are from the 1870 U.S. census, population schedule, Terrebonne Parish, La., National Archives microfilm publication M593, roll 533; 1920 U.S. census, population schedule, Terrebonne Parish, La., T625, roll 634.

Appendix 1

LETTERS

[From John Anthony Munnikhuysen to his son, William][1]
Harford Saturday Jan 14th 1860
Dear William

As it is a rainy day and I am in the house laid up with a bad cold I thought I would strain a point and write you a few lines your letter to your Sister Fanny came to hand yesterday evening but she was not at home which you know is no new thing she is at Stevey Archers[2] Mitt and doctor [George] Archer went up there yesterday and we sent the letter to her

well now I suppose you want to know how we are geting along we are I think doing as well as anyone under similar circumstances we have to hire in doors and out which you know makes it come hard on a poor fellow[3] we had a fine pen of Hogs we had ten and they weghed nearly 15 hundred your ma will make her jack selling Bacon next summer we have lofted 147 barrels of corn and we have about 15 barrels to get in the corn house is full top and bottom and some over at the old house George Gover offered me 100 dollars last Tuesday for 30 barrels he would haul it but I refused to take it Your Uncle Parker thinks I can do better[4]

now dear William you see how we are getting along I am getting old the 9th day next month if I live to see it I will be 60 years old and I have felt age more this last year I am getting quite grey

In the following letters, I have largely left capitalization and punctuation as they are in the originals. When changes have been made, they are noted. Most of the people mentioned are identified in the list of Principal Friends and Family. If a person is not in the list and I have been able to identify them, I provide detail in a note.

1. I have added paragraph breaks to improve readability. I have left the sentences as they were written, however, with no ending punctuation or capitalization to signal a new sentence.

2. Stevenson Archer.*

3. Instead of owning enough slaves to farm his land, John Anthony had either to hire slaves from local slave owners or to hire free black laborers. Bond indicates in her diary and letters that that her family had financial difficulties, and in this letter her father also writes of relative hardship.

4. Parker Lee.*

dear William I know you have a hard time of it but try and bear with Josh Bond while you are with him he is a base man and I want to see him once more to give him a piece of my mind Well William you know you always have a home to go too while I have one so when ever you see fit you can come home I dare say the old proverb is verified in your case their is no place like home, Howard Bond has asked for Mit by letter but I have not given him an answer yet.[5] I don't see how I can object but I don't think I will ever consent to her going out there, Mit has never been used to see negroes flayed alive and it would kill her, Mit is her own Woman and can do as she pleases now

William I must close this letter it so dark I can hardly see I sent you 3 papers you don't mention that you got them I sent you the paper that had the Harper Ferry affair in it, your ma just handed me the girls invitation to Miss Virginia Richardsen wedding to Mr Nelson L Bead

[From Bond to her sister Fannie]

My own dear sister

It is nearly five o'clock, and the evening before my marriage. You have asked me to write you some thing you may look at in after years.

I am hurried and know not what to write. Had I the gift of a ready writer I could fill pages of *heart felt wishes* for your happiness. But, you know, my dearest sister, what the nearest and dearest wish of my heart has been, and still is, for you. That you may be a *christian*. Not in *name* only, but *indeed*. *Tomorrow* I shall resign myself to another—to one I believe to be worthy of me. As the poet says, "The dearest spot of Earth to *me* is *home* sweet, sweet *home*." And I can verify the truth of it. You know how my heart has always clung to my dear old home. And *now* it has become dubbly dear, as I look around on each object so dear to my sight—my heart clings more fondly than ever to the associations of my childhood. I know it is a sad trial to all to give me up. But you all are together, I shall be far away from all my *people*.

It is true there is one who will sympathize my grief. But the heart will often grow sad—and long for the "Loved ones at home." But it is a sweet thought, that there is a place of meeting where parting is no more. My heart is sad to night—sister Fannie, and oh! the memories that throng it. It is filled with sweet, sad memories—

The inserting future is before me. I am going out in the world—leaving the loved of my childhood home. Who can tell the changes that shall take place before I return, should it ever be my good fortune to visit those dear ones again.

But into God's hands I put my trust. *He* has guided me, and I believe He still

5. See Bond's diary entry of 1 December 1859, in which she records the receipt of Howard's letter.

will. Let us never forget to remember each other in our daily supplications at the Throne of Grace. Let us go where we may, the same watchful eye is upon us, the same arm stretched out for our protection, It is indeed a sweet thought that "Our Father" watches over *us all, home,* or a broad, I now say good bye. May God's riches blessings attend you is the prayer of your devoted Sister Mitt

Jan 14th 1861.

[From Bond to her mother]

"Crescent Place" Feb 27th 1861

My darling ma,

I have just this afternoon received, and read your *dear, dear* letter. It was indeed a *treat.* I was feeling a *little* sad, and it has dispelled all *such* feelings. I also got at the same time brother's letter and one from aunt Rebecca [Bond], Hers was one of her *choices gems,* You may imagine the contents. My own ma—your letter of the 16th seemed so like you—so like the manner in which you always speak when talking to me. I was lost to all around me, and imagined myself once more beside your dear side, in *my old home.* O! my ma, my pen can not tell how much I wish to see you and all the ones at home. I do not allow myself to dwell on the theme, less I get too homesick, and if I do not express my feelings of loved ones oftener; do not attribute it to forgetfulness or want of *love.* My love is deeper—purer, and more sacred for you & all, than ever I knew it to be.

I was indeed *truly sorry* to hear you were suffering with your back again. Ma dear do take good care of yourself do not work so hard. You will injure yourself. *None* of us can do without you yet. Even me—so far away, if you were gone—life would almost be a burden to me—although I have dear Howard to live for—yet I believe I should want to die. Ma I imagined I saw you penning my letter, seated on "your old chair," occasionally looking over your "specks" out of the window—perhaps to gain an idea.

I was not very much surprised to learn Pink Norris was dead. It was what I had been looking far. O it is a warning to us all especially the young. God grant—he may be better off. Perhaps his death may be the salvation of his brothers. What does Juliet say about it? Did you see the death of Ben Bond in the paper? He died on the 11th.

Dear Lizzie I suppose will be the next I shall hear of—but what a blissful exchange will be hers.[6] What hope in her death to her relatives. May our last days be like hers. I received a long letter from Ann Lee, the very day I sent one to her; so tell her she must not wait for me to reply to this one—but receive this any and other I should write to the rest, as to her too. Howard and I had hearty laughs over

6. Bond refers to Lizzie Webster, who Bond, in her diary, frequently describes as being ill.

her letter. I am sorry pa's under the painful necessity of chasing the hens to make them lay eggs; for when I left they were performing their duty admirably—and then too I hear pa is so *fat*, he surely must have been very much fatigued from *the exersise*. I'm sorry to hear pa has gotten so very fat, as his *pants* are in danger of having to be turned *hind past before* if not—ma will have to do some patching—and I am sure she has sufficient to do of that kind of work.

Brother wrote me quite a laughable letter, says you, sister Fannie & Ann Lee are quarling over old *chimese*, and have divided all my old ones. I do not remember to have left many. What few things I did leave—sister Fannie & Peggie [Bond] were kind enough to burn *before I left*. I wrote Peggie some time since, am looking for an answer soon. And now my dear ma, I have written nearly four pages—and have not told you how I was—but you may know I'm not very sick—or I should have "said so sooner." I am feeling as usual—gaining strength—I take iron yet, I drink the strongest kind of coffee, after I have finished my dinner, It is always handed after dinner. Laura [Bond] takes it before she's up but I have not gotten so *frenchy yet*. It agrees with me *splendid*. And another thing we have nearly every day—that is oyster gumbo, It is the nicest thing. I have fried oysters for my breakfast nearly every day—they are the nicest—and largest—I ever saw—get them right fresh from the gulf. I want you to have me some sassafras gathered and dried—then rub it fine and keep it till next fall, and if cousin Josh goes on he will bring it to me. They have to pay very high for it here. Get just as much as you please. I will send you a recipe how to make Gumbo—soon. At least how they make it here. They do have elegant eating here, that's the truth. Had some turtal soup the other day, it was splendid. Wellie [Bond] caught some frogs the other day, and had them nicely cooked for breakfast, tried to pass it off for chicken, but I suspected some thing, and did not eat any. It looked very nice—but the *thoughts*. Mr. Stickney (the Episcopal minister dined here on Monday) he is trying to convert me over to his and the church but—I fear I am too far gone a *Methodist* for that. He sent me some books to read, but instead of drawing me to "The church" it shows me more clearly the uncharitableness of its doctrine. No if I ever [chose an]other than the one I now belong, it will be the Presbyterian, Still I can never be any thing but a Methodist at heart.

I wish Pa would get a sertificate from Mr. Valiant for me to join else where, & send it to me. What my conscience dictates to be done—that I will endevor to perform. All here (in this house I mean) are inclined to the Presbyterian church. Even cousin Josh likes it best, And perhaps it is best for me to be with all the rest, For as the good book say, They who are for me, are not against me. It is so dark I can not see—

Howard left yesterday morning about 7 oc to put up the mail, I have not seen him since, and it is now half past six in the evening. He went last night about 15 miles to sit up with the young man that was shot.[7] He is a seckon *Dr. Dance* he will accommodate any body in the world, even if it disobliges himself. I miss him so much. It is the first time we have been sepperated since the 15, I tell you I don't believe I will get a *desease* I must make haste & finish this before he comes, or I want be able to get it done. Howard has just come, the young man is dead, he's name is David Phips, the other died several days ago—his name was James Hagers. He was buried with military honors. Mr [Mathern] McConnell is to preach his funeral sermon on next Sunday. I should have loved to have heard Mr Valient preach Pink Norris's funeral sermon.

Give my love to him & his good kind wife. I have not taken the Protestant yet[8]—will soon. Cousin Josh has just asked me who I was writing, I told him, & he says, "give my love to all" cousin Rebecca sends hers to each one and *all*. Howard sends his to you especially and *you* in *particularly,* Cousin Josh told me to day, he had a barrel of sugar for *me* to send home, I thanked him and told him he should send it—in his name—but he insist not—so I will send it to you—with the promise to put me up some *apples & grapes* next summer, I do not know when he will send it—when he sends the others—as he has several to send to friends now is not that kind? Surely I should feel thankful, and I do. Dearest ma pray for your *children,* I think of you especially on Sunday when I go to church, I go every Sunday that's fit. Love to each one and all—tell pa to write soon. I am looking for sisters Fannies answer—God bless and keep you my own dearest ma

Your devoted child Mitt

Laura says I slept with her last night and through my arms around her, and said now give me a kiss—But I say I did not, she made me write this—so good bye Your child Mitt[9]

[From Bond to her mother]
Sunday May 19th 1861 "Crescent Place"[10]
My own darling ma,

It is now five minutes past four oc by my watch—I have been sitting here up in my room, in the rocking chair, reading your *dear* letter, & looking at your sweet face; till I almost imagined I heard you repeat those words over "Be a true woman

7. See Bond's diary entry of 23 February 1861.

8. She refers to the *Protestant Vindicator,* a periodical that expressed anti-Catholic sentiment. See the introduction for further detail.

9. This note is inserted in the top margin.

10. Bond does not write in her diary in May 1861.

Mitt." For it seems to me I shall never forget them. They surely were words spoken in season, as many others of yours have been.[11] My dearest ma, I have written this much without even telling why I have not answered your dear missive ere this; which I received on Wednesday. I was in bed sick—and you may be sure tiding from home were even hailed more joyfully—if possible—than ever. With yours I also received one from Ann Lee & one from aunt Rebecca. All so *dearly appreciated.*

I said I was sick. Yes, very. I went to bed early Sunday night after being sick enough to have been there several days before but tryed to keep up. I was suffering terrably with boils under my arms three under one arm, two as, or nearly as large as a hen egg. They had to be lanced several times, which of course was very painful. And I *very nervous.* The last one I had lanced, I jumped as the instrument was being applied, and inflicting a very deep & rather dangerous wound. Howard thought at first he had cut a large artery, which he knew to be near there, as the blood gushed out in great quantities. But fortunately it was not so. He was very much frightened, and became very sick; had to go out in the open air to keep from fainting. Wednesday night about two oc I was taken with dreadful neuralgia in my stomach. Cousin Rebecca was up with me three or four hours applyed mustard till it drew a blister but did not release me, she and Howard took a light, went out in the garden and got some horse raddish leaves soaked them in hot water, and applied them to my back & stomach in less than 15 minutes I felt greatly released. I felt very sick all the time, and at final—thought I had a solise but there was no window, my stomach, before breakfast—I commenced hickcoughing & throwing up just as I did once before when Lizzie Watters stayed with me (dear good kind girl) don't you remember? It was when Dr. Archer gave me *Velerian* I became also very cold & nervous. Dear cousin Rebecca & Mrs. Campbell were so kind—not saying around about dear Howard Mrs Campbell, had some hot water & mustered brought and placed my feet in—washed & rubed them herself, and covered me up with blankets. I shall never forget her kindness. Howard sent off for Dr. Hemlick, who did pretty much as Dr. Archer did. I continued very sick till late that evening. Howard did not leave me all day. Truly I had reasons to thank God that he had given me such a husband, and had raised me up such good friends.

Had I been cousin Rebecca's own child, she could not shown more feeling. Ill as I was I cold not help noticing the heartfelt tears she wept or feel the warm kisses she pressed on my brow. And Mrs. Campbell too would bathe my face with cologne, and kiss me to show her deep feelings. It may *read foolish* to others ma,

11. Bond also mentions her mother's advice to be a "true woman" in her diary entry of 29 September 1861 and in a letter to Ann Lee on 4 December 1863.

but not to you to see how *your child* was cared for when far away from her who alone can feel and understand her suffering child. And *know* though out of your reach was cared for and loved, the same she could have been at home. But my own dear ma do not think for a moment *you* were forgotten. Ah, no, how oft did my heart yearned for the caress of *that* hand, be it smoothe or *rough*. None in the world is like it. None so gentle—so loving—or loved as that. None can administer consolation, sympathize like you. And never deem you are for one instant forgotten, or less appreciated by me. Every day I learn how to prize you more. And I pray those you have around you, may now appreciate & love you more & more and my dear sisters & brother, let me say to you now, there is no one in the wide world like you own mother—let her be educated or uneducated, pretty or ugly, rich or poor, it is all the same, there is none who will love, bear with your little faults, over look the *many things* in you like her; she is ever ready to excuse you, and make the best of your faults, and short-comings. Nor will you ever know what a treasure she is till you have lost her. I feel what it is now to be sepperated from her for a while, therefore I know in a measure what it would be altogether. I pray she may be spaired to us, as well as our dear pa—for *both* deserve our *deepest love*—for many long and happy years yet. Rather abruptly did I leave off telling you of my sickness but it is sufficient to know I am much better now. I got up yesterday but did not go down stairs till today when cousin Josh gave me a hearty welcome—and seemed glad to see me down again. The night after I was so sick; he would not go to sleep till cousin Rebecca went up stairs to see how I was, it then being about 11 oc and he in bed. That showed what he thought of me. Mrs. Barrow came to see me. She is a very kind lady. I was truly sorry it so happened I was sick last week, as the week before the ladies of Terrebonne met in Houma at Mrs. Goods, and organized a sewing society for the getting and making up clothing for the "Guirot Gards" of this parish, now at Pensecola, I had taken six shirts to make; but only made one when I was taking sick. But Howard so good & kind—subscribed 10$ for me so they would not think hard of me.

I am truly glad to hear all are well at home; or at least much better. Tell cousin Lizzie I could not begin to say how glad I was to get her dear letter,[12] she shall hear from me as soon as I feel more in the spirit of writing though from the length of this one would suppose I *was*. I'am writing home now which makes a difference. Howard wrote to sister Fannie while I was sick. Howard looks thin and badly, is not very well. He will take the one for sister Fannie soon, and send it her. Tell her not to dispair of getting it.

Cousin Josh will not be on this summer that is, there is not much chance of his

---

12. She could refer to either Lizzie Lee or Watters.

traveling North. I am distressed about dear old Maryland, I *still hope* she will come with her *sister states,* and not allow herself to be ruled by an *Abolition President, Every* drop of blood in my veins is *southern* It is impossible for Maryland to get off either way without war she will have [a] fight, and that for the south. I will not till compelled believe she will go with the North, there are many warm hearted southerners there to keep her true. Every body here are eagerly watching Maryland—hoping for her, and longing to see her bravely acknowledge herself independent of "*Old Abe.*" For my part, if she allows herself to be governed by Black Republicanism I would not live on her soil. I would feel myself under a *despot*—an *arbitrary tyrant.* I think Maryland of all other states has put up with enough and now if ever, she should no longer be subject to such laws. The Union in proper hands was a glorious one—but in such as now reigns over it—makes it a despot's country—where neither land or people are safe, one confiscated—the other murdered. But all I might write or say will never make it better. All, as you say, to be done now is to leave it in the hands of an all wise God—I do pray he may not be against us but with us, to direct and sustain us in every condition. My dear ma, my letter has grown long and not much to interest you. Could I be near you—how I could *talk.* I try to imagine I see you all, and fancy cousin George [Glasgow] and Dr Archer there. Is it so? I do hope all are well this lovely Sabbath eve. Howard going to take me riding after it gets cooler, for this has been the warmest day this summer. Dear Ma I feel so sorry I did not get the sugar off before, but so it is, It can not be sent now—I do hope the time will soon come when we will be able to do so. Tell pa to keep in good spirits about hard times. Better days will come. Give my love to him and tell him he don't know how I would prize a letter from him—to write soon your letters do me so much good I will write home soon again if the mails continue. Love to every body who ask for me—tell them *not one* are forgotten by *me.* Howard sends his best love to you and each one. Tell the girls & brother to *write me* soon and often. I also got another letter from Ann Lee. Receive the devoted love of your

child Mitt

Cousin Rebecca sends her love, sis hers also, says she is going to write to cousin Wm. Now my dear ma good bye once more. May God in His wisdom watch over and protect you all, is the sincerest prayer of your child Mittie Bond[13]

13. In the top margin Bond writes a lengthy list of family and friends to whom she sends her greeting.

[From Bond to her father]

May 24th 1861

My dear pa,

It is very late at night—I have only a few moments to pen you a few lines so you may get them, when you receive the bag of peas Howard sends you, also some okra—it is very nice plant—plant it like you do beans, in the corn, it will run on the corn, I mean the corn peas, The okra you plant like you do peas, only it does not run. It makes elegant soup—and is very nice boiled, with butter, sault pepper & vinegar on it.

I thought I better tell you about it, for fear you would not know its use. I have been looking for a letter from *home* every mail day this week. I hope I shall not be disappointed next.

Are you all well at home? I sincerely hope so. I'm suffering with my back, otherwise I am well. I hope dear pa you are entirely recovered from your recent attack, and that your health will be hereafter *good*. You can not imagine how much I think of *you all*, and now that *war* is a settled thing in our land, It is hard to be sepperated, at such a time. But we have the same kind Providence over us where ever we may be. Let us still place confidence in Him, who lets not a sparrow fall unnoticed to the ground. I should like much to send you by this mail a long letter but can not—I will endever to write by next mail, which is tuesday. Howard joins me in much love to you, ma, and *all all.*

Let me hear from you soon, dear pa, and

Believe me your affectionate child Mitt

Oh! if the mails are stopped what shall I do!

[From Bond to her mother]

Crescent Place June 5th 1861[14]

My dearest Ma,

Again I am permitted to pen you another letter with the hope of your getting it, as the mails will continue North till the 8th of this month, It goes through Tennessee. I hope then the Southern Confederacy will be able to carry it to Baltimore any how. And now my dear ma, how are you?

You can not conceive how much *I do* want to see *you all.* I try to fancy how you all look & how inployed. I find fancy is not like *reality.* But before I go farther, let me tell I am well, though have not been very well for several days. I have not gained any in flesh since I came south. If anything thinner. I do not suffer with neuralgia like I did. I tease Howard about my being thin, as much as I did you. Howard is

---

14. Bond writes no diary entries in June 1861.

well, & looking better than I ever saw him—*real handsome,* I think. He sends his *best love,* and says I am a very bad girl; so I've written what he said. You need not fear he will not take good care of *me.* Cousin Rebecca says now he has spoiled me.

Cousin Josh, & sis have been spending the day at Mrs. Pearce's have just got home,[15] and we all are under the bar, and such talking, I can scarcely write I said we, now who are we? Cousin Josh & cousin Rebecca, Mrs. Campbell, Howard, Wellie, Barrow, & myself. Howard is chief talker, and is talking how to get rid of old Lincoln. I wish some one would invent some means to give him a *pill.*

O, ma is it not dreadful, our country. It is getting worse—instead of better. O ma will I ever see dear old Maryland again! It seems some times as though I shall never see it again, Yet I will hope I may have that privelage. I do not feel as disappointed, not getting home this summer, as you might suppose; for when I parted from you, I felt it would be many long weary days before I should enter that dear old homestead. I can not dwell on the thought of *home,* without a heartache, therefore I forbear talking of it. Is there prospects of very hard times in Harford? There is here. Every body cryes "*hard times*" Pork is 26$ a barrel, and anything else according. Dark clouds seem indeed right over our heads when & where will they burst? I do often think of poor pa, O how I should love to help him along alittle. But alas I can't now. Tell him he must comfort himself, he has one less to support these hard times.

When did you hear from grandma? Has Anne been confined yet? I feel anxious to hear from *all.* I owe aunt Rebecca a letter, also Peggie. Tell Howard [Munnikhuysen] I will write to him soon as I can. The weather is very warm, and musquitus very troublesome. It is with difficulty I write, even under the bar, The postage raised, to ten cts, beside three cts for "United States" postage.

Cousin Rebecca sends great deal of love to you & all. O, she is a dear good Mother to me, just as good as she could be to her own child. Brother can tell you what a fond mother, to her children, she is. In fact *all* are as good & kind to me, as they can be. Tell brother, I persuaded cousin Josh to have shutters for the parlor, he had them done and then I asked for curtains he gave me beautiful lace muslin ones. So you see he tryes to please me.

I got the certificate of membership, It does indeed seem the last link which bound me to Harford is now broken. I have not joined church, but expect to, in a few sundays. I feel very much at home in the Presbyterian church. The people are very kind. I mean the members. I still feel like a *Methodist* and expect always to feel so.

When did you see cousin Cass Gover? Give her my love, and tell her I often

---

15. Phoebe Pierce, a Terrebonne Parish plantation owner from South Carolina.

think of the many *talks* we have had together, and wonder if we shall ever have another.

Give my love to cousins Juliet and George. Juliet & all the children. Uncle Jim & aunt Dillie, Uncle Parker aunt Mary all the children. Mr. Watters and family, Tell dear cousin Lizzie not to think I have forgotten her, I think of her often, and shall never forget her kindnesses to me. Love to aunt Nancy and family. Mr. Hendows and family. Cousin George, Mr. Stump, and Dr. A- Tell sister Fannie to write me soon & oftener. O the letters from home are so dear to my heart—do send them often.

Ann Lee must write me soon I love to get her letters. I must now stop. It is quite late. I will try [to] write a longer [letter] next time.

Ma do write soon to your poor child, and give her good advice—for she needs all she can get—to help her along.

May God in His mercy take care of my dear parents, brother & sisters, is the prayer of your devotedly attached child

Mittie Bond

Love to each one & *all*.

[From Bond to her sister Ann Lee]
Houma April 13th 1862[16]
My darling sister

I have written many letters home, since last Fall but none so yet have reached me. I feel well assured you all, have tried every means to get letters to me—nor do I know if one of mine has ever reach home. I will still trust to God I may hear shortly from you; and that this may go safely to you. I do not feel very much encouraged to write—but will indever to cheer you up all I can. In regard to the state of my health; it is quite good indeed. I'm much better than I ever thought I should be again. And they say I am looking much improved. Tell my precious ma, not to give herself an uneasiness about me. If I knew she & all of you were doing as well as I, I should feel very much happier about all at home. But I can not help feeling very uneasy sometimes. I fear some one is sick and dear, dear Ma, is seldom out of my mind. I am looking every day for a letter from my old friend Dr [Archer] I hope to hear some tidings from home he nearly always gives me some news from old Harford. I heard from him a few weeks since—he was quite well then—but had been a *little sick*. I have sent two letters to him to send home for me & do hope they may have reached you ere this. You will see, Ann Lee, by the date of this, I am in town.

16. Bond writes no diary entries for April 1862.

I am staying with Mrs. Helmick—came sunday morning. I have been here since. Dr. H has gone to "Corinth" to render all the assistance he can to the poor wounded soldiers there. I suppose he will be home the last of this, or first of next week. I am doing an *act* of *charity* by staying with his *old* woman while he is gone. She is a Virginian by birth, and a very sweet and estimable lady. One I think a great deal of she & the Dr. Tell Ma they are *Methodist.* I know that is a good recommendation to her. Howard too is in Houma all day attending to the store whilst Mr. Calhoun is away on business. He was here to breakfast, Is very well, would send his love if he knew I was writing, but I will let him know before I close. They are all well at Crescent Place, except cousin Josh. I suppose he never will be much better, as I wrote before—he has Paralysis. The Dr does not believe he can possibly get over it—his age if nothing else will prevent his recovery. Poor fellow! Death seems far from his thoughts; nor do I dare venture a reproof—or a word of warning. Oh! it is so distressing to hear him blassfeaming God, when we do not know but that may be his last word.

Dear cousin Rebecca is in constant dread all the time. O, she is so good to me—so kind & all I could desire a mother in law to be. I do indeed feel myself to be fortunate in obtaining such a Mother. Wellie & Barrow are going to school. Wellie is *taller* than Howard. Barrow grows too but slowly. Sissie is a dear little loving child—not as pretty as she was when I first came, her hair is cut short on her neck & not so becoming as curles. Laura is at Mrs. Barrows, spending some time with a lady from Orleans—a Miss Bright. They seem to be taking life easy riding a horse back before breakfast & late in the evening. Laura has grown very fleshy—she is about my height. Is considered quite pretty and I believe has a *serious* beau, a cousin of Mrs. Barrow's & bearing the same name[17] I could like Laura much better if I did not know so much about her that is not very *flattering in its nature,* I hope none of you will speak of the latter to any one. Well here I have written ever so much, and have not talked about any one of my dear ones at home. O! I could fill pages telling how much I wish to behold your dear faces but what is the use—for that you know and I will not distress any one by the distress I feel at this terrible seperation. I do love you all so dearly and feel this seperation to be almost unbearable some times. Truly has God said, "As our days so should our strength be." I have heard of Mary Cass's Death, but only that she died with scarlet fever, & left a little babe. I feel so anxious to learn all the particulars of her death. Oh!

Give my love to all who ask for me. I have not heard from Dr A for a long time—suppose I shall not now. God bless you. Pray for your sister & brother Howard.

17. Josh Barrow; see the diary entry 25 December 1861.

[From Bond to her mother]
Crescent Place May 4th 1862[18]
My very precious Ma,

Again with pen in hand am I seated to write you, tho fearful this may never reach you. O! how little we prized the privelage of holding free converse with each other, even twice a month and now are almost if not completely deprived of that blessing—truly blessings brighten as they pass from us. How is my precious ones this day? O how my heart longs once more to behold their dear faces! But my dear ones, I can bear it better if I know all were well and cheerful & not grieving about you. Do not grieve for me precious ma, God will never leave or forsake your poor child. He has strengthen'd me thus far & He still will—only pray more for me & be steadfast with the *Faith*. "Bless the Lord O my soul and forget not all his works, bless his Holy name." O how off that portion of scripture comes up in my mind. It is so beautiful O! my precious pa & ma every time you bend the knee at the throne of Grace—pray for your poor children here that the path of duty may be made clear to us & we may walk here in with a steady faith, looking into the hills from whence cometh our help. O how difficult it is to pursue the right path besieged as we are by so many paths which are smooth and flattering to our mortal sights. Had I you my precious ma to give a word a sweet council in season, how much easier could I surmount my troubles. Truly may it be said every heart knows its own sorrow. Mine has various ones some times. Our national troubles make my "soul dark" then this dreadful separation from loved ones cut off from ones hearing whether they are dead or a live. That, without another thing is enough to fill ones soul with sorrow. And nothing but the grace of God could have help me bear up under it. "His grace is all sufficient." I do not allow myself to dwell upon those sad things often. I know it is not right. I have given you all in the hands of the Lord. His will be done I try to say—and yet I fear my heart is still filled with a sorrowing spirit. We have troubles at home too, of which I have in several letters home mentioned—or at least in part. It is the ill health of cousin Josh. He you know has had the palpatation a number of years & the Drs say it is the cause of the stroke of paralysis. It has been about three months since he was taken. He is not getting any better but continues about the same. It is a thing mortally impossible for him to get over it. It is all over his body *inside* & *out* but can use his limbs yet but with some difficulty. But the most dreadful thing is Death seems so far from his thoughts, no one dare venture to speak to him on the subject for fear of exciting him and the Dr says he must be kept from all such—but O, if you were to hear the

---

18. With this letter Bond begins cross-writing, using paper sparingly by writing both horizontally and vertically on the page.

oaths & curses heeped upon every thing that don't suit him, it would make your blood run cold.

My heart stands still almost sometimes. When I first came here, I use to talk to him about right & wrong—but I soon found it would do more harm than good. I pray God I will not be held responsible for any of his sins. I pity him from the bottom of my heart, but I can [not] love or respect him. I try to pray for him but I feel *so little hope* in his ever turning from his idols, that I fear it will do no good.

Dear cousin Rebecca is kept so anxious all the time—truly she has drained sorrows cup. The rest of the family are very well—Laura is at home now she is fat & hearty—has not had a day sickness since she's been here. She does not seem to be affected by being blockaded from home. I can not think she has natural feelings for her *home people*. In fact she does not seem to have any *real right* affection for any one but Mrs. Barrows—and Mrs B- is blinded to her *faults*. Laura has some *few* redeemable traits and others are *abominable*. They are heartily tired of her here, and she seems not to care wether she's loved or liked, so she gets what she wants. If I had been in her place, I should have left long ere this, while I could have got home. If she had any sensibility, or self respect she would. But do not for the world speak of this out of the house—I only intend it for *your household*. Howard is very well, sends lots of love to *you & all all*. He is still with me & you may be sure I will keep him as long as I possibly can. In fact he could not well leave the plantation now his father is confined to his bed—and is not willing for Howard to leave the place. He finds a great deal of fault with H- but is never sadisfied if he goes away till he comes back & watches for him, equal to *pa for brother when he goes to Balto* Wellie & Barrow go to school. Wellie has many noble traits of character but they need culture *sadly*. O the example these children have had set them from their cradle. What an account their parents will have to answer. I fear it will be a fearful day with them, more *especially* cousin Josh. Sissie is a dear little affectionate child— as delicate as a flower. Perhaps it would be a mercy if she should be transplanted, ere the heart becomes corrupted by her surroundings to the garden of Eden. It seems to me parents should never grieve for their little ones, when God takes them to be with him—to know no sin, nor sorrow. I feel thankful *I have* here not one to be subject to such surroundings.

Doubtless dearest ma, you have felt some uneasiness on that score; let me release your mind. I am not in *any way* calculated to make you grandma, nor do I ever expect to be. I feel thankful I have not any such *responsibilities*. Please don't let any one see this.[19]

I have just got a lovely boquet—I wish I could give it you. Ma I was sick the

---

19. Bond draws a box around this information to call attention to its personal nature.

other day & while being on the bed thinking if you were thinking of me—some verses, or rhymes, popped in my head, & I wrote them down. I will send them to you, don't show them to any one. They are only for your benefit. *Are you thinking of me Mother*[20]

Are you thinking of me Mother,
    Are you thinking of your child?
We have not seen each other,
    For a very long, long while.

My heart aches badly Mother,
    To hear your gentle voice;
To feel thy loving kiss Mother
    That makes my heart rejoice.

Oh! that I was nere by Mother
    Close kneeling at thy side
My faults are very many Mother
    And I wish thou, me to chide.

Oft I think of that sad morning
    When I bid you all adieu;
My sky was dark and lowering,
    And my joys very few.

But I'm happier far dear mother,
    Than when I gave my hand;
To leave *you all*, my Mother,
    For this strange and distant land

My husband's kind and true Mother,
    As man can be to woman,
But in all the world there's no other
    I love like I love you.

The last stanza does not rhyme, but it will do, they are "my sentiments exactly." I have written a long letter and have not given any war news. But I had better drop—such subjects, perhaps they might strand my letters progress home. It is enough to say New Orleans is in the hands of the *Yankees*. And we are cut of from all communication from the rest of the world. We live surely in a little world of our own. How comes on brother & sister Fannie & Ann Lee are they well. God bless them

20. Bond writes this poem in her diary on 26 July 1862.

all & you my dearest Ma & Pa. I still pray for a letter from home. I sent Ann Lee one by way of Houma. I hope she will get it. How are all of my dear friends in Balto? My love to all especially dear old grandma if she is yet living. God bless her & strengthen her in this day of sorrow. Mary Cass's death truly is sad our loss is her gain no doubt. I have not told you that I still enjoy a good share of health. My back ache has nearly left me very seldom indeed have one.

We have plenty to eat if we are blockaded, of course there are some luxuries we are deprived of but what of that these times. We can not get flour. I often wish I could give you some sugar for flour. I do sincerely hope you are not suffering for the comforts of life. God will take care of you all.

I am busy knitting stockings for Howard.[21] I think you will call me an industrious and economical wife when I tell you I have made all the Howard's clothen, since the war, I finished a vest for him last night, it fits beautiful—I feel quite proud of my efforts. Well how is all the good & bad folks of our neighborhood? Give my love to each and all of my relatives & friends. I have not time to particularize and except, The hearts best love, pa ma sister Fannie, brother & Ann Lee. And may god in his infinite goodness grant we may meet again on earth is the daily prayer of your devoted child. If you think you can get letters to me, direct Mittie P Bond. Give my love to Charlotte & Betsy, hope they are still with you.[22] This is Monday I imagine [them] doing the washing tubs in the kitchen. I can picture Mondays better than any other day.

[From Bond to her mother]
Abbeville Nov 2nd 1863
My dearest ma,

Not long since I sent you a few lines but as I have another chance of sending one I will except it. It almost seems useless to write for I never get any answers. I'm still trusting in Providence & hope I may get a letter from you soon. Oh, is it not dreadful to be sepparated & not even the privlage of hearing from each other these *dreadful times!* I pray all are well at my *dear old home.* God bless its peaceful habitation—may no cloud darken its hearth! I hope my dearest ma & pa that your health is better than it usually is, & my dear brother—what shall I say to you—I hope you are still under the parental roof. I hope you may be able to remain at home—for I do not see how dear pa could do without you. Oh! how I should love to know how every thing is going on at home. Is sister Fannie & *Ann Lee not married?* O! It seems to me I would give anything were it mine to give—to see & hear

21. The sentence that follows in the original letter is not readable. I have omitted it.

22. Charlotte and Betsy are the Munnikhuysen's household servants; see the introduction for further detail.

them talk. Do *talk & think* about me *often*. It does me good to think I am thought of at home—& *missed too*. I often visit "the dearest spot on earth to me," in my dreams—& some times feel your arms & kisses my dearest ma. Oh! shall I *ever* on earth see you my precious ma? If not I'll know you in Heaven—yes my ma, we'll meet never more to part, & O! may we be a *joined family there*.

Ma I got acquainted with a poetist some time since, a lovely creature—who like myself was "away from home," & *mother* & like me not long married—she wrote a piece to her Mother—which is touchingly beautiful more so because it was the last piece she wrote. I will copy & send it you—and my ma consider they are my sentiments to you expressed by another. She has passed away in the spring time of youth—I hope to bloom in the garden above. Her maiden name was Carrie Plumlee.[23] Oh! she loved me so.—I have some long sweet letters from her—one, the last she ever wrote—came after her death! Begging me to come to her—her life was lonely & *uncongenial* with her husband. I then was at the *point of death*—but see, the angel of death left me & took her. One year my dearest ones since I first took sick death seemed to stand waiting for my spirit a long time—the lamp of life seemed almost out. I was given up by two Physicians & the third had little hope—but God has raised me up—Perhaps it was the prayers of the "loved ones at home" that he heard. I *knew* you were praying for me my dear pa & ma, It comforted me so, whilst I suffered—the thought *they are praying for me at home*. Blessed be God! He does hear, & will answer the prayers of *His children*. My health is better—If I get well it will be God who cures me—for man can have nothing to do with it. There are no medicines here for me—"All things are possible with God." *I will* trust in his *mercy & love*.

Cousin Rebecca & sis are well we are keeping house here very cozily together. The rest were well when we heard from them. I have just eaten a dollars worth of oranges—how many do you suppose I eat? Only *2. Cheap!!* You can form no idea I don't suppose how high every thing is. I paid this morning the rate of 10$ for claret wine per bottle. I wish I could get some flannel—I can not get it here—I have to wear it all the time. Tell sister Fannie I sold my red popplen for 40$ & could have gotten more. I often imagine I see in the store room at home—how different is ours—I have not seen flour for an age—my friend Mrs. Robertson (from the E[astern] S[hore] of Md) sends me *real* Md biscuits occationally. When I get it, I pay 1.25 per lb. When you have light bread or roles & good butter think of *Mitt*. Corn bread & beaf is what I live on, not a vegetable except sweet potatoes—I want irish potatoes badly. It is so warm here now I expect it is real cold in Md. Have you got Charlotte with you yet? give her my love & tell her she must not leave *you* How

---

23. Bond records some of her friend's poems in her diary entry of 2 January 1864.

does Betsy come on? Give my love to all my dear relations a double share to G ma & your sisters—my aunts. Write me often and tell me all the news.

[From Bond to Ann Lee]
Abbeville Vermillion Parish
Friday afternoon Dec 4th 1863
My darling sister

My delight for so great and unexpected pleasure as hearing from *home* is far better imagined than described. It seemed as though I should never hear again. Although Hope had *not entirely forsaken me.* Peggies letter was so hopeful so lovely— Oh, how I thank her for it, and my God for His tender care over my darling ones at home! Truly there are no clouds however dark & gloomy, but have some rays of light. Oh to know all are well at home—to know time has not made sad changes around that hearthstone that has been made around others is indeed enough to fill my soul with joy. Peggie writes Ma looks the same—trips about the house like only ma can, letting fall such words of counsel, and reproof as "Oh Coz" "My dear baby" Oh! how those words carried me home. I seemed to be there & heard them as they fell from her lips. My heart yearned for home then so badly I could not help exclaiming, "Oh my home, my home!!" But thank God my strength has been as my day. My troubles & affliction has brought me nearer to the *cross of Christ.* They have convinced me I am a child of Gods & am heir of Heaven—they have convinced me through tribulations only I am to see God & dwell in that house not made with hands.

Darling Ann Lee Peggie writes you are devoted *to your church.* Am I to understand you have come out from the world—& professed love for your savoir? Oh! my sister, God grant it may be so & that my darling brother & sister F- are also partakers of the Heavenly calling. Oh! my blessed sisters & brother perhaps I shall never behold your dear faces on Earth & never clasp your hands in sweet fellowship, here. But O Let us be an undivided family in that better world where parting never causes tears to flow. The wish that lies deepest in my heart is that we all may meet above. I'm rejoiced to hear time has delt gentle with dear pa. Peggie says he never looked so well & in good spirits also sister Fannie & brother she speaks of. Sister Fannie so lively & stays at home a great deal. Oh it seems to me if I ever get home, I'll never want to leave it. Home sweet sweet home. I have not felt like I had a home since I left my old one. My darling sisters prize your house you have never felt the want of one. I have—you have ever had to battle with cold world & receive cold unkind words when you should have had kind ones—I have. Oh your heart has never swelled to bursting for the want of *ma our dear ma* to sooth you by her gentle words, when pain has racked your frame, & your days of Earth seemed so few you never felt your life seemed ebbing away—that never again should you behold that dear face or receive one word of love from those dear ones so far away. I have—all all, I have felt & more too. At such times when those thoughts filled my mind not only was I separated from all my loved ones at home, but from my husband. Those true dear & loving ones were around my bed doing *all* that was in their power to relieve me. But my heart felt a void! It was then I turned to my Savior, who seemed gazing upon me with so much pity and love. I felt I had *a friend above all others*. And Oh! the thought was such a sweet one. I laid my burden at the Cross when thoughts filled my heart. My Savior stood near—I had nothing to fear—home seemed not so far off. *I felt there* were prayers offered up for *me* that *would be answered* and so I was sparred. And I have reasonable hopes that I may yet live to see you all again. My health is better; if my cough was not so bad, I would feel almost well—the disease appears to be confined to my throat. I have no medicines—have given myself up entirely in the hands of my Heavenly Father. I do not pray to live, for I know not the future were I to do so, I might sorely regret it in after years. "Thy will be done." Is my prayer. Do not let my dear ma (I mention her in particularly because pa is more hopeful in disposition) imagine me unhappy for I am not—my mind—thank God is free from care—I never *never* allow myself to be distressed by any occurance—my entire trust is in Him—he doeth all things well. It has not always been in this happy frame; nothing but affliction has brought me to it. The only thing that grieves me is my own proneness to sin. I find it hard many times to take up the cross & put down the Advasary. But I do feel *eager*. God will perfect the work He has begun in me, even if it is through a firey ordeal. My dearly beloved sister—need I tell you how much I want to see you all! And how fervently I pray the unholy war may be ended, & all be permitted to be together an unbroken household? Oh, I need not attempt that I should fail in my pen is inadequate. Three long months have passed since I heard from dear Howard; *hundreds* of miles separate us I trust he is well. I thought when he left I could not live—my sorrow was so great, for I felt it would be along time ere we should meet and I was inconsolable. But "Be a *true woman Mitt*" has helped me in many such instances. Those precious words of my dear ma's. How they have roused every dormant feeling in my breast & prompted me to action—not to give up—but bear bravely on—others had crosses as well as I. But enough. I am delighted to hear grandma, dear grandma is still alive.[24] Give her my love & many kisses. Tell her she is never forgotten by any of us. And my dear aunts—give my love. I feel sorry Ann has a intemperate husband. Oh! I have much to be thankful for in mine. He is so good to me—there never was a better husband. Do not think sister Mittie

24. She writes of her maternal grandmother, Mary Bond.

has grown to be blind—no I can see his faults, but who has not got them. None are perfection. Cousin Josh & the boys are in Texas—we have not heard from them for a long time. Laura writes she is going home soon. She will tell you many things *I can not write.*

I am glad brother is still at home. Give my love & a kiss—If he won't let you give it—Tell *Laura Moores* she must be my deputy. I have not got a letter from any of you for more than two years. You and sister Fannie must write me long letters, send them to cousin Asbury Jarrett & perhaps he can send them to some one in the Federal army & I can get them by flag of truce—

If they knew how much I want to hear from home they surely would let my letters pass. Cousin Rebecca sends much love to you & all—says she never expects to see old Maryland again, Says tell Ma—I don't look much like a sick girl I've got so fat & *rosy*—My complexion it is true is very clear.[25] I am accused of roughing, some times, but I attribute the roses to a sore in my arm which is kept constantly running. Sissy sends her love to *all* particularly cousin Wm says she has not forgotten how he used to carry her up & down the gallery in his arms—but she is too big for that now. She goes to school & is learning french, brother would not know her she is growing very fast—will be *tall* I think. She is naturally a very good child—but of course a little spoilt, Cousin R- is very fleshy—She is very kind & good to me & says she is going to turn all her business over to me as I have more judgment than she. She is certainly the poorest manger I've seen. What would some of my relations think if they knew I was speculating in sugar, I bought two hhd of sugar the other day paid 600$ for the two. I'm obliged to do something for I do not know when I shall see Howard. He gave me 300 when he left, I speculated till I had 1100 then I got my sugar. I am at enormous expense; it is only to pay as I go prompts me to do so. I don't know what H- will think of me. But he generally lets me do as I please; so I have not much to *fear.* I want you all to show Laura some attention when she goes home—she was very kind to me when sick, and I believe would do anything for me. I would love to go on with her—but my *duty* calls me here. Do send me your likeness, & brothers as I have the rest. Is Charlotte still here? Tell here I would give any thing to hear her laugh and Betsy I hope is a good girl—give my love to all who ask after me. Particularly *all* my relations, how is cousin George? Is he in Dixie? Now I must stop. When shall my eyes be regaled with a "letter from home?" I enclose a piece of poetry—they are *my sentiments.*[26] Give my love best love to Ma, pa , brother & sister Fannie. May God in

---

25. Fevers that accompanied consumption often caused the patient to have a flushed or ruddy complexion. The pink cheeks created a deceptive appearance of good health.

26. The poem is no longer with the letter.

his infinite mercy & goodness spare us to meet again. May our Father in heaven protect you all is the prayer of the absent one. Kiss cousin Lizzie W[atters] for me, & give the family much love, I can not now mention all but as they inquire—just give them my love.

Ever your affectionate sister.

Mitt

[From Bond to her sister Ann Lee]
Abbeville Sept 21st 1864
My Darling Ann Lee

I have again taken my pen to try scratch a few lines to my beloved sister. It has not been very long since I sent letters home since then I have I believe been nearer the gate of death than ever was before, but God has raised me up again for what wise purpose He alone knows. I suffered several months with diarrhea but I am now well of that. The last attack was a violent inflammation of the bowels. I had the cramp in my stomach about three days. I came near dieing one day. The Dr considers my being better. I do not cough near so much as I did. I try to keep out of bed as long as I possibly can, & take every care of myself for *all* your dear sakes & my dear Howard's. That is all I have to live for in this world. I pray to be spared to live to go home just to see you all once more, & lay my weary bones down in the grave. I try my precious sister to put my entire trust in that *one* who knows what is best for me & say in all truth "thy will O Lord be done." And I hope you do the same. God knows best what is for us all. I often wonder of what use I am in the world. I can not see I am any except, I suppose, when with dear Howard, I adore him & comfort in trouble. He says I am all the world to him, sick or well. With all my trials & troubles I have so much to be truly thankful for. Howard is the *kindest & best*. There is no sacrifice he would not endure for my sake & when he is with me I do not feel half my pain. He often says "what would Ma say if she saw me petting & waiting on you so." I tell him she would say "Howard dear good child." He was with me nearly three weeks but has gone to his business again—but expects to come for us in about five or six weeks—then if the Lord directs we will move up to Mount Lebonon about 350 miles from here. I dread the journey but I comfort myself if it be right for me to go there God will give me strength to stay the trip. If I am too sick it will be all right I should not go. I try to ask His direction with faith in everything. Oh! my precious, I come so far short of what I should be, that it makes my very soul sorrowful. Surely God is merciful to bear with me as he has. The more I look into my heart, the more I see of sin, folly & ingratitude. If we poor short sighted sinners trusted for salvation in our own merits, what lost wretches we would be. You know my darling Ann Lee—the good book says "Strive to enter in," we must *strive* by watching ourselves—every emotion of our hearts every sin that besets us easily & every evil thought & action. I know I love my Savoir—that it is my chief desire to be a true and faithful servant of the *Most High* & yet I fall so far short of it I wonder God bears with me as He does. You all must pray for your afflicted one—that God will not give her to the snares of the Evil one. Oh, how it rejoiced my heart to hear all were there & well—that dear ma's health was better last winter than it had been for a long time. I pray it may continue so. I suppose Laura has paid you a visit before this, & told you every thing. Do not let my precious ma grieve on my troubles tell her they are the best thing for me. God is my *Father,* the more sorrows I have the nearer His wing of love [that] lifts up dear ones—let us praise him for all he has done & trust Him for all that's to come.

I hear Mrs. Barrow has moved to the city—I fear my chances of hearing from home are very uncertain—but perhaps there will be some way, after awhile, I have not received my flannel yet am all in rags—but rags does better than none. I have parted with good many of my clothes to get something to eat. I can not eat just corn bread & beef all the time—it goes against me. I find I can [get] more things with sugar than money. I paid this morning seven lbs of sugar for 4 half grown chickens, & was glad to get them for that. I paid $1.25 for a lb. of coffee—in silver & it is so bad I can't drink it. When I had this last spell I did not eat for three days & then I was so hungry—but Dr. Young allowed me so very little it did not do me much good. I laid there Ann Lee & thought of *all* the good things I ever eat at home. I particularly wanted some of ma's anise coddled apples & cream. Oh, what would I not give for an apple. I think of all the nice things you all have there to eat. I even can't get an irish potato—I can't eat sweet ones. If we go to Lebonon we can get more to eat—plenty of flour which is a great consideration for me & there I will be with H- all the time. His pay is 25,00$ a year, he is State Chemist of La & I think it suits him better than any thing else.

Wellie is in the fourth Texas & thinks he has seen the [word is illegible] his father & Barrow are still in Texas but talk of coming back this fall—I expect they will go to Terrebonne. If you will write to me & put it in another envelope and address it to Dr A. S. Hemlick Houma care of R. R. Barrow St Charles Hotel New Orleans. I believe I stand a good chance to get it.

Cousin R- sends great deal of love—& says she keeps as fat as a pig on corn bread & beef. Sis looks thin & puny but I believe quite well. Tell dear aunt R I will try to write her a letter by writing to grandma. I know she will be glad to hear from her grandchild. It is such an exertion on my part to write now—that I can not write as I use too. I hope all will write to me, I can not write much at a time—I do my very best when I write home—but my hand trembles & ideas so confused that I expect you scarcely make them out and Peggie must write she always hears from me when you do, & she must consider them partly to herself. I will enclose a letter in here to grandma, please send it her the first chance. To show you how old I am I put a gray hair combed out of my head this morning; keep it as the first silvery line Time has wrought upon my head, & remember youths sunny noon is fast growing into twilight. Tell brother to take good care of *"Jim cat"* for me. I had forgotten, amid *all my troubles,* there ever existed such a *cat,* till sister Fannie spoke of him in her letter & then I remembered my former *pet.* What has become of little Betsy? What are the names of Ann's & Mary Cass children? Where is Jack & Juliet? Tell me everything. Did *you* get an *appointment at Conference?* How does grandma look what has become of uncle Henry? What does ma say & pa—just tell me something they say to live upon—Does sister Fannie have as many beaux as ever—who is the *right* one. And has Ann Lee still a heart? You must tell me everything—O! I want to know so much. You must give my love to every body that ask for me especially my relations & particularly my *favorite ones*—Kiss & hug ma for me—tell her she is seldom out of my mind—and I have had many a remorseful tear over my girl hood life. My dearest Ann Lee, be good to your parents—love & cherish ma for my sake—never speak *cross to her*—love to stay with & help her—you will never regret it, should you be separated I urge this upon you dearest sister, because I never want you to feel what I have. Tell dear brother I play on [the] table occasionally & think of the time it use to worry him & the only way I had to put him in a good humor was to tell him—"now I'm going to play *like Sallie."* I always then could detect a smile lurking around the corners of his mouth, Oh Ann Lee how I should love to see you all. Tell dear pa I fully appreciate his offer to send me money to come home but I know how little able he is to afford it. I think if I should go to Terrebonne again next spring (if my life is sparred) I shall surely go home & I hope I will have the means to go on—but I shall be obliged to spoung upon you all—I know none of you will consider it in that light but you will find one more troublesome than you have an idea of. I hope peace will soon be declared, & there won't be such difficulty in traveling. Do [you] ever have apple dumplings for dinner? Eat one for me. I want something good to eat so badly this evening. I did not eat much dinner—I eat a little piece of beef—a piece of cornbread & a cup of tea. What had you? I'm sorry to hear Blanche [Archer] is in such ill health give her my love. Give my love to cousin Richard [Lee] & tell him I think if he would come see me here, he would do me good. Oh, for the sights of a Harfordsman! Tell Laura to write me. Give her my love. I head all about she & Mr. J.

Now my darling sister I must bid you all good bye—I hope all may be cheered by my letter—Take courage my life is still left where there's "life there's *Hope."* Oh!

May our Father grant *our* prayers that we may yet be a unified family on earth. Oh! it is so consoling to me to know the same kind Father is watching—knowing he will hear us & is there around us.

Love to pa, Ma, sister Fannie & brother receiving all mercy good wish & prayer of your loving & afflicted sister.

Mitt

P.S. Cousin R says tell sister Fannie as I can't come this winter she must come out & stay till spring with us & then I'll go home with her in the spring—Oh sister Fannie do come—my very heart aches for you tell pa to give you the means he would send me on—if he has not got it get cousin George Presbury to let you have it & Howard will pay him after the war. After you get here you will not be at any expense—Ann Lee will be everything to ma I know she will—ma's health is always better in the winter—you can come by flag of truce from New Orleans. Tell cousin George Presbury I know he has the means he can give you to come see a dieing sister,[27] & if he does listen to the cry of a home sick heart & let my sister come to me he conferes the greatest favor under Heaven to me. Tell him he will never loose any thing by it—God will reward him for it. O my sister come to me if its only to close my dieing eyes—what a comfort would it be to have you by me. I hope & pray you will be able, then you can take good care of me *going home.* I leave it all to our Father. God grant you may come. Your loving sister Mitt

27. George Presbury was related to Bond through the Lee family. He lived in Baltimore and was married to Priscilla Moores.

Appendix 2

BOND KEPT THE FOLLOWING two lists of books she had read; she mentions some of the books in her diary.

BOOKS I HAVE READ, 1864

Vivian, or the Secret of Power. Mrs Southworth
"Initials" . . . . .
David Copperfield[1]—Charles Dickens
Dombey & Son "Cricket on the Hearth"
Christmas stories . . . .
Old Curiosity Shop
One year after Marriage . . Arthur
A Serious Call to a devout & Holy Life——by Law
Bennett's letters to a young lady——
Prince of the House of David——Graham
Laird of Norlan—a Scottish story
Dunallen——
The Two Guardians—Marian Harland
"Lamp Lighter"——
The Fair Maid of Pearth—Scott
Castle Dangurous, Anne of Geisnetein—Scott
Martyar Wife F. G. Arthur
The Vicar of Wakefield, She stoops to conquer—Goldsmith
Montgomery's & Mrs Hearman's poems, partly
Anecdotes on the New Testament by John Whitecross——

1865 BOOKS READ THIS YEAR

Adele——
Vale of Cedars by Grace Aquillar

---

1. The dashes appear as Bond wrote them.

Bibliography

"Abstract of Title Numbers, Seventeen Hundred and Ninety 'C.'" Robert Ruffin Barrow Papers, ser. H, reel 19. *Records of Ante-Bellum Southern Plantations from the Revolution through the Civil War.* Microfilm. Frederick, Md.: University Publications of America, 1996.

Apsley, William J. E. "The Educational Concerns, 1816–1861." In Baker, *Those Incredible Methodists*, 121–46.

Ashworth, Suzanne M. "Susan Warner's *The Wide, Wide World*, Conduct Literature, and Protocols of Female Reading in Mid-Nineteenth-Century America." *Legacy* 17, no. 2 (2000): 141–64.

Baker, Gordon Pratt. "Fragmentation." In Baker, *Those Incredible Methodists*, 229–80.

———, ed. *Those Incredible Methodists: A History of the Baltimore Conference of the United Methodist Church.* Baltimore: Commission on Archives and History, the Baltimore Conference, 1972.

"Bayou Black." *Civic Guard*, 9 June 1866.

Becnel, Thomas A. *The Barrow Family and the Barataria and Lafourche Canal: The Transportation Revolution in Louisiana, 1829–1925.* Baton Rouge: Louisiana State University Press, 1989.

Bergeron, Arthur W., Jr. *Guide to Louisiana Confederate Military Units, 1861–1865.* Baton Rouge: Louisiana State University Press, 1989.

Bleser, Carol, ed. *In Joy and in Sorrow: Women, Family, and Marriage in the Victorian South, 1830–1900.* New York: Oxford University Press, 1991.

Bleser, Carol, and Frederick M. Heath. "The Clays of Alabama: The Impact of the Civil War on a Southern Marriage. In Bleser, *In Joy and in Sorrow*, 135–53.

Booth, Andrew C., ed. *Records of Louisiana Confederate Soldiers and Louisiana Confederate Commands.* 3 vols. 1920. Reprint. Spartanburg, S.C.: Reprint Co. Publishers, 1984.

Bragg, Jefferson Davis. *Louisiana in the Confederacy.* Baton Rouge: Louisiana State University Press, 1997.

Brevard, Keziah Goodwyn Hopkins. *A Plantation Mistress on the Eve of the Civil War: The Diary of Keziah Goodwyn Hopkins Brevard, 1860–1861.* Edited by John Hammond Moore. Columbia: University of South Carolina Press, 1993.

Brooksher, William Riley. *War along the Bayous: The 1864 Red River Campaign in Louisiana.* Washington, D.C.: Brasseys, 1998.

Brugger, Robert J. *Maryland: A Middle Temperament, 1634–1980.* Baltimore: Johns Hopkins University Press, 1988.

Bunkers, Suzanne L. "Diaries and Dysfunctional Families: The Case of Emily Hawley Gillespie and Sarah Gillespei Huftalen." In Bunkers and Huff, *Inscribing the Daily,* 220–35.

———, ed. *Diaries of Girls and Women: A Midwestern American Sampler.* Madison: University of Wisconsin Press, 2001.

Bunkers, Suzanne L., and Cynthia A. Huff, eds. *Inscribing the Daily: Critical Essays on Women's Diaries.* Amherst: University of Massachusetts Press, 1996.

Burge, Dolly Lunt. *The Diary of Dolly Lunt Burge, 1848–1879.* Edited by Christine Jacobson Carter. Athens: University of Georgia Press, 1997.

Burr, Virginia. "A Woman Made to Suffer and Be Strong: Ella Gertrude Clanton Thomas, 1834–1907." In Bleser, *In Joy and in Sorrow,* 215–32.

Bynum, Victoria. "Reshaping the Bonds of Womanhood: Divorce in Reconstruction North Carolina." In Clinton and Silber, *Divided Houses,* 320–34.

Calkin, Homer L. "The Slavery Struggle, 1780–1865." In Baker, *Those Incredible Methodists,* 192–228.

Cashin, Joan E. *A Family Venture: Men and Women on the Southern Frontier.* New York: Oxford University Press, 1991.

———. "'Since the War Broke Out': The Marriage of Kate and William McLure." In Clinton and Silber, *Divided Houses,* 200–212.

Cassedy, James H. *Medicine in America: A Short History.* Baltimore: Johns Hopkins University Press, 1991.

Clinton, Catherine. *The Other Civil War: American Women in the Nineteenth Century.* Rev. ed. New York: Hill and Wang, 1999.

———, ed. *Southern Families at War: Loyalty and Conflict in the Civil War South.* New York: Oxford University Press, 2000.

Clinton, Catherine, and Nina Silber, eds. *Divided Houses: Gender and the Civil War.* New York: Oxford University Press, 1992.

Collins, Vicki Tolar. "Women's Voices and Women's Silence in the Tradition of Early Methodism." In *Listening to Their Voices: The Rhetorical Activities of Historical Women,* edited by Molly Meijer Wertheimer, 233–51. Columbia: University of South Carolina Press, 1997.

Crete, Liliane. *Daily Life in Louisiana, 1815–1830.* Translated by Patrick Gregory. Baton Rouge: Louisiana University Press, 1981.

Culley, Margo. "Introduction to a Day at a Time: Diary Literature of American Women from 1764 to 1985." In *Women, Autobiography, Theory: A Reader,* edited by Sidonie Smith and Julia Watson, 217–21. Madison: University of Wisconsin Press, 1998.

Davis, Gayle R. "Women's Frontier Diaries: Writing for Good Reason." *Women's Studies: An Interdisciplinary Journal* 14 (1987): 5–14.

Edwards, Laura. *Scarlett Doesn't Live Here Anymore: Southern Women in the Civil War Era.* Urbana: University of Illinois Press, 2000.

Elmore, Grace Brown. *A Heritage of Woe: The Civil War Diary of Grace Brown Elmore, 1861–1868.* Edited by Marli F. Weiner. Athens: University of Georgia Press, 1997.

Faust, Drew Gilpin. "Altars of Sacrifice: Confederate Women and the Narratives of War." *Journal of American History* 76 (March 1990): 1200–1228.

———. *Mothers of Invention: Women of the Slaveholding South in the American Civil War.* New York: Vintage Books, 1996.

———. "'Trying to Do a Man's Business': Slavery, Violence and Gender in the American Civil War." *Gender and History* 4, no. 2 (Summer 1992): 197–214.

———. "'Without Pilot or Compass': Elite Women and Religion in the Civil War South." In *Religion and the American Civil War,* edited by Randall M. Miller, Harry S. Stout, and Charles Reagan Wilson, 250–60. New York: Oxford University Press, 1998.

Faust, Drew Gilpin, Thavolia Glymph, and George C. Rable. "A Woman's War: Southern Women in the Civil War." In *A Woman's War: Southern Women, Civil War, and the Confederate Legacy,* edited by D. C. Campbell Jr. and Kym S. Rice, 1–28. Charlottesville: University Press of Virginia, 1996.

Fields, Barbara Jeanne. *Slavery and Freedom on the Middle Ground: Maryland during the Nineteenth Century.* New Haven: Yale University Press, 1985.

Fox-Genovese, Elizabeth. "Family and Female Identity in the Antebellum South: Sarah Gayle and Her Family." In Bleser, *In Joy and in Sorrow,* 15–31.

———. *Within the Plantation Household.* Chapel Hill: University of North Carolina Press, 1988.

Fox-Genovese, Elizabeth, and Eugene Genovese. "The Divine Sanction of Social Order: The Religious Foundations of the Southern Slaveholders' World View." *Journal of the American Academy of Religion* 55 (June 1987): 210–23.

Friedman, Jean E. *The Enclosed Garden: Women and Community in the Evangelical South, 1830–1900.* Chapel Hill: University of North Carolina Press, 1985.

Gannett, Cinthia. *Gender and the Journal: Diaries and Academic Discourse.* Albany: State University of New York Press, 1992.

Genovese, Eugene D. *A Consuming Fire: The Fall of the Confederacy in the Mind of the White Christian South.* Athens: University of Georgia Press, 1998.

———. *Roll, Jordan, Roll: The World the Slaves Made.* New York: Vintage Books, 1972.

Gorham, Deborah. *The Victorian Girl and the Feminine Ideal.* Bloomington: Indiana University Press, 1982.

Harrison, Kimberly. "Rhetorical Rehearsals: The Construction of Ethos in Confederate Women's Civil War Diaries." *Rhetoric Review* 22, no. 3 (2003): 243–63.

Herndl, Diane Price. *Invalid Women: Figuring Feminine Illness in American Fiction and Culture, 1840–1940.* Chapel Hill: University of North Carolina Press, 1993.

Heyrman, Christine Leigh. *Southern Cross: The Beginnings of the Bible Belt.* New York: Knopf, 1997.

Hollowak, Thomas L., comp. *Index to Marriages in the (Baltimore) Sun, 1851–1860.* Baltimore: Genealogical Publishing Co., 1978.

Holmes, Emma. *The Diary of Miss Emma Holmes, 1861–1866.* Edited by John F. Marszalek. Baton Rouge: Louisiana State University Press, 1979.

Jimerson, Randall. *The Private Civil War: Popular Thought during the Sectional Conflict.* Baton Rouge: Lousiana State University Press, 1988.

Kelley, Mary. "Reading Women/Women Reading: The Making of Learned Women in An-
  tebellum America." *Journal of American History* 83, no. 2 (September 1996): 401–24.
Kirsch, Gesa. *Women Writing in the Academy: Audience, Authority, and Transformation.* Car-
  bondale: Southern Illinois University Press, 1993.
Laas, Virginia Jean. *Love and Power in the Nineteenth Century: The Marriage of Violet Blair.*
  Fayetteville: University of Arkansas Press, 1998.
Leonard, Elizabeth D. "Mary Surratt and the Plot to Assassinate Abraham Lincoln." In
  The War Was You and Me: Civilians in the American Civil War, edited by Joan E. Cashin,
  286–309. Princeton: Princeton University Press, 2002.
Lyerly, Cynthia Lynn. *Methodism and the Southern Mind, 1770–1910.* New York: Oxford
  University Press, 1998.
Lystra, Karen. *Searching the Heart: Women, Men, and Romantic Love in Nineteenth-Century
  America.* New York: Oxford University Press, 1989.
MacKenzie, George Norbury. *Colonial Families of the United States of America,* vol. 2. Balti-
  more: Seaforth Press, 1911.
Malone, Ann Patton. *Sweet Chariot: Slave Family and Household Structure in Nineteenth-
  Century Louisiana.* Chapel Hill: University of North Carolina Press, 1992.
Mathews, Donald G. *Religion in the Old South.* Chicago: University of Chicago Press, 1977.
Mattingly, Carol. *Well-Tempered Women: Nineteenth-Century Temperance Rhetoric.* Carbon-
  dale: Southern Illinois University Press, 1998.
McCandless, Peter. "Mesmerism and Phrenology in Antebellum Charleston: 'Enough of
  the Marvellous.'" *Journal of Southern History* 58, no. 2 (May 1992): 199–230.
McLoughlin, William G., ed. *The American Evangelicals: 1800–1900.* New York: Harper
  and Row, 1968.
McPherson, James M. *Ordeal by Fire: The Civil War and Reconstruction.* New York: Knopf,
  1982.
Menn, Joseph Karl. *The Large Slaveholders of Louisiana, 1860.* New Orleans: Pelican Pub-
  lishing, 1964.
Morgan, Sarah. *Sarah Morgan: The Civil War Diary of a Southern Woman.* Edited by Charles
  East. New York: Simon and Schuster, 1991.
Moss, Elizabeth. *Domestic Novelists in the Old South: Defenders of Southern Culture.* Baton
  Rouge: Louisiana State University Press, 1992.
Pace, Robert F. "'It Was Bedlam Let Loose'": The Louisiana Sugar Country and the Civil
  War." *Louisiana History* 39 (Fall 1998): 389–409.
Peña, Christopher G. *Touched by War: Battles Fought in the Lafourche District.* Thibodaux,
  La.: CGP Press, 1998.
Poovey, Mary. *Uneven Developments: The Ideological Work of Gender in Mid-Victorian En-
  gland.* Chicago: University of Chicago Press, 1989.
Preston, Walter W. *History of Harford County Maryland.* 1901. 2d ed. Baltimore: Clearfield
  Co., 1990.
Price, Rev. H. B. "Terrebonne Parish, Louisiana." *Debow's Review* 8, no. 2 (February 1850):
  146–50.

Rable, George C. *Civil Wars: Women and the Crisis of Southern Nationalism.* Urbana: University of Illinois Press, 1991.

———. "'Missing in Action': Women of the Confederacy." In Clinton and Silber, *Divided Houses*, 134–46.

Reid, Whitelaw. *After the War: A Tour of the Southern States, 1865–1866.* 1866. Edited by C. Vann Woodward. New York: Harper and Row, 1965.

Roberts, Giselle. *The Confederate Belle.* Columbia: University of Missouri Press, 2003.

Rodrigue, John C. *Reconstruction in the Cane Fields: From Slavery to Free Labor in Louisiana's Sugar Parishes, 1862–1880.* Baton Rouge: Louisiana State University Press, 2001.

Roland, Charles P. *Louisiana Sugar Plantations during the Civil War.* 1957. Reprint. Baton Rouge: Louisiana State University Press, 1997.

Rothman, Ellen, K. *Hands and Hearts: A History of Courtship in America.* New York: Basic Books, 1984.

Rothman, Sheila M. *Living in the Shadow of Death: Tuberculosis and the Social Experience of Illness in American History.* New York: Basic Books, 1994.

Royster, Charles. *The Destructive War: William Tecumseh Sherman, Stonewall Jackson, and the Americans.* New York: Random House, 1991.

Ruether, Rosemary Radford, and Rosemary Skinner Keller. *Women and Religion in America.* Vol. 1: *The Nineteenth Century.* San Francisco: Harper and Row, 1981.

Schneider, A. Gregory. *The Way of the Cross Leads Home: The Domestication of American Methodism.* Bloomington: Indiana University Press, 1993.

Scott, Anne Firor. *The Southern Lady: From Pedestal to Politics, 1830–1930.* Chicago: University of Chicago Press, 1970.

Sewell, Jane Eliot. *Medicine in Maryland: The Practice and Profession, 1799–1999.* Baltimore: Johns Hopkins University Press, 1999.

Sinor, Jennifer. "Reading the Ordinary Diary." *Rhetoric Review* 21, no. 2 (2002): 123–49.

Smith-Rosenberg, Carroll. "The Cross and the Pedestal: Women, Anti-Ritualism, and the Emergence of the American Bourgeoisie." In Smith-Rosenberg, *Disorderly Conduct*, 129–64.

———. *Disorderly Conduct: Visions of Gender in Victorian America.* New York: Oxford University Press, 1985.

———. "The Female World of Love and Ritual: Relations between Women in Nineteenth-Century America." In Smith-Rosenberg, *Disorderly Conduct*, 53–76.

———. "The Hysterical Woman: Sex Roles and Role Conflict in Nineteenth-Century America." In Smith-Rosenberg, *Disorderly Conduct*, 197–216.

Solomon, Clara. *The Civil War Diary of Clara Solomon: Growing Up in New Orleans.* Edited by Elliott Ashkenazi. Baton Rouge: Louisiana State University Press, 1995.

Sontag, Susan. *Illness as Metaphor.* New York: Picador, 2001.

Stone, Kate. *Brokenburn: The Journal of Kate Stone, 1861–1868.* Edited by John Q. Anderson. Baton Rouge: Louisiana State University Press, 1995.

Stowe, Steven M. *Intimacy and Power in the Old South: Ritual in the Lives of the Planters.* Baltimore: Johns Hopkins University Press, 1987.

Taylor, Joe Gray. *Louisiana Reconstructed, 1863–1877.* Baton Rouge: Louisiana State University Press, 1974.

Theriot, Nancy M. *Mothers and Daughters in Nineteenth-Century America: The Biosocial Construction of Femininity.* Lexington: University Press of Kentucky, 1996.

Thomas, Ella Gertrude Clanton. *The Secret Eye: The Journal of Ella Gertrude Clanton Thomas, 1848–1889.* Edited by Virginia Ingraham Burr. Chapel Hill: University of North Carolina Press, 1990.

Tracey, Karen. *Plots and Proposals: American Women's Fiction, 1850–90.* Urbana: University of Illinois Press, 2000.

Tonkovich, Nicole. "Rhetorical Power in the Victorian Parlor." In *Oratorical Culture in Nineteenth-Century America: Transformations in the Theory and Practice of Rhetoric.* Edited by Gregory Clark and S. Michael Halloran, 158–83. Carbondale: Southern Illinois University Press, 1993.

Twain, Mark. *Life on the Mississippi.* New York: Harper and Brothers, 1923.

U.S. War Department. *The War of the Rebellion: A Compilation of the Official Records of the Union and Confederate Armies.* 70 vols. in 128 pts. Washington, D.C., 1880–1901. http://cdl.library.cornell.edu/moa/browse.monographs/waro.html/.

Vermilion Historical Society. *History of Vermilion Parish Louisiana.* Dallas: Taylor Publishing Co., 1983.

Walker, Henry. "Power, Sex, and Gender Roles: The Transformation of an Alabama Planter Family during the Civil War." In Clinton, *Southern Families at War,* 175–92.

Warboys, Michael. *Spreading Germs: Disease Theories and Medical Practice in Britain, 1865–1900.* Cambridge: Cambridge University Press, 2000.

Weiner, Marli F. *Mistresses and Slaves: Plantation Women in South Carolina, 1830–80.* Urbana: University of Illinois Press, 1998.

Welter, Barbara. "The Cult of True Womanhood, 1820–1860." *American Quarterly* 18 (1966): 151–74.

Whites, Lee Ann. *The Civil War as a Crisis in Gender: Augusta, Georgia, 1860–1890.* Athens: University of Georgia Press, 1995.

Williams, T. Harry. *The History of American Wars: From 1745 to 1918.* Baton Rouge: Louisiana State University Press, 1981.

Winters, John D. *The Civil War in Louisiana.* Baton Rouge: Louisiana State University Press, 1963.

Wright, C. Milton. *Our Harford Heritage: A History of Harford County, Maryland.* Baltimore: French Bray Printing Co., 1967.

Yrigoyen, Charles, Jr. "Methodists and Roman Catholics in Nineteenth Century America." *Methodist History* 28, no. 3 (April 1990): 172–86.

Zboray, Ronald J., and Mary Saracino Zboray. "Books, Reading, and the World of Goods in Antebellum New England." *American Quarterly* 48, no. 4 (1996): 587–622.

CENSUS RECORDS CONSULTED

1850 U.S. Census. Free schedules, City of Baltimore, Wards 5–7, National Archives microfilm publication M432, roll 283.

1850 U.S. Census. Free schedules, Harford and Kent Counties, Maryland, National Archives microfilm publication M432, roll 294.

1850 U.S. Census. Free schedules, Terrebonne Parish, Louisiana, National Archives microfilm publication M432, roll 241.

1850 U.S. Census. Slave schedules, Harford County, Maryland, National Archives microfilm publication M432, roll 301.

1860 U.S. Census. Free schedule, Harford County, Maryland. National Archives microfilm publication M653, roll 476.

1860 U.S Census. Free schedule, St. Mary Parish, Louisiana, National Archives microfilm publication M653, roll 425.

1860 U.S. Census. Free schedule, Terrebonne Parish, Louisiana, National Archives microfilm publication M653, roll 425.

1860 U.S. Census. Free schedule, Vermilion Parish, Louisiana, National Archives microfilm publication M653, roll 426.

1860 U.S. Census. Slave schedule, Harford County, Maryland, National Archives microfilm publication M653, roll 484.

1870 U.S Census. Population schedule, Harford County, Maryland, National Archives microfilm publication M593, roll 588.

1870 U.S. Census. Population schedule, Terrebonne Parish, Louisiana, National Archives microfilm publication M593, roll 533.

1880 U.S. Census. Population schedule, Terrebonne Parish, Louisiana, National Archives microfilm publication T9, roll 472.

1920 U.S. Census. Population schedule, Terrebonne Parish, Louisiana, National Archives microfilm publication T625, roll 634.

U.S. Bureau of the Census. *The Seventh Census of the U.S., 1850: Embracing a Statistical View of Each of the States and Territories and Arranged by Counties, Towns, Etc.* 1853. Reprint. New York: Norman Ross Publishing, 1990.

U.S. Bureau of the Census. *Statistics of the United States (including mortality, property, &c.) in 1860: compiled from the original returns and being the final exhibit of the eighth census, under the direction of the Secretary of the Interior.* 1866. Reprint. New York: Norman Ross Publishing, 1990.

Index